May Day Festivals
in America,
1830 to the Present

ALSO BY ALLISON THOMPSON

*Dancing Through Time: Western Social Dance
in Literature, 1400–1918: Selections*
(McFarland, 1998; paperback 2012)

May Day Festivals in America, 1830 to the Present

Allison Thompson

McFarland & Company, Inc., Publishers
Jefferson, North Carolina, and London

The present work is a reprint of the illustrated case bound edition of May Day Festivals in America, 1830 to the Present, *first published in 2009 by McFarland.*

LIBRARY OF CONGRESS CATALOGUING-IN-PUBLICATION DATA

Thompson, Allison, 1955–
May Day festivals in America, 1830 to the present / Allison Thompson.
p.   cm.
Includes bibliographical references and index.

ISBN 978-0-7864-7722-7
softcover : 50# alkaline paper ∞

1. May Day — United States — History. 2. May Day — England — History. 3. United States — Social life and customs. 4. England — Social life and customs. I. Title.
GT4945.T47   2013   394.26270973 — dc22   2008045974

BRITISH LIBRARY CATALOGUING DATA ARE AVAILABLE

© 2009 Allison Thompson. All rights reserved

No part of this book may be reproduced or transmitted in any form or by any means, electronic or mechanical, including photocopying or recording, or by any information storage and retrieval system, without permission in writing from the publisher.

Front cover: Dancing around five maypoles in Mendon, Utah, 2006 (photograph by Karole Sarensen)

Manufactured in the United States of America

*McFarland & Company, Inc., Publishers
Box 611, Jefferson, North Carolina 28640
www.mcfarlandpub.com*

Acknowledgments

This book would not have been possible were it not for all the college and university librarians and archivists who provided copies of photographs, student newspaper or alumnae bulletin accounts, May Queen reminiscences and other ephemeral documentation of their institutions' May Day festivals. I am deeply grateful for all your hard work.

I am particularly grateful to Carol Yeager, the coordinator of Grove City College's Parents' Weekend (the weekend in which the May King and Queen are crowned and a spectacular dance performance is put on in the Queen's honor). Carol introduced me to several of the college's May Queens. Thanks also go to Wanda Finney, archivist of Wilson College, and her associates in the Office of Alumnae Affairs who assisted me in contacting several former Wilson College May Queens.

Fellow folklorist and historian Stephen Corrsin gave me encouragement throughout the lengthy research and writing of *May Day Festivals in America*. He also served as a valuable sounding board on the issues of tradition. Thanks also go to Daniel Walkowitz, New York University, and Susan Merskey of the Elsie J. Oxenham Society.

My greatest thanks are to my children, Christopher and Emma, who put up with their mother's long-standing and peculiar obsession with comparatively little eye-rolling. Veterans of the maypole dance themselves — they each performed it in both kindergarten and eighth grade — perhaps they will now better understand the history and significance of May Day in America.

Table of Contents

Acknowledgments v
Introduction: "I'm to Be Queen of the May, Mother!" 1

Part I: May Day

THE MAKING OF MERRIE MAY DAY

1. *Celebrating May Day in England before 1800* — 15
2. *The Making of May Day in Merrie England* — 23
3. *John Ruskin and the Whitelands College May Queen Festival* — 32
4. *Merrie May Day in the New World* — 38

SETTING THE STAGE FOR PERFORMANCES

5. *Physical Education for Girls and Young Women* — 49
6. *"As the Child Plays, So Will the Adult Perform": Progressive Reformers and the Playground Movement* — 58
7. *The Educational, Hygienic, Civic, and Moral Benefits of Folk Dance* — 67
8. *The Pageant and Festival Movement* — 75
9. *The Urban Child's May Day* — 85

THE COLLEGE MAY DAY FESTIVAL

10. *The Making of the College Girl of 1900* — 91
11. *Origins of the College May Day Pageant* — 98
12. *The Play's the Thing — College May Day Pageant Themes* — 107
13. *Corydon in Arcadia — Men and May Day* — 120
14. *Maypole Dances and Drills* — 129
15. *Crowning the College May Queen* — 139
16. *The May Queen Unthroned* — 148

May Day Festivals of Today

17. *May Day as Labor Day, Loyalty Day, Law Day, Child Health Day, and Lei Day*   156
18. *Celebrating an Old English May Day Today*   164

Conclusion: "The Merriest Day of All the Glad New Year!"   177

Part II: The College Festivals

College	Page	College	Page
Agnes Scott College	185	Kent State University	212
Albright College	187	Lebanon Valley College	213
Auburn University	187	Mary Baldwin College	213
Bates College	187	Meredith College	214
Berea College	188	Miami University	215
Bluffton University	189	Mills College	215
Brenau University	189	Mount Holyoke College	217
Brown University	190	Muskingum College	218
Bryn Mawr College	190	Newcomb College, Tulane University	219
Bucknell University	191	New Mexico State University	220
Carleton College	191	Oberlin College	221
Case Western Reserve University	193	Oklahoma State University	222
Chatham University	194	Oregon State University	222
Colby College	195	Pennsylvania State University	222
College of Wooster	196	Randolph College	223
Columbia College	197	Rockford College	223
Converse College	198	Rollins College	225
DePauw University	199	Russell Sage College (The Sage Colleges)	226
Duke University	200	Salem College	226
Earlham College	201	Scripps College	227
Elmira College	202	Simmons College	227
Goucher College	202	Skidmore College	228
Grinnell College	203	Smith College	229
Grove City College	204	Sweet Briar College	229
Hollins College	206	Trinity University	230
Hood College	207	University of California at Berkeley	231
Indiana University	208	University of Charleston, West Virginia	231
Iowa State University	209	University of Colorado	231
James Madison University	210	University of Denver	233
Judson College	210		
Kansas State University	211		

University of Idaho	234	University of South Carolina	239
University of Illinois at Urbana-Champaign	234	University of Tennessee	239
		Ursinus College	239
University of Kansas	235	Valdosta State University	240
University of Maryland	235	Wartburg College	241
University of Minnesota	236	Wellesley College	241
University of Missouri	237	Wells College	242
University of New Hampshire	237	Westminster College	243
University of Puget Sound	238	Wilson College	244
University of Richmond (Westhampton College)	238	Winthrop University	246

Chapter Notes 249
Selected Bibliography 261
Index 265

Introduction: "I'm to Be Queen of the May, Mother!"

> You must wake and call me early, call me early, mother dear;
> To-morrow 'ill be the happiest time of all the glad New-year;
> Of all the glad New-year, mother, the maddest merriest day,
> For I'm to be Queen o' the May, mother, I'm to be Queen o' the May.
> —"The May Queen," by Alfred, Lord Tennyson*

May First, 1910, Collegetown, USA: Spectators swarm the grounds of the college campus, or stand precariously on the seats of the buggies lined up along the road, hoping for a better view. Here comes the procession of the girls in their dainty white dresses decked with flowers. Some are costumed as milkmaids or gypsies; others carry wreaths of flowers. The trumpets announce the arrival of the Queen of the May, the prettiest, nicest, most popular girl in the college. After the coronation, the girls swear obeisance to their Queen, who bids them enjoy their day of revelry. Girls perform well-known folk dances from many countries, and one adventuresome soloist, barefooted, with her hair streaming down her back and sporting a skimpy Grecian tunic, skips joyfully in an interpretive dance that represents the song of the robins in spring. Then there is the maypole dance — will they wind the ribbons (in the college colors) correctly? This year there is also to be a play: *Robin Hood and His Merrie Men*. What a treat! Everyone looks forward to the college's annual pageant of an Old English May Day in Ye Olden Tyme.

At the same time, across town, a state senator canvassing for reelection has brought 5,000 children from the wrong side of the tracks, where the foreigners live, to the city's only park. Faces beaming, the ragged children wave little American flags and cheer shrilly when the senator strolls by. There are cake and ice cream and the crowning of little May Queens and the performance of the maypole dance held on the green grass that some children have never seen before. Young girls perform the folk dances that they have learned in school, and a few adults, red-faced and embarrassed in the heavy clothes of the old country, demonstrate a national dance. Little Biddy and Stefan and Antonio return home that night reluctantly; they will not have the opportunity to play in the park again until next May Day.

Maypoles decked with multi-colored streamers, the flower-garlanded May Queen and her court, dainty girls tripping to and fro on the green or tenement children frolicking in the park — it may surprise the reader to realize that this is a picture of May Day not in Merrie

---

*This is the first stanza of the first of three related poems collectively titled "The May Queen." This poem and its companion, "New Year's Eve," were published in 1832; "The Conclusion," in which Alice dies of consumption, in 1842. As Chapter 2 relates, this popular poem cycle was an important factor in shaping the image of May Day in Merrie England.

Old England, but in the Merrie New World. Middle-class, religious Americans of the nineteenth century were not, in general, interested in the wholesale importation of English traditional customs, especially any of the low-class ones that involved begging for money or drink. But, beginning about 1830 and accelerating at the turn of the century, a phenomenon of old English May Queen or May Day festivals sprang up in the United States, almost as it were from thin air. Thousands of young women and children participated in these festivals, held both at colleges and universities and in urban parks. May Day festivals were usually a re-enactment of a golden idyll of a pastoral village in Merrie Old England. But, in what one is compelled to think of as a typically American, bigger-is-better fashion, our May Day festivals could incorporate hundreds or even thousands of participants and thousands or tens of thousands of spectators.

Whether held at a college or in an urban playground, the May Day festival was a consciously re-created tradition that deliberately evoked the perceived moral and aesthetic values of an imaginary and better earlier time. It was also, from its inception in the 1830s until at least World War II, a tradition that was felt to bestow upon participants, and, to a lesser degree, spectators, certain well-defined moral, social, educative, aesthetic, Americanizing, or hygienic benefits.

Why study this holiday? First, in part, for its own merits — the May Day festival in all its forms was a colorful and entertaining spectacle that few today realize was either so long-lived or so widespread, as shown in the responses of 80 colleges and universities from across the country that did — or still do — celebrate May Day.

But, more than this entertainment value, an examination of the May Day festival provides insight into interesting questions pertaining to the roles and education of girls and young women in the United States. These questions include the following: What were the common elements of the image of a Merrie English May Day and why was this image relevant to an American girl of the 1830s, the 1890s or the 1950s? Why was the image of the May Queen so powerful that it overcame the taboos of conservative,

Interpretive dance welcoming the spring, Chatham University, May Day 1910. This dancer has abandoned her corsets for light slippers, a shockingly short Grecian gown and an attitude of merry gaiety (Archives, Chatham University, Pittsburgh, Pennsylvania).

Victorian-era parents about seeing their daughters perform in public? How could a festival with origins that many today erroneously aver as pagan be so compelling that it was unquestioningly accepted, even by students and strait-laced administrators of the colleges and communities of the Quakers, Methodists, Mennonites, Baptists and Mormons? Once initiated, how and why did these colleges and universities continue with the tradition for decades, modifying it over time to suit their changing needs and goals? Why was it not the English or the Fine Arts departments but the Physical Education department that sponsored and organized the elaborate college May Day celebrations? Why did participants and spectators alike feel that the early festivals conveyed such strong moral, social and aesthetic values? Why did settlement workers, politicians, and playground directors organize thousands of urban children, most of them immigrants or children of recent immigrants, into May Day festivals? How did the two World Wars and the socialist workers' celebration of May Day affect the imagery and the performance of the festivals? How were the changing roles of women after World War II reflected in the May Queen crowning ceremonies? Why did many college May Day festivals end, comparatively abruptly, in the late 1960s? What is the contribution of the re-created May Day to the discussion of the nature of tradition? Was the girl-oriented May Day a feminist celebration, or did feminism kill it? And, finally, why, in what fashion, and by whom is an old English-style May Day — or elements thereof — still celebrated today?

Before attempting to address these questions, it is useful to examine what this book is not about. It is not a straightforward history of higher education for women nor of the history of physical education for women in the United States, though it touches on both topics. It is not about the settlement house movement in the U.S., nor is it about the history of the Playground Association of America or the American Pageant Association, though, again, it refers to these important organizations. It is not an analysis of the changing cultural and economic status of girls and women in this country nor is it about an examination of the popular conception of beauty and image, though it touches on these topics intermittently and importantly. It is not a history of feminism, though most of the festivals were discontinued around 1967 due in part to the women's liberation movement. It is not about War, though the festivals could express strong feelings of patriotism; it is not about Peace, though many of the festivals expressed unifying feelings of melting-pot Americanism. It is not about religion, as the festival was originally nonsecular, though today it could be seen as moving slowly toward a sort of Creative-Paganism.

The May Day festival serves as a prism to capture any particular period's attitudes toward all of the above topics. But, overall, it must be remembered that while today we can see in the festival a reflection of important social issues, most participants at the time saw it simply as great fun. Girls created the college May Day festival, the principal focus of this book, in order to celebrate the coming of spring and the approaching end of the school year. Girls wrote the pageant scripts, performed the dances and songs, made the costumes, and sold the tickets. It was a celebration of a world apart, a world in which women could succeed by themselves and be admired for the pretty and inspiring performance that they presented. In this sense the festival may well have been personally empowering for a young participant, but it should be noted that the themes of the pageants themselves were in no way feminist by modern standards; on the contrary, they expressed and reinforced the conservative and sentimental popular image of the dainty maiden whose principal goal in life was Love.

The college May Day was an event that satisfied women's (and occasionally men's) needs for continuity and entertainment so that it remained a satisfying tradition for nearly 200 years. It was also a festival that was easily personalized by each generation of students. This can be seen by the change in theme of the elaborate pageants that were part of the festivities, from the retellings of Greek or Oriental myths that were popular in the early 1920s, to the stories of Peter Pan or Alice in Wonderland in the 1930s, to versions of the Wizard of Oz or Bobo [sic] Baggins in the 1950s to "A Mad, Mod, Merry May Day" in the late 1960s. This flexibility can also be seen in the gradual accumulation to the festival of formal dances, athletic events, plays and art shows, father-daughter or mother-daughter teas, alumnae reunions, or other activities that filled a long spring weekend.

Some historians have looked at women's history as an evolution or progress from repression to a pinnacle of modern consciousness. The girls' May Day festival certainly would not represent a step on this evolutionary ladder, but it should not therefore be ignored: in fact, quite the reverse. Regardless of their feelings about votes or jobs for women, from 1830 to roughly 1967 girls took pride in their festivals and in the honor of being elected Queen of the May.

Most — though not all — of the college May Day festivals ended in the late nineteen-sixties due to the major social changes of the era: in particular the changing perceptions of women's roles and their attitudes toward their bodies, protests surrounding the Vietnam War, and, to a lesser extent, the perceived inaccessibility of the festival to students of color. Students themselves changed during the decade of the sixties, becoming hostile to old conventions and traditions associated with white, elite privileges. Parietal rules ended at most colleges and there was a new gender consciousness on campus. The elaborate festival was also threatened by coeducation, typically that of men being admitted to a formerly women's college, and by the lure of the male sports-oriented festivals like Homecoming; by the loss of faculty wife labor on the pageants as these women entered the workforce themselves; as well as the post–Kent State Massacre changes in many college calendars which resulted in moving examinations from June to May — all of these factors left, as the Earlham College historian has put it, "not enough May for May Day."[1]

I say generally, because it would be a tidier story if all of these festivals had in fact vanished in the late 1960s in the spirit of rebellion, liberalism, and feminism. But they did not. Some of them remained, often in the hands of folk dancers and enthusiasts, or in the hands of those committed to Paganism or Wicca but also — though admittedly more rarely — in the hands of those who still see the festival as a legitimate expression of a communal celebration of spring that incorporates certain, self-selected elements of English folk traditions. In this category we find eight out of the 80 colleges in the study group, some K–12 schools, and several communities, notably that of Mendon, Utah.

It is important to note early on that the girls' May Day — whether celebrated on the college green or in an urban park — had almost no connection to the sometimes violent protests or marches of workers and socialists on May First. I have found only a handful of contemporary examples that link the two events: the Walter Crane Socialist maypole described in Chapter 17, a Socialist magazine cover from the 1940s that shows both children dancing around a maypole and workers protesting, and the inception of a May Festival in the 1950s in Moscow, Idaho, as an action that was clearly attempting to disassociate that town from its Russian counterpart. While it is possible that some adults were aware of the irony of the juxtaposition of the girls' festival with worker protests and Communist displays of might, they left no discovered record of their feelings.

May Day (along with Christmas, Thanksgiving, and St. Patrick's Day and other holidays) falls in the category of an invented tradition, as described by Eric Hobsbawm and his associates in their study of 1983, *The Invention of Tradition*: a set of practices of a ritual nature which seek to inculcate certain values through repetition and a reliance on continuity with a suitable historic past. But this argument tempts us falsely to think that if a tradition is invented it is somehow therefore tainted, that is, not really authentic. This questionable argument assumes that before there were invented traditions there were real ones — however one would identify or measure these — that were not invented, and that these would *ipso facto* be better. But not only is this not historically possible, it is irrelevant. No useful aesthetic or historical line divides invented traditions from real ones.[2]

However, the concept of an invented tradition, as Hobsbawm and his associates defined the term, is still a useful one in that it allows us to step away from the activity itself to examine the motives and feelings of its sponsors and participants. The girls' May Day increased in popularity in the late 1890s and early 1900s because of prevailing concerns about the New College Girl on the one hand, and the plight of the urban poor on the other. It remained popular, especially in the conservative, patriarchal South, because after the suffrage amendment was passed, the feminist movement collapsed for several decades. May Day vanished, for the most part, in the late 1960s because of the profound social upheavals — and, in particular, the changed view of the role of women in society.

May Day Festivals in America is divided into four sections. The first section of this book discusses how and when the image of Merrie May Day came into being. Many people today

It's a cold May Day at Elmira College in 1924. Note the "Gothic"-inspired building in the background, helping to set the stage for old-time romance (Elmira College Archives).

assert that May Day is a pagan holiday and that the maypole was a phallic symbol. Both assertions are incorrect, and Chapter 1 examines why. The modern reader already has a mental picture of an old English May Day. But this image is really just a charming fantasy created by decades of romantic enthusiasts repeating and embroidering upon each other's legends and theories. In the last twenty years, folklorists and historians have provided us with rigorous and detailed examinations of the origins and practices of English rituals and customs in the historical record such as the maypole, the morris dance, Robin Hood and the Jack-in-the-Green. Chapter 1 summarizes recent findings about the celebration of May Day in England prior to the early nineteenth century. These practices varied significantly over the centuries or over geographical regions. They might be practiced differently in towns versus villages, and they could also vary depending on the tastes and budgets of the local gentry who sponsored the events. Chapter 1 provides the reader with a basis to compare documented historical practices with the re-created idyll of the nineteenth century or the romantic beliefs of modern enthusiasts.

By the end of the eighteenth century many of the actual May Day practices in England — dancing in front of the maypole, morris dancing, and so on — had fallen into disfavor with those individuals who formerly engaged in them. The inflation and social disruptions caused by the Napoleonic wars, the increase of manufacturing that caused so much suffering, and the migration of the workforce from the country to the crowded cities that occurred throughout the nineteenth century, led many in both England and America to look back to an idealized Golden Age, one located hazily at some point between the reigns of Good King Arthur and Queen Elizabeth I. Starting in the 1770s with the craze for Gothic architecture and lurid Gothic "horrid" novels such as Ann Radcliffe's *Mysteries of Udolpho*, poets, romantically inclined antiquarians, and even some English politicians began the process of creating a "Merrie England," an imaginary, vaguely Elizabethan world in which both peasant and lord knew his place, and all participated happily in the gay holidays of the year. Chapter 2 describes the creation of Merrie England, a term that became so well-known that by the 1850s, just those two words alone conjured up a precise mental and emotional picture for English and American men and women. Here we will find that English poets and writers such as Scott, Tennyson, and Ruskin, as well as the American writers Nathaniel Hawthorne and Washington Irving, were important in creating the remarkably cohesive and clear picture of Merrie May Day that the average nineteenth-century American girl could describe as well as an Englishwoman.

Chapter 3 reviews in detail art critic and social commentator John Ruskin's influence on May Day both through his writings on his ideals of girlhood as well as his contributions to the famous Whitelands College May Queen celebration. This festival, first celebrated in 1881 and still celebrated today, was reported on frequently in English periodicals for girls, and was also described in an American publication as early as 1886. Ruskin's ideals, and the details of the Whitelands festival, formed one of the inspirations for the college May Day festivals that proliferated at the turn of the century.

For how and why did the image of Merrie May Day cross the sea? Chapter 4 discusses the fact that the writings of English antiquarians and poets were as almost well known in America as in their home country. In this chapter I also discuss two uniquely American antecedents of the picturesque May Day: the maypole of Merrymount, the most famous maypole erected in the New World prior to the nineteenth century, and the popular Ring Tournaments of the ante- and post-bellum South. Given all these sources, by the 1830s the romantic image of an old English May Day was well-developed enough to cause the spontaneous appearance of May

Day celebrations in America, and this chapter concludes with some descriptions of early May Day festivals, most of which were organized by young girls at their finishing academies, and blessed by their teachers and administrators.

Having established the creation of the image of Merrie May Day, the book's second section examines some important aspects of the Progressive reform movement of the 1890 to 1920 period: in particular the activities of the American Pageant Association and the Playground Association of America. The moral, social, educative, artistic and symbolic theories of the leaders of these two groups shaped both the elementary school and college physical education programs and, therefore, the dances, drills, and pageants performed at May Day festivals, whether held in city parks or on college greens.

Chapter 5 addresses the topic of physical education for girls and college women. The maintenance — or improvement — of physical health was seen as a critical corrective for the perceived stresses of higher education for women at the turn of the century. By 1900, dance, rather than calisthenic drills or machine-based exercises, was seen as a safe, beneficial and pleasing form of healthful exercise for girls. Physical education instructors focused on folk dance and, shortly after the turn of the century, aesthetic (modern) dance as a prime means of conveying good health and grace to their students. Trained in the arts of pageantry, these teachers organized May Day festivals in part to demonstrate the year's work in dance and drill.

Chapter 6 turns to the activities of the Progressive reformers, and their connection to May Day, which, as the beginning to this Introduction shows, had an important role in both pedagogy and politics. One of the reformers' concerns was the need for poor, urban, mostly immigrant children to have a safe place in which to play; another was to ensure that these immigrant children played games that would inculcate them with Anglo-American values and prepare them for citizenship in a democracy. Thus in 1907 the Playground Association of America, formed under the auspices of the Russell Sage Foundation, began campaigning for the construction of playgrounds in the teeming tenements and the teaching of folk dance to girls in elementary and upper schools as part of a much-needed physical hygiene program. Another item on the Association's agenda was to urge local civic and school leaders to present annual community holiday festivals, especially May Day festivals, in order to give a taste of beauty and pleasure to slum children. In a separate but related movement, settlement houses, modeled in part after London's Toynbee Hall and staffed by that new creature, the college-educated woman, were founded in cities and, later, rural areas across the nation. Settlement houses offered educational and recreational classes and events, mostly to immigrant women and children. These reformers taught a select group of folk dances and organized children in May Day pageants and plays.

The May Day of Merrie England — something vaguely and charmingly Elizabethan — was a favored holiday of these social workers and civic reformers who were concerned about the horrors of childhood in the immigrant sections of American cities in the early 1900s: the inescapable heat or cold; the lack of space to play; the poverty, hunger, and despair. Many argued, of course, that more than a May Day masque was needed to change these children's lives: they knew that jobs for their fathers, clean water and TB-tested milk, education and opportunity were more important. But, working from a modest "social housekeeping" platform, they noted — not entirely ineffectively — that the May day jollities might serve to expose a social ill, by demonstrating to the unconvinced the extreme pleasure that the pleasure-starved children took in it. These social reformers felt that while major social ills might indeed require greater measures to cure, such little windows of play and culture could help to bring in a new order, especially to the masses of poor Catholic or Jewish immigrants whom these Protestant Progressives were determined to Anglo-Saxonize. For while these social workers were sensitive to the desires of immigrants to retain certain aspects of their native traditions (especially the colorful and benign ones of song and dance), their fascination with May Day lay in part both in its English origin and because it would teach good, hard-working Protestant American values to the teeming hordes of new arrivals with their reputedly dubious sexual and work ethics and their possibly Bolshevistic tendencies.

Folk dance was a recommended form of exercise for girls and women, and the theories of influential educator Dr. Luther Halsey Gulick (1865–1918) would be translated directly into the folk dance manuals that proliferated from 1905 on. Many of the new women instructors of physical education, a relatively new discipline, were influenced by Gulick's teachings and went on to sponsor elaborate May Day festivals at their new positions. These festivals incorporated the folk dances recommended by Gulick and his associate, the famous folk-dance collector Elizabeth Burchenal (1877–1959). Chapter 7 discusses the perceived hygienic, moral, civic, and physical benefits of folk dancing. Not all folk dances were perceived to be equally beneficial, and Gulick's and Burchenal's recommended dances were reflected not only in elementary and secondary school curricula, but can be seen again and again in the college May Day programs.

Chapter 8 examines the influence upon May Day festivals of the American Pageant Association, active between 1905 and approximately 1925. This movement sought to unite democracy with art by organizing enormous civic pageants that united high social ideals with democratic reform actions. These pageants often involved several hundred local participants and thousands of spectators. Numerous books and articles detailed the aesthetic and symbolic principles of the Pageant Association of America, and the Bryn Mawr College May Day, among others, was singled out as a particularly expressive type of springtide pageant. Many of the college May Day pageant themes discussed later in Chapter 12 and Part II exhibit clearly the principles of the Pageant Association of America.

Weaving together all these elements of pageantry, the benefits of folk-dance in general, and the specific dances recommended, Chapter 9 describes the urban May Day festival that began just before the turn of the century, providing further detail as to the nature and purpose of these celebrations, particularly as a way to indoctrinate foreign-born young people into the American way of life. Under the Playground Association's urging, cities in the Northeast and Midwest sponsored enormous festivals in which thousands of school children performed folk dances: for example, 8,000 children performed in Schenley Park in Pittsburgh, Pennsylvania, in 1908; 10,000 children danced in a May Day festival in Central Park in 1910; while 9,000 children in seven different parks performed folk dances simultaneously for the benefit of 42,000 spectators in Omaha, Nebraska, on May 1, 1927.

The third section of the book turns to the college girl and the college May Day pageant. While girls had held modest celebrations in their seminaries and finishing schools from the 1830s onward, May Day became truly popular and widespread in the late 1890s, when the college girl, the so-called "New Girl," embraced the festival. The 1890s saw a sea change in the type of girl who went to college, and the kind of experience she sought there. Compared to her poorer, more serious predecessor, who sought a degree in order to support herself by teaching, the New Girl was more casual about her studies, wealthier, more fun-loving, and more eager to engage in the social life of college such as debating and dramatics clubs and the new sport of basketball. So that we may understand how May Day fit into college life, Chapter 10 discusses the making of the College Girl: from her beginning, when higher education was something that women fought for, through the changes in both the country and the girl herself that created the New Girl and, later, the New Woman.

Throughout this work the use of the word "girl" rather than "woman" is a deliberate and important distinction. The word "girl" had a precise meaning at the turn of the last century, a term used consistently in popular fiction and academic writing and one that meant something different to late Victorians than it does to us today. A "young lady" was at home, husband-hunting. A "girl"—of a certain class, at least—was an almost unsexed being between the ages of eight and thirty: young, unmarried, innocent, virginal, and enjoying an idyllic period between childhood and adulthood. As Claudia Nelson and Lynne Vallone point out, the girl of 1890 is not a twenty-first century teenager in period costume: profound differences separate her from the young woman of the 1970s or later. They add that the use of the word "girl" also reminds us that we must be careful not to impose our conceptions of what it means to be a young woman today upon these inhabitants of an earlier time.[3]

The College Girl of the 1890s was a new creature, and one that rather frightened her parents and suitors. An absorbing concern of many parents and social commentators of the turn of the last century was the reluctance of the first generation of college women to marry and, once married, to have children. Frequently cited statistics showed that the college-educated woman was choosing to marry late or not at all and, when married, was not producing Anglo-Saxon children at a rate comparable to the alarming fecundity of the recent immigrants. Had college made her too picky in her requirements for a husband? Was she too absorbed in a career? Had her education somehow made her *unwomanly*?

With its emphasis on feminine beauty, pageantry, dance, and dramatics, the college May Day festival must have reassured these anxious parents. The College Girl might possess a rigorous education, a new feisty personality, athletic prowess, and the career ambitions that were rarely, if ever, realized in real life. But the May Day pageants assured spectators that underneath it all, the College Girl was still a dainty maiden who conformed to the prevailing sentimental view of girlhood, and who would eventually make a good wife and mother.

Chapters 11 through 16 address the origins and nature of the college May Day festival. In many cases the girls themselves initiated the festival, and accounts of the origins of the festival at different colleges sometimes point to one girl who conceived of the idea: sometimes apparently spontaneously, sometimes directly influenced by her reading of a poem or an account of an English May Day, and sometimes influenced by the celebrations of nearby or famous colleges, as documented in popular periodicals. She would then convince her classmates to join her in the festival, a festival that sometimes was a way to honor the graduating senior class, or was designed to raise funds for a women's building or other cause. At other colleges, a girls' club or organization—the Young Women's Christian Association (YWCA) or a dramatics or literary club—initiated the festival. These events often served as fundraisers for the women's special interests, such as a women's gymnasium, the endowment fund, or a women's religious mission.

Once a May Day festival was initiated at a given women's college or coeducational university, faculty and administration usually embraced the event for two reasons. First, since so many of these institutions of higher learning for women were so newly created, administrators were consciously seeking ways to create their own college traditions: strawberry breakfasts, mountain days, step-sings, big sisters-little sisters, pumpkin parades, the carrying of the daisy chain at commencement, and so on. These traditions were deliberately conceived of and/or supported both to create solidarity within individual college classes as well as among the entire college community. A second reason for college administrators to support May Day was that the spectacle attracted thousands of spectators to the college each spring. In some cases special trains were laid on to accommodate the visitors, who invariably reported being impressed at the beauty and erudition of the college girls. In other words, it was tremendous advertising for the college.

While each college May Day festival had its own unique features, all had five key elements: the procession of the costumed participants, the crowning of the Queen, the maypole dance and its attendant folk or aesthetic dances, and the pageant or play given to honor the Queen. These pageants were ambitious, creative and exhausting to mount. Almost invariably the pageants were directed by the head of the women's Physical Education department and incorporated dance: in particular, folk dances and Greek, interpretive or aesthetic (modern) dances.

Chapters 11 and 12 address the creation of the college May Day festival and its evolution into the elaborate pageant. I review the varying criteria for the choice of the May Queen, and describe the additional characters sometimes seen, such as the May King or Robin Hood — both of which roles were usually played by girls — the Maid of Honor, the Court, Jesters, Trumpeters and Pages. I review some of the pageant themes from the 1920s and 1930s, discuss the music used in these performances, and review the types of dances from the Physical Education classes that spectators could see. These ranged from garland drills through the folk dances espoused by the Playground Association of America, classical (Gilbert) dances, "fancy" dances, aesthetic (sometimes known as Greek or natural) dances and, on occasion, tumbling or light gymnastics.

Chapter 13 examines the role of men in May Day, a role that ranged from passively (though usually enthusiastically) viewing the festivities to participating as an escort or a patron, to one of mockery or dis-May.* Chapter 14 discusses the ultimate symbol of the festival: the maypole dance, a dance that, contrary to what many believe today, neither dates back to those famous mists of pagan antiquity, nor has an invariable, fixed form, nor, until very recently, had any elaborate post–Freudian fantasies associated with it, such as that the winding of the ribbons represents a symbolic journey through the birth canal.

By the 1950s, especially in the South, May Day festivals had become essentially a beauty pageant. The Queens wore elaborate white gowns that frequently doubled a few weeks after graduation as their wedding gowns. They had large courts of honor, male escorts, formal dances, and huge bouquets of flowers. Details of their lives, aspirations and beauty secrets were published in local newspapers, and some May Queens achieved brief national fame.

There are still many May Queens alive today and some of these have provided documentation of their feelings about the event. The Queens of the 1940s and 1950s continue to value and treasure their election and the crowning ceremony itself, though they now look back at the ceremony and regard it as sexist — or at the very least, as non-feminist. But they say that while the event might not appeal to their daughters or granddaughters, it remains a happy and important memory for them. Chapter 15 addresses the process of selecting and crowning the Queen, and includes the reactions and impressions of some living May Queens.

By contrast to the Queens of the 1940s and 1950s, the opinions and recollections of May Queens from the early 1960s — the transition years — already reveal greater ambivalence about the custom. And by 1967 there was widespread, though by no means complete, rejection of the election of the May Queen and her court: of the 50 colleges in the respondent group still

---

*The term "DisMay" was used at Randolph-Macon Woman's College (now Randolph College) as early as the 1940s, where students and faculty performed skits and parodies as part of the DisMay Court. Today, perhaps, we tend to hear the word more aggressively as "dissing," or "disrespecting."

celebrating May Day at the beginning of the sixties, 24 held their last festival in just the four springs between 1967 and 1970. At many colleges the event simply ceased without much explanation or fanfare. At others, faculty expressed regret at its demise or students themselves were divided on the issue. In some cases very strong negative feelings — for or against the celebration — were expressed. Chapter 16 reviews the demise of the May Queen.

The final section of this book examines some other aspects of the celebration of May First. Chapter 17 reviews May Day as it is, or has been, celebrated as Labor Day, Loyalty Day, Law Day, Lei Day and Child Health Day, and touches on the un-related Mexican and Mexican-American festival of Cinco de Mayo. Yet May Day is far from dead — Chapter 18 reviews five types of existing celebrations: the remaining celebrations held at colleges; the celebrations within communities or in schools for young children; the celebrations of folk- and morris-dancers; and the celebrations of Pagans and Wiccans. I conclude the work with some observations on the nature and importance of the May Day tradition in our lives today.

Part II of this book provides details of the May Day celebrations of 80 colleges and universities. These 80 colleges form a sample that is neither comprehensive nor scientifically determined. I started with the assumption that any women's college or one that accepted women circa 1900 would have celebrated May Day and simply contacted as many as I could. Internet searches revealed other candidates, including a surprising number of large, co-educational universities. While in many cases the archivists were unable to determine the beginning or ending dates of the festival, or provided, at my request, only sample pageant programs or themes, the materials presented attest to the depth, the pervasiveness, and the coherence of the prevailing image of both the Merrie May Day of Old England and of American girlhood.

*The maypole's image of purity, childhood and innocence made it useful in advertising wholesome products such as Pears soap, Carter's children's underwear, Lifesavers' candies and, as in this ad, breakfast cereals (*Munsey's Magazine, *May 1903. Collection of the author).*

The celebration of May Day in the United States illustrates longitudinal stability: in the context of the larger society, it was a satisfying custom for decades until the major social upheavals of the sixties. In the context of an individual college or city the festival exhibits geographic and temporal variations: each community was able to take a common concept and adapt it to fit its own needs. Above all, the celebration of May Day in America represents an important and hitherto unappreciated facet of girls' and women's lives during the nineteenth and twentieth centuries.

A final factor in the creation of this study that I must acknowledge — and celebrate — was my own personal involvement in the 1977 Big May Day of Earlham College in Richmond, Indiana. It was my senior year and, as a folk-dancer and musician, I was the student dance coordinator for the event. I helped to make the costumes for the men's morris side, and turned up my nose at the coed morris side. I taught my fellow students the English country dances "Gathering Peascods" and "Sellenger's Round," and worked with other dancer leaders to help train the five, simultaneous performing groups of maypole dancers. I rehearsed fellow recorder players — The Tudor Tooters — in a handful of Elizabethan tunes. On the big day itself the May Queen (one of my house-mates) and I were awakened at six a.m. by the morris men, who danced on the lawn in the Queen's honor. From this distance of time I cannot remember if I was then aware of anti–May Day protestors, who were sponsoring a Prune Queen of their own, or whether my memory of that comes from a *New York Times* article on the topic from an earlier year.

The rest of the day is a blur: the procession of the 1,600 costumed participants, the successful winding of the five maypoles, the increasingly tremulous tootling of the recorders, all culminated for me in a crashing headache. But it was fun. It was hard work. It was an amazing festival to have participated in. And even then I knew that May Day was a special event and that I wanted to write about it someday.

Part I: May Day

THE MAKING OF MERRIE MAY DAY

1. Celebrating May Day in England before 1800

> *The Maypole*
> The maypole is up,
> Now give me the cup,
> I'll drink to the garlands around it;
> But first unto those
> Whose hands did compose
> The glory of flowers that crown'd it.
> — Robert Herrick, *Hesperides*, 1648

Ask most inhabitants of Britain or North America about the origin of May Day and you will probably get the confident answer, "It's an ancient pagan fertility holiday," followed by a nudge-nudge, wink-wink: "*And we all know what the maypole stands for!*" Whether these respondents are thinking of pagans as black-haired Romans in bed-sheets or blond-bearded Druids in nightgowns, they are firmly convinced that, while the holiday's origins are lost in the primeval mists of time, its primary purpose was fertility, especially human fertility, and that the maypole is a phallic symbol.

These beliefs would have surprised those Celtic and Roman pagans who, while they knew about sex, were unacquainted with maypoles. It would have surprised the American girls of 1830 and even the girls of the early 1960s who danced enthusiastically around the maypole. It would also have surprised their Baptist, Mormon, Methodist, and Quaker college administrators, who certainly would not have endorsed the festival had they felt that it was principally about sex, especially pagan sex.

It is true that the Puritans had denounced May games and especially the maypole as pagan, but their assertion was based not on evidence but, to paraphrase historian John Forrest's analysis of morris dancing, on a syllogism of guilt by association: the maypole is the work of the devil, paganism is the religion of the devil, therefore the maypole is pagan.[1] In fact most of the Puritans' specific complaints about May Day festivities focused on drinking, dancing, fighting and holding games on the Sabbath, rather than on idolatry. By dint of repetition, however, this belief in pagan origins continued throughout the early twentieth century in academic circles, and remains firmly planted in the mind of the general public. These general beliefs in pagan fertility rites have been strengthened in recent years due to the activities of modern Pagans, a movement that has its origins in the now largely discredited theories of late nineteenth-century folklorists.

It is true that the origins of May Day are indeed lost in the mists of time, in the sense that there is no historical reference to one year when the May was not celebrated and the next year when it was. Historian Ronald Hutton has concluded, however, that there is no documentation of any aspect but one (and that a minor and fairly localized one) of any aspect of the English May Day as being celebrated by pagan Romans or Celts. Instead, May Day was a holiday that was celebrated with enthusiasm by Christian Englishmen and women from at least 1240 through today.

The Romans indeed had a springtide holiday, but it bore no resemblance to the well-documented May Day activities practiced in England from the thirteenth century onward. Pliny reports that in 238 B.C., at the direction of an oracle in the Sibylline books, a temple was built in Rome to honor Flora, an ancient goddess of flowers and blossoming plants. It was dedicated on April 28 and the *ludi Floralia* (games) instituted to solicit her protection. Some years later the annual festival was discontinued, to be revived again in 173 B.C. after a cold spring that shriveled the blossoms. The Floralia included officially recognized farces and mimes, and were known for their licentiousness. The prostitutes of Rome, who regarded the day as their own, performed naked in the theater and even fought in the gladiatorial arena. By A.D. 303 the origins of the festival had become obscure; one commentator then ventured the idea that it was begun by an actual famous and wealthy prostitute, named Flora, who left an endowment so that her birthday might be celebrated by bawdy public games. This writer then accused the senate of conspiring to cover up this exaltation of harlotry by pretending that the festival was really intended to honor a goddess of flowers and crops. In any event, other than an association with flowers and young women, the Floralia bear no relationship to the recorded May Day practices of early modern England. It is also not clear to what extent the Floralia were celebrated outside Rome, and there is no mention of them being celebrated at all in Roman Britain.

Later descriptions of the Floralia were bowdlerized to suit more genteel tastes. For example, the brief article that accompanied the picture of May Day in the May 23, 1874, issue of the American popular magazine *Harper's Weekly* talks about "our Anglo-Saxon ancestors" going forth to the woods on May morning to gather greenery, describes the maypoles that "had their place equally with the parish church or the parish stocks," and added that "[t]he custom of having a Queen of the May, or May-queen, looks like a relic of the heathen celebration of the day. This flower-crowned maid appears as a living representative of the goddess Flora, whom the Romans worshipped on this day."[2] It was this picture and article that directly influenced two young Quaker girls to institute a May Day festival at Earlham College; a festival which, however, did not invoke the Romans. Instead, the girls made speeches describing the more demure May-tide activities of Henry VIII and Catherine of Aragon.

Another common modern assertion that May Day originated with the pagan Celts and their priests, the Druids, has even less validity, for we have no knowledge of what these peoples thought or believed. A non-literate people, the pre–Christian Celts left no textual messages behind. A handful of Greeks and Romans, writing over a period that spans the beginning of the second century B.C. to the fourth century A.D., did comment on various unpleasant attributes of the Celts, particularly those of Gaul: they drank their wine neat, not well-watered as a decent Greek or Roman would; they did not build temples; they were somehow associated with wild woods; and they were barbarous and practiced human sacrifice, something the Romans themselves had only comparatively recently given up. These glimpses are, however, insufficient to theorize much about the Celt's religious practices and beliefs.[3]

When we move to the British Isles of the post–Christian conversion period, information on pagan Celtic celebrations is similarly scanty and unreliable. The old religions in England appear to have been maintained until the mid-fourth century, declining and vanishing sometime in the fifth century, while Celtic paganism collapsed in Ireland sometime in the sixth century. The earliest Irish literature, a handful of hero tales, date from a period of at least two centuries later and were, in addition, written in Latin by Christian monks familiar with the conventions of the Latin classic genre. These tales provide glimpses of a pagan pantheon, but they must be regarded with caution, as they provide only a shadowy glimpse of a past that would, especially in the area of religious practices, have been heavily redacted by the writers. However, some of these references do seem to record a genuine pagan springtide custom consisting of the rekindling and blessing of fire. Historian Ronald Hutton argues that there is no evidence that the old Irish engaged in any sort of solstice or equinox celebrations; they were concerned more with the opening and closing of the agricultural year rather than with the movements of the sun.[4]

It is true that May 1 is also Beltane, one of the four great festivals of the medieval Irish year (the others were Samhain, Imbolc, and Lughnasadh, held, respectively, on the first days of November, February, and August). Of these festivals Samhain was the most important, a day when local leaders would settle disputes or arrange alliances. Beltane, as the word is commonly modernized today, was the second-most important feast day. The first written reference to Beltane does not appear until about A.D. 900 and was made by Cormac of Cashel in Munster, possibly a churchman, who wrote that men built two bonfires, "lucky fires," and drove the cattle between them on May 1. Other references to Beltane fires come from eighteenth- and early nineteenth-century sources. The fires seem to have lingered in areas of Gaelic influence: Ireland, parts of Scotland, Wales, and the Isle of Man, as well as in two places in England in which native British culture lingered longest.[5]

Hutton argues that the Beltane fires are in fact the only survival of pagan activities in the English ritual year. The survival of this folk custom, designed to ward away malignant spirits, is documented as occurring in many parts of Ireland, Scotland and Wales and in a few parts of England. Farmers lit fires in the fields and drove their cattle over or between them; people might jump or walk over the coals to obtain good luck or avoid bad. Indulgence in these luck-practices does not mean, however, that the participants were pagan; there is nothing to suggest that they were anything but devout, practicing Christians. Hutton adds that Beltane fires, while common in some northern parts of the British Isles and Europe that the Celts inhabited, cannot precisely be termed "Celtic," since not all Celts — a widespread people — practiced them. He concludes that the fires were a common way of protecting livestock and humans from evil forces at a critical part of the agricultural year, the time in which animals penned for the winter were released into the fields; arguing that the belief in supernatural danger on May Eve and May Day were strongest in the cold, northern parts of the Celtic world, where the people practiced a pastoral economy. In more southern areas of Britain and Europe, the opening of summer was a less anxious time, and its rituals were "far more celebratory and less defensive." Most of England, at that time, fell into this latter category.[6]

Thus, the possibility of the Beltane fires aside (fires that were *not* widespread in England), we cannot say that the English May Day originated in paganism, whether Roman or Celt. There is simply no evidence, written or iconographic, and it is pointless to assume origins and practices beyond the historical record.

The earliest historical evidence of May Day activity in the British Isles comes from a reforming English bishop circa 1240, who complained to his archdeacons about priests who demeaned themselves by joining in "'games which they call the bringing-in of May.'" Thereafter there are numerous references to the expenses involved of buying greens to bring in or make the May. Hutton notes that the term "bringing in the May" appears to have been shorthand for flowers and greens brought in from the woods to decorate houses and sometimes churches to celebrate the coming of summer.[7] Bringing in the May was an activity that allowed townspeople to reconnect with the natural world. Thus, in 1603 John Stow wrote:

> In the month of May, namely, on May-day in the morning, every man, except impediment, would walk into the sweet meadows and green woods, there to rejoice their spirits with the beauty and savour of sweet flowers, and with the harmony of birds, praising God in their kind.[8]

From Tudor England on, we are in a territory of familiar May Day images, as more and more writers described the day and the gradual joining to it by Robin Hood, morris dancers, May Lords and, more rarely, May Ladies, and that great icon of the holiday: the maypole. Increasingly abundant documents describe May Day activities: church records show payments for greens, costumes, ribbons, bells or performers; diaries record various antics or complaints about noise in the streets; polemics condemn improper behavior like the fights of rival village youths over the maypoles; and poems and tales paint a fanciful picture of youth and spring. From these sources it is evident that from 1240 through the early nineteenth century, May Day was celebrated in a variety of communal ways, these waxing and waning in popularity with changes in tastes, politics and religion. The Catholic church at various times supported the festival by sponsoring May Ales, a communal brewing of beer the proceeds of which benefited the local church. Records from the fifteenth century on that show that women in some areas made money by making or displaying May garlands. At some periods May Lords or Summer Lords, or, more rarely, May Ladies or Summer Ladies were invested to preside in state over the festivities. These Lords and Ladies, who rarely appeared as a couple, were neither attired nor acted as symbols of marriage or fertility; they were simply jolly representations of earthly authority who presided over games and farces, or used their royal roles to demand donations.[9]

Hutton writes that references to May games and activities — which despite the name did not always occur on May First or even in the month of May — multiplied as English literature increasingly included background descriptions. Scenes of going forth to the woods to gather flowers for garlands appear in Chaucer's *Court of Love* of 1346 and Malory's *Morte D'Arthur* of 1485. In a well-publicized account, King Henry VIII and Queen Catherine of Aragon rode out to picnic in the greenery on May Day of 1515. Hutton comments that Edward VI, Mary I, James I, and Charles I all seem to have been in different ways too prim for such activity, but Elizabeth I loved to dance at country houses on May Day, and did so up to the last years of her life.[10]

The origin of the maypole, the icon of the holiday, is obscure. Hutton observes that by the period 1350–1400 the custom was well established across southern Britain, in town and country and in both Welsh-speaking and English-speaking areas. He adds that maypoles were not found uniformly throughout the British Isles; they are recorded only in areas of English, as opposed to Celtic, influence and language. Hutton further argues that to these pre–Freudian people, the maypole did not represent a phallic symbol: "[t]hey were not carved to appear so, and their original stark outline was always concealed by layers of decoration when they were actually in use." He also provides evidence to dismiss the suggestions of the late nineteenth-century folklorists that the poles represented a survival of a fertility-giving tree spirit, concluding that the maypole simply represented a focal point for the rejoicing of the returning strength of vegetation.[11]

Huge maypoles were erected in permanent locations by cities and market towns where they might stand for decades: the "new" maypole erected in the Strand in April 1661 after the restoration of the monarchy was 41 yards high.[12] The maypoles were often decorated with garlands of flowers twining down the shaft; an engraving of 1769 shows such a pole with a large wreath hanging vertically about a quarter of the way down the pole. A group of young people are dancing in a circle with linked hands around the maypole. Little is, in fact, known about the dances performed in front of or around the maypole, though none before 1836 involved holding and plaiting ribbons (see Chapter 14). Poets simply described youths dancing, smiling, and kissing. An engraving of 1852 shows a far larger and more elaborate maypole: four X-shaped crosspieces in diminishing sizes are set at intervals along the pole, while numerous garlands or wreaths hang lushly from the crosspieces. There are no long ribbons. A flag and what looks to be a crown adorn the top of this huge maypole in the village of Burley, Hants, as depicted in the *London News*.

*A satirical political print of 1832 that shows a maypole decorated with garlands as was common prior to the adoption of ribbons. Note that the maypole extends proportionately more than three times the height of the men. One musician has just ceased playing a "whittle-and-dub"—the three-holed pipe and tabor—while the seated musician plays upon a triangle. (*McLean's Monthly Sheet of Caricatures, or, The Looking Glass*, June 1, 1832. Collection of the author.)*

The varying waves of the Protestant Reformation caused some May activities to go in and out of favor. Under Elizabeth I, some evangelical Protestants attacked the bringing in of May as an empty frivolity bringing with it the risk of debauchery; the best-known of these, extremist Philip Stubbes, averred pruriently in 1583 that of the maidens who went out, "scarcely the third part of them returned home again undefiled." While the reputed behavior of the young people served as both a scandal and a titillation — Stubbes' comments still appear in print and on websites as a basis for some modern Pagan sexual practices — demographic historians have revealed that there was, in fact, no rise in pregnancies at this season; the increase in conceptions came later in the warmer summer.[13] Elders have always criticized their juniors, however, and Stubbes' complaints might be seen as the equivalent of saying that playing video games will incite all teens to violent rampages.

As the sixteenth century wore on, and fears of social disorder grew, maypoles became a focus for municipal and religious complaint: rival village youths fought over the maypoles; there were instances of drunken behavior or Sunday merry-making; the owners of the trees were not always consulted before the poles were cut (in addition to simple issues of trespass, the owners' grievances probably came from the fact that the tall, straight trees sought after for maypoles could also have been sold for ships' masts). From 1570 to 1630 maypoles were banned in some major English cities. Yet during that same time, and after, the Stuart kings James I and Charles I explicitly lent support to the maypole by permitting dancing around it on Sundays — which was anathema to the Puritans. Banned for twenty years during the Puritan interregnum, the maypoles were triumphantly resurrected after the restoration of Charles II.

Maypoles continued to be common in England and Wales during the eighteenth century, as they were now firmly associated with the restoration of traditional order in Church and State.* They were still decorated with flags and garlands and were still a focal point for occasional raids and riots and landowner complaints. By the late seventeenth century, however, Hutton notes that a new theme of abandonment creeps into the historical record: maypoles have been blown down or rotted and are not being replaced. The last maypole in London was removed in 1795, leading him to conclude that the poles were simply going out of fashion at last.[14] As we shall see, however, maypoles — decorated at last with ribbons — did enjoy a revival under the Merrie England movement.

Morris dancing is another activity associated in our minds with May Day, though the association of the dance with urban May Day festivities did not occur until the middle of the sixteenth century.[15] While there are several distinctive regional styles, the style of morris that the influential late-nineteenth century folklorist Cecil Sharp somewhat arbitrarily determined to be the "most representative" is known today as the Cotswold morris. The dance collected by Sharp at the turn of the last century typically involves six dancers, with bells on their legs and either staves or handkerchiefs in their hands. A musician and, on occasion a Fool, a Hobby Horse and a Betty or Maid Marian — a man dressed unconvincingly as a woman — accompany the dancers and assist in amusing the crowd and collecting money.

For various complicated political and personal reasons, Sharp was committed to the theory that the morris was a relic of ancient pagan practices, left embedded in the minds of simple peasants rather like a fossilized seashell in limestone. Recent research has disproved this theory. In 1999 John Forrest concluded that the references to morris dancing are scanty prior to 1480; that they peak at royal venues in the period 1480–1510, at urban venues such as guildhalls from 1541 to 1570, and at church venues from 1571 to 1600. Morris dances were also performed at village, public house and open country venues from 1601 to 1990, while performances at private houses expand in importance to the end of the examined period, 1721 to 1750. He concludes, therefore, that the morris was an entertainment that originated at court and then slid

---

*The word maypole was also used as a derogatory term for a tall woman: when the 54-year-old, non–English speaking George I landed in England in 1714 to accept the throne after the death of Stuart Queen Anne, he was accompanied by his two mistresses whom the English, unimpressed with their new sovereign, rapidly dubbed "the Elephant and the Maypole" due to their distinctive physiques.

slowly, but not uniformly, down the socioeconomic ladder until it ended up where Sharp saw it, in the hands of out-of-work English laborers who performed in front of the gentry for money.[16]

Furthermore, the morris of 1480 was not Sharp's morris: save for the fact that the dancers wore bells attached either to their garments or their arms or legs and that it involved energetic gyrations, details of the actual dance are scanty and appear to have evolved over time. In some early cases in a royal or noble setting the morris appears to have formed a miniature romantic drama, in which a set of young male dancers compete for the hand of a Lady, who chooses instead to give her favors to a Fool. The point of Forrest's analysis, however, is that from its inception the dance was ever-changing, in terms of how it was performed, who performed it, and who watched it.

Robin Hood and his merry men appear as a pillar of the re-created Merrie May Day, and indeed, Robin was, historically, linked to that holiday, as well as to later summertime celebrations. Robin Hood's initial popularity may have lain in the fact that he was both farcical (he is routinely defeated at bouts of the quarterstaff at the hands of sturdy potters, tanners, etc.) and anti-authoritarian (he triumphs in his encounters with greedy bishops or false knights).[17] Recent research has shown that Robin's story was as evolutionary as that of the morris: he was already famous by 1262, and by 1470 his "games" had become linked to parish finances over a very wide area of England. These games might range from a simple costumed procession of Robin and his stock characters — Little John (from the beginning) and Friar Tuck and Marian (after 1500) — to a full-blown play. Hutton notes that if the morris traveled outward from royal and aristocratic households, Robin Hood plays made the opposite journey, climbing up the social ladder to reach the court of Henry VIII in 1510 in an elaborate entertainment.[18]

Yet, within two generations of entering the court, Robin Hood plays fell out of fashion even when maypoles and the morris did not. Forrest suggests that, for Protestants, his story had become both anti-episcopal and dangerously mocking. Friar Tuck, in Forrest's analysis the major link between morris dancing and May games, was triply objectionable: he was drunken and lecherous, he was a representative of the old Catholic faith, and he was a friar, and thus exempt from local episcopal jurisdiction.[19] The character of Marian remained tied to the morris, however, in the form of cross-dressing comic relief.

The historical record of May Day shows many other forms of celebrating the May: some more or less long-lived; some regional and some local. These range from "garlanding"— girls and young women making and displaying garlands of flowers to collect money — to the mock battles between Summer and Winter held briefly in the eighteenth century on the Isle of Man and in parts of Wales. As a final example of the mutation of tradition, let us turn to the Jack-in-the Green.

The Jack, who appeared at some American college May Day festivals in the 1920s and 1930s, is a man hidden inside a wooden framework completely covered by greens and flowers: only his feet can be seen. The Jack is "traditionally" accompanied by a band of chimney sweeps: yet, while to modern eyes the flower-covered Jack is romantically interpretable as a spirit of vegetation, the connection with his ragged boys is harder to make. Early folklorists like Violet Alford romantically claimed (without showing any evidence) that he was an "old" character, older than the Summer Lord or Lady, "for he is the Spring itself and [has] his counterpart all over Europe in the persons of Green George and the Wild Man from the Swiss forests."[20] In fact, historically, the Jack is a relatively modern creation, dating back no further than 1770, and was not connected to any sort of fertility spirit.

In his landmark study of 1979, *The Jack-in-the-Green*, Roy Judge found that the figure had its origins in the practices of mid-seventeenth century London milkmaids, who delivered buckets of milk daily to their customers. On May Day they would dress in their finest clothes and carry around a sort of pyramid, called a "garland," of silver cups and plates on their heads in order to amuse their customers and collect tips. Over time, these garlands got too elaborate and heavy for a young woman to carry; the milkmaids then were accompanied by a man who would carry the heavy tray full of plate while fiddlers provided music for the women to dance to. Competing bands of chimney sweeps and bunters (rag-pickers) also carried around garlands, often decorated with greenery as well as silver. Judge suggests that the Jack, completely decked in greenery, appeared independently around 1770, but in the 1830s became associated with the bands of youthful chimney sweeps. While the popularity of the Jack dwindled in subsequent years, due to concerns about rowdy groups of men and boys cavorting around town demanding money, he was revived in the romantic late nineteenth-century. And, in England, when May Day was again made a Bank Holiday in the late 1970s, after ceasing to be so celebrated in 1871, some morris teams revived the figure once again.[21]

From this brief overview we must conclude that, with the possible exception of the Beltane fires, which were confined to certain, Celtic-influenced parts of the island, the English May Day prior to 1800 had nothing to do with pagans, whether Roman or Celt. From 1240 until the early part of the nineteenth century, there were wide variations in how any individual May Day custom was observed in England: variations over time, variations between villages or between village and city, and variations based on individual tastes and prejudices as influenced by the budget of the sponsor of the festivities. By contrast to this historical pattern of diversity and evolution, we will see that the elements of the consciously recreated Merrie May Day in England and America are both well-defined and comparatively static.

2. The Making of May Day in Merrie England

"Robin Hood"
... Gone, the merry morris din;
Gone, the song of Gamelyn;
Gone, the tough-belted outlaw
Idling in the "grenè shawe;"
All are gone away and past!
And if Robin should be cast
Sudden from his turfed grave,
And if Marian should have
Once again her forest days,
She would weep, and he would craze:
He would swear, for all his oaks,
Fall'n beneath the dockyard strokes,
Have rotted on the briny seas;
She would weep that her wild bees
Sang not to her—strange! that honey
Can't be got without hard money!
—John Keats, Poems, 1820

While the May Day of historical record shows wide variations in practices over time and location from 1240 to the mid-nineteenth century, Merrie May Day, a creation of the early nineteenth century, was a remarkably homogeneous construct. Located hazily in the imagination somewhere between Arcadia, Avalon and the Golden Age of Elizabeth I, Merrie May Day was ineradicably associated with a maypole, a May Queen, Robin Hood, morris dancers, robust English games like wrestling, fencing and archery, and dancing and merriment on the village green. Puck, Shakespeare, Venus, Pan and Milton might also make an occasional appearance in this mélange. But how was this sturdy image created — and why at this particular time?

The epigraph to this chapter hints at the answer: while in the mid-sixteenth century poets like Robert Herrick wrote only of pretty pastoral customs in poems like "Corinna's Going a-Maying," or "Sweet Country Life," in 1820, Keats laments the money-grubbing, degenerate tendencies of the modern world, and looks back to a vanished idyll of English greatness as represented by Robin and Marian. The nineteenth century was a watershed time, particularly in the areas of population statistics and economics. The century began with social and economic dislocations caused by the Napoleonic wars. The transformation from an agrarian to an industrial economy, with its resulting migration of workers from the country to the city and the human cost in a society without social safety nets, took a terrible toll. While only one in four Americans lived in cities at the end of the Civil War, for example, by the end of World War I more than one out of two Americans lived in a city, a result not only of immigration patterns but of the movement of workers from the country to the city, cities that were ill-equipped to handle issues of sanitation, education and entertainment. Inflation and periodic economic and crop failures broke banks and destroyed livelihoods, making the nineteenth century in both England and America a time of turmoil. As a result, many individuals in both countries sought comfort in an idyll of the past. They looked longingly back to Merrie England, a dream-time bathed in mellow hues, inhabited, as Gillian Bennett notes, "by contented yokels with picturesque customs, and glorying in a checkered landscape of fields and woods and quiet farms."[1] This was an England—nineteenth-century America's spiritual mother—untroubled by economic and class strife.

If the nineteenth century was so troubled by these issues, and so longing for a return to a Golden Age, we should expect to find that it was a time that other romantic and value-oriented holidays were invented or increased in popularity; and this is indeed the case. Nineteenth-century America saw the creation of, or the heightened celebration of, Thanksgiving, St. Patrick's Day and the political holidays of Washington's Birthday and the Glorious Fourth. Chief among the new holidays in America and England, however, was that of Christmas, and several influential Americans had important roles to play in the creation of the image of Old English Christmas as well as of Merrie May Day.

Holidays exist and evolve because we need them. During the first two hundred years of white settlement in the United States, no one celebrated Christmas. The Puritans felt that there was no biblical proof that Christ was born on December 25, as this date had been so ordained by the church in the fourth century, and they also believed that the holiday had been tacked onto pagan solstice celebrations. Indeed, for twenty years in the late seventeenth century, celebrating the holiday was illegal in the colony of Massachusetts. Moreover, as Stephen Nissenbaum notes, the holiday that the Puritans forbade was not the genteel one we think of: instead it involved rowdy public displays of excessive eating and drinking, the mockery of established authority, and roving gangs of young men and boys aggressively begging for money or food, often even threatening householders or invading their homes.[2]

Nissenbaum argues that the celebration of Christmas as a family, not a public, holiday began in New York City in the early 1820s as a response to social changes that seemed both threatening and overwhelming. While the middle-class creators of the private Christmas read Canto VI of Sir Walter Scott's poem "Marmion," published in 1808—"England was merry England, when / Old Christmas brought his sports again"—they were particularly influenced by the publication in 1819 and 1820 of *The Sketch Book* of American writer Washington Irving. Irving was a member of the Knickerbocker set: a group of patrician gentlemen, members of the Episcopal church, and politically conservative, even reactionary. His book included five stories about the celebration of Christmas at the fictional Bracebridge Hall in England. However, even Irving's hero, the Squire, is aware that he is *re*-creating a tradition of a Merrie Olde Christmas: the Squire has found himself unable to exactly reproduce what he felt were the genuine rituals of Christmases past, for the country people "did not understand how to play their parts in the scene of hospitality." Consequently he has been forced to scale back his festivities, but even in his scaled-back version, the country lads laugh at him behind his back: they know it is just play-acting.

In a later version of his *Sketch Book*, Irving himself admitted that he himself had never seen such a festivity; regardless, his popular stories were one of the foundations of the enduring imagery of Christmas, to be joined in 1823 by fellow-Knickerbocker Clement Moore's famous poem, "A Visit From Saint Nicholas," that gave us the unthreatening, family-oriented, gift-bringing Santa Claus. Nissenbaum notes that in 1843, Charles Dicken's *A Christmas Carol* would then suggest to mid-century Victorians how to celebrate the holiday properly with, respectively, the poor (alms), one's workers (a goose), and one's family (dinner). And as for the Christmas tree, that icon of the holiday, there is no credible evidence of its existence earlier than the 1810s, and its later popularity can be traced to a short story by Caroline Sedgewick published in 1836.

Christmas was an artifact of conservative artists and patrician New Yorkers. Merrie May Day in Merrie Old England was similarly a construction of romantic poets, nostalgic antiquarians, and politicians with varying agendas. Not all of these individuals were English: several Americans — among them Washington Irving, Nathaniel Hawthorne, and Howard Pyle — were instrumental in creating the shared image of the day. And each poet, artist, or antiquarian built on the images of the prior ones; historian Roy Judge has argued that that the continuous process of plagiarization was an important, self-preserving influence on the development of the festival. He observes that

> once an event [describing May Day] had entered the repertoire as contemporary it tended to remain so, and to be used as such, however long ago it had actually happened. Some, like Herrick's poetry, represented a recent discovery of what seemed, perhaps misleadingly, to be deliberate descriptions of old custom. Some, like Washington Irving's writings, immediately assumed an entirely spurious authority, based on no more than their attraction for the popular imagination.[3]

Judge observes that three points could be made with some certainty about Victorian English May Day celebrations. First, there was a great deal of varied activity, much of it very localized. Second, there was a growing consciousness of a decline in approved May Day activities and a corresponding appreciation of the moral values of this holiday. Finally, accompanying this sense of decline was a strong conviction that something needed to be done about it; that a revival was not just *desirable* but *necessary* for modern Englishmen.[4]

Despite the fact (or perhaps because of it) that there were active customs of Maying or morris dancing still extant in parts of England, mostly in the hands of the laboring class, the middle- and upper-class creators of Merrie England and its Merrie May Day did not care to examine these, but turned instead to the more romantic Tudor and early Stuart literary references to May games. These they presumed were more pure and authentic and more closely tied to the social function that they held in the Middle Ages, a golden time that was believed to lack the class strife of the 1830s.[5] Poets of the past, especially the Stuart poet Robert Herrick, were rediscovered and lauded; lines from Herrick's poems, such as "Corinna's Going a-Maying," appeared in numerous American college May Day programs or in the newspaper articles covering the events. In their eyes, the past was more pure than the present: a philosophy supported by the fact that when late-nineteenth century folk song collectors published genuine May carols, sung in recent memory in English villages as part of the still-living tradition of "garlanding" (carrying around garlands of flowers in hopes of earning tips), these songs do not appear in the American May Day pageants. This might be due to the fact that, unlike the morris dances that were also collected and published at this time, the songs were not presented as particularly "aunciert"; moreover, their lyrics are undeniably rustic by comparison to the elegancies of the Stuart poets.

Enthusiastic antiquarians contributed as much as did the old poets to the creation of Merrie England and its Merrie May Day. Antiquarians copied and re-copied written accounts of quaint British customs and traditions, rarely, however, identifying where and when such traditions occurred, nor whether or not they were still extant. One of the first contributors to the May Day mythos was the antiquarian Joseph Strutt, whose novel *Queenhoo-Hall* was completed in 1808 by Sir Walter Scott after Strutt's death in 1802. Judge argues that the first chapter of *Queenhoo-Hall*, on "The May Game," immediately became the standard authority on its subject. Strutt's larger work on English customs of the past, *Sports and Pastimes*, was first published in 1801 and went through at least five editions between 1830 and 1841. Excerpts from his works were cited in numerous popular articles; they appear, for example, in the American Jennette Carpenter Lincoln's *The Festival Book; May-Day Pastime and the May-Pole* (1913). In addition to Joseph Strutt's *Sports and Pastimes*, Chambers' *Information for the People* was published in 1841–1842, Horatio Smith's *Festivals, Games and Amusements* was published in 1831, and Hone's *Every-Day, Table, and Year Books*, between 1825 and 1832.[6] Journalists in America and England eagerly seized upon these quaint materials and published snippets of them in popular periodicals, thus, for example, the article on "May Day" by M. C. Hungerford in *The Outlook*, May 4, 1895, or Laurence Hutton's article "May-Day Customs in Ancient Times," in *Harper's Weekly*, April 28, 1894.

Washington Irving was also a significant contributor to the imagery of May Day. In 1822, he published a set of several loosely linked stories describing the May Day revels of the Squire of Bracebridge Hall. In these tales the villagers have summarily felled, somewhat to the Squire's dismay, a tree from his lands to serve as a maypole decorated with garlands of flowers but not ribbons or streamers. The Queen of the May, a "fresh, rosy-cheeked" village girl, is enthroned in a bower of green branches and flowers. Morris men accompanied by a boy dressed as Maid Marian dance while gypsy women tell fortunes. The Squire and his guests pass among the peasantry, who — well aware that they are play-acting for the Squire's benefit — wink and nod knowingly when his back is turned. At first all is well; the village May Queen shyly gives her chaplet of flowers to a lovely young lady bride. Alas, the day ends in fisticuffs, and Irving's fictitious narrator has his doubts about the possibility of a return to Merrie England.

> this was but a faint shadow of the once gay and fanciful rites of May. The peasantry have lost the proper feeling for these rites, and have grown almost as strange to them as the boors of La Mancha were to the customs of chivalry in the days of the valorous Don Quixote. Indeed, I considered it a proof of the discretion with which the squire rides his hobby, that he had not pushed the thing any further, nor attempted to revive many obsolete usages of the day, which in the present matter-of-fact times, would appear affected and absurd. I must say, though I do it under the rose, the general brawl in which this festival had nearly terminated, has made me doubt whether these rural customs of the good old times were always so very loving and innocent as we are apt to fancy them, and whether the peasantry in those times were really so Arcadian as they have been fondly represented.[7]

Even Irving refers to the re-creation of these old English customs as the romantic Squire's "hobbyhorse." The Squire can only keep the holiday going "in a forced state of existence" at his personal expense, and he finds "great difficulty in getting the country bumpkins to play their parts tolerably." He manages to produce a May Queen, but has had to give up on her companions: Robin Hood, the Dragon, the Hobby Horse, and Friar Tuck. Irving's narrator concludes by saying that, as an American, he is not a bigoted admirer of old customs just for their antiquity, but he is sorry to see May Day fall into disuse for the following very specific reasons:

> I cannot but regret that this innocent and fanciful festival has fallen into disuse. It seemed appropriate to this verdant and pastoral country, and calculated to light up the too pervading gravity of the nation. I value every custom that tends to infuse poetical feeling into the common people, and to sweeten and soften the rudeness of rustic manners, without destroying their simplicity. Indeed, it is

to the decline of this happy simplicity that the decline of this custom may be traced; and the rural dance on the green and the homely May-day pageant have gradually disappeared, in proportion as the peasantry have become expensive and artificial in their pleasures, and too knowing for simple enjoyment.[8]

The peasants have grown intractable, artificial, and ungrateful; their masters no longer care for them in the feudal way. The social dislocations of war, industrialization, and urbanization have made significant changes in the way the rich and the poor interact. There is no more lordly and generous hospitality flowing down to humble and grateful recipients. In Irving's analysis, the modern world is degenerate and the peasants are all revolting, in both senses of the word. However, Irving's readers missed his point: while he suggested that the past, no matter how lovely, cannot be re-created, his readers glossed over this observation and instead fastened happily upon the pretty images of the squire's May Day and Christmas festivals. Now well-launched under the apparent antiquarian authority of Strutt and Scott and with the romantic blessing of Irving, the image of May Day swiftly entered the popular consciousness.

Another major contributor to the May Day mythos was the poet Tennyson, who in 1832 published the first of three related poems now collectively titled "The May Queen." Saccharine by modern standards, the first poem, apparently written in 1830 when the poet was twenty-one, was a great favorite with early reviewers for its pathos, sweetness and simplicity.

> You must wake and call me early, call me early, mother dear;
> To-morrow 'ill be the happiest time of all the glad New-year;
> Of all the glad New-year, mother, the maddest merriest day,
> For I'm to be Queen o' the May, mother, I'm to be Queen o' the May.

Wild little Alice is to be crowned Queen of the May in the first poem of the cycle, but by the third, as she is dying of consumption, she bequeaths both her May Queen crown and her lover, Robin, to her more biddable younger sister. The poems do not provide much specific detail about the festival she is looking forward to: simply a brief mention of a crown of flowers and dancing around the maypole on the green. While Roy Judge concludes that Tennyson was not describing an event that he had personally witnessed, and was probably basing his poem on literary references, possibly even upon Irving's essays, he notes that the poem — so popular that it spawned at least thirty-seven parodies — had a formative influence on the development of the Victorian May Day.[9] The poem's first stanza was often cited in American college pageant programs, and the entire poem cycle was even acted out as, for example, at the Earlham College May Day celebration of 1896.

American author Howard Pyle's popular book, *The Adventures of Robin Hood,* published with his charming illustrations in 1883, provided further inspiration for a woodsy English springtime idyll involving Robin and Marian. Pyle followed that successful novel with romantic stories such as "A May-Day Idyll of the Olden Time," published in *Harper's New Monthly Magazine* of 1884. Replete with "prithees," "peradventures," and "by my troths," the story depicts the romance of a gentleman of 1610 who proposes to his mistress, the Queen of the May, in the course of a masque.

Physical images were as important as the word paintings. The first significant image of a Merrie May Day, according to Judge, was that exhibited at the Royal Academy in 1821 by Charles Leslie, an American painter and an acquaintance of Washington Irving. It was called *May Day in the Reign of Queen Elizabeth*, and included representations of the maypole, a May Queen, morris dancers, a pipe and tabor player, a fool, a dragon, a hobby horse, and so on.

Judge believed that the details of the picture came from Leslie's imagination as fueled by Strutt's *Queen-hoo Hall*. Certainly Sir Walter Scott, to whom Irving introduced Leslie, saw the picture as it was being painted, and, given his antiquarian interests, it seems reasonable to assume that he would have had comments upon it.[10] Other such images included those such as Gleason's *Pictorial—Drawing Room Companion* for May 7, 1853, with its three engravings titled "A Scene Descriptive of May Day in Olden Time," or the *Harpers' Weekly* image of "May Day in the Fifteenth Century" that inspired the Foulke sisters to inaugurate a May Day celebration at Earlham College in 1875.

Concurrent with the creation of a May Day in Merrie England, social historian Mark Girouard has identified a Cult of Chivalry that originated in the mid-eighteenth century but accelerated in popularity in the nineteenth with the publication of Sir Walter Scott's novels, especially *Ivanhoe*, published in 1819. *Ivanhoe* was immediately dramatized: in 1820 there were at least five versions of it running simultaneously in London, including one at the famous Astley's Amphitheater. Girouard describes the rise of the cult of chivalry and the taste for medievalism, a taste that looked back to a time that stood for tradition, authority, stability and romance. This preoccupation was both fueled by and contributed to Scott's popular medieval Scottish novels, the coronation of George III in 1821 at which almost all the participants sported pseudo-Elizabethan garb, and the fad for building medieval castles that took off after 1800 and peaked in the 1820s. These trends built upon each other to recreate an image of a new Golden Age: a better England, a Merrie England. With all this interest it was inevitable, as Girouard notes, that someone would give a tournament, complete with a Queen of Beauty; and this indeed occurred in 1839, under the aegis of a young, sporting Tory earl, Lord Eglinton. All the Tory smart set were seized with a passion to participate in his tournament, though the strenuous practice necessary to joust with success rapidly whittled down the initial 150 contenders to the thirteen knights who finally entered the lists. Tens of thousands of spectators purchased tickets to attend the elaborate affair, which ended in the disaster of a pouring rain.[11]

The failure of the Eglinton Tournament did not kill the spirit of chivalry; less than three years later, the Queen and Prince Albert gave a fancy-dress ball whose theme was the medieval court of Edward III and Queen Philippa. Other tournaments and medieval fêtes followed, including, as late as 1912, a great tournament held as part of the tercentenary "Shakespeare's England" celebrations organized by the American-born Lady Randolph Churchill—or Mrs. George Cornwallis-West as she had now become.

The point of these chivalric and medieval excesses? First, that members of the upper class in England enjoyed dressing up and playacting, especially playacting about a time that was perceived to be happier, more secure and more romantic than their own. Second, it is apparent that they felt that by doing so they might, as individuals, actually absorb the high ideals of that better earlier time. Girouard argues that the absorption into of these chivalric ideals into popular psyche is what made the nineteenth-century gentleman what he was, with his slogans of "women and children first," and "play up, and play the game." Finally, while the cult of chivalry is perhaps only indirectly connected to May Day in England, it was more directly so connected in the Southern United States, as we will see in Chapter three.

Politics were also bound up in this search for a stable past; different groups of reformers focused on the principles of chivalry to address the plight of the poor. The so-called "Young England" movement of the 1840s had four influential Conservative members of Parliament as spokesmen: Benjamin Disraeli, Lord John Manners, Alexander Baillie-Cochrane and George Smythe. These reforming activities sought to emulate desirable aspects of medieval

England: the return to the country, the principles of shared work and work-as-holiday, the revival of physical activity, and the return to principles of craftsmanship.[12]

In the 1840s and 1850s the influential art critic and philosopher John Ruskin also called for a return to Gothic architecture and the ideal of the craftsman, criticizing modern life for its ugliness, its soul-killing emphasis on money-making and its lack of closeness to nature. In addition to galvanizing social reformers and artists in both England and America, Ruskin had a direct impact on the image of May Day through his connection to the Whitelands training school for teachers, a connection discussed further in Chapter four.

Images of Merrie May Day and Merrie England could be seen on the stage as well as in the houses of the great. While teams of morris dancers in the living tradition were slowly dying out due to lack of interest from antiquarian-oriented gentry, the Old English Morris Dance could be encountered in theaters in the first eighty years of the nineteenth century. Roy Judge has described how theatrical morris could be encountered as an integral part of a play, ballet, opera or pantomime; as the interlude between the play and the afterpiece; and as an attraction in the pleasure gardens. He also noted that theatrical morris fell into three broad categories: as a comic or grotesque dance, usually performed by men and associated with pantomimes and circuses; as a country dance, often for mixed couples; and as a more balletic dance with graceful and aesthetic quality and often linked with maypole dancing. All of these forms of the dance affected later developments in those dances performed by street buskers. Judge also discusses how the theatrical presentation of the "Old English Morris Dance" was greatest during the height of the Merrie England movement, from the 1830s to the end of the 1840s.[13]

It is also notable that the maypole dance with plaited ribbons, a dance that in the popular mind is so old and so quintessentially English, first captured the English interest in 1836 at a production of J.R. Haines's romantic medieval drama *Richard Plantagenet* at the Victoria Theatre in London. After a morris dance earlier in the play, the second scene of the second act is described thus:

> A Superb Gothic Ball-room, splendidly illuminated ... a handsomely-decorated May-pole, center, with an elegant light on the top, and glittering streamers of different colours appended.... Music.— The Knights and Ladies advance, and the "Ancient May-Pole Dance" is performed. At its conclusion, a flourish of trumpets — the King drinks to all under the garlanded tent formed by the streamers of the May-pole — the dancers kneel and extend the colours, and the scene closes.[14]

Both the morris and the maypole dances in this production were choreographed by a professional dancing master to deliberately re-create a time that was felt to be simultaneously picturesque and ancient as well as peculiarly English in character. The spectacle proved immensely popular and subsequently appeared in many other theatrical productions. By 1840, according to Judge, the maypole dance had left the stage and was being used to lend additional color to the well-dressing ceremony at Buxton in the Derbyshire Peak District. During the 1850s and beyond the dance appeared at festivals in southern England, and the plaiting of the maypole became a popular attraction in a wide range of public situations.[15] We will examine the evolution of the plaited maypole dance in more detail in Chapter 14.

While the Golden Era that was being invoked by the phrase "Merrie England" was chronologically vague, its attributes were constant, as Keith Thomas notes: "a contented, reveling peasantry and a hierarchical order in which each one happily accepted his place and where the feast in the baronial hall symbolized the ideal social relationship."[16] Thus, as the image of Merrie England coalesced into a firm uniformity, the interest in revivals increased. The 1840s through the 1860s were rich in May Day revivals in England, most organized by local clergymen or gentry. Some were short-lived — sometimes because they became *too* popular and led to vandalism and rowdyism; others were very long-lived indeed. For example, the town of Knutsford, England, first celebrated its May Day festival in 1864. In 1887, upon attendance by the Prince and Princess of Wales, the event became known as the Royal May Day, and Knutsford continues its celebration today. Another famous and well-publicized festival was that created by John Ruskin in collaboration with the Reverend Faunthorpe, principal of Whitelands College, a training-college for teachers. This festival, described in detail in Chapter three, also continues today.

As another example of the intense interest in Merrie England, in 1885 and 1886 a musician from Cheltenham, D'Arcy Ferris, produced a series of popular revels and pageants — Harvest Queen, Summer Queen, or Christmas — employing a grab-bag of picturesque dances and customs. In addition to running these revels, Ferris, who titled himself the Lord of Misrule, revived the Bidford morris side, training young village men and sending them touring. He choreographed at least one dance for them, Bluff King Hal, set to an old tune, "Staines Morris." Some years later Cecil Sharp gleefully collected this dance and used it as prime evidence for his theory of cultural survivals until Ferris corrected his error, but not his theory.[17]

The image of Merrie England — now a shorthand term for all that was best about England — flourished throughout the century. Visions of Merrie England appeared on the stage as a ballet written by Sir Arthur Sullivan in 1898 to honor Queen Victoria's sixtieth anniversary. Running for six months (a long run for the time) at the Alhambra Theatre, *Victoria and Merrie England* boasted scores of druids, mummers, a depiction of May Day in Queen Bess's time complete with a solo dance for the May Queen and a maypole dance, Christmas revels, a tableau of Victoria's coronation, and a dance celebrating "Britain's Glory." Four years later, in 1902, Edward German's two-act operetta *Merrie England* established the composer as a possible successor to Sullivan in the world of English operetta. His operetta dealt with love and rivalry in the days of Good Queen Bess and Sir Walter Raleigh and included a May Queen and her faithful and faithless champions.

By 1896, one can find an occasional article decrying the artificiality of the recreated May Day. In her account of "Latter-Day Cranford," published in *The Atlantic Monthly* in April 1896, Alice Brown describes a trip to the village of Knutsford. Miss Brown found Knutsford's well-known May Day festival artificially "decked out in modern fripperies for the public entertainment." The May Queen rode in state,

> a pygmy lady of fashion, clad in white satin, elaborate, frosty, like a wedding-cake. But one would fain have seen her in simple white muslin enriched only with posies of her own plucking, gathered with the dew on them while even Corinna slept. "Wake and call me early," that I may hook myself into a ball dress and send for my wired bouquet! Some bathos comes with time.

Miss Brown found similar artifice in the maypole dance presented by a set of "decorous little girls.... They tripped it prettily, they braided and wove their ribbons round the pole, but the spontaneous joy of Old and Merrie England was not in them. A dancing-master had trained them for the public eye."[18] Clearly, spirit and enthusiasm were to be preferred over technical dexterity. However, while the article decries the artificiality of the Knutsford pageant, it nowhere suggests that the *idea* of May Day is silly or worthless — in fact, Miss Brown's criticisms reinforce the image of a verdant, spontaneous, youthful celebration.

The intense interest in Merrie England culminated in Joseph Deedy's creation of the Merrie England Society in 1911, which was responsible for running ambitious May Queen festivals in London. Children paid a penny a month to join, and were divided into districts called realms. Each realm chose its own Queen, and from these girls "the choicest one" was selected as May Queen of London. Judge reports: "In 1915 there were five realms (and queens); in 1917 there were fifteen; in 1918 there were twenty; by 1930 there were one hundred." He notes that the event became self-perpetuating, with the Queens from one period becoming the mothers and organizers of the next, and so on.[19] The event still continues; in the London borough of Bromley in May 2007, five local May Queens walked in procession with the London May Queen, her retinue, and a band.

The last great contributor to the image of May Day and Merrie England was the Anglo-American poet Alfred Noyes who, in 1913, published the poem "A Song of Sherwood" ("Sherwood in the twilight, is Robin Hood awake?") as well as a Robin Hood play in five acts. Lines from the poem appear frequently in American May Day programs or the newspaper articles describing them, and the play was performed at numerous May Day pageants.

Well before 1900 then, the term *Merrie England* was a patriotic emblem, a phrase that, without any further elaboration, conjured up a composite image in the minds of both Americans and Britons of the best and finest of English life, culture, and character. The Christmas Revels on the one hand and Merrie May Day on the other were the two prime anchors of this image, one that was fastened upon both by romantic aesthetes as well as Progressive reformers. "The ordinary person might well feel a misplaced confidence that he was well-informed about May Day," Judge concluded, "while the reality was that he was simply accepting an established repertoire of material created by romantic imagination."[20]

3. John Ruskin and the Whitelands College May Queen Festival

> Perhaps one of the most characteristic features of the art teaching of Professor Ruskin, founder and first master of the Guild of St. George, is that it is the duty of women and girls — of girls especially — to be as pretty, and as prettily useful, as ever they can. Like all men of great mind, he is an implicit and explicit believer in the Divine influence of girlhood, of womanhood, and wifehood. And in various ways he has let this appear — in his devotion to his own mother; in the personal pleasure he has taken with and for many of his pets [girls]; in his teaching; in many of his writings, notably "Queen of the Air," "Ethics of the Dust," and "Fors Clavigera"; and besides all these, in his May Queen Festival at Whitelands College, Chelsea.... All our girl readers cannot be Queens of May, but they can all be queens in their own homes, diffusing brightness and joy and happiness.
> — The Reverend John Faunthorpe, Principal of Whitelands College and co-founder with John Ruskin of the Whitelands May Queen Festival, in "Professor Ruskin's May-Day Festival," *The Girl's Own Paper*, April 20, 1889

If the cult of chivalry and honor was to define the nineteenth-century English or American gentleman, what then would define the lady? Philosopher and art critic John Ruskin filled the gap in 1865 with the publication of his popular book *Sesame and Lilies*, a romantic treatise on the education of the girl, in which he declared that "queens you must always be; queens to your lovers; queens to your husbands and your sons; queens of higher mystery to the world beyond, which bows itself, and will for ever bow, before the myrtle crown and the stainless scepter of womanhood."[1] Ruskin's philosophies and his romantic view of girlhood, especially as embodied in the still-ongoing May Queen festival at Whitelands College, Chelsea, England, had an important effect on the evolution of the American May Day celebrations at colleges and schools in the late 1890s.

For many years folklorists of the early twentieth century such as Violet Alford asserted that Ruskin had personally introduced the plaited maypole dance to England from Italy as part of his Whitelands College May Queen celebration.[2] However, this claim is erroneous. Both Roy Judge, in his study "Tradition and the Plaited Maypole Dance," and the archivist and historian of Whitelands College itself provide evidence against this claim. As detailed in Chapter 14, the plaited maypole dance first became popular in England as a result of an 1836 theatrical production. Judge concluded that in the nineteenth century, Whitelands College was simply making a successful takeover bid for the responsibility of originating the school May Day, adding that its well-publicized festival certainly gave significant encouragement to any already flourishing set of activities.[3] It is certain, however, that Ruskin's involvement with the Whitelands festival gave it and other May Day celebrations both publicity and a stamp of approval.

John Ruskin was born to wealthy, middle-class parents in 1819. During his life he witnessed firsthand the disruptions attendant upon the nineteenth-century migration of rural workers and their families to the cities and factories. Ruskin felt that industrialization had robbed the worker of control over his work, and of joy and beauty in general. Factories were ugly, they created nothing but ugliness, and they made the workers dull and ugly as well. Many of his writings addressed the need to reject the industrial era and called for a return to an idyllic, rural, medieval past. Ruskin and his follower William Morris were influential creators and proselytizers of the craftsman ideal, an ideal that strove to reunite the worker with his work and with his recreation. Ruskin's writings and philosophies were extremely popular in America: by 1855 Ruskin apparently felt that he had a more significant audience in America than in England. While his published works do not describe or directly address the May Queen festival, his books *Sesame and Lilies* and *Queen of the Air*, both sentimental treatises aimed at the ideal education of girls, were readily available to American readers. It is not difficult to observe how Ruskin's insistence on any girl being the natural queen of all those surrounding her translates into May Queen or Queen of Beauty Festivals.

Ruskin's conception of a May Queen celebration was a demonstration of the ideals of youthful rural innocence and the innocence and beauty of young girlhood. The philosopher was, in fact, unable to relate in a normal and realistic way to real girls and women, and he developed early in life an eccentric attitude toward an idealized femininity. He had attempted to institute a May Queen celebration more than once before 1881, when he then began correspondence with the Reverend John Faunthorpe, principal of Whitelands College, a training school (at that time called a "normal" school in the United States) for future schoolteachers and governesses. Whitelands had been founded in 1842 with the mission to produce parochial schoolmistresses not only to communicate knowledge but to cultivate Christian tempers and dispositions. In 1881 Ruskin and Faunthorpe began to discuss the form that the May Queen ceremony should take. While Ruskin had envisaged a rather simple ceremony that the girls organized and ran themselves, Faunthorpe successfully argued for one involving a special chapel service. The college's historian, Malcolm Cole, notes that Faunthorpe was a high-church clergyman fond of elaborate ceremonies, and that it was natural that he should choose to formalize the election of a May Queen with a religious service and that the Queen herself should be elected based on Ruskin's principles of "natural and uncontending worth." Faunthorpe also felt that the elected Queen should undertake some sort of charity work. Finally, Mrs. Faunthorpe and the governesses of the college inaugurated the custom of dressing the Queen in a suitable gown. These three elements—worth, charity and attire—remain an integral part of the Whitelands ceremony even today.[4]

Ruskin, who took a great interest in all the details of the ceremony for those whom he called his *little pets, girlies, White girls, sirens, little students,* and *perfectly beautiful girls,*[5] was particularly keen to ensure that the Queen was given a permanent memento of her office. At first he considered a golden fillet for her head, but he then settled on a cross, decorated in the early years with his favorite hawthorn, as more expressive of both his personal religious feelings and the college's religious foundation. Artists Edward Burne-Jones and Arthur Severn provided early designs for the crosses.

At first, Faunthorpe and Ruskin had some disagreement as to whether a junior (a first-year student) or a senior should be eligible to be Queen. In a style that evidences his sentimental and romantic obsessions, Ruskin wrote:

If I were a girl, I'd like to see anybody calling *me* a "Senior"!! They should have their faces scratched if I was put in a coalhole for it. Also if I were a Principal, I'm not sure whether I shouldn't ordain that the Queen was to be chosen *among* the Juniors!

Of course there's to be a Cross every year! The being the likeablest or nicest girl of 160 is surely a thing which deserves memory, from all who care for her or will care, worth at least so much fastening of it as may be in a little gold trinket!⁶

Faunthorpe acceded, acknowledging Ruskin's recommendation that a first-year girl be chosen as Queen, since she would still be in college the following year when her term of office ended. And the concept of choosing "the nicest or likeablest" girl as opposed to the prettiest, smartest or richest one was to cross the ocean and reappear in the criteria for selecting a May Queen at many American colleges.

The first May Day festival at Whitelands was held in 1881, when Ruskin was recovering from one of his periodic bouts of depression. To sit for the official photograph that was to be sent to Ruskin, the Queen, who was dressed in mourning for her father, was hastily swathed in a white shawl and decked with flowers. In subsequent years a loose gown, suitable to fit any girl who was chosen Queen on the momentous morning, was devised. Ruskin did not approve of the design of the early gowns and commissioned his protégée Kate Greenaway to design one, decorated with the pansies (heartsease) for which she was well-known. The Whitelands Queens wore this gown between 1888 and 1891.

In 1889, Faunthorpe described the crowning ceremony for *The Girl's Own Paper*, a popular periodical published in Manchester, England:

> Flowers and evergreens are bought, and by the 1st of May the chapel, the college rooms, and the students present such an appearance of May, and May morning, and going a-Maying, as would do anyone's heart good, who likes flowers, and greenery, and pretty smiling faces, and white dresses, better than bricks and mortar, gas lamps and pavements.

After morning chapel, the girls voted for a junior girl to be elected Queen and the lucky girl was taken away to be robed. The Queen received volumes of all forty of Ruskin's works, specially bound by his publishers in purple calf and gold. As Ruskin wished, she kept *Queen of the Air* "by right" for herself and gave the rest, suitably inscribed, to her friends; and "if by chance it [the inscription] expresses rather what the girl ought to be, than what she actually at present is," Faunthorpe remarked austerely, "she has a life-long reminder of what she must strive to attain."

As each girl advanced to the Queen's dais to receive her book, the students sang May Day songs, danced around the maypole, or recited from Shakespeare. The Principal then made a suitable address. In an 1889 article in *The Girl's Own Paper*, Faunthorpe sycophantly related that in the prior year he had given

> some account of "Merrie England" as it was once, and as it shall be again when the writings of Professor Ruskin are more widely known and his teachings more extensively followed. The text, if we may say so, was this: "To please is woman's work." Women and girls can give and make pleasure. All right pleasure is praise and praiseworthy. They can give pleasure by making rooms clean and pretty, by kindly sympathy with all with whom they come in contact, and by carrying about the "Human face Divine" with a smile on it. "God has made you girls to take pleasure in the use of your eyes, and of your wits, and of your bodies. And foolish creatures are continually trying to live without looking at anything, without thinking about anything, and still more without doing anything," says Mr. Ruskin, and of course they fail, and become soured and discontented and miserable; and what is worse, they make everybody else miserable also.

A distinctive feature of the Whitelands celebration after the first few years has been that the

Queen wears a crown of flowers: ideally at first Ruskin's favorite hawthorn, which, however, is rarely in bloom on May 1, then, for many years, apple blossom. As the tradition evolved, the Queen chose flowers to match with or contrast with her dress. Regardless, at the investiture of the new Queen, her original, faded crown was removed and she was given a new floral crown of forget-me-nots. A bouquet of flowers similar to her original choice is still given to each of the former May Queens who return to walk in the procession.

As Ruskin had wished, the Queen declared a half-holiday. She and her maidens were photographed, copies of the photos being sent to Ruskin, who made many comments as to their relative comeliness or lack thereof. At Faunthorpe's urging, the girls then took down the wreaths and made them into bouquets to give to local hospitals "so there is May Day also kept, with flowers at hundreds of bedsides."

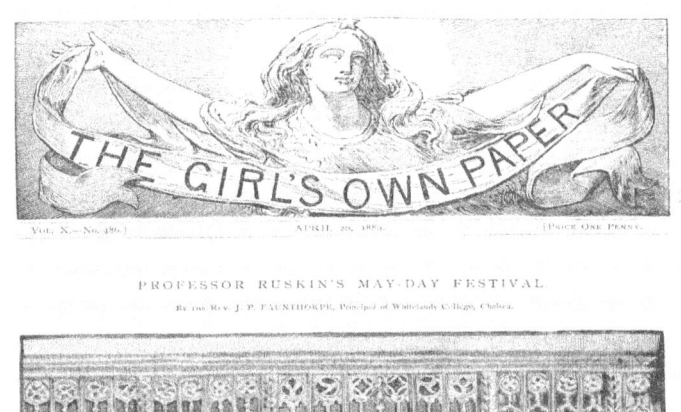

The Whitelands College May Queen distributing Ruskin's works to her subjects. She wears the pansy-embroidered gown designed by Kate Greenaway. (The Girl's Own Paper, April 20, 1889. Collection of the author.)

Faunthorpe concluded that that one of the "happiest features" of the Whitelands May Queen festival was that many of the graduating girls tried to institute the May Queen festival in their own schools, "and to try is to succeed. No one knows what help she will have in giving pleasure to others until she begins. All our girl readers cannot be Queens of May, but they can all be queens in their own homes, diffusing brightness and joy and happiness."[7] Shortly after Faunthorpe's article appeared, Ruskin entered his final bout of depression, dying insane in 1900. Although he was often at the college and gave money for several stained-glass windows designed by Burne-Jones and executed by William Morris's company, Ruskin never actually attended a Whitelands May Queen ceremony.

Within five years of its inception, an account of the Ruskin-Faunthorpe Whitelands May Queen festival appeared in an American periodical: the issue of July 10, 1886, of *The Living Age* contained the article "Mr. Ruskin's 'May-Day,'" by Eric S. Robertson. The article repeated all the details noted above, adding the instructive reflection that "'Girls,' says Mr. Ruskin, 'should be like daisies, nice and white, with an edge of red if you look close, making the ground bright wherever they are.'"[8]

Many American May Day celebrations implicitly followed Ruskin's ideals of worth or service, though only one referred to the philosopher directly. Accounts of May Day celebrations at numerous American colleges made explicit reference to the fact that the elected Queen should represent the spirit or ethos of the college, or that she should be the *best*— not necessarily the prettiest or the smartest — of all the girls. Only one of the respondent colleges, Rockford College in Illinois (then known as the Rockford Female Seminary, a training ground for Christian missionaries and the alma mater of settlement house founder Jane Addams), made explicit reference to Ruskin's ideals and to the details of the Whitelands ceremony. In 1902 Rockford began the custom of giving a pin and a small gold cross with a sprig of hawthorn on it to the Queen. A 1924 account of the giving of the pin noted that this was a "May Queen badge of 'sovereignty of service,' an old token revived by Ruskin." This account noted further that

> as the years went by the symbolism of the ceremony has been more and more emphasized. The choice of May-Queen is now determined, not by personal beauty or scholarship alone as it used to be, but by the worth and character of the girl. Ruskin's idea of the sovereignty of the May Queen being the sovereignty of service, has come to be the foundation of the May-Party, until today our Queen is a symbol to us of the finest and fairest in character, unselfish, serving all — the symbol, as she stands violet-crowned, of the best in Rockford College.[9]

The Whitelands College May Day festival continues even today, and an impressive aspect of the festival is the gown in which the newly elected Queen is presented. As mere men, neither Ruskin nor Faunthorpe had given any thought to this vital topic at the first ceremony in 1881, when Queen Ellen wore black. And after a few years of the suspenseful May mornings, the festival was modified, as it was too much nervous strain on the girls to wait until the day itself to know which of them was to be elected Queen. Thus since 1890, the Queen has been elected prior to May Day, an arrangement that permits each Queen to design her gown and choose her flowers. Since fine embroidery was a specialty of the early college curriculum, the elaborate gowns were usually beautifully embroidered, often with flowers or symbols of personal significance.

A distinctive feature of the continuing Whitelands celebration is that all the prior May Queens who are able to attend walk in the procession wearing their gowns and crosses, thus providing, as Cole comments, "a charming and fascinating cavalcade of dresses usually spanning some fifty or so years of May Queens.... The procession of May Queens, past and present, is therefore something much admired and commented on yet never ridiculed by those fortunate enough to witness it."[10] In 2003, for instance, Queen Beatrice celebrated her seventieth year as Queen while Queen Vera celebrated her fiftieth year by wearing a replica of Queen Elizabeth II's dress to commemorate the Jubilee year. In addition, the grandchildren of Queen Muriel (1903) participated in the ceremony as well as Queen Jean, who was celebrating her fortieth year; Queen Frances, her thirtieth; Queen Sharon, her twentieth; and King David, his tenth year. This continued involvement and emotional investment of the college monarchs, as well as the fact that numerous important personages, including royalty as well as literary and political notables, have attended the ceremony or presided over the crowning, gives gravitas and legitimacy to the celebration.

One American college, Grove City College in western Pennsylvania, also adopted the custom of honoring previous Queens: at least as early as 1925 it honored its Returning Queens. Now, every four years, all the former May Queens are invited to return to campus to be treated as "Queen for a day," and to walk in the procession. In 2004, for example, 19 former Queens, the oldest from 1938, returned out of 67 invitations sent. The college similarly honors its Homecoming Queens on a five-year basis.

Whitelands College is now one of the four constituent colleges of the Roehampton University of Surrey. The college, no longer purely a teacher-training college, admitted men in 1966, and men can now be elected May King. The spring of 1997, for example, saw the installation of the sixth May King, a young man from Ghana who wore his traditional Ghanian robes in the procession and the maypole dance. The ceremony is not just about the gowns, however; in fact, one of the several reasons why the custom has endured for so long is that there is a real function for the monarch to perform. Whitelands' modern May monarchs have increasingly turned to charitable services: the 2002 Queen, for example, raised over one thousand pounds for the hospital of her choice. The monarchs organize blood donation drives, assume responsibility for flag days, and welcome new members of the college.[11]

A final aspect of the Ruskin-Whitelands May Day ceremony is acknowledgment of the popular novels of the prolific novelist Elsie J. Oxenham (1880–1960), who wrote more than ninety books for girls and young women. Forty of these well-loved books are known as the "Abbey Girls" series, beginning with *The Girls of the Hamlet Club*, published in 1914. In this series a group of girls spontaneously create their own May Queen ceremony, one that incorporates several key elements of the Whitelands festival: specifically, the beautiful gowns elaborately embroidered with the flower of the Queen's choice, the Queen's choice of special flowers in the bouquet and crown, the procession of the former Queens in their gowns, and the removal of the faded wreath of the retiring Queen and its replacement with a wreath of forget-me-nots — though Oxenham added the feature that the thickness of this wreath indicated how well the girl was loved by her peers during her tenure as Queen. The Queens act as leaders of the school, taking care of younger or new girls, and teaching them the English folk dancing that they all love. When graduated and married, they still maintain an informal sorority, as did the actual Whitelands Queens.

Oxenham was a participant in the early days of the folk revival under Cecil Sharp, and she greatly admired Helen Kennedy, one of Cecil Sharp's key dance teachers. Kennedy was briefly a physical education instructor at Whitelands. Since Oxenham lived in London until 1922, it is possible that she saw the Whitelands ceremony firsthand, read about it, or that Kennedy described to her the key details of the event. Oxenham's biographer Monica Godfrey also suggests that the writer, who was deeply influenced by actual settings, buildings, and people, may have created her version of the ceremony from seeing crownings, maypole dancing, and morris dancing in other parts of the country.[12] Whatever the sources of her inspiration, Elsie J. Oxenham's books were, and still are, very popular in the Great Britain, Australia, South Africa, and Canada, and it is quite possible that they have, over the years, contributed to inspiring girls and women to initiate or support a school or community's celebration of a so-called traditional May Day.

I have reviewed the components of the Ruskin May Day festival at length because so many of them appear in the college or urban May Day: the tension inherent in choosing a worthy as well as a pretty Queen, the drama of the selection process, the roles of the current and retiring Queens, the gifts given by or to the Queen, the songs, dances and plays performed to honor the Queen, and the Queen as an exemplar of perfect girlhood. These ideas, combined with new American notions of the relationship of dance to physical hygiene and the emergence of the art of pageantry, would all contribute to creating the spectacle of the American May Day.

4. Merrie May Day in the New World

> *"Song of Sherwood"*
> Sherwood in the twilight, is Robin Hood awake?
> Grey and ghostly shadows are gliding through the brake,
> Shadows of the dappled deer, dreaming of the morn,
> Dreaming of a shadowy man that winds a shadowy horn....
>
> Merry, merry England is waking as of old,
> With eyes of blither hazel and hair of brighter gold:
> For Robin Hood is here again beneath the bursting spray
> In Sherwood, in Sherwood, about the break of day....
> Alfred Noyes, "Song of Sherwood," 1913

When and why did the celebration of an old English May Day come to the United States? It didn't arrive with the Pilgrims — while not quite as dour as they are sometimes represented to be, they certainly disapproved of dancing on the Sabbath and the drinking and fighting that often accompanied seventeenth-century May games. Five early manifestations of May Day in America can be found prior to the whole-hearted embracing of the image of Merrie England that began in the 1830s: May First as moving day, the famous Maypole of Merrymount, the maypole as a Liberty Pole, the Ring Tournaments of the ante- and post-bellum South, and the informal May Day celebrations of young girls at their finishing schools and academies.

May Day as Moving Day

From the eighteenth century until the early twentieth, May First was celebrated, at least in New England cities like Boston and New York, as a moving day for renters, a day that caused all kinds of confusion and pandemonium. This commotion was referred to as early as May 19, 1787, at the James Theatre in New York, where the Old American (theater) Company presented a two-act comic opera by Royall Tyler entitled *May Day in Town; or, new-York in an Uproar*. The libretto has not survived, for the opera was performed one night only. A contemporary review of *May Day in Town* found that while its plot and incident were "as good as any English farce," it failed because the principal character was a scold and some New York ladies were alarmed that everyone would think them the model for the character.[1]

Even as late as 1853, the "Editor's Drawer" column of *Harper's New Monthly Magazine* could comment on the confusion in the streets as everyone prepared for the annual clearances: the burning of straw mattresses and their attendant vermin, the finding of lost articles, the proliferation of wagons, carts, and wheelbarrows. "We once knew a wag," the editor commented,

> who, on the evening before the first of May, put up two "Number Eighteens" on two houses that were just alike, and that adjoined each other, in the same street. Two families were moving out, and two coming in; and, as he lived opposite, in his own dwelling, the wicked joker sat at the front window and watched the inextricable 'confusion worse confounded' that ensued.[2]

The manifestation of May Day as moving day appears to have died out sometime after 1900.

The Maypole of Merrymount

Maypoles in the New World under the Puritan regime were rare, and the most famous of these stood for only a few months before being torn down in 1627. It would take two more centuries before the works of Irving, Hawthorne, and the English poets would make May Day and the maypole popular in America.

The famous Maypole of Merrymount was an actual maypole erected for a few months in Quincy, Massachusetts. Its importance, however, lies less in what it was at the time, than in how it was romantically perceived in the nineteenth century, especially as interpreted by the New England writer Nathaniel Hawthorne:

> Bright were the days at Merry Mount, when the Maypole was the banner staff of that gay colony! They who reared it, should their banner be triumphant, were to pour sunshine over New England's rugged hills, and scatter flower seeds throughout the soil. Jollity and gloom were contending for an empire. Midsummer eve had come, bringing deep verdure to the forest, and roses in her lap, of a more vivid hue than the tender buds of Spring. But May, or her mirthful spirit, dwelt all the year round at Merry Mount, sporting with the Summer months, and revelling with Autumn, and basking in the glow of Winter's fireside. Through a world of toil and care she flitted with a dreamlike smile, and came hither to find a home among the lightsome hearts of Merry Mount.

Hawthorne's short story, "The Maypole of Merry Mount," influenced the popular imagination of Americans by adding more images to the celebration. It first appeared in 1835, in a Gift Book (a collection of poems, tales, and essays designed to be given to a young person by the newly invented Santa Claus at the newly invented holiday of Christmas) that also included a short story by Catherine Sedgwick that was the first to popularize the idea of

With gauzy wings and short skirts, these little girls look like fairies in this illustration of a May Day festival in New Orleans in 1866. The Queen's escort, the only boy in the room, stands to the left in a Grecian tunic and wreath. (Harper's Weekly, June 23, 1866. Collection of the author.)

the Christmas tree.[3] Because the Maypole of Merry Mount appears reinterpreted at several times during the nineteenth and twentieth centuries, it is worth examining its story, as well as the subsequent literary treatments of the event.

In 1625, one Captain Wollaston established a trading post called Mount Wollaston and located about twenty-five miles north of Plymouth, Massachusetts. The post was staffed mostly by indentured servants. The post did not produce Wollaston's expectation of wealth, however, and in 1627, with several indentured servants, he left the area for Virginia, where he realized a handsome profit by selling the men for the term of their indenture to the Virginian planters. He wrote back to Massachusetts, requesting that more of his men be sent, but a partner in the venture, Thomas Morton, instead led a peaceful rebellion among the servants, persuading them to join him in a colony where they would live together in equality. A gentleman adventurer, fond of erudite puns, Morton renamed Mount Wollaston as Mare Mount, or mountain by the sea. The nearby Puritans, hearing of the frolics held there, called it Merrie Mount.

Morton was on excellent terms with the local Native Americans, whom he admired. He provided them with liquor and firearms, both prohibited items, and in return, they helped him corner the lucrative beaver skin trade. As a symbol of his new colony, Morton caused a maypole to be raised. According to Morton's own account, the maypole was to act both as a beacon so that travelers (or runaway indentured servants) could find the colony, and was also to honor Maja, "the Lady of Learning." Morton invited the neighborhood to his festival and composed several songs and poems, including one to Hymen, as the young men with him were eager to have wives sent over to them. According to Morton's own account in his book of 1637, *The New Canaan*, these men, aided by the Indians, and to the rough music of guns, drum and pistols, erected an eighty-foot-long pine tree with a pair of buck's horns nailed to the top. They then broached the beer and wine and, in company with the Indian men and women, danced about the maypole.

Such was Morton's version. But according to Puritan Governor William Bradford, this was not a onetime frolic; instead the men were "drinking and dancing about it many days together, inviting the Indian women, for their consorts, prancing and frisking together, (like so many fairies, or furies rather) and worse practices. As if they had anew revived and celebrated the feasts of the Roman Goddess Flora, or the beastly practices of the mad Bacchanalians."[4]

Enraged by these reports of licentious behavior around and seditious tracts nailed to the pole, by the forbidden sale of liquor and arms to the Indians, by the concern that nearby Puritan settlements would not be able to retain their indentured servants, by the political insubordination that the maypole represented to the Puritan regime, and finally by the fact that Morton's company controlled the lucrative and desirable beaver skin trade, Wollaston and Captain Miles Standish captured the self-styled "Lord of Misrule" in 1628 and destroyed the maypole. Though they feared to execute Morton outright because of his powerful friends in London, the Puritans abandoned him for several months on an uninhabited island until he could be sent back to England for trial.

Morton and Bradford each wrote their own account of the incident, and these documents were available, at least to educated men, for the next two hundred years. The subject, for example, formed the basis of several letters of inquiry and discussion between John Adams and Thomas Jefferson.[5] (They both disapproved of Morton.) But in 1835, with the publication of Hawthorne's short story, the significantly revised tale, embellished with Hawthorne's poetic imagery, became available to the general public. And, in contrast to the facts as reported by the contemporary protagonist and antagonist, Hawthorne's tale itself created imagery for May Day fêtes of the nineteenth century. For example, he described the maypole of Merry Mount — that plain, almost prosaic, eighty-foot pine tree with a buck's antlers nailed to the top — as a colorful and picturesque pole, one not yet decked with long ribbons for dancing, but still a pretty sight:

> From its top streamed a silken banner, colored like the rainbow. Down nearly to the ground the pole was dressed with birchen boughs, and others of the liveliest green, and some with silvery leaves, fastened by ribbons that fluttered in fantastic knots of twenty different colors, but no sad ones. Garden flowers, and blossoms of the wilderness, laughed gladly forth amid the verdure, so fresh and dewy that they must have grown by magic on that happy pine-tree. Where this green and flowery splendor terminated, the shaft of the Maypole was stained with the seven brilliant hues of the banner at its top. On the lowest green bough hung an abundant wreath of roses.

Hawthorne described the maypole's "votaries" as dressed in fantastic, animalistic costumes in contrast to the Lord and Lady of the May, who were "two of the fairest forms that had ever trodden on any more solid footing than a purple and golden cloud. One was a youth in glistening apparel, with a scarf of the rainbow pattern crosswise on his breast. His right hand held a gilded staff, the ensign of high dignity among the revelers, and his left grasped the slender fingers of a fair maiden, not less gaily decorated than himself." The English priest who is to marry them is also decked with flowers in heathen fashion and "by the riot of his rolling eye, and the pagan decorations of his holy garb, he seemed the wildest monster there."

Hawthorne clearly identifies these revelers as idle dreamers and wastrels (if not worse). Even those who are simply innocently gay in the full flush of their youth, like the Lord and Lady of the May, are deserving of censure. The revelers worship their maypole at least once a month throughout the year, and soon come into conflict with the grim, strict and stern Puritans. Hawthorne identifies Governor Endicott as the force behind the felling of the maypole and the individual who orders a whipping for all its votaries. Endicott spares the May Lord and Lady, however, in part because of their beauty, but principally because, in true Christian fashion, each offers to sacrifice himself for the other. Endicott orders his men to cut the young man's Cavalier-style lovelocks and dress the couple in more seemly garb, and with his own gauntleted hand throws the faded wreath of roses from the ruin of the Maypole over the heads of the espoused lovers. "It was a deed of prophecy. As the moral gloom of the world overpowers all systematic gayety, even so was their home of wild mirth made desolate amid the sad forest." The young couple then work their weary way heavenward, never wasting a regretful thought "on the vanities of Merry Mount." As in others of his works, Hawthorne wrote of those who seek pleasure only to suffer the pains of its consequences. But the importance of this tale lies less in its religious moral than in the colorful imagery of the forbidden festival.

In 1877, forty-one years after the publication of Hawthorne's tale, Charles Francis Adams, Jr. (1835–1915), the grandson of John Quincy Adams, published two articles that provided readers with more of the facts behind the tale. These articles were undoubtedly submitted in order to support Charles Adams' re-issue of Morton's *New English Canaan*. Adams concluded that though the Puritans were admirable, they were not attractive, and that between "us and them" the intervening two centuries and a half were none too much. He further commented that in no respect was the sour and unattractive side of the Puritan character brought out more clearly than in their dislike of innocent and joyous relaxations, such as those of the maypole.[6] Such a critique from such an eminent historian may well have helped pave the way for a late nineteenth century re-creation of the formerly frowned-upon custom.

In 1912, during a time when there was a common perception that Americans did not know how to play and enjoy themselves and that the Puritans had left us too dour and gloomy a heritage, the tale of the Maypole of Merrymount resurfaced again under the aegis of the Pageant Association of America, an organization discussed further in chapter eight. At this time, Esther Willard Bates provided scripts for five different pageants, including a Colonial Pageant that incorporated nine scenes such as the Discovery of Manhattan, a Witchcraft Interlude, a Virginia ballroom, and the Maypole of Merrymount. A brief and quite cheerful scene in pantomime, the latter began with the following prologue:

> Not only goodly elders crossed the wave,
> But wastrel, spendthrift, vagabond, and knave
> Came hither once, and dwelt in merry mood,
> And many pranks played they from lustyhood.
> They raised a pole, and there in motley dight,
> With rout and revelry and vain delight,
> They danced a Maypole dance, and tried therein
> The Indian girl and Plymouth maid to win!

Wearing costumes from several different periods, these merry damsels dance with their shepherd swains, who wear late-Victorian smocks and gaiters, in the cover illustration of The Household Magazine, published in Boston in May 1894. The accompanying article tells the reader exactly how to organize a May Day festival. (Collection of the author.)

The scene opens on a background of forest greens. The "rout of revelers" runs on, the men in "dilapidated cavaliers' dress with as many incongruities as possible." The girls are to include a few Indian maids, a runaway Puritan and the rest, gaily-dressed English lasses. Two Indian boys "imperturbably" hold the maypole in place. The dancers perform "any of the well-known maypole dances to old-fashioned music and wind up the ribbons as they dance." They then run off the stage, laughing merrily. There is no further action or speech.[7]

Finally, twenty-one years later, in 1933, the Maypole of Merry Mount appeared as the opera *Merry Mount*, with libretto by Richard L. Stokes and music by Howard Hansen. Stokes took some aspects of the Hawthorne version of the story but darkened it considerably, perhaps to fit the mood of the Depression era. In his version of the story, the fiery young Puritan pastor, Wrestling Bradford, is indeed wrestling with his feelings about issues of the flesh. While he is advised for his own salvation and benefit to marry Puritan Patience

Tewke, he is suddenly enamored of a Cavalier girl, Lady Marigold Sandys, who is engaged to Sir Gower Lackland.

The cavaliers, who are determined to found a new colony devoted to pleasure and to call it Merry Mount, dance and sing with their Indian friends around the maypole (which Bradford denounces as a "staff of Hell"). Enraged by this sign of un-godliness, the Puritans attack and Gower is killed. Bradford then tries to force his attentions upon Marigold, who repulses him. Bradford sells his soul to the devil and eventually sinks into a bower of flames with the swooning Marigold in his arms.[8] *Merry Mount* was apparently one of the Metropolitan Opera's most successful essays into new American works in the 1930s, both artistically and with the public. At its premiere, the opera received a total of fifty curtain calls, a house record.

The Maypole of Merrymount thus represents a duality of the American psyche: the desire for pretty gaiety and the anxiety surrounding giving in to it. Perhaps because of its negative ending, I have only once — at Ursinus College in 1947 — found the story depicted in any of the thousands of pageants given at colleges or in urban settings. But the images of the beautiful flower-decked maypole and the Lord and Lady of the May who are the most beautiful of their companions undoubtedly contributed to the nineteenth-century image of the festival.

The Maypole as a Liberty Pole

Maypoles, which had become a symbol of opposition to Puritanical rule, were restored to favor in England when Charles II ascended to the throne. They appeared from time to time in the colonies as well, but took on new political life in the 1770s when the poles, first called "Liberty Trees" and then "Liberty Poles," began to be used as convenient points to nail up seditious tracts or to act as rallying points for colonists in their opposition to British rule. Dance historian Kate Van Winkle Keller reports that British soldiers would cut down the poles, only to have the colonists replace them. Even as late as 1798, a group of protesters calling themselves "Buck Skins," and claiming to be neither "*Scotch*, English or Turks, but Americans," complained that "a man of law and order" had ordered them not to attempt to erect a maypole "which should be a rallying point for all *Insurgents*." Americans have the right to erect on their own property what they please, they argued, and continued: "How frequently have may poles been erected and danced around too, without raising the citizens to arms; but the time has now arrived, when even the raising of a log of wood, is to be construed into raising a rebellion, and the sound of a child's drum as a token of opposition."[9]

Keller further documents a relatively short-lived custom of having a May King who took on the name and attributes of a Delaware Indian Chief named Tammany (?1625–?1701). She writes, "[S]ubject of many myths, Tammany was credited with supernatural exploits and was chosen in the 1770s as the figurehead of May Day ceremonies that combined elements of British May Day and seasonal visiting traditions with native American references, the patriotic resistance movement, and dancing." Thus, on May 2, 1774 (May first was a Sunday) in Norfolk, Virginia, an elaborate ball was given on "the anniversary of Saint Tamminy, the tutelary saint of the American colonies." Nearly 400 people attended and after the ladies retired, the "sons of Saint Tamminy" danced a mysterious war dance around their leader.[10] Later, in 1778, during the war, Dr. James Thacher noted in his diary:

> Last evening [April 30] May poles were erected in every Regt in the camp and at the revelle I was awoke by three cheers in honor of King Tamany. The day was spent in mirth and jollity the soldiers parading marching with fife and drum and huzzaing as they passd the poles ... one serjeant drest in

an Indian habit representing King Tamany ... in the evening the officers of the aforesaid Regt [Lord Stirling's] assembld and had a song and dance in honour of King Tamany.[11]

St. Tamany Societies were established in many cities as patriotic and sometimes charitable organizations, although it appears that the King's connection to May Day grew weaker after 1800.

Southern Romanticism and the Ring Tournaments

While the Maypole of Merrymount provided fodder to the romantic imagination of Northerners, residents of the South enjoyed a different romantic fantasy of Merrie Olde England: one that involved horses, a manly competition that included the spice of danger, and the crowning of a beautiful girl by the victor. The ante- and post-bellum "ring" tournaments of the South, while only loosely tied to May Day, nonetheless provided a precedent for the selection and crowning of a Queen of Love and Beauty, a popular figure in festivals, pageants, competitions, and other festivities in the nineteenth century, especially in the South.

It was Mark Twain who first bitingly argued that blame for the Civil War could be laid directly at novelist Sir Walter Scott's feet, with his popularization of romantic notions of chivalry, honor, and fighting as the best test of a man's prowess and nobility. Indeed, for some years after Twain's comment, the famous "tripod" of the South was considered to be cotton, the slave trade, and the cult of chivalry. Historian Rollin G. Osterweiss agreed with Twain's thesis to some extent, but preferred to modify the third leg of the tripod from chivalry *per se* to a general Southern romanticism which included "the cult of chivalry as its most persistent manifestation and the idea of Southern nationalism as its most ambitious impulse."[12] He also felt that the chief utility of the cult of chivalry was to bring color and entertainment into the monotonous routine of rural existence. Osterweiss noted that certain trappings were associated with the medieval ideals in their Southern form: the duel, the use of fine horses in the hunt, the tournament and the race; romantic place-naming; heraldry and ancestry; and lavish hospitality. A final aspect of the ideal of Southern was the romantic cult of Womanhood: an intense adoration of the pure maid, the mother, the hunting goddess. Osterweis was to add that, even as of 1949, "[t]he cult of manners still exerts a rigid rule in Dixie and the place of woman is not that sought by Susan Anthony and Carrie Chapman Catt."[13] The elaborate May Day festivals of Southern colleges in the 1940s and 1950s would confirm his observation.

Other observers have also noted that one aspect defining Southern "honor" for both men and women was the idea of bodily appearance as outward sign of inner merit.[14] In other words, if one appeared externally attractive and chivalrous or ladylike then it could be assumed that one also held these attributes inwardly. The reverse theory also held true: it was almost inconceivable that someone louche and ugly could possess a superior intellect or a refined sensibility. While not a new concept — this philosophy dates back to at least the early Renaissance — it contributed greatly to the idealization of the beauty of a Southern woman as a measure of her worth.

The physical manifestation of these Southern Romantic ideals — Chivalry and Womanhood — were the ring tournaments, simulated "jousts"— more accurately, tilting contests — that took place all over the South from the 1830s, through the Civil War and well into the 1930s. Jousting in fact remains the official sport of the state of Maryland today. The modern knight or "maid," as female contestants are known today, wears conventional English riding attire topped with a bright colored *gipon* or sash depicting the armor worn by his or her medieval counterpart and registers and rides under a title of his or her own choosing such as "Sir Knight of Cedar Lane," "Maid of Dragon's Lair," or even, if humorously inclined, something on the order of "Sir Knight of Will If I Can."[15]

The ring tournaments with their exotic pageantry found particular favor at spas and resorts where young people congregated. Esther J. and Ruth W. Crooks, who provided exhaustive documentation of these events in their book of 1936, *The Ring Tournament in the United States*, suggest that idea of the tournament in the United States came from the elaborate tournaments held in Europe, such as that at Maur, France, in 1828, and Eglinton Castle, England, in 1839. While some ring tournaments were held north of the Mason-Dixon line, ring tournaments were particularly popular in the South because, according the Crooks, the idea of winning the favor of a beautiful woman by being the victor in a gallant contest of arms appealed to the Southern gentleman. The latter's interest in horse breeding and fine horsemanship was another contributing factor.

To compete, the young man galloped on horseback while aiming the lance held under his right arm at three rings, each ranging from a mere two inches to one-half inch in diameter. These rings hung from hooks placed in a straight or curved line about 25 or 30 yards apart. The entire course of 100 to 125 yards was to be covered in a given time, usually 10 seconds. The Crooks noted that the tournaments were usually performed on horseback, but in the twentieth century there were occasional bicycle or automobile tournaments. Occasionally the participants engaged in other tests of strength or skill, such as saber or pistol shot exercises.[16]

Between twelve and twenty riders, or knights, competed at a tournament, though thirteen was the usual number. The knights took chivalric names from Scott's novels, Spenser's *Faerie Queene*, or Tennyson's *Idylls of the King*, in honor of the battles of the Confederacy or occasionally, in lighter vein, after local geographic features. Exotic costumes and elaborate pageantry were common. The winner of the tournament was rewarded with the honor of crowning his inamorata "the Queen of Love and Beauty." Girls vied for the honor, and, to be correctly attired in case that distinction fell to her lot, most were accustomed to wear white dresses to the tournament. An element of romance was connected with the selection of the Queen and her maids as the knights were almost always unmarried men, or, if married, they typically waived their right of selection to a bachelor friend.[17]

After the tournament there was often an elaborate supper and a ball, with additional entertainment such as tableaux, exhibition numbers by a dancing school, or a woman's tilt in which women tried their skill at removing tiny rings with miniature spears. There were burlesque ring tournaments, in which the riders came fantastically garbed on broken-down hacks or donkeys, or dressed as Don Quixote de la Mancha. In one burlesque tournament in Maryland, the men were mounted on mules and rode at suspended nail-keg hoops using saplings, brooms, and fence rails for lances. "The queen and maids were young men dressed in women's clothes and were carried around the tracks mounted behind their respective knights."[18] Southern black churches also sponsored "colored tournaments" as a means of raising funds. These were conducted throughout, including the crowning, exactly as the white tournaments.

Even the War Between the States, as the Crooks termed it, did not halt the ring tournaments: they continued in places, especially spas, where troops were stationed. During the one hundred or so years of their greatest popularity, tournaments were often given as benefits for churches or war memorial funds. Crowds of as many as 5,000 spectators were apparently not uncommon. Leading men of the community were often instrumental in providing funding or guidance for the tournaments. And, finally, tournaments often occurred on holidays, such as Christmas. The Crooks noted that before the Civil War, Washington's Birthday was a popular tournament day, but in the later years of the nineteenth and early twentieth centuries, May Day and Labor Day became more popular; however, the Fourth of July remained the most popular tournament day.[19]

The relevance of these ring tournaments to May Day as it was later celebrated in the South is not difficult to trace: the concept of a man's chivalry and a woman's passive acceptance of his protection; the image of crowning the girl whose grace and beauty most deserved the honor; the association of colorful costumes and fantastic imagery and names with an entertainment event; and the community orientation of the festival. It will come as no surprise that many Southern girls' academies and colleges warmly embraced the May Day festival and, in particular, the crowning of the Queen.

Early May Day Festivities in the New World

When did Americans actually first start celebrating a re-created May Day festival? The earliest reference that I have found to date of a May Day "fair" was that held in Boston in 1833. This crafts fair involved young ladies selling their drawings and needlework, just as Meg March experiences in Louisa May Alcott's *Little Women*, published a few decades later. The fair was presided over by a maypole erected on the central table, a pole fifteen feet high, according to the newspaper account, "dressed after the true Old English fashion." Evergreens, interspersed with red and white roses, twined around it and the pole was surmounted by small branches of spruce. "Four feet from the top hung a circle of evergreens, clustered with festoons of roses, and suspended by beautiful garlands. It was the most appropriate and interesting ornament of the hall, from the circumstance of its being a perfectly correct copy of the Maypole so famous in the holiday sports of our father-land."[20]

Four years later, on May 1, 1837, came the first coronation of a May Queen that I have identified to date, one described in the journal of Susan Nye Hutchinson, an educator at a girls' academy in Barhamville, South Carolina. Mrs. Hutchinson was apparently instrumental in creating the celebration at her school. She wrote, "The queen was led to a high rock where surrounded by a dozen maids of honor the address was read, the crown placed, the whole followed by the song which was most delightfully sung."[21] Later events held at this same academy involved the marching drills performed by a squadron of young cadets, the maypole dance, spectators from town, feasting, and dancing. Mrs. Hutchinson always wrote the Queen's speech, as the latter gave an embroidered flag to the cadets, and other local notables also delivered elegant addresses.

Historian Christie Ann Farnham notes that the crowning of the May Queen rapidly became a traditional event at Southern female schools and a ritual incarnation of the South's ideal of femininity. She observes that these romantic events, that afforded "unique opportunities for personal display," were popular with the students, who organized the festivities themselves if the administration failed to do so. She notes that the Queen was usually elected by the students on the basis of "sweetness" and beauty, although her father's status often played a role.[22]

In another early example, the Roanoke Female Seminary, one of Hollins University's precursors, existed from 1820 to 1841. Little information about the Seminary survives, though a letter from one student, the niece of the headmaster, notes in 1838 "a delightful party here on the 1st day of May, which day is generally celebrated with great rejoicings in nearly all female schools."[23] It is apparent that the festivities became both widespread and widely reported enough in America that, by 1840, Englishman Boleyne Reeves included in his *Kalendar of Amusements* the comment that

> Annually on May-day, in America, a very pretty custom is observed at the ladies' schools. The scholars select a favourite and beloved schoolmate whom they crown with a coronet of flowers, and create "Queen of May and Priestess of the Holiday." ... It is a sweet custom, calling forth sweet sympathies, and we wish nothing better than to lead to its adoption in old England.[24]

Apparently American girls had out–Englished the English!

In other early references, an inhabitant of the city of Buffalo, New York, recalled with pleasure a May Day party of 1840, with the elected Queen presiding over "dancing and other sylvan sports" while boys under military age armed with long spears marched in her honor.[25] Other contemporary onlookers waxed more cynical about the holiday: whole romantic boarding schools "do sometimes and in damp verity," sourly commented the editor of *Harpers New Monthly Magazine* in 1854, "go to the woods and fields, and dismally dance around a wretched pole hung with shivering flowers, and return chilled, sad, and weary, with rheumatism and tic-douloureux established permanently."[26]

One early and detailed description of a May Day festival was that of a celebration held on Monday, May 2, 1853, in San Francisco, California, just scant years after the Gold Rush of 1844 that opened up the far West. At that time the city boasted seven schools, fifteen teachers, of whom the writer of the account was one, and an unknown number of children. The school superintendent wished "this first celebration of a May Day ... *to be ushered in with all time-honored May Day customs*, and desired all the seven schools to combine, to inaugurate the event for all future observance of the day, and as a reminder of the homes they had all but recently left behind" (emphasis added). The phrase "time-honored" implies that the superintendent was sure that all the participants knew in fact what these customs were without any further description, an indication of just how securely the image of an English May Day was established in the American imagination.

The celebration began with a parade of the schools through the city to the party ground, each school led by a banner carrier. The teachers gave a bunch of wildflowers to each child. These were apparently much appreciated by those children who had just made the arduous voyage around Cape Horn. After a song, the May Queen was crowned by a "Bishop," a "fine, sturdy youth" from a different school, and there were additional participants such as a Scepter Bearer and Maids of Honor, one chosen from each school. "Next was the planting of the flagstaff to do duty as a May Pole, and when the American flag was hoisted all the children cheered; such cheering had never before been heard on this shore." A luncheon followed. According to this author, other glorious May Day gatherings were held over the subsequent years.[27]

An example of another early and spontaneous May Day celebration is that of the small town of Mendon, Utah. The town was founded as a Mormon community in 1859 with twenty families hailing mostly from England and Denmark. In 1863, the first spring after the U.S. Army's massacre of several hundred Indians in their winter camp, thus "resolving" the Indian problem, some young girls walked out to gather flowers. They voted to make the youngest of them, nine-year old Ingeborg Kirstine Larsine ("Seny") Sorensen, the Queen of the May. (Seny's mother had, in fact, been a May Queen in her home village in Denmark.) After this inauguration, the adults, in particular Seny's father and other male members of the Sorensen family, formalized the festival and continued to oversee and sponsor it continuously to the present.[28]

"May Day in Merrie England," the 1874 engraving published in Harper's Weekly *that directly inspired the Earlham College May Day festival of 1875. (Collection of the author.)*

The first acknowledged May Day celebration held at an accredited college (as opposed to a girls' academy) was that held in 1875 by the women of Earlham College, a Quaker college located in Indiana. The college was a conservative one in the nineteenth century: the students dressed soberly and spoke "plainly," saying "thee" and "thou." Men students were forbidden tobacco, and plays or even dialogues were banned at the college until 1899. Even the superintendent's acquisition of a parlor organ, to which the students might listen for one hour each week, was regarded as a dubious and frivolous innovation.[29] In light of this strictness of living it is amazing that two young women, the Foulke sisters, who were influenced by a picture and brief article that appeared in *Harper's Weekly* of May 23, 1874, were able to convince the matron that the girls should celebrate May Day.

The two-page engraving by C. J. Staniland that so influenced the Foulke sisters bears the caption "May Day in 'Merrie England.'" It is a romantic drawing of people sporting quasi-Italian Renaissance clothing and mid-nineteenth century hairstyles: a Lord of the May carrying a flower-decked staff and arm-in-arm with the May Queen (or, more likely, Robin Hood and Maid Marian), a tonsured friar (Tuck?), a Fool with a bladder, a Wild Man, morris dancers with bells on their jerkins, and a hobby horse, all dancing before well-dressed ladies and gentlemen who view the scene from the broad steps of a great house. The accompanying short article describes the custom of "the middle and humbler classes" to go forth in the morning to collect blossoms, dance, and crown the May Queen. It also reviews the history of maypoles, and explicitly (though incorrectly, as we have seen) describes the May Queen as a heathen relic and the incarnation of the goddess Flora, whom the Romans had worshipped "on this day."[30] (Curiously enough, Staniland's engraving had been originally published in *The Illustrated London News* on May 2, 1874, with a quite different article accompanying it that focused on the feasts of King Edward IV and Henry VIII and made no references to the Floralia.)

That these young Quaker girls were able to re-create even on a modest scale festivities that were explicitly, though erroneously, connected with Roman paganism is a triumph of the romantic and sentimental image of the holiday that existed in mid-nineteenth-century America. Another important characteristic of all these accounts of early May Day celebrations is that, whether the students organized part or all of the affair themselves, it was held with the tacit approval or the direct support of the adults: matrons, principals, teachers, and parents. A Merrie May Day in Old England was something that middle-class American girls were *supposed* to celebrate.

Setting the Stage for Performances

5. Physical Education for Girls and Young Women

> The aim of physical training for the woman receiving a university education should be more than the body training alone. It should educate and train the body to express the inner self: a woman should be not only strong, but graceful, and that grace should come from an inner prompting.... The May-pole ... serves much more than a picturesque purpose. It ... shows in the grace, precision and harmony of movement which it evokes, the immeasurable benefits of corrective, hygienic and educative exercise.
>
> Jennette E. Carpenter Lincoln, *May-Pole Possibilities with Dances and Drills for Modern Pastime*, 1907[1]

From the 1890s through World War II, college and urban May Day festivals fell under the purview of the Physical Education department, not, as might perhaps have been expected, the Theater or English departments. Physical Education instructors—many of whom were graduates of eastern women's colleges and/or the Columbia University Teachers School—used the May Day program as a showcase for the year's work in dance and drills and to demonstrate, as maypole-dance expert Jennette Lincoln noted in 1907, "the immeasurable benefits of corrective, hygienic and educative exercise." But why did physical education have such a prominent place in the college curriculum? And why did the May Day pageant fall under that department's aegis?

The emphasis on physical education for women in the 1890s and beyond was a direct result of both the increase in number of women attending college, and the continuing opposition to their doing so. Some doctors argued that women's constitutions were too weak to support the rigor of study, and that college would result in hysteria, mental breakdown and the total collapse of the woman's reproductive system. In 1873, for example, a former Harvard professor of medicine, Dr. Edward H. Clarke, stated that the "identical education of the two sexes is a crime before God and humanity that physiology protests against, and that experience weeps over."[2] Even more dramatically, another physician, Dr. A.L. Smith, wrote in 1904 that

> the duties of wifehood, and still more of motherhood, do not require an extraordinary development of brain, but they must absolutely have a strong development of body. Not only does wifehood and motherhood not require an extraordinary development of brain, but the latter is a decided barrier against the performance of these duties. Any family physician could give innumerable cases, out of his experience, of failures of marriage directly due to too great a cultivation of the female intellect, which result in the scorning to perform those duties which are cheerfully performed and even desired by the uneducated wife.

Dr. Smith went on to declare that most ill-health in women was due to overeducation, because

Top: *"Wand Drill," part of "The Quest of Youth; A Masque of May," the 1924 May Day pageant of Trinity University. The girls replicate the formation of a maypole with their long wands. (Special Collections and Archives, Elizabeth Huth Coates Library, Trinity University.)* Bottom: *A different group of girls perform a "Ball Drill," Trinity University, 1924. According to the program, these girls are either elves or Bacchanalians. (Special Collections and Archives, Elizabeth Huth Coates Library, Trinity University.)*

it overdeveloped the nervous system, taking blood to the brain and away from the generative organs. He argued that college educated women had overdeveloped nervous systems, causing them to lead abnormal lives and not marry until 26 or 27, if then, whereas, according to him, they ought to marry at age 18.[3]

The result of arguments like these was to cause women's colleges to require their students to take an extensive program of physical health and hygiene, in order not only to preserve, but to improve their health. Physical education at colleges for women went through a trial-and-error experimentation. Prior to the 1860s, dancing, walking, light calisthenics, and the performance of domestic duties were the principal forms of education in girls' and women's seminaries.[4]

In the 1860s and 1870s, physical education for women was seen to be corrective in nature, used to cure distortions of the spine and other maladies thought to be the unavoidable result of too much studying. Some colleges experimented with the German system of gymnastics, brought to the United States in 1848 by political refugees, who formed exercise clubs called *Turnvereine*. Others experimented with the wand and bean-bag exercises of Dio Lewis. In the 1880s and 1890s, educators turned to the apparently more scientific and measurable system of Dr. Sargent of Harvard University, who opened a teacher-training school in 1881. His system involved a thorough physical measurement of the student before and after the course of exercise. Student-specific exercises were prescribed in order to develop those specific muscles perceived to be weak. The improvement of each student could thus be measured and averaged with that of the class, leading to impressive annual statistics of improvement and change.

However, in addition to a rather negative philosophy that regarded each student as inherently defective, the Sargent system required a large gymnasium space and expensive equipment. While popular in both men's and women's colleges for many years, educators eventually challenged the system on the grounds that the development of certain parts of the body did not necessarily lead to better coordination in general. Finally, neither the Sargent system, nor any of the competing German or Swedish exercise systems, were suited to the crowded classrooms and playgrounds of the urban elementary schools, as we will examine in Chapter 6.

In 1893, Lida Rose McCabe observed that colleges were still divided as to the relative benefits of the Swedish, German and American (i.e., Sargent) systems, but that the women's colleges had begun to add fencing, equestrianism, lawn tennis, rowing and other outdoor activities, while physicians gave the girls lectures on physiology and anatomy. The girls' attire is suited to their activities, McCabe claimed, describing this cumbersome and bulky outfit as

> Black Turkish trousers with divided skirt effect, blouse waists with sailor knots of varied hue at the throat, black stockings and heelless Oxford ties [shoes] complete the gymnasium costume. A pretty girl in this Oriental garb is very attractive. Much diffidence was manifested in donning the trousers at first, and the unexpected appearance of Mark Twain in the gymnasium at Bryn Mawr, when a class was exercising, brought every girl instantaneously to her knees![5]

In the 1890s the emphasis in physical education shifted to creating general well-being of the body, rather than upon the increase of any particular sets of muscles. In addition, character training came to be considered as one of the aims of physical education: that is, the discipline of formal gymnastics or — possibly — athletics could be carried over into general life to give a girl greater self-control and poise. During this period many women's colleges also adopted sports such as archery, swimming, rowing and tennis, although these sports were usually not taught by the physical education instructors, whose focus was on drill and individual student improvement. Dancing and fencing came into the curriculum in the first decade of the twen-

Milkmaids with cow at the elaborate May Day festival held in 1911 at the University of Minnesota, an event that attracted 3,000 spectators plus the governor of the state. Robin Hood's Merry Men stand behind the girls. (University Archives, University of Minnesota.)

tieth century because they required definite organization and instruction, and because they could be done in winter when outdoor exercise was difficult.[6]

Athletic games, organized by the students themselves until well after 1900, were seen as a competition to the formal course of physical education instruction — and as a possible threat to the girls' health and mental well-being. Indeed, Sherrie A. Inness has suggested that the aggressive female athlete posed a problem for college officials, who were openly concerned with denying the allegations that girls who competed at basketball or softball were coarse and masculine and that, upon graduation, they would neither marry nor bear children in sufficient numbers to do their part in maintaining the Anglo-Saxon race.[7]

By 1910, however, the ideal of a physical education class was to develop muscular response and control that would carry over into self-control and self-direction outside of class — that is, development for life. In this theory, the behavior of the student was as much a part of the responsibility of the department of physical education as was the efficient use of her body. Dance, with its emphasis on enjoyable movement, self-expression, and artistry, fit nicely into this philosophy, and avoided the issues of competition and athletic aggression as well.

Thus, with its emphasis on folk and aesthetic dances, light tumbling, drills and other gentle forms of movement, the May Day program formed a perfect opportunity for the physical education instructor to demonstrate how her charges had improved during the year. For example, the director of the Berea College women's physical education department, who originated that college's May Day dance demonstration in 1935, was concerned with the number of girls entering college in the fall with a posture grade, as measured by silhouettes, of D or D+, and pleased that they left with a C or B-. "To the health of the individual, strength and beauty should be just as indispensable as imagination and creative power are to the soul of the artist," she wrote to the president of the college, adding that if beauty meant grace and ease;

> I think we saw it in the May Day program; it was symbolized by groups in their rhythm, formation, and movements; by individuals in their poise, action, and freedom. To the girls has come the realization and satisfaction that the tedious, monotonous hours they have spent trying to improve their body mechanics, to get their bodies supple, flexible, and strong, have been most worth while.[8]

Types of Dances as Physical Education

While, as we will see, the urban May Day festival principally showcased folk dances, the college programs refer to at least six forms of movement, and often two or three different types appeared in one program. These movement categories included marching drills, light tumbling, fancy dances, Gilbert or classical dances, folk dances, and the form of what we now call modern dance that was then titled variously Greek, aesthetic, rhythmic, interpretive or natural dance. While in this section I attempt to separate the forms of dance, there was a considerable overlap of terminology and perhaps even of movement. Thus, for example, a "fancy" dance with balletic steps, performed in what was perceived to be Welsh costume and set to a Welsh air, could appear to the uninitiated to be very similar to folk or character dance.

DRILL

Marching drills are exactly what they sound like: participants march about in complex patterns and formations: sometimes to music, sometimes to a count. To work the upper body, participants typically wielded props such as Japanese fans, hoops, parasols, balls, Indian clubs, "wands" (sticks ranging from one foot to about three feet, often decorated), garlands, wooden guns, flags or lanterns. Precision of movement was key. "To secure ... success two things are absolutely essential," wrote one author in 1907, "viz., exactness in marching, and motions and uniformity in dress. Indifference of attitude, corners carelessly turned, as well as varying shades of color in costume or differences in length of skirt, will detract seriously from the results of any drill, and waste the time and effort spent in preparation."[9] Indeed, the complex patterns evident in the manuals required considerable effort on the part of students and instructor alike. Drills were considered suitable for young people of all ages though they grew more complex as the participants grew older. College May Day programs refer to, for example, Milkmaids' Drills with buckets and sometimes with a cow (presumably acting as a focal point, not a performer), Gun Drills (performed variously by women, by men, or by a mixed group), or Japanese Lantern Drills (particularly effective at dusk).

AESTHETIC DANCES, GILBERT DANCES, CLASSICAL DANCES, DANCING CALISTHENICS, AESTHETIC CALISTHENICS

These terms apply to the form of dance created by Melvin Ballou Gilbert (1847–1910) and continued by his pupil Emil Rath. In 1893, Gilbert was asked to provide a form of vigorous dance to the Harvard Summer School of Physical Education. Gilbert simultaneously founded in Boston his Normal (teacher-training) School of Dancing. The form of dance that he developed was known variously as Gilbert dancing, aesthetic dancing, aesthetic calisthenics, or classical dancing. This dance type, a combination of ballroom steps and ballet without the pointe work, emphasized simple rhythmic movements of the body and arms, and was designed to cultivate grace and elegance as well as to promote physical hygiene.

Gilbert's work was continued by Emil Rath, who held the position of director of the Normal College of the American Gymnastic Union (formerly the Turnverein Seminary) from 1907 to 1932. Rath's works, *Aesthetic Dancing* (1914) and *Theory and Practice of Physical Education: Vol. I, Gymnastic Dancing* (1916), provide a more systematic approach to the theory and practice of aesthetic dancing than Gilbert's collection, offering detailed descriptions of the various movements of the feet, arms, head and trunk. Rath's more scientific work elaborates on the physical benefits in terms of endurance, coordination and poise that aesthetic dancing can give. He provided detailed descriptions and analysis of the arm, torso and leg movements of different steps and then informed the reader how best to connect one step sequence with another — a relatively challenging skill, and one which may in part explain the apparently limited appeal of classical dancing following Gilbert's death.

While Gilbert was an influential force — several important modern and folk dance leaders and writers studied with him, including Gertrude Colby, Mary Wood Hinman, and Elizabeth Burchenal — it is not clear how frequently that his compositions were used in practice: only a few of them appear on college May Day programs of the period, for example. Only Jennette Lincoln Carpenter's maypole dance book references one of Gilbert's dances — the "Faust Waltz." One reason for this may be that his manual of dances appeared posthumously, another may be that the music that he chose to choreograph his works to is, generally speaking, challenging. Unlike the very simple rhythms of the folk dances, the Gilbert dances would demand a skilled accompanist.

Figure and Fancy Dances

A form of dance similar to Gilbert dances in that their choreographers employed ballet steps, but dissimilar in that they did not necessarily promise a scientific regime of physical hygiene, were the "Figure" or "Fancy" dances, which blend into the "Character Dances," as described below. Fancy dances featured simple ballet steps set to familiar ballroom rhythms as well as props and fairly elaborate costumes. Englishwoman Elizabeth Turner Bells' book of *Fifty Figure and Character Dances* (published by A.S. Barnes in the United States in 1925) includes, for example, six "Dainty Dances Set to Olden Tunes"; or dances like "The Merry Milkmaids," a "Stately Measure" such as a shepherd's dance with crooks or an early Victorian crinoline dance with parasols, or a variety of dances of many nations, such as a Welsh dance set to the air in waltz time, "The Ash Grove." While the May Day festival of the urban children explicitly eschewed fancy dances, the early college programs often featured them.

Character Dances, National Dances, and Folk Dances

In the late nineteenth century there was some ambiguity among these three terms, though by the early twentieth century they had separated into distinct components. *Character dance* is the phrase used in the earliest years, and comes from the world of ballet, in which choreographers would prepare a dance exhibiting some national characteristics: this concept is well exhibited, for example, by the second act of the *Nutcracker Ballet*, in which there are the dances of Spain, Arabia, China, Russia, and so on. Most of these composed character dances bore only a slight resemblance to an actual folk dance; instead, they exhibited movements or postures felt to be "racial expressions" or "characteristic" of the people, performed to any type of vaguely characteristic music. Thus, in her book of 1912, *The Festival Book; May-Day Pastime and The May-Pole*, Jennette Carpenter Lincoln provided a handful of "character dances," such as "Japanese Dance," which could be set either to an unspecified aria from Puccini's *Madama Butterfly* or to "The Japanese Love Song."

In the United States, the term *folk dance* was used beginning shortly after 1900 as educators such as Dr. Luther Halsey Gulick and Elizabeth Burchenal made them more popular. The term referred to those dances directly attributable to people of specific countries or regions thereof, and presented with music unique to a specific dance. The practice of collecting folk dances, both on the continent abroad and from immigrants to the U.S., burgeoned after this date, and numerous folk dance manuals were published, particularly by Elizabeth Burchenal, who was a major contributor to the field, considered by Ida Tarbell to be one of the fifty most influential women in America.[10]

After more true folk dances were collected, the term *characteristic dance* began to fade away to be replaced by what was at that time considered to be a clear distinction between folk dances and national dances, a distinction felt to be similar to the distinction between a national anthem and folk song. For example, each "great people," as Gulick opined, had its characteristic folk music, and these musical characteristics were most fully worked out and presented in the national anthems. Similarly, folk dances of a given country were more varied and mutable over time, whereas the national dances were more static, more uniform and more elaborate.[11] National dances were those most characteristic of the country: for example, the "Italian Tarantella" and the "English Sailors' Hornpipe." In this view, theoretically all citizens of a given country would be familiar with their national dance, though their folk dances might vary from region to region.

Thus, in 1908, in connection with the Playground Congress of that year, an exhibition of folk and national dances was given in Van Cortlandt Park, New York City. Dr. Gulick described the differing values of the folk and national dances as follows:

> The children's part of the program consisted of folk dances, that presented by the adults of national dances. This distinction between folk and national dances is similar to the distinction between folk music and the various national anthems. Each great people has its characteristic folk music. These characteristics are more fully worked out and presented in more adequate form in the national anthems, which represent the same motifs as the folk music elaborated by the genius of trained artists ... we know in a general way that these folk dances have grown up gradually, not only embodying in themselves racial characteristics of movement, but represent-

An aesthetic dance with scarf, May Day 1910. (Archives, Chatham University, Pittsburgh, Pennsylvania.)

Graceful attitudes mark these Greek or interpretive dancers in the play Antigone *by Sophocles, part of the 1919 or 1920 May Day pageant at Converse College. (Archives and Special Collections, Converse College, Spartanburg, South Carolina.)*

ing in symbolic form race ideas, just as does the folk music. Like folk music again, these folk dances vary in detail with each group that employs them, while the national dances, like the national anthems, are more uniform as well as more elaborate.[12]

This distinction between folk and national dances continued for some time, and can occasionally be heard today. In 1925 Esther Willard Bates noted in her book on pageants that national dances were intricate and highly dignified, "beautifully performed by gifted and practiced soloists," as opposed to the simple folk dances of the children or even the "richly-colored, beautifully-costumed dances to which men and women have laughed in their native lands over the sea."[13] The numerous benefits of folk dance over other forms of dance will be discussed in Chapter 7.

Aesthetic Dances, Natural Dances, Greek Dances, Rhythmic Dances, or Interpretive Dances

This category of dance has a confusing and somewhat overlapping terminology; the terms do have some distinctions, but for the purposes of this work are used interchangeably to mean modern dancing, and to distinguish this type of dance from ballroom dances (quadrille, foxtrot, waltz), jazz dances (animal dances, rough dancing), folk dance or ballet. Aesthetic or interpretive dancing became popular after Isadora Duncan's triumphant return to the United States from Europe in 1908. Duncan based her barefoot dances, interpreting moods or emotions such as spring, sorrow, or joy, on her understanding of ancient Greek dances. Such dances featured light skipping movements or ponderous dragging steps as well as ecstatic attitudes of head, torso, and arms. Photographs from college yearbooks and May Day programs show young interpretive dancers in bare feet or white stockings and black slippers with laces that crossed up the shins and short Grecian-style tunics, with unbound hair and bare arms. The abstract drapery formed on the Greek model offered variety and undoubtedly the titillation of novelty to the dancer still accustomed to the corsets, high heels, and long skirts of normal life.

Greek or natural dances were typically performed to classical music. While occasionally the dance instructions provide details of movement measure by measure, frequently the dance is simply described as a brief story, such as the sun rising after a rainstorm or the death of

Narcissus. In some dance manuals, such as those of Mary Wood Hinman, photographs, sometimes as many as ten to a page, show the characteristic poses to be associated with the different figures of the dance. This vagueness allowed the individual dancers or their teacher to work out the specific details of movement as they pleased, in fact creating their own dances.

Most college May Day pageants in the first few decades of the century featured interpretive dances of various types. But these dances, so beloved by pageant-producers and educationalists, also had their critics. In 1914, one observer noted that

> The use of the word "natural" in describing this kind of dancing has tended to a belief that it can be successfully undertaken by anyone with good looks and a fine figure. For a time it seemed that anyone — especially if with some social backing — need only go on to the stage with bare feet and a minimum of clothing to secure instant success as a dancer. Indeed, signs are not wanting that the classical dancer may, for this reason, follow the skirt dancer into obscurity.... It is not uncommon just now to see performers on the stage who, under the blessed name of Greek art, do little more than run and romp about; young creatures in flimsy classic drapery, picking imaginary roses and throwing and catching balls. This is certainly very often pretty and attractive, and it can be made use of as a quite admirable educational exercise, but it is not a serious art.[14]

And the art form had its satirists, as well. In 1917, the young humorist P.G. Wodehouse poked fun at classical dancing in a romantic novel, *Uneasy Money*, in which a jolly former chorus girl now married to an impecunious English Earl is earning her living dancing in bare feet "and not much else" at a restaurant in New York City. Her dance — "The Dream of Psyche" — is described as "a truculent affair ... not so much dancing as shadow boxing," and in one paragraph, Wodehouse gives us a clear picture of what this natural dancing looked like.

> It began mildly enough to the accompaniment of *pizzicato* strains from the orchestra — Psyche in her training quarters. *Rallentando*— Psyche punching the bag. *Diminuendo*— Psyche using the medicine ball. *Presto*— Psyche doing road work. *Forte*— The night of the fight. And then things began to move to a climax. With the fiddles working themselves to the bone and the piano bounding under its persecutor's blows, Lady Wetherby ducked, side-stepped, rushed, and sprang, moving her arms in a manner that may have been classical Greek, but to the untrained eye looked much more like the last round of some open-air bout.[15]

Thus the college physical education instructor of 1910 had numerous forms of dance and exercise available to her for the physical and aesthetic improvement of the girls in her classes. Often these instructors had also received training in the art of pageantry, which, with its emphasis on symbolic dance, also fell under the physical education curriculum. These instructors used the May Day festival as a natural showcase to feature the improved grace, strength and talents of the young college performers.

6. "As the Child Plays, So Will the Adult Perform": Progressive Reformers and the Playground Movement

> Perhaps the greatest of the values of games in both child and adult life is their contribution toward keeping the Emotional life properly aroused, self-disciplined, and health fully coordinated with integrity of thought and Right Action. As the child plays, so will the adult perform.
> "What Pittsburgh Junior High School Pupils Read," in the series, *The Heart of Youth*, The Henry Clay Frick Foundation, 1931[1]

> "Amusement is stronger than vice, and it alone can stifle the lust for it."
> Jane Addams, cited in the 1924 edition of the handbook of *The Victrola in Physical Education, Recreation and Play*, published by the Victor Talking Machine Company

Omaha, Nebraska, May 1, 1927: Workmen from the Nebraska Power Company scramble to lay the last few power lines in each of the seven city parks, while local radio dealers warm up the radio tubes. Harassed parents and teachers escort more than 9,000 children to the parks, over roads clogged with automobiles, trolley cars, and taxi-cabs carrying more than 42,000 spectators to the same locations. After some announcements, the children, organized by school, begin dancing *simultaneously* in all seven parks to the music broadcast over the airwaves: the "well-known" folk dances "Csebogar," the "Irish Jig," the "Dal Dance," the "Scotch Reel," the "Bummel Schottische," an English morris dance titled "How Do You Do, Sir?" and, as the grand finale, the maypole dance.[2]

How this organizational *tour de force* came into being as part of a May Day celebration and how the folk dances became *well-known* both in city parks and college campuses is the combined story of the Playground Association of America, the Child Hygiene Department of the Russell Sage Foundation, the American Pageant Association, and the compelling image of a youth-centered May Day. The folk and maypole dances performed by thousands of children each spring represented, in part, a Progressive ideal for the amelioration of the problems of the city.

The Problem of the City

The Progressive reformers active between approximately 1880 and 1920 found reason for despair both in the nation's large cities and in its poor, rural areas. If rural life was isolated and stultifying, the transfer of the workforce from the farm to the city, combined with waves of immigration, strained the social fabric of the city. Sanitary systems were ineffectual and typhoid, diphtheria and tuberculosis were endemic. There was no access to clean milk or water. Morbidity rates were high, but no one knew how exactly high since city officials did not maintain birth and death records. Parents labored in the sweatshops while their children took care of younger siblings and got into trouble on the streets. The city was blazing hot in the summer and bitter cold in winter. Gangs roamed the streets and both juvenile and adult crime rates were high.

The city was becoming ever larger, more anonymous and threatening, and more dirty and dangerous. The sense of change, of chaos, of looming destruction — whether from Bolshevist forces, labor strikers, or suffragists — was overwhelming, and native-born Americans of Protestant stock observed these conditions with fear and anxiety. A particularly overwhelming problem was the difficulty of absorbing millions of immigrants, mostly peasants, from alien cultures. The year of peak immigration was 1907: 1,285,000 immigrant entries were recorded. Three years later, 13.3 million foreign-born persons were living in the United States, almost one-seventh of the total population.[3] "We have become the world's melting pot," one critic despaired.

> The scum of creation has been dumped on us. Some of our principal cities are more foreign than American. The most dangerous and corrupting hordes of the Old World have invaded us. The vice and crime which they have planted in our midst are sickening and terrifying. What brought these Goths and Vandals to our shores? The manufacturers are mainly to blame. They wanted cheap labor: and they didn't care a curse how much harm to our future might be the consequence of their heartless policy.[4]

The newer immigrants were predominately peasants from unfamiliar countries. Mostly poor and uneducated, their languages and customs were different from those of the native-born white population, they lived in appalling conditions in the tenements and they could be — as the Haymarket and other riots showed — dangerous threats to law and order. Progressive reformers recognized that the immigrants needed jobs, but they also felt that these newcomers needed to be made fit for democracy: they needed to be Americanized, to absorb the commonly perceived attributes of Anglo-Saxon Protestants that included good work ethics, high moral values, a reverence for womanhood, and a regard for the process of democracy and the value of education.

The Progressives felt that one avenue to Americanization was to provide the immigrants with an improved moral character through greater access to culture and the arts. These reformers were convinced that the arts could uplift and transform workers on a personal level as well as improve their democratic principles. Culture could ennoble, elevate and purify these workers and provide them with a refuge from the turmoil and the feelings of alienation of modern life.[5] To help themselves cope as well, the American middle-class turned to personal culture and self-improvement, Delsarte exercises, Arts and Crafts, and the founding and support of parks, museums and symphony orchestras.

Yet culture itself was under siege. What *was* American culture? Did we actually have one? Even as late as the 1880s, observers felt that there was no distinctive American art form: no American opera, no literature, no drama. Critics like Henry James and Charles Eliot Norton felt that as a people, Americans lacked refinement, and our democratic society militated against our ability to remedy the deficiency.[6] For example, Constance Cary Harrison's popular novel of 1890, *The Anglomaniacs*, confirms that Americans themselves felt that they had no culture or refinement. The novel's plot centers on a nouveau riche, ill-bred American woman who tricks and manipulates her beautiful daughter into marrying a spendthrift, amoral, titled Englishman. Along the way, characters—both English and American—comment on the relative uncouthness of the latter at the time. An Englishman says that Americans think of nothing beyond "heaping up colossal fortunes and laying so many miles of railroad." The American responds calmly that "We'll catch up with history and the arts by and by.... Pictures and statues will come along.... In the last few years our grand new houses have been filled with treasures you were glad we had dollars enough to pay for.'"[7]

The crusade for culture took American artists back to a contemplation of a traditional civilization from which the earliest Americans sprang and to which all Americans were heir.[8] These artists called for a return to Anglo-Saxon ideals, readings of Beowulf, and the medieval tales of Scott and Pyle. Progressive artists indulged in nostalgic depictions of the peaceful small towns of a past that, as Robert M. Crunden notes, "always seemed to exist about the time [they were] born."[9] A merry Elizabethan May Day was certainly a part of this imagined ideal.

The Progressives felt that not only could Art be a panacea for society's troubles, it could work to ameliorate them. Calling on the shades of Ruskin and Morris, American Progressives John Dewey, Frank Lloyd Wright, and others argued that a democratic society needed to have all of its citizens able to express themselves creatively. Thus, for example, the Pageant Association of America (discussed further in Chapter 9) regarded community art as not only aesthetically satisfying, but as an instrument of creative democracy.

But, first, Progressive reformers had to tackle the pervading physical problems of the overcrowded city. Children—the hope of the future—were an important target, as well as being a malleable target and one easily organized in groups. "It is to improve the quality of citizenship that the city is gradually extending its protectorate over childhood," reformer Mabel Daggett wrote in an article of 1912 titled "The City as Mother." Daggett argued that even with the advent of compulsory education and labor laws that kept young children out of the factories, city children were still too mentally and physically weak to concentrate on their studies, forcing them to have to repeat grades. Her argument was not purely an emotional one, but an economic one as well—a strong selling point in the era of big business: "The attempt to put education into physically defective children is not a paying venture," she concluded.[10]

Reformers like Daggett successfully argued for the institution of compulsory education, child labor laws, school doctors and nurses, free lunches for schoolchildren and other ameliorative efforts. Other reformers founded settlement houses, where college-educated women (and men) lived in the slums and trained and nurtured the local population: two famous and influential settlements were Jane Addams' and Ellen Gates Starr's Hull House founded in Chicago in 1889, and Lillian Wald's and Mary Brewster's Henry Street Settlement founded in New York City in 1895.

The Progressive Answer: Health, Education and Recreational Reform

If health and education were two issues that demanded reform, recreation—in a well-organized form—was seen as one solution. "Play, games and physical training have become a necessity for school children if health and future intellectual efficiency are to be obtained," wrote one observer in a 1911 article titled "Recreation and Industrial Efficiency."[11] Play organizers wished to counteract the crowded conditions of the slums, the perceived social limitations of the Southern and Eastern European immigrants, and the moral corruption of capitalistic individualism: hence their preference for team sports—at least for boys.

The "problem of play" was not a small issue. Children who had no place to play were more likely to be juvenile delinquents, claimed Henry Street founder Lillian Wald in 1915. Recreation "may afford wholesome expression for energies which might otherwise be diverted into channels disastrous to peace and happiness," she observed, adding that "that clean sport and stimulating competition can replace the gang feud and even modify racial antagonisms."[12]

Public playgrounds for children were an unknown quantity in 1890; children played in the streets whenever the policemen's backs were turned. But play reformers were gradually successful in obtaining play spaces. In 1893 Jane Addams and Ellen Starr established the first public playground in Chicago the city. In 1895 Philadelphia became the first city to take over the administration of playgrounds, and by 1912, there were 257 cities, mostly in the Northeast and Midwest, that maintained playgrounds. Historian Dominick Cavallo reports that between 1880 and 1920, municipal governments spent over one hundred million dollars for the construction and staffing of organized playgrounds.[13]

The settlement houses, with their safe programs for children and teenagers, were also perceived as a beneficial counter influence to the attractions of saloons, dance halls, and movie parlors. By 1891 there were six settlements in the United States; by 1900 there were over 100; by 1910 there were over 400. Three-fifths of all settlement residents (workers) between 1889 and 1914 were women and almost nine-tenths of them had been to college. The settlement house thus acted as an important source of jobs or post-college activity for the New College Woman who desired to improve community life.

Settlement workers soon found that the most useful things to focus on to improve the lives of the urban poor were childcare and kindergarten classes for children whose mothers worked all day. Other classes brought in the mothers as well for classes in English, and homemaking, handicraft or vocational skills.[14]

Reformers and organizers adopted a variety of strategies to occupy, train, or, depending on your point of view, indoctrinate the children. For example, several cities offered "vacation schools" held during the summer at playgrounds and schools. The vacation school offered singing games, arts and crafts, and mild physical activity, such as marching and drills.

As Dominick Cavallo notes, Progressive reformers believed that mental, moral, and physical development for children went hand-in-hand. If the reformers could control the children's muscles, they would control their minds and morals, molding them into an agreed-upon Anglo-Saxon ideal of behavior and morality. Thus, in 1907 George E. Johnson, then the Superintendent of Recreation of the Pittsburgh playgrounds, reported optimistically that

> By catching children at the opportune period of development of any particular power or emotional interest, we may secure for them the highest possible development along right lines. In other words, we may in education, in a measure, assume control of individual variation. This thought suggests to us the tremendous importance of play in education and places in our hands a new weapon in the battle for the uplift of humanity.[15]

Children were thus the new battleground for a right-thinking democracy. Reformers like Dr. Gulick felt that the immigrant home was inadequate to teach the basic American tenets of fair play and democracy. He believed that racial antagonism was, in his words, "fostered, rather than discouraged" at home and in the streets. In addition, there was a generation gap: the dapper young Americanized children of foreign-born parents were ashamed of their parents' broken English, dowdy clothes, and strange customs. Gulick argued that the playground was the place to resolve these issues in a natural way, as the playground was a training school for development of individual character, democracy, and the qualities that make good citizens.

He put forth his theories in an article of 1908 titled "Teaching American Children to Play: The Significance of the Revival of Folk Dances, Games and Festivals by the Playground Association," published in *The Craftsman*.* There he stated that

> A fundamental condition for the permanent development of a free people is that they shall in childhood learn to govern themselves,—self-government is to be learned as an experience, rather than taught as a theory. Hence in a permanent democracy adequate playgrounds for all the children are a necessity.[16]

While some individuals questioned the value of organized play over free play, arguing that a spirit of self-reliance and the power of initiative required independence to develop, Gulick disagreed:

> While that is doubtless the case where other influences tend towards the right kind of physical and mental development, it hardly obtains when applied to the children of the crowded districts in a modern city. The lessons taught by the street, and too often not counteracted at home, are hardly those of manliness, courage, decency, unselfishness and fair play.[17]

As a result of theories like these the first few years of the twentieth century saw the creation of child- or youth-centered groups that taught morals along with healthy outdoor or crafts skills. The Boys Clubs of America were founded in 1906; in 1910 the Boy Scouts of America, based on Sir Baden Powell's Scouts, were founded under the direction of Ernest Thompson Seton (himself the founder of the Woodcraft Boys, an Indian-based outdoors organization) as Chief Scout; Gulick and his wife founded the Camp Fire Girls in 1912; and Juliette Low founded the Girl Scouts in 1912. While founded in the nineteenth century, the YMCA and the YWCA expanded their activities in the early part of the twentieth century, providing safe, cheap housing and middle-class activities for young men and women alone in the big city. Working girls' clubs, such as those started by Grace Hoadley Dodge, a wealthy young philanthropist and reformer, also stressed self-improvement and middle-class social graces, manners, and morals.

One result of these influential reformers' activities was the increase in public playgrounds for children. But just building some playgrounds was not enough — there were still too few playgrounds for too many children. Moreover, unorganized free play did not appear to provide the desired moral and social results. Gulick observed that if one hundred children were turned loose in a playground, the biggest and toughest of them would dominate the space, forcing the shyer or smaller children — those that needed the exercise the most — onto the edges as passive spectators. What was needed was both a factory-like, *efficient* use of the playground and one which taught the *desired* social skills: that is, the organized playground, or, in factory-floor terms, an efficient throughput of fun.

To have a properly organized playground, you need a playground organization. The Playground Association of America (PAA) had its origins in the spring of 1906 in an organizational conference that included Joseph Lee, a philanthropist and theoretician of play movement, Henry Curtis, Jacob Riis, Jane Addams, Lillian Wald, Luther Halsey Gulick and others. In 1907 these reformers formed the PAA with Theodore Roosevelt as honorary president, Riis as honorary vice-president, Gulick as president, Curtis as secretary, and Addams

---

*The Craftsman *began publication in 1901 under the direction of Gustav Stickley, the furniture manufacturer and chief American acolyte of Ruskin and Morris and the English Arts and Crafts movement. The first few issues directly acknowledged intellectual debts to Ruskin, the Gothic revival, and the guilds. By 1906, Stickley broadened the subject matter to include all contemporary art and social reform, as if to prove that craftsmanship led to total "right living": he changed the subtitle of the magazine to "Better art, better work, and a better and more reasonable way of living."*

and Lee as vice-presidents. The purpose of the PAA was to secure for urban children "'their natural birthright — play,' under the auspices of 'elevating leadership.'"[18] This agenda was more than just keeping children off the streets; it was a tool in urban reform and struggle against poverty, vice, and political corruption.

The PAA would not have been successful without the financial support of the Russell Sage Foundation, whose head, John M. Glenn, invited Gulick to become director of the foundation's education and recreation department. Instead, Gulick suggested that the foundation create a playground extension committee, with himself as chair, to act as liaison between both organizations. The PAA acted as a federation of autonomous playground associations located in major cities, each of which carried out its own research and activities with regard to play.

The overall goal of the Playground Association of America was to promote normal wholesome play and public recreation. One way to achieve this goal was to develop communal celebrations, such as the popular May Day festivals and other community or holiday pageants whose missions were to develop civic and social spirit, such as the community pageant in Thetfort, Vermont, in 1910 in that was cited by the Sage Foundation as a great success "in bringing the entire population of the town together in harmonious utilization of community resources."[19] Thus Gulick opined that: "The conscious restoration of such festivals as that of May Day, and the creation of suitable forms in which to express the spirit of liberty on the Fourth, are examples of how the community need for aesthetic expression is finding itself."[20]

The Theory of Play

Of course the Progressive reformers had a well-developed theory of play, and one which would directly lead to the urban girls' May Day festivals. This theory was articulated by the influential Dr. Gulick, and was based on the work of psychologist G. Stanley Hall, who had made child study a national movement under the premise that the science of psychology could modernize the practice of education, that a modernized child education could radically improve the prospects of humanity, and that the key to progress in these domains was to conduct child rearing and schools in conformity with the principles of natural human development, as determined by science. Hall's highly influential 1904 study of the child titled *Adolescence: Its Psychology and Its Relations to Physiology, Anthropology, Sociology, Sex, Crime, Religion and Education* combined scientific data with intensely personal reflections and observations to conclude that the adolescent had needs that were different from those of the younger child, and that both groups were ill-served both by current educational practices or by the too-early departure from school to work in the factory. The United States might lead the world in industry, commerce, and capitalism, but Hall argued that it had forgotten that "for the complete apprenticeship to life, youth needs repose, leisure, art, legends, romance, idealization, and in a word humanism, if it is to enter the kingdom of man well equipped for man's highest work in the world."[21]

Hall's theory was summed up in the phrase, "ontology recapitulates phylogeny," a theory based on now-discredited studies of embryonic development that suggested that the human fetus passed through different "lower" animal forms before achieving human form: in other words, that each successive stage in the physical development of an individual repeats the evolutionary development of the species. Hall believed that the child's physiological and psychological development also recapitulated what he called the development of the race: that is, as the child passed through stages of life he expressed certain hierarchical inherited instincts: the three-year-old made mud-pies like the most primitive of societies; the restless ten- or eleven-year-old expressed behaviors corresponding to the nomadic period of social organization; the adolescent's peer-group orientation and clannishness were redolent of tribal psychology. In addition, Hall believed that play itself rehearsed or recapitulated racial history; in fact, that play was the principal medium through which both the habits of physical movement and the spirit of the past persisted in the present.[22]

Luther Halsey Gulick supported Hall's theories and applied them to the science of physical education. Gulick's own ill health as a young man as well as his upbringing by missionary parents had already interested him in the spiritual and physical benefits of physical education. One of his philosophies was that good bodies and good morals went hand in hand; that there was a relationship between physical discipline and moral rectitude. As Cavallo observes, one of Gulick's most important theories was that "'[m]uscular contraction appears to be closely related to the genesis of all forms of psychic activity.'" Thus the little child should play cooperative ring games, the ten-year-old "Big Injun" should practice its racial memory by games that involve running and chasing, and the adolescent should engage in clannish team games and dances.[23]

Gulick felt strongly that play should not only re-invigorate these ancient "racial" traits, but that it should have a symbolic, emotional, or aesthetic component. Play should be "for the whole child—for his heart, mind, and imagination, as well as for his arms, legs, and chest."[24] While Gulick felt that gymnastics (at that time often simply stretching exercises performed at the children's desks) were beneficial in offsetting some of the unavoidable bad effects of school life—such as the hunching over desks that produces rounded shoulders and narrow chests—these exercises were primarily for the body, and had none of the equally important social, psychic and moral elements of play.

Thus, organized play was the answer, both to address the conditions of the crowded playground as well as to provide moral and social benefits. As Gulick observed, "organized play is freer than free play. In organized play, where every child is a unit in a larger, mutually responsible, mutually responsive whole, all reach a higher and more significant state of individual freedom than is possible on the unorganized, free-for-all playground."[25]

And Gulick's answer for boys was relatively easy: competitive team sports. Gulick was a proponent of the value of athletic and competitive sports for boys and men due to the fact that "[w]e are the survivors of those whose very lives depended upon their ability to run, strike, and to throw, and whose mental and moral qualities of endurance, pluck, team work, fair play, and the like were developed in connection with the playing and earnest use of those activities."[26] Thus in 1903 Gulick organized the Public School Athletic League of Greater New York to encourage participation in athletics (which hitherto had been in the hands of the boys themselves), in order to promote all-round physical development and "to foster clean sport between gentlemen."[27] By 1905 this league was providing recreation as well as moral learning to 100,000 boys.

Play and Physical Hygiene for Girls

If participation in team sports civilized the young man and made him more fit for life in a democratic and mechanized world, what about the girl? In the Hall-Gulick theory, women's inherited racial tendencies are different from those of men. "It was not the women who could run, throw, and strike best who survived," Gulick argued. "The women who were the best mothers, who were most true to their homes, who were the best workers, were those that survived. So athletics have never been either a test of or a large factor in the survival of women.

Athletics do not test womanliness as they test manliness."[28] Indeed, Gulick and his followers believed that that vigorous exercise and, especially, competitive exercise was bad for the girl and the young woman.

> Athletic games — at least as we Americans rush into them — are not good for girls. Nature forbids womankind to run and leap and strike to the verge of exhaustion, as men do, and the girls who violate this law by indulgence in strenuous athletic contests pay a heavy penalty for the violation in later life.[29]

Reformers like Gulick viewed askance the recent increase in competitive games and track and field events for girls. They felt that it was bad for girls to be traveling far from their families to play games, and they also decried the fact that strange men could come watch the girls in their short gym skirts play. There were also still some on both sides of the Atlantic who felt that athletics could make a girl "coarse": "Loud voices, loosened hair, rough words and gestures, the contemptuous application of the term 'crock' to any girl not skilled in athletic games, these ... are not beautiful; neither are big, reddened hands, large feet, to be admired," wrote one critic in 1902.[30] Thus in her study of athletics for girls, Elizabeth Burchenal, Gulick's protégée, cited a testimonial from a woman, now married and a mother, who as a girl had a boyish build and who could and did practice exercises "usually possible only for men." Indeed, this woman was "allowed to follow unrestrained her own desires" in athletics. As an adult this woman reported morosely that her "internal derangement" — a polite catch-all for symptoms that could include depression, hysteria or sterility — had been caused by the "violent" physical exertions that had sapped her vitality.[31]

Gulick felt that engaging in competitive sports was both physically and morally bad for a girl, but he acknowledged that some new activity was needed for young women: "in the new era, which is already upon us, the same demands with reference to the larger movements of the community are being made upon women as have been made upon men; yet the same opportunities are not being given to women for learning the lessons of cooperation."[32] Girls and women as well as boys also needed to learn the moral qualities of team play.

As a final compelling argument, Gulick turned to the example of ancient Greece, a time when he felt that human life was most brilliant and full. A fundamental and essential part of the ancient Greek education that produced these "balanced and brilliant lives," Gulick assured his readers, was dancing

> that dancing which united body and soul in the expression of high emotion; that dancing which represented in social form those virtues which it desired to stamp upon the soul ... through these cadenced rhythms, these expressions of strong and virtuous emotions, that poise — mental as well as physical — becomes wrought into the tissue of character.[33]

Thus dance was the key to moral, social, emotional, and physical growth for girls and women.

As a result of these concerns, in 1905 Gulick and several influential society women formed the Girl's Branch of the Public Schools Athletic League of New York City. In a typically Progressive reformer fashion Gulick and the league engaged in "scientific" study of the best form of exercise, carrying out careful experimental work along three lines: athletics, gymnastics, and folk dancing. "It soon became evident that of these three," Gulick wrote,

> folk dancing was the most interesting; that by a judicious selection of dances a larger number of children could secure exercise in limited space and time than in either of the other forms of exercise; and that the folk dances afforded opportunity for cooperation with other activities of school and home in a way not afforded by either of the other activities.[34]

Gulick had initially feared antagonism to his use of folk dancing in the New York City public schools, as many conservatives were concerned that girls who could dance beautifully would end up in the dance halls that were popularly — and sometimes correctly — seen as dens of prostitution, and that the public schools would become feeders to vice. He noted that "[t]he boy who can beat all the other boys by a foot in a running high jump is not exposed to the same kind of temptation that is likely to face the girl who can dance beautifully."[35] He was encouraged, however, by the support of his influential society patronesses. In addition to the support of these society leaders, Gulick also collected and published numerous of letters of commendation regarding the use of aesthetic, folk and fancy dancing from various school principals, city superintendents, and the influential folk dance teacher Mary Wood Hinman.

In part to forestall complaints from conservatives, the Girls' Branch leaders encouraged girls to perform in gym tunics and suitable shoes rather than fancy dresses to give greater freedom in movement; they deplored the use of costumes, which they felt tended to make the folk dancing more of an exhibition than a form of exercise and were, in addition, expensive. They approved of a "reasonable" degree of competition but wished to avoid the notoriety of inter-school games, and thus argued against basketball and other competitive sports and games. The Girls' Branch adopted certain fundamental principles about the type of play desired for girls: that everyone present should take part, that no individual should have a starring role that would make the rest "subservient," and that the exercise should be of a "measurably all-round character," involving not just physical improvement, but permitting the girl to develop "the qualities of skill, quickness of perception, readiness to meet emergencies, and the like."[36]

As a result of Gulick's arguments, in late 1909, the New York City Department of Education appointed Elizabeth Burchenal, an alumna of both Earlham College (with its May Day festival) and the Gilbert Normal School of Dance, to the post of inspector of athletics for the public schools. By 1910, the Girls' Branch of the Public School Athletic League employed five assistants for her. According to *The Playground*, in 1910 Burchenal held eleven after-school classes training 1,051 teachers from 246 schools, and these efforts reached 325,000 girls in New York City.[37] That year, the initiative culminated in a performance in Central Park in May 1910, in which 10,000 school-girls demonstrated folk and maypole dances.

But why folk dances for urban girls and not other forms of dance, like the aesthetic, natural or Greek dances that were in vogue after Isadora Duncan's triumphant return to America in 1907? The answer lies in the next chapter that describes the perceived social, educative, moral, and physical benefits of folk dance.

7. The Educational, Hygienic, Civic and Moral Benefits of Folk Dance

> *"Merry May-Day as in Merrie England; Girls' Gymnasium Class Will Wind the May-pole with Cream and Crimson Streamers May 1"*
> The gymnasium will assume its most festive appearance to greet the merry May-Day frolickers. The scene will be one of unusual beauty, when on that day, twenty-four co-eds, clad in white, join in winding the May-pole with cream and crimson streamers [the school colors]. The graceful, yet stately movements of the dancers will recall the days of "Ye Merrie England."
>
> The revival of the old folk dances, which for some time have been a prominent event in most universities, is a beautiful and interesting custom and the program promises to be a great success at Indiana [University] Friday afternoon. The old Norwegian and Danish costumes and the weird music make one forget that the girls taking part in the dances are not really Norwegian.
> — Two Indiana University student newspaper accounts,
> April 16, 1908, and April 30, 1908[1]

Folk dances of many lands were a highlight of the urban May Day program and an important component of the college May Day program. But *why* folk dances? That is, what were their peculiarly beneficial attributes? And, equally importantly, *which* folk dances? From about 1910 on, May Day programs showcased the same handful of folk dances, a selection influenced by the theories of Hall, Gulick and Burchenal. These educators believed that folk dance conveyed innumerable social, emotional, aesthetic, and even moral benefits along with the purely physical benefit of healthful and efficient exercise.

Some educators felt that any dance form was valuable, as its expressive or emotive aspect enabled the dancer to develop personal grace or even an improved character. For example, Englishwoman Elizabeth Turner Bell, author of *Fifty Figure and Character Dances* (published in the U.S. by A.S. Barnes in 1926) noted that dance in general was "capable of imparting notions of grace and beauty with facial expression in accordance with the varying moods of the dance." Educators like Bell felt that the girl who danced beautifully was expressing her inner beauty of character. Similarly, with regard to folk song, noted folksong collector Cecil Sharp averred that a young person's ability to sing well both required and demonstrated the "right" mental and emotional attitude, and that singing folk songs well was a good test of not only the intelligence but the moral character of the singer.[2]

The Progressive reformers agreed with these theories, but they had a more complicated agenda. G. Stanley Hall had espoused folk and national dances specifically because he believed them to be condensed expressions of ancestral and racial traits and embodiments of the eth-

"Bow to your partners"—a Western square dance at the Judson College May Day festival in 1950. (Judson College Archives.)

ical, religious and moral temperament of the various peoples. Hall particularly approved of imitative dances, especially those of nature (storms, spring, the coming of dawn, etc.). Hall believed that educational dance should also include religious dances, love dances, and war dances —each presented to the child at her correct stage of development as she recapitulated the rise of the human race from primitive savagery to civilization.

Dr. Luther Halsey Gulick elaborated upon Hall's principles and, working with Elizabeth Burchenal, made them concrete by selecting the folk dances they considered most beneficial for children and girls. They promulgated these specific dances both in Gulick's writings, in accounts of performances described in the Playground Association of America's journal, *The Playground*, in Burchenal's extensive array of folk dance manuals, and in the dances taught under Burchenal's direction to the girls in public schools in New York City beginning in 1905. Gulick and Burchenal's collective influence was so strong that it is this select group of folk dances that we see in innumerable college and urban May Day programs from approximately 1907 on.

Gulick, Burchenal and their supporters had many arguments in favor of teaching girls and adults folk dances. One of Gulick's arguments, for example, was Hall's assertion that folk dances were valuable because they embodied "racial characteristics" of movement, and because they also represented "race ideas" in symbolic form.[3] This theory averred that the dances of a people expressed something unique about their national character. Gulick offered as "proof" the Cossack dances of the Russians, which used large movements of the body, deep flexions of the knees, an upright torso, and high leaps into the air. He claimed that these characteristic movements represented the spirit of the Russian people, "which, while it soars to heaven, secures for itself power and vitality from the earth." He felt that the "Scottish Reel," on the other hand, exhibited more deliberate and economical movement. "The carefully regulated joy of the Scottish, their canniness, their consideration of each step before taking it" formed a sharp contrast to the "abandon" of the Russians or the "languid grace" of the Spanish.[4]

This view that each nation or race (as these educators employed the term) expressed its unique character through its characteristic dance was not confined to Hall and Gulick. For example, in 1910 Englishwoman Grace Kimmins, whose books on the games, dances, and festivals of the London slum children organized by the Guild of Play were popular in the United States, described the English "Sailor's Hornpipe" as the dance most characteristic of Englishmen, a race of brave sailors. By contrast, she categorized French dances thus: "Order, and a fine sense of proportion, have always been the characteristics of French dances, and even in provincial dancing were more or less observed." In her view, any dance of the Spaniards, no matter how brisk, has a "certain dignity"—"it never tires, but seems to rest the performer and spectator alike," while the Scottish reel exhibits an "economy of movement":

> Contrast it for a moment with the joyous abandonment of the *Irish jig*, with its patter and go, or with the *Russian dance*, with its vigour of movement, and at once there is given an insight into the racial meaning of these dances, which is better grasped by this means than any other. The canny Scotsman hoards his breath whilst fully considering each step; and the rhythm, balance, and sense of proportion throughout the dance, makes the learning and using of it of real educative value to children.⁵

Perhaps because the Scots — holding or perceiving to hold desirable values such as belief in a Protestant God and a dedication to thrift, education and success in business — were an admired "race," these early dance educators commonly perceived the Scottish dances as vigorous yet cannily controlled. There was little consensus, however, on what, exactly, the characteristics of other nationalities were or how they were exemplified in dance.

Gulick did not unduly stress the idea of nationalism as expressed in the dance, preferring to focus on the second part of his argument as to the value of folk dances. He believed that these dances, with their symbolic gestures and movement, represented the particular activities "that have been useful in the preservation of the race." This statement is a direct reference to Hall's theories of development, suggesting that, unlike pure social or fancy dances, the performance of folk dance was not just a physical exercise, but one that stimulated the "neurological combinations upon which intelligence rests." By stimulating these "racially old neurological coordinations," the dancer would create in herself wholesome moral and emotional feelings. It is thus from the moral and emotional standpoint, and not the purely physical one, Gulick argued, that the folk dances are valuable. Each folk dance represents "in symbolic form, a long history of human activity." In his view it is this symbolism that gives preeminent educative value to folk dances over other forms of dance: since bodily movement has an effect on the mental state, "bodily movements of the folk dance type aid toward wholesome thinking." In his view, unlike made-up fancy dances or the jazz or ballroom dances of the period, folk dances enabled the dancer to feel and express the ancient and valuable emotions of joy, triumph, and vigor.⁶

Gulick also praised folk dances for their social benefits: because dancing is noncompetitive and permits or even requires large groups of girls to work together, he felt that it was beneficial in breaking up cliques of girls and creating harmony in the classroom. "The social aim [of folk dancing] is thus quite as

Scottish Lassies in a characteristic pose and costume ready to dance the Highland Fling in 1909. (Photograph, 0002992.tif, courtesy of the University of Illinois at Urbana-Champaign Archives.)

prominent as is the physical one," Gulick wrote in 1911.[7] Grace Kimmins of the Guild of Play agreed, suggesting that dance could in fact develop good citizenship, "for no dance can be taught alone ... and ... the great virtues of courtesy and chivalry and self-restraint, and, nowadays so necessary, of modesty, are likely to be unconsciously impressed upon the children by means of such play as this." In order to dance, the children learn to "sink their own personal ends or ambition for the sake of the side or the set, of which they form only one."[8]

The benefits of teamwork aside, Gulick further asserted that because the girls enjoyed the dances so much, they eagerly embraced the hard work needed to master them, and this improved work ethic spilled over into their regular schoolwork (in Hall's psychology, a child's interest in a topic was confirmation of its racially old validity).[9] Since not everyone could join the public school folk dance clubs, the dancing could become a motivational tool as well. In his book of 1910, *The Healthful Art of Dancing*, Gulick cited one New York public school principal as noting that a girl's membership in the "Burchenal Athletic Club" (the after-school folk dance club) was dependent on good school performance. Thus, he opined, "we find in many instances a wayward, troublesome, idle girl often spurring up to a high standard in her class lessons and deportment, in order to be permitted to enter the folk-dancing class."[10] The folk dancing appeared to improve girls in many dimensions; Gulick cited the supervisor of the Children's Playground Association of Baltimore, Maryland, as stating in 1910 that:

> Physically, [the folk dance class] improved the children in poise, lightness of step and grace. Socially, it broadened their interest in each other and enlarged their vision. Morally, it brought much happiness, kindness, spirit and less selfishness. In fact, we could see improvement in every direction.[11]

Unlike the couple-centric popular social dances of the period, folk dances had a natural ability to force participants to mingle: another important benefit, even (or perhaps especially) for adults. The Progressive folk dance leaders, in particular Mary Wood Hinman in Chicago and Elizabeth Burchenal in New York City, regarded folk dance as a useful mechanism for breaking down artificial social barriers among older participants, such as those attending settlement house classes. In 1909 Hinman wrote that she used folk dancing in the Chicago high schools and at the University of Chicago quite specifically "to meet [i.e., resolve] the problems of girls' societies and fraternities and those who were not members, and to insure social intercourse between Jew and Gentile, rich and poor."[12] Folk dances could lure young people away from the vices of the streets and teach them American values while they were still young enough to absorb them readily. Hinman reported that she taught a combination of ballroom and folk dancing at Hull House and various schools and settlements in Chicago, and that as a result of these classes, the men gained the American attitude of respect for women "which they knew nothing of in their life in the other country." She felt that well-run dances were beneficial in teaching self-respect to young people and that, in fact, there was "no better, quicker, or surer way" to bring them in from the streets and into an embrace of the values of the settlement house reformers.[13]

Gulick and Burchenal also noted that folk dances were an important way to tie those Americans who had been here longer with the waves of new immigrants. In 1920, Burchenal argued in favor of using folk dance in everyday life, emphasizing the opportunities which folk dance offers as "*recreation for adults*, its possibilities as a *democratic socializing agent*, and its value as a form of *real 'Americanization'*" (emphasis in the original).[14] She noted that in these simple folk dances participants changed partners changed often, dances were learned easily and provided a "universally appealing play element," which, because dances need no translation, as do songs, could immediately create an atmosphere of good fellowship. Burchenal argued that folk dancing for the adult community was particularly valuable because it enabled longtime Americans to mix with more recent citizens, thereby gaining a common ground of interests. "The latter may thus come within the magic (and to them usually closed) inner circle of real American life and feel that they are recognized as belonging; both acquire the respect, appreciation and friendly sympathy for each other that comes through a close acquaintance."[15]

Gulick and Burchenal also believed that in addition to giving beauty and meaning to general American culture, folk dances could also help tie immigrant parents with their scornful, newly Americanized children. They asserted that when the foreign-born parents saw their children demonstrating the dances of the old country, they came to feel that there were ties between themselves, their own children and the historic past of their own people. The children themselves then came to understand — and value — their parents and the meaning of the dances better.

Burchenal and other reformers also argued that folk dancing could provide a more wholesome form of entertainment than the disreputable jazz dance performed in dance halls. In 1926 she condemned the modern jazz dance evil, an "evil of sensuality that stops short of immorality, but that comes to grip young people like a habit-forming drug, developing appetites against which they are almost powerless." She argued that this form of couple dancing caused overly narrow social contacts, and was innately unaesthetic, ugly, and unmusical. She suggested that a program "based on universal human needs" would instead develop forms of the dance that were suitable for all ages, that joined the family and the community together, that gave each individual contact with all others in the group, that were aesthetically pleasing, and that provide suitable exercise "for the whole body and for everybody."[16]

Some romantically inclined dance leaders felt that folk dances could bring families together, and bring them in greater touch with their neighbors. In 1912, for example, Helen Storrow, later a leading member of the Country Dance & Song Society of America, looked forward to the vision of the family at home after supper. How pleasant it would be, she wrote, when "grandpa and father lay down their papers, grandma her knitting, mother the family stockings, auntie her picture puzzle and their children their school books and someone starts the gramophone, to see all the family join in a Scotch Reel or a Danish Firetue." If there is no room in the tenement, the family will go to the nearest school house and join with their neighbors "in the merry mazes of a dance." Now, however, she noted sadly, it was only the children and their teachers who knew the dances.[17]

These enthusiasts and reformers felt that folk dancing, along with the practice of other arts and crafts, could provide a significant source of pleasure to every American citizen. Like Ruskin, Gulick also rebelled against dreary urban life and an overemphasis on making money. "There is now going on a great revolt against materialism," he wrote in 1910, "and the folk-dancing movement is part of that reaction. Folk dancing means the pursuit of that thing which is ideal — the joy of living — that which is more real than the drudgery of everyday life, that which makes human life interesting and significant."[18]

Finally, Gulick and Burchenal argued that folk dance was intrinsically beautiful and aesthetically pleasing and satisfying. Folk dances are "the wild flowers of the dance world, unspoiled by the hand of man," Burchenal wrote in 1913. She valued the dances from the standpoint of their possibilities "as a form of self-expression and play rather than as a means of 'showing off' for the benefit of the onlooker."[19] One contemporary observer noted that dance — more than music, literature or art — had an immediate and accessible appeal to children whose lives were devoid of beauty.

> [W]e are so constituted that while we are executing beautiful and graceful movements our minds turn subconsciously to the gentle and sweeter channels. Watch the faces of the children as they dance and see how they refine and sweeten. I do not remember ever to have seen a coarse or vulgar expression on any face of the hundreds who danced [in the New York May Day festivals].[20]

Despite these numerous and frequently asserted arguments in favor of folk dance, some detractors continued to worry about the girls' interest in dancing, suggesting that it might lead to an interest in public dance halls, popularly seen as a place of debauchery. Gulick's response was that, on the contrary, folk dancing could actually improve a girl's moral sensibilities, as once a girl was exposed to *good* art, she would voluntarily eschew jazz and other elements of (low) popular culture.[21]

Thus, when a lady who observed the mass demonstrations of folk dancing at a May Day festival in Central Park in 1911 noticed disapprovingly that one girl was particular was enjoying herself in the dancing (enjoyment being implicitly suspected as an indication that the girl would end up in a public dance hall — or worse), Elizabeth Burchenal was quoted in a *Harper's Weekly Magazine* article as responding that

> I am convinced that any girl or any thousand girls will be so developed and strengthened, physically, mentally, and morally, but the dancing and games taught in our public schools that the resisting power to temptation is greatly strengthened. Moreover, everything possible is being done to avoid anything resembling ostentation or display in the dancing. Fancy costumes, for example, are absolutely prohibited by a rule of the Board of Education.[22]

Types of Folk Dances Recommended for Girls and Young Women

While Gulick and other educators felt that folk dances in general offered numerous benefits to the children and young women who performed them, they did not regard all folk dances as equally beneficial: some dances contained or promulgated superior characteristics more than others.

Thus, per Hall's theories, Gulick and Burchenal recommended singing games and those dances or games that involved pantomime like Roman Soldiers or Carrousel for the youngest children. Vigorous yet simple group dances, especially those that invoked the "racial memories" of weaving, harvesting, and so on, such as the Swedish weaving dance Reap the Flax or the mock-combat Oxdansen, were suitable for older children, while they recommend more vigorous pattern dances like the "Sailor's Hornpipe," an English morris dance or the "Highland Fling" for the older boys and men, and social dances like the "Tarantella" or the "Scotch Reel" for adults.

Gulick and Burchenal were in fact very specific about the types of folk dances that would provide the greatest physical hygiene value. Gulick recommended dances in which most children were vigorously active most of the time, so that a dance such as the "Virginia Reel" (the "Sir Roger de Coverley"), though socially beneficial, was unsatisfactory for hygienic purposes, since so many "players" stood still during it. He felt that certain dances, such as some of the Russian ones, were too vigorous for growing bodies, while others required too much of the precious playground space to perform. He recommended dances with large movements of the trunk and limbs, excluding, therefore, dances from Java, which emphasized small motions of the hands. He picked dances that would reinforce aesthetic principles, noting that "[a] consideration is that the body positions in the dances shall be graceful and such that do not tend in any way to the forming of habits of movement or posture that are disadvantageous from the standpoint of health." This principle excluded as a whole the dances of the American Indi-

7. The Educational, Hygienic, Civic and Moral Benefits of Folk Dance 73

Girls perform an English morris dance with handkerchiefs as part of a late 1940s May Day pageant. (Archives, Chatham University, Pittsburgh, Pennsylvania.)

ans, "in which ... the body is bent forward, the individual dancing with bent knees and in a crouching position."[23] He and Elizabeth Burchenal picked dances "eliminating the element of personal display and choosing those dances in which large numbers can take part, and which have, in addition to a social element, the virtues of (one) simplicity, (two) vigorous action, (three) wholesome, natural, out-of-door spirit."[24]

Folk dances also had to be simple enough for children to learn and enjoy quickly, in part because their time on the playground was limited, and in part because Gulick was sympathetic to the need for the activity to be fun for them. Finally Gulick rejected a large number of folk dances that were unsuitable from the moral or emotional standpoint, such as, for example, "the love dances of the East, [which] however beneficial they may be from the standpoint of the bodily movements involved, are entirely unsuited from the standpoint of their emotional content and their relation to the morals of our civilization."

Given all these constraints, there were, as Gulick ingenuously remarked, really only a few folk dances—"perhaps five percent"—that met the hygienic, aesthetic, and moral needs of children and young women. "Neither is it yet certain," Gulick added, "what dances will prove the best suited for our American conditions. Some of the spirited and characteristic folk-dances of Sweden and Russia have so far seemed to make the very greatest appeal to the children."[25]

Following Gulick's theories, Elizabeth Burchenal's first folk dance manual, *Folk Dances and Singing Games* (1909), contained dances from the culturally familiar countries of Norway, Sweden, Denmark, Russia, Bohemia, Hungary, Italy, England, Scotland, and Ireland. It must be remembered that the collecting process was still in its infancy; many more dances from other countries were collected as the century wore on. However, the dances contained in this influential book were those that fit Gulick's criteria by being relatively easy, pleasant to perform, referring to "ancient" occupations or activities, mimetic and/or vigorous. They included:

BOHEMIAN: "Komarno," "Strasak"
DANISH: "Ace of Diamonds," "Dance of Greeting," "Shoemaker's Dance"
ENGLISH: "Bean Setting," "How Do You Do, Sir?" "Laudanum Bunches" (morris dances); and "The Maypole Dance"
FINNISH: "Bounding Heart," "Harvest Dance"
HUNGARIAN: "Csardas"
IRISH: "Jig," "The Lilt"
ITALIAN: "Tarantella"
NORWEGIAN: "Mountain March"
RUSSIAN: "Comarinskaia"
SCOTCH: "Highland Fling," "Highland Reel," "Highland Schottische"
SWEDISH DANCES: "Bleking," "Clap Dance," "Fjalnas Polka," "Oxdans," "Reap the Flax," "Trollen," "Varsouvienne"
SWEDISH SONG PLAYS: "Carrousel," "Hey," "Little Lassie," "How Do You Do, My Partner?"; "I See You, Kull Dance," "Ma's Little Pigs," "Nigare Polska"

In the early years, up to World War I at least, folk dancing was very popular in the city schools of the Northeast and Midwest. In 1911, Helen Storrow, Chairman, Committee on Folk Dancing of the Playground and Recreation Association of America, wrote:

> All [the young people from age five to twenty in Mary Wood Hinman's folk dance classes] love it, all look forward to the lessons with joy. There is no self-consciousness. Apparently the girls think neither of their clothes nor of the boys, nor do the boys think of the girls nor of the size of their own feet, so absorbed are they in what they are doing.... Awkward children become easy, shy children lose their self-consciousness, hasty-tempered or quarrelsome boys take it out in the oxdans [a Swedish mock-combat dance for two], all sorts and conditions of children dance together simply and naturally, the rough mannered become gentle, and the gentle do not deteriorate. All the teachers are enthusiastic over the results.[26]

By 1916 the benefits of the use of folk dance in the schools was decisively proven, for in that year, Dr. C. Ward Crampton, at that time director of physical training for the New York City public schools, averred in the foreword to his own *Second Folk Dance Book* that "Folk Dances have ceased to be a fad. They are now used in connection with formal physical training as a delightful means of obtaining hygienic, educational and recreative results of normal exercise."[27]

The early urban children's May Day programs showcased folk dances almost exclusively. By contrast the college programs depicted a combination of the common folk dances listed above, along with various interpretive dances, character dances, and drills performed with gauzy scarves, hoops, balls, or long sticks. Thus, for example, at the 1920 celebration of the University of New Hampshire, the crowning of the May Queen was followed by the performance of a minuet, 13 folk dances (most from the list above) and two fancy dances: a parasol dance and the dance of Pierrot and Pierrette. The finale of the program was the maypole dance, performed by the good and bad characters in the accompanying pageant titled "The Spirit of Americanization," including Liberty, Love/Queen of the May, Health, Christianity, Education, Culture, Science, Poetry, Art, Genius, Pleasure, Rest, Recreation, Music, Industry, Success, Poverty, Dishonesty, Ignorance, Political Jealousy, Immorality, Laziness, Gluttony, Crime, Disease and H.C.L. (*sic*: the High Cost of Living).[28] We will learn more about the maypole dance, that exemplar of teamwork, unity and the blending of the individual into the harmony of the whole, in chapter 14.

8. The Pageant and Festival Movement

> Pageantry — the new Pageantry — is not only the birth of a new art, or the rebirth of a lost art. It is the birth of a new educational idea. It is the forerunner of a distinctly different and a distinctly higher civic and social life.... The historical definition of Pageantry means merely a pompous and evanescent ceremonial parade.... But the Pageantry developed in recent years is anything but a meaningless parade. It is community drama, as distinct from individual drama. It symbolizes in a thousand possible ways, the growing and striving community gathering up into its soul the growing tradition and idealism, the strivings and hopes of its generations of men and women. Pageantry, viewed by this idea, is the great modern art ... and is made possible only through the existence of imminent potentiality of the new social idea. It rests on community consciousness and brotherhood.
> — John Collier, cited in the American Pageant Association *Bulletin*, May 14, 1913.[1]

For four performances, from May 28 through June 1, 1914, nightly audiences of more than 100,000 gathered out-of-doors on Art Hill overlooking the city of St. Louis to view a cast of 7,500 of their fellow citizens perform *The Pageant and Masque of St. Louis*. The pageant, written by Thomas Wood Stevens, depicted through various "episodes" the history of the city, beginning with the Mound Builders and concluding with the end of the Civil War. After dusk, audiences then viewed Percy MacKaye's *Masque*, a symbolic and poetic presentation that interpreted the relationship of St. Louis to the life of America and humanity. The *Masque* featured a giant puppet named Cahokia, spectacular illuminated effects and special efforts to portray water scenes. Despite the throngs of people, newspaper accounts emphasized the orderliness of the crowds: there was only one arrest and no calls on the fire department. More than mere entertainment, however, reformers and intellectuals claimed that *The Pageant and Masque of St. Louis* did wondrous things for the community, uniting its citizens and having far-reaching social effects. Thus Lotta Clark, the secretary of the American Pageant Association, praised the 1914 pageant and claimed that

> When its pageant was in preparation every kind of help was secured through the appeal of the magic words, "For the honor of St. Louis! For the good of our city!" After it was all over people asked just what good the city had received. It had produced a marvelous spectacle ... but were the results of such stupendous effort and expense to be of no lasting good to the city? St. Louis had been trying for years to get a revised charter, but it had been bitterly opposed on account of a provision for municipal ownership of the street railway. This year the charter was passed, street-railway clause and all. Her western neighbors envy St. Louis her charter and there are those who believe that it was secured this year because the idea of the "the good of the city" had been so firmly fixed by the pageant in the minds of the people.[2]

Both the college and urban May Day programs were strongly influenced by the artistic and

An Oriental potentate greets a supplicant in this scene from a May Day pageant give in the 1920s. (Archives and Special Collections, Converse College, Spartanburg, South Carolina.)

symbolic principles of the American Pageant Association (APA), under whose aegis enormous community pageants such as this — spectacles in which hundreds of local townspeople performed to illuminate a great movement in their town's history — were performed from 1905 to approximately 1925. By 1920, pageants had been performed in all 48 states.[3] The APA was intimately connected to the Playground Association of America, and both entities labored to promulgate the performance of pageants in schools, colleges and, particularly, in communities across the nation.

Many college physical education instructors, especially those graduating from Columbia Teachers College, were trained in pageantry symbolism and aesthetics, and they took their knowledge and their enthusiasm to the schools, colleges, and universities at which they subsequently directed May Day pageants. Most college May Day pageants of this period and later adhered to the aesthetic and symbolic principles outlined in the bulletins, books, and articles produced by the American Pageant Association and the Playground Association of America.

Not just entertainment, pageants of this era reflected the goals of Progressive reformers, who saw them as a powerful tool for change in American life by uniting art and democracy. Articles such as "The Value of Outdoor Plays to America: Through the Pageant Shall We Develop a Drama of Democracy?" (which appeared in a 1909 issue of *The Craftsman*) argued that the people must be involved in the creation of their own art, and that both art and the people could be transformed by following the key principles of pageantry. On the simplest level, pageantry could turn the people away from their obsession with cheap jazz and tawdry plays and movies. However, pageant leaders not only wanted to develop popular art of quality in every community, they wanted to use the pageant as a vehicle for social reform. By bringing people of all races, economic levels, and creeds together they hoped to break down ideological differences within the community. "Anything that tends to bring the residents of the city together as a great family has untold value in the making of good citizenship," reported the Playground Association of America's Committee on Festivals in 1911.[4]

Thus, one Independence Day pageant held in Springfield, Massachusetts, in 1908 featured a parade of thirteen immigrant groups, most in floats representing national heroes: Leif Eriksson for the Swedes, Socrates and Plato for the Greeks, William Tell for the Germans, Christopher Columbus for the Italians and so on. Black Civil War veterans participated by reenacting the Battle of Fort Wagner, in which they had played a key role. As one contemporary observer noted, with this glittering spectacle before his eyes, how could any citizen of Springfield fail to have "his outlook broadened by some glimpse of the American of the future that is to come out of this mingling of races and of race ideals, or ... fail to see the general possibilities for improvement in the amalgamation of many of these people, bringing traditions of such beauty and nobility?" The writer firmly averred that

> practically every citizen [of Springfield] was interested directly or indirectly in the conduct of the celebration, and all shared in an inspiring and uplifting entertainment. Lessons of cooperation and community service were taught in the best possible way, that is, by doing; and the various elements of the population were united in the bonds of a common endeavor. Civic pride was stimulated, and the day was replete with suggestions of the meaning and value of human liberty.[5]

This pageant wasn't just a parade of fancy costumes, it was a display of safe ethnicity, a statement of melting pot internationalism, and a call to liberty, community, and the future.

What exactly was a pageant? In an article titled "What the Pageant Can Do for the Town," that appeared in the *Ladies Home Journal* in April 1914, Professor George Baker of Harvard University called it "something between a play and a procession," noting that it contained any or some of the elements of fancy costuming, dramatic scenes in prose of verse, instrumental or vocal music, dancing, pantomime, and tableaux.[6] Pageants were typically epic-scale productions of three to seven self-contained episodes. They were usually performed out-of-doors and typically celebrated an occasion or a person important to a particular community, or an idea such as Peace, Progress or Industry. Pageants were locality-based — that is, the physical surroundings were congruent with the theme of the pageant — secular, and largely performed by amateurs. The pageant usually began with a spoken prologue, and incorporated poetry, vocal and orchestral music, expressive and symbolic movement, and dance. Symbolic interpretive (modern) dance interludes often separated the episodes and further illuminated the main theme, while the standard list of folk dances discussed in Chapter 8 could be incorporated into episodes on Brotherhood or the Unity of Nations.[7]

Early in the movement, pageant leaders emphasized the benefits of the actual process of creating the pageant as the community's citizens took charge of all aspects of the production. One of the APA's original goals was that the process of creating the pageant would help to erase class or money distinctions. Thus the pageant *Cave Life to City Life*, presented in Boston in 1910, was cited by contemporaries as an excellent example of how more than 1,200 local organizations grouped themselves into thirteen categories (Civic, Fine Arts, Education, Business, etc.) As the pageant was written and rehearsed, it was reported that the planners worked together to address practical issues of concern to the city.[8] Women had an important role to play in organizing and producing pageants, even early in the movement: in the preface to an 1895 article on festivals in American women's colleges, the editor noted that "in all parts of the country is to be noticed of late years an increase of interest in gay and beautiful pageants, of one sort or another, on land or water. Women have in these a great part, and this new tendency in our rather hard and strained American life is surely one to be cultivated at school, in our homes, and in our communities."[9]

Contemporary advocates such as Esther Willard Bates perceived the pageant as having many moral and social values. She wrote that the pageant's prime value was that it represented "the presentation of American ideals. It promotes patriotism. As Americanization work, it is almost the only civic movement which brings all classes, races, creeds, districts, and political groups into a working unit where all may be equally represented." (At this time, the term "race" was used where today we would use the word "nationality" or "ethnicity.") A successful pageant was a force that could unify the many recent arrivals and blend them into an American whole. Bates argued that the social values of pageantry enriched not only individuals but the community: according to her new city charters, playgrounds and buildings would spring up in the wake of pageantry. Pageants would increase the spread of democracy and improve the spiritual health of the community.[10]

The APA and the Playground Association of America felt that the building of community was one of a pageant's most important benefits. Reports in *The Playground* of various successful (they were always successful!) pageants often included the comment — offered as confirmation of the importance that the people placed in their pageant — that during its presentations there were no calls upon the local fire department and few on the police. "No advertisement of a community is more legitimate and effectual than a splendidly organized pageant," wrote playwright Percy MacKaye in an article titled "American Pageants and their Promise" that appeared in Scribner's *Magazine* in 1909.[11] "What is a pageant for but to unite a town and to keep it united and moving along the road of its best welfare?" pageant master William Chauncy Langdon asked rhetorically, ignoring any examples of class or labor conflict. In the Progressive spirit of the unification of art, reform, and democracy, he argued that for its best effect, a pageant should not confine itself to the depiction of the past but should present the answers to the public questions of the present: "here in the present and the future lie the greatest civic value and the most thrilling dramatic opportunity of the pageant."[12]

Pageants had educational value, as Esther Willard Bates argued in 1925: "Collegiate pageantry preserves myths, traditions, customs, and observances more beautifully than any other kind." Religious pageants could teach spiritual lessons. Finally, Bates wrote, pageants could enrich, beautify, and unite a formerly apathetic community:

> cooperation, local pride, and progress are found in a town where democratic festivals are recurrent. Beautiful lagoons enrich the landscape. Unsightly vacant lands are cleared. Bandstands are no longer clumsy wooden structures but pillared temples of music. These are the visible results. But the invisible and imponderable ones are greater. There is healthy activity among the youth where formerly there was restlessness. Minds once closed are more open. Nobler appeals touch the heart. The community spirit, her wings folded, has come to dwell unseen."[13]

Besides these benefits to the community, pageants and seasonal festivals had other, more individualized benefits, especially for young people. In 1912, pageant leader Percival Chubb claimed that educators were concerned that children wanted to quit school as soon as possible, as they found the large classes and rote learning dull. (Others might have argued that they left school to obtain jobs; while some child labor laws were on the books at that time, they were not well-enforced, nor were they integrated with the school age requirements.) Chubb felt that festivals could provide an interesting antidote, especially if they were fully integrated into the curriculum. He also argued that the 250-year heritage of the grim Puritans had left native-born Americans, especially those in rural areas, unable to play and to enjoy themselves. Pageantry and festivals would help to address this problem as well. Echoing Ruskin's ideals, Chubb noted the increasing dehumanization of factory work that gave no pleasure or pride to the worker. Americans lacked the joy of refined and edifying leisure activities, he argued, "such joy as was expressed in the folk festivals of the past through folk song, folk dance, folk drama, and folk ritual." Chubb also reiterated the Progressives' concern that popular culture encouraged licentiousness and asserted that introducing children to "quality" performances would surely make them less susceptible to the influences of libidinous jazz or "vaudevillanous" plays. Finally, pageants and festivals could help address the fact that many homes (i.e., those of the immigrants) were not promoting the right values: the Protestant Anglo-Saxon values of democracy, respect for women, and hard work. The home, Chubb sorrowed, "so far as the great masses of our workers are concerned, is becoming less and less a center of play and amusement. It has no nursery, no yard; the school, the playground, and the social center must take its place."[14]

The Pageant Movement in America

The Pageant of Sherbourne (England) in 1905 is generally considered the model for the pageants that quickly emerged in the United States. In 1905 the first important American pageant, Percy MacKaye's *The Gods and the Golden Bowl*, sometimes referred to as *The Saint-Gaudens Masque*, was given in Cornish, New Hampshire, to celebrate the twentieth anniversary of the founding of an artists' colony there. By 1910, William Chauncy Langdon, hoping to establish a Bureau of Pageantry, was corresponding with Dr. Luther Halsey Gulick, who was at that time head of the Department of Child Hygiene for the Russell Sage Foundation, established in 1907 for the purpose of improving social and living conditions in the United States. While Gulick supported Langdon, viewing pageants as a form of creative play with an important role to play in social reform, the Foundation was not yet willing to give money for such an enterprise.

By early 1913, however, Langdon, along with Lotta A. Clark, chair of the History Department at Charlestown High School in Massachusetts, George Pierce Baker of Harvard University, and Dr. Gulick, then president of the Playground Association of America, organized a conference of pageant leaders which subsequently led to the creation of the American Pageant Association with Langdon as president, and Lotta Clark as secretary.

The Sun God, from a May Day pageant of the early 1920s at Converse College. Elaborate costuming was a feature of many of the early pageants. (Archives and Special Collections, Converse College, Spartanburg, South Carolina.)

Almost immediately, the APA began publishing helpful bulletins addressing topics such as how to employ effectively the symbolism of color, music, or dance. One such article gave a detailed description of the Bryn Mawr College May Day celebration and praised it as a prime example of that springtide holiday. Another listed the titles of the 41 pageants given in the United States between January and October 1914. These were held in communities from the northeast through the Midwest to California, though none were held south of the Mason-

Dixon line. There were, in addition, 17 festivals and masques (not including Christmas festivals). Themes ranged from those of written pageants that could be purchased for such a purpose, such as *A Pageant of Trees*, and a *National Y.W.C.A. Pageant*, to specialized local histories of towns, colleges and rivers, to expository statements such as *The Romance of Work*, presented by the Association of Working Women of New York City, or *A Dream of Freedom (A Woman's Suffrage Pageant)*, held in Cleveland.[15]

University courses in pageantry, especially at the influential Teachers College of Columbia University, influenced the development of American dance from 1911 through 1925, and several dance-education pioneers attended Teachers College during this period and acknowledged the experience as having a significant impact on their teaching and writing. Courses offered there from 1911 through 1921 addressed various aspects of festival and pageant dancing.[16] Some of these physical education instructors subsequently taught courses in pageantry to their college students: for example, at Ursinus College, from at least 1941 to 1959, women could choose an elective, two-semester hour-long course called Pageantry that gave them training and experience in the management of their May Day pageant. Similar courses were also taught at Berea College.

A pensive "Napoleon" contemplates defeat in the 1920 Chatham University May Day pageant, Victory Through Conflict. *(Archives, Chatham University, Pittsburgh Pa.)*

The Playground Association of America published many accounts of civic and communal pageants and festivals in its journal, *The Playground*. Within a few years of the inception of the pageant movement, readers could also turn to books like Percival Chubb's *Festivals and Play* (Harper & Brothers, 1912) or *Pageants and Pageantry* (Ginn and Co., 1912) by Esther Willard Bates. Other texts included *The Technique of Pageantry* (A.S. Barnes, 1921) by Linwood Taft, then director of the American Pageant Association; and *The Art of Producing Pageants* (Walter H. Baker Co., 1925), also by Esther Willard Bates.

These articles and books all gave arguments as to the value of the pageants and festivals as well as reading lists and practical advice on how to write and produce a pageant. This advice covered topics such as how to devise effective color groupings of the costumed participants while maintaining the aesthetic principles that certain colors denoted moods or characteristics, how to organize the musicians, how to run rehearsals, and how to address other administrative and business details.

The familiar cadre of folk dances could be used as dance interludes in pageants, especially when the theme was something along the lines of the Brotherhood of Nations. More commonly, however, pageant dances were modern dances, usually ones that told a story, such as the dances of Mills College's 1914 May Day pageant, *California*, described thus:

In the beginning the Creatures of Drought rule the Pacific Coast. Mother Nature brings Rain and Sunshine and then the Green Things and Spring Dance. Without warning, the Creatures of Drought reappear and the flowers droop. Mother Nature brings great Water, and as it advances, the Fruits of Cultivation appear and triumphantly cast their mantle of flowers about California, while all join to do her homage.[17]

The natural landscape was an important player in the pageant drama: local spectators and participants were expected to be more firmly tied to their community through seeing its history reenacted on local ground. Landscape was such an important part of the college May Day pageant that administrators spent sizable sums in planting trees, erecting permanent bridges to islands or building bleachers to accommodate the audience. The college buildings appear as "players" in the dramas: photographers tended to pose dancers or performers in Greek costumes in front of Greek-pillared buildings, or performers in Elizabethan costumes in front of Tudor- or Gothic-style buildings.

Symbolism was a key aspect of pageantry: symbolism in color, costume, dance, and theme. In 1915, for example, one writer advised that in using color,

> [p]urity must be white or silver; hatred, black or red; harvest, yellow and white for grain; or orange, brown and red for autumn fruits.... It is not enough that it should be red, blue or green; it must be just the right shade of red, blue or green. To use a blue purple where a red purple should go would make all the difference between a crude and a charming color harmony.[18]

The use of symbolism in pageant themes may easily be seen in the accounts of various college May Day pageants, such as that held in 1915 at Chatham University, a women's uni-

Aesthetic dances in the May Day pageant, Paskennodan, *or The City of Smoke Vapor or The City of Mist, given in 1915 at what was then Pennsylvania College for Women. Perhaps these are the River, Fog and Mist Maidens mentioned in the text. Note the well-dressed crowd in the foreground, and the staging of the pageant in the beautiful grounds which served as an important component of the spectacle. (Archives, Chatham University, Pittsburgh, Pennsylvania.)*

versity in Pittsburgh, Pennsylvania. *Paskkennodan*, or *The City of Smoke Vapor or The City of Mist*, was written to symbolize the growth of the city of Pittsburgh. It depicted the city's geological history, its industrial and educational life, and its "future promise." The pageant incorporated many aesthetic or interpretive dances, such as the "Dance of the River, Fog, and Mist Maidens" (set to Strauss' "Beautiful Blue Danube Waltz") that represented the meeting of the two great rivers that shape the city, and a symbolic dance of fern trees living and dying and turning into coal, at that time a principal product of the city. The science portion of this pageant included a representation of Madame Curie, accompanied by radium dressed in dazzling white and emitting alpha, beta, and gamma rays. It also incorporated a dance of physics, depicting heat converting ice into water. It is interesting — and indeed typical of the college May Day pageants — to note that this historical overview, presented by students at an elite college to their elite parents and friends, made no mention of the local bloody Homestead strike or other class and labor issues.

The earliest pageants focused on historical themes, but soon pageants, especially those organized by members of the Playground Association, became allied with seasonal festivals. In 1910, at the fourth annual Congress of the Playground Association of America, the Festival Committee gave its report and recommendations on the status and value of community festivals. Unlike the early leaders of the APA, however, they did not desire these events to be either spontaneous or community-led; instead, they felt that wise guidance was needed in many of these communities so that the right principles of democracy, hard work, and so on were emphasized clearly. The committee consisted of community leaders from many cities, as well as Percival Chubb, pageant director, and folk-dance leaders Elizabeth Burchenal, Caroline Crawford, and Mari Ruef Hofer. The committee conducted research, sending out more than a thousand questionnaires to cities large and small. They concluded that many communities did not understand the true meaning of the major national celebrations, and that neither the national holidays nor the regional or local celebrations, such as a community's "Pioneer Day," adequately involved children. The committee concluded that May Day, Independence Day and Labor Day were the festival days most closely connected with the goals of the Playground Association.

> Your committee is impressed with the desire on the part of a great number of communities to change May Day from its tendency toward a moving day back to the joyous festival as known to history, song and story, associating it with festivals, flowers, processions of happy children and trips to the spring woods. The desire is strong for a serious Decoration Day, a day of commemoration rather than one of sport and commercialism. Everyone wishes to see July Fourth teach the significance of loyalty and liberty in these United States in a safe and sane way. Labor day should be an American play day for all the people. Workingmen of all types and political belief might well work to this end.[19]

The Playground Association then pledged to provide more information to the reader: sample programs, pamphlets on "how to arouse interest," and "how to secure funds," study guides, bibliographies and so on. A spate of detailed publications indeed followed, both as separately published pamphlets and as articles in the association's monthly journal, *The Playground*.

Schools and colleges embraced the idea of play and pageantry with enthusiasm. In 1911, for example, the principal of the Clarion State Normal School in Clarion, Pennsylvania, described the commencement pageants of 1905 through 1909, pageants that steadily grew more elaborate. In the first year there was only a simple drill; in the second year each class, under the direction of the physical education instructor, performed different folk dances: the Danish "Dance of Greeting," the Russian [*sic*] "Varsovienna," the Swedish "Weaving Dance" and the English "Maypole Winding." In 1907 there was a four-part pageant that concluded with the crowning of the Pageant Queen who typified Spring. The pageant of 1908 was a *Plantation Holiday*; that of 1909 was a re-creation of Merrie England with the story of Ivanhoe; while that of was 1910 a *Roman Holiday*. The principal noted that

> The splendid influences these pageants have had upon the school and the community can scarcely be over-estimated. While only an incident in the work of the Physical Department, they have served to arouse greater interest in that work.... [The pageants'] educational value lay in the fact that students were urged to familiarize themselves with the customs, manners, costumes and history of the times they were to represent.

The principal added that the pageants did not take much time from regular classwork, the costumes were inexpensive and made by the students themselves, and no professional talent was used.[20]

Seasonal pageants and festivals could and did range over many topics, but a favored festival was May Day. In 1909 Elizabeth Burchenal wrote a pamphlet titled "May Day Celebrations," published by the Russell Sage Foundation. She quoted descriptive passages from Brand's *Popular Antiquities*, Chamber's *Book of Days*, and Strutt's *Book of Sports and Pastimes*, but noted that the "vital point ... is not so much to imitate what people of the olden days have done, as to inspire the [happy springtime] feeling from which this celebration sprang." She then gave suggestions for an urban celebration that was to begin with the children going out into the nearest woods or countryside for flowers and greenery and to make wreaths, garlands, wooden whistles, and bows and arrows. Upon their return to the city, they were to set up and decorate the maypole, crown a May Lord and Lady, and process through the streets. May Games, which were to include speeches, dances of all the countries represented among either the participants or the spectators, the winding of the maypole, running games and archery, were to occur next, followed in the evening by the hanging of the May baskets, dramatics and music.[21]

The early days of the pageant movement were filled with inspiration and hope. Successful pageants did please and entertain many people in communities across the Northern and Western states; more rarely in the South, where the Progressive movement was less influential. In her book of 1912, Esther Willard Bates anticipated the future with enthusiasm:

> American pageantry will be so ordered as to possess a constructive influence on the people. There will be entertainment with splendid effects in color, form, and music to both please and improve the popular taste; the spectacle will stimulate pride in town, state, and nation; a broad sympathy for all lands and peoples will underlie and dominate the scenes; and finally there will be a definite educational aim to make real the great deeds of the fathers and to quicken the aspirations of the sons for right living and for devotion to country. In this last appeal the need of our immigrant population will be kept fully in mind.[22]

Pageants were a popular and inspiring form of entertainment, blending art, music, dance poetry, and high ideals in a new art form. Whether the pageants truly had the effect of permanently or even temporarily uniting a community is debatable, although on at least one occasion a pageant or play festival had more than just a spiritual effect on a city. When the Playground Association of America held its third annual congress in Pittsburgh, Pennsylvania, in May of 1909, 12,000 children gave a play and dance festival in Schenley Park, witnessed by 25,000 spectators, among whom was Miss Helen Frick, daughter of prominent businessman Henry Clay Frick. The program details a long list of the schools, settlement houses and recreation centers that organized and sent the children, who gave mass performances: for example the play-dance Looby Loo was danced by 1,000 children aged five to six; 2,000 older boys and girls performed a figure march and drill, and so on. The festival was such a success that the next month, when Mr. Frick asked Helen what she would like as gift to celebrate her debut into society, she responded that she would like to give a park to the poor children of the city. This initial gift of $500,000 plus subsequent endowments resulted in the beautiful Frick Park, now comprising nearly 500 acres in the center of the city, a pleasant irony given Frick's local negative reputation, even today, as a harsh employer and strike-breaker.[23]

World War I and the decline of optimism among Progressive leaders put an end to the American pageant movement, and the last true community pageant was held in 1925. Stilted and unimaginative dialogue contributed to the decline in interest, and the symbolic dance interludes which seemed so daring and innovative in the first two decades of the twentieth century looked dated and silly by the 1930s.[24] The somewhat less ambitious May Day pageants given at colleges could and did last for some time, but, as we will see in Chapter 18, as student interests changed and as the first wave of physical education instructors — those who had been trained in pageantry and dance — retired, many college May Day pageants dwindled or vanished as well.

9. The Urban Child's May Day

> Up oily in de mornin' we,
>   Ter trip ut o'er de green,
> Wid dance an' mirt' an' ruv-el-ree
>   An' love ter grace de scene.
> Up oily in de moinin' we,
>   Ter trip ut, trip ut mur-ril-lee.
>   — Zona Gale, "Robin Hood in Jones Street,"
>   *Outlook Magazine*, 1909[1]

While popular novelist Constance Cary Harrison described informal May Day festivals as taking place in the parks of New York City as early as 1895,[2] the urban May Day festival truly blossomed there around 1905, and by the 1920s such festivals were being held in cities as far apart as Omaha, Nebraska, and Pittsburgh, Pennsylvania. The urban festival had a different purpose from that of the colleges: it was ostensibly a philanthropic event designed to allow poor slum children to experience a day of perfect happiness in the parks that were theoretically theirs to play in, but which they rarely got to use. Yet while appearing to be a day of pleasure for children, the festival could also fulfill a political agenda both in the sense of buying votes for local politicians as well as in demonstrating and inculcating precepts of democracy and brotherhood in action to a receptive and captive audience: schoolchildren.

The festivals began when sponsors such as local merchants, a Hibernian society, or politicians sent children from the lower East Side and other poor districts to Central Park in Manhattan for a day of frolic, games, and food. These celebrations could be held at any time during the months of May and June. Some events were relatively informal: a white-gloved policeman would grant written permits to use a part of the park space to "any properly organized party with its Queen, maids of honor, and train of courtiers and subjects duly escorted by 'grown-ups.'"[3] These parties began with the raising of the maypole and the crowning of the Queen, followed by some type of games or dancing and food.

At more formally organized festivals there was reportedly keen rivalry among the New York election districts for the record of parading the greatest number of children at their annual May party. In 1905, for example, New York State Senator James Frawley was the proud benefactor of 25,000 children *plus* their parents. "His diamonds scintillating, a bouquet as big as a head of cauliflower in his button hole, and an American flag tied to his gold-headed cane, Senator Frawley marched to the Park at the head of his battalions, a proud and beaming figure of a man," reported a writer for a popular magazine. Once assembled, the children all sang "My Country, 'Tis of Thee," thus transforming the English idyll into an Americanizing experience. "Stocky little Germans, black-eyed babies lisping in Yiddish, excited little

Italians, more placid Scandinavians, their yellow pigtails plaited with brand-new ribbons, and Irish lads and lasses running about like spilled quicksilver—*all were American on this day*" (emphasis added). Indeed, every little girl carried a flag and every little boy had a paper cap of red, white and blue, part of the conscious method by which "their patron and host sought to make them good Americans and loyal voters." After the maypole dancing, the crowning of the May Queens and the games, the senator's young guests consumed five tons of cake, two and a half tons of ice cream, six thousand gallons of lemonade, five tons of candy, and twenty-five thousand oranges.[4] One imagines that there were also 25,000 tummy-aches that night.

The procession of the May Queen through the city streets by Charles Dana Gibson, 1898. Two boys carry a garland-decked banner or canopy over the Queen. The genteel clothes of the children and the smiling Mama who accompanies them probably means that the poor boy next to the out-of-work man asleep on the bench will not participate in the festivities. (Collection of the author.)

Politicians were not alone in sponsoring May Day fêtes. The spring of 1905 marked the first time that the public school girls trained by Elizabeth Burchenal and her teachers performed folk dances as well as the maypole dance in Central Park as part of a non-competitive, multischool celebration. These were so popular that by May of 1911, for example, eight thousand girls from sixty different schools danced around forty-five maypoles erected in Central Park.[5]

Educators and reformers valued the May Day dance festivals for many reasons: immigrant parents had a chance to show off the riches of their heritage to their children, girls had a rare opportunity to enjoy their girlhood, and lessons in democracy, cooperation and fellowship could be learned. Thus, in an article titled "The Value of Outdoor Plays to America: Through the Pageant Shall We Develop a Drama of Democracy?" published in *The Craftsman* in 1909, one observer discussed why she valued the dancing every spring of "public-school immigrant children" on the lawn of Van Cortlandt Park in New York City:

> The dances are of peasant origin, and the audience, mainly immigrant parents dressed in strange undesirable garments of modern cut, find with pathetic pleasure that there are memories of their own childhood not despised by their mongrel children. The children dancing gaily the Highland fling, the Irish clog, the Hungarian czardas, the Americans applauding, and the peasant women with tearful smiles are all welded in this outdoor festival into closer nationality in this intimacy of enjoyment and exchange of sympathy. It is a simply and homely pleasure, but one productive of better human relations, and so worthy of our consideration.[6]

These springtime park fêtes formed an objective for the activities of a school district during the school year. Ideally, though, they were not simply an exhibition of the dances and songs that the girls had learned during the school year, but an expression of their rightful heritage of youth:

[They are] a spontaneous expression of that lively joy of girlhood which even swarming streets and dark rooms on air-shafts, early responsibilities and early sophistication cannot quench. So long as a hurdy-gurdy comes to Delancey Street [in the slums of New York City], Mary McToole will shuffle happy feet over the pavements. But on May Day she finds her true heritage of sun and sky, color and laughter and motion. She is the thousandth part of a harmonious and beautiful whole, that is all hers to grasp and to remember.[7]

Another contemporary observer observed that once one had seen the springtime festivities in Central Park, he could forget the fact the all the joy and laughter was intimately bound up in the "intricate machine of party politics. Whatever the motive," he observed in 1906,

one fact brightly shines though it all. Thousands upon thousands of little children are transported from streets where there is little sunshine and gladness, to one day of perfect happiness in the free out-of-doors. The parks were made for them, not for the children of the rich. But were it not for these May parties, a great multitude of the children of New York would not know that Central Park existed.[8]

In addition to politicians, playground directors and settlement house workers also sponsored May Day celebrations, sometimes held in the crowded streets themselves. In a 1909 article titled "Robin Hood in Jones Street" published in *Outlook Magazine*, Zona Gale gave an account of a Robin Hood May Day masque in Manhattan. She noted that the seasons were not well recognized in Jones Street: summer was cruelly hot, winter bitterly cold, and autumn and spring hardly recognized since there were few trees to mark the season — spring especially always seemed to be somewhere else. But the festival, for which the children practiced several hours a week for a month, gave the children back their childhood. On this magic day, "Oh, we are jawly outlars," the ragged immigrant children sang. "Green Shoiwood is our ho — ome." In a concentrated month of practice, the children learned their dances, the Robin Hood story, and the songs, such as "Up oily in de mornin' we," which they declaimed in a strong New York accent. Gale described the scene with pathos and whimsy, but the article extolled the reforming virtues of the May Day masque:

To add another to the list of gayeties and activities which make the settlement [house] attractive to the neighborhood; *to familiarize the children with an English classic*; *to stimulate their interest in the things mentioned in the Masque*; *to instruct them in music, in form, color, dance*; *to tell them about beauty*; *to give them the benefit of the drill and the influence of the rehearsals*; *to help in various developments of social consciousness*— all these counted for something. But the reason for the Masque and its chief value lay in providing the children in Jones Street with a bit of their rightful heritage — Play [emphasis added].[9]

The emphasized passages show that Gale believed that participation in this masque would improve and Americanize these children. She concluded her article by suggesting that the Robin Hood masque also served to expose how the city was failing poor children, by demonstrating the extreme pleasure the pleasure-starved children took in it. She suggested that, while social ills might require greater measures to cure, such little windows of play and culture could play a part in bringing in a new order.

By the 1920s, the urban or rural May Day festivals (rural festivals had the added responsibility of drawing far-flung communities together and teaching the dull and apathetic country children, as they were typified, to see the beauties of nature) became more elaborate, incorporating pantomimes or sentimental little plays and including as much color and beauty as possible. Each year, *The Playground*, the journal of the Playground Association of America, recommended numerous books and activities to school organizers and physical education instructors. The pageant director had her choice of a variety of plays and pageants, some incorporating dance or song, some specifically cast for as few as 18 little girls or as many as

The Chief Hollyhock crowning the American Beauty Rose as Queen and the most beautiful flower in the world in this one-act, juvenile pageant-operetta, Flowers of the Nations. *An example of one of the many May Day plays or pageants for children available for a festival organizer to use. (Collection of the author.)*

150 characters.[10] Schools, libraries, settlement houses, athletic associations, or playgrounds, many of which were under the direction of a salaried playground director, sponsored these kinds of festivals.

In accordance with G. Stanley Hall's philosophies, *The Playground's* authors felt that nature themes, such as pageants that celebrated the changing of the seasons, or myths and fairy tales in which nature played a big part, appealed most to children and were the best suited for these spring-tide events. Aesthetic appeal and symbolism, ideals of the American Pageant Association as well as the Arts and Crafts movement, were also important, as Constance D'Arcy MacKaye noted in 1920:

Great care should be exercised in the costuming of symbolic characters. *The colors must coincide with the mood that is to be created for the audience. Failure* should be in robes of black and grey, with an ashen grey veil over her face. *Success* should be in robes of soft-shot-silk or chiffon in which orange gold and flame-tossed scarlet should mingle. *Hope* should be in robes of faint luminous green representing the eternal power of Earth to renew [emphasis in the original].[11]

Miss MacKaye also recognized the perennial problem of "producing a good effect for very little money." It was difficult to impart aesthetic appeal to masses of children dressed in their best clothes instead of picturesque costumes. "There is a deadly monotony about this which discourages the ambitious worker," she wrote in discouragement. She urged that the girls all be dressed in white and the boys wear white shirts and black trousers and suggested that one should use lots of flags and pennants if giving a folk festival, and that flower festivals were easy to produce using crêpe paper for flower hats and skirts.[12]

These urban and rural community-based May Day celebrations continued throughout the 1920s and through the early 1940s, though they apparently diminished in frequency, size, and ambitiousness of scope during and after the Depression. Every year *The Playground* reported on communal festivals and festivities such as the following four examples.

In 1911 the Rev. Ernest Bradley, dean of Tamalpais Centre, in Southern Marin County, California, reported that the rural work center was "born" on May Day 1909 as a gift to the people. Its annual May Fête was at that time the largest gathering in the county. In 1910 there were 6,000 people on the grounds and more than 100 track and field events for boys and girls. The popular band of the St. Vincent's Orphanage led the procession, and the sports contestants passed by the May Queen's throne.[13]

At the May Festival on May 21, 1926 held in Parkersburg, Virginia, 5,000 children from all grades and the high school performed before an audience of 10,000. The lower grades danced folk dances such as the Swedish Klapdans, the English Gathering Peascods, and Looby Loo to the music of the high school band. Six hundred of the Junior and Senior High School Boys performed a mass formation boxing drill. The older girls performed maypole dances, after which the May Queen was driven around the field in a decorated float followed by all the girls who had taken part in the dance. The local Rotary, Kiwanis, and Lions (men's civic) Clubs donated cars to take the children to and from the stadium.[14]

A *May Day Revel on Nottingham Green* was given by the Eaton Girls' Club of the T. Eaton Company, Toronto, in 1926. The Queen was chosen from among the 14,000 employees of the plant, with a golden-haired girl winning the most votes and the much sought-after honor. The festivities took place on Lady Eaton's estate. There were several Robin Hood scenes, culminating in a village fair scene that included May Day Mummers with their Jack-in-the-Green, morris dancers, and the maypole dance. Robin Hood then crowned Maid Marian to be Queen. (The original play they used was then made available for sale through the Playground Association for $1.50.)[15]

A later example, in 1936, was *May Day as Play Day* as held in Palo Alto, California. An article in *Recreation* (as *The Playground* was now called) noted that the festival had originated sixteen years earlier, and during that time was under the "jealous" chairmanship of novelist and philanthropist Kathleen Norris. A principal feature of the event was a parade, with zoo animals, pets, military bands, a May Queen, "juvenile organizations in uniform," and children riding decorated bicycles or wheeling flower-covered doll carriages. Prizes and awards, a "locally written dance drama depicting either a fanciful or an historical event," a vaudeville show, food, and sports and drama events rounded out the day.[16]

New York City public schools and many public schools in other cities continued to hold less elaborate May Day festivals at least until the early 1960s — perhaps later. In a recent letter to the *New York Times*, one reader reminisced about maypole festivities in New York public schools in the 1940s and 1950s. "It was a very enjoyable activity, and the girls looked forward to it every year,"[17] she wrote. There is also an unconfirmed report that in 1957, when New York City celebrated its fiftieth May day festival, every maypole was painted gold, and more than 12,000 children took part in the festivities. And springtime dance festivals, sometimes called May Fetes and now featuring dances like the "Macarena," the "Hokey-Pokey" and the "Alley Cat," still take place in some New York City public schools, according to a *New York Times* article of June 2006 article titled, "Styles Change but Dance Tradition Endures in Schools."[18]

And what of the children themselves who participated in these festivals? After the first few years, when the adult supporters of pageants and festivals and folk dance training in the public schools described the girls' enthusiasm and their despair should they not be able to participate, there is little documentation. In informal conversations with adults today, many remember fondly May Day celebrations with the maypole dance at their elementary schools, and recall their pride and pleasure when they were finally old enough to wind the maypole. No one lately reports having been "improved" by this participation, however, and it seems safest to conclude that after the Progressive reform era, folk dancing at school festivals in the spring sank to being merely an enjoyable event.

THE COLLEGE MAY DAY FESTIVAL

10. The Making of the College Girl of 1900

> With dew-drenched roses in her hair,
> With jeweled girdle, rich and rare,
> Arrayed in gown of dazzling white,
> Our May Queen, vision of delight,
> As she danced gaily up the street
> So daintily on slippered feet,
> It was indeed a lovely scene —
> The progress of a royal queen.
> —Albert H. Macy, written in honor of fourteen-year-old
> Tennessee Tomlinson, Earlham College's first May Queen in 1875[1]

From the 1830s on, girls celebrated May Day in a modest way at their finishing academies and seminaries. It was not until 1875 that the girls of an accredited college first celebrated May Day, and the festival soared in popularity in the 1890s and thereafter.

But why did May Day flourish in the college environment, appearing at institutions of such very different size and character as the intellectual Bryn Mawr College in Philadelphia, the then-Southern-belle Agnes Scott College in Decatur, Georgia, and the huge, co-educational, land-grant University of Colorado in Denver? And why did the festival become more popular at the turn of the century?

There are four interlocking answers to these questions. First, women were attending college in ever-increasing numbers in the 1890s and thereafter, numbers that encouraged them to create traditions that celebrated girlhood as well as their shared college experience. Second, as a result of more middle-class girls attending college, there was increased social and parental anxiety about the nature of the College Girl. This anxiety may have caused administrators and parents to embrace the girlish May Day festival as an exemplar of traditional femininity. Third, there is ample evidence the spirit of the College Girl herself changed dramatically at the turn of the century, when girls focused more enthusiastically on the entertainment aspects of their college lives.

A final reason for the popularity of an Elizabethan May Day was that middle-class America in the last decades of the nineteenth century was in the grip of Anglomania in general. These were the days when it seemed as if American millionaires' daughters traveled by every boat to England to catch impoverished but titled husbands; Edith Wharton's *The Buccaneers* (published in 1938 after the author's death, but set in the 1870s) and Constance Cary Harrison's *The Anglomaniacs* (1890) describe this marriage fever. Everything English — especially old English — was delightful and desirable, romantic and upper-class. If the former Lady Ran-

Carrying the Daisy Chain at Commencement— another beloved tradition of College Girls in the days when only a handful graduated each year. (Collection of the author.)

dolph Churchill (née Constance Vanderbilt) could play with her titled friends at a medieval tournament in 1912 as part of a Shakespeare tercentenary celebration, why shouldn't American girls have an old English May Day of their own?

The College Girl of 1900 was not a young woman of 2000 in a corset and a long skirt; fundamental differences separate these two individuals. She was, in the words of a writer of 1900, regarded "curiously and a little askance" by others. "She is subjected to three processes which in the eyes of the world at large are occult and mysterious, separating her from her kind, fraught with possibilities and dangers: she passes through a terrible ordeal known as the entrance examination; she plunges into the abyss of intellectual work; she is surrounded by the strange enchantments of college life."[2] This chapter examines how the college girls who initiated and enjoyed the May Day festivals came to be.

Throughout the nineteenth century, educators opened institutions of higher learning for females. These colleges were small, and the studies were not particularly rigorous. In the early years, girls could be admitted as young as fourteen, the age gradually advancing as the century wore on. The youth of the girls, and their relatively poor academic preparation, had a distinct bearing on the entrance studies and curriculum. A girl entered as a sub-freshman and had to pass examinations to determine if she could take the college work, or if she were conditioned (required to do extra work) in any subject.[3]

Moreover, each of these colleges was experimenting with a different model and curriculum for female education. Many of the land-grant colleges funded by the Morrill Act* accepted women, partly due to shortages of male students during and after the Civil War, but they

---

*The Morrill Acts of 1862 and 1890 funded institutions to teach agriculture, military tactics, and the mechanic arts as well as classical studies so that members of the working classes could obtain a liberal, practical education. The first Morrill Act provided grants in the form of federal lands to each state for the establishment of a public institution to fulfill the act's provisions. There is now at least one land-grant institution in every state and territory.

tended to offer so-called "Ladies Courses" to their women students: watered-down versions of selected portions of the men's curriculum. It was not until Smith College opened in 1875 that we see a women's college beginning at the outset to provide a course of study almost identical to the men's. Wellesley College soon followed.[4]

Coincident with the opening of Smith College, not only did women's college curricula grow more rigorous, but women began attending college in ever-increasing numbers: the number of women college students throughout the country increased from 11,000 in 1870 to 85,000 in 1900. While the overall proportion of American women who attended college was still very small, women had a big impact on campus: in 1870 women represented 21 percent of the college population, by 1900 they represented 35 percent, and by 1920, women made up nearly 50 percent of all enrolled college students.

The increasing numbers of college-educated women, and the increasing visibility of the College Girl led inevitably to public concern about the value and appropriateness of higher education for women. The general social anxiety over the role of the college girl expressed itself in debates about whether college would "de-sex" or "de-womanize" her. Would it ruin a girl's physical and future reproductive health, or would it make her discontented with her lot and therefore disinclined to marry and have children? One statistic that alarmed society at the turn of the century was the reported decline in the marriage rate and subsequent birthrate of college-educated women: in the 1880s and 1890s, nearly 50 percent of women graduates did not marry, compared to the approximately 10 percent of single, non-graduates in their age groups. This decline in the marriage and birthrates of white, Protestant, middle-class women was regarded with extreme anxiety, as the immigrants flooding the cities appeared to be doing more than their share to keep the birthrate up. The apparent failure of the college-educated woman to procreate was a potent argument against sending one's daughter to college.

Pro-college arguments, even those made by women, were conservative: a college education would make the young woman better fit to be mistress of her home, children and social circle. In her study of 1905, *The College Girl of America, and the Institutions Which Make Her What She Is*, Mary Caroline Crawford argued that higher education was valuable for women because

> [t]he future of American culture depends upon the women. They alone have the leisure for it. And upon the college woman who has been laying up stores of intellectual wealth rests the duty of redeeming the over-commercial tone Americans are in danger of acquiring.[5]

The Angel in the House should be a well-educated one, fit to redeem her businessman husband. Conservative arguments like these — buttressed by the many articles in popular magazines about the frolics and girlish fun to be had at college — gradually allowed both men and women to think of a woman's college education as something that would not threaten the status quo.

For while a middle-class, Protestant, white woman's ability to obtain higher education — whether in single-sex or coeducational colleges — increased dramatically from 1870 onwards, it did not result in an increase of a modern-day feminist spirit. Suffrage was not an issue on campus in the 1890s and the early 1900s: the undergraduates of Wellesley College, for example, continued to vote overwhelmingly against their own enfranchisement until 1910, after the states of Washington, Utah, Idaho, Colorado and Wyoming had actually granted the ballot to women.[6] Women college students had only a minimal impact on the suffrage movement before the formation of the College Equal Suffrage League in 1906, and the connection in general between higher education and feminism remained tenuous.[7] Even as late as 1918, and after several generations of college women had graduated, none of the apparently progressive Eastern women's colleges were producing, in Roberta Frankfort's words, "militantly sexless Amazons." College might provide a more sophisticated academic training, but it did not permanently challenge the cult of domesticity, continuing to prescribe to women the traditional role of dedication to home and family.[8] Indeed, historian William D. Jenkins argues that the precepts of the Progressive movement itself limited the potential changes of the suffrage movement.[9]

While many observers feared that college would de-feminize a girl, others feared that the advent of women on campus might effeminize their men. Many men's colleges banned women students altogether; some, like Stanford University, adopted quotas for the admission of women; while other colleges established separate (sometimes termed "coordinate") women's colleges. Once admitted, the women's access to libraries, gymnasiums, and certain science classes were often restricted. Under one administration at the University of Missouri, for example, the women were marched to class with teachers as guards at the front and rear. Under another president, female students were required to wear uniforms in order to distinguish them from other women in the town.[10]

The college men were often actively hostile to the women students: at the University of Rochester they stamped their feet loudly when a woman entered the classroom, slammed doors in their faces, and formed crowds in front of campus buildings to prohibit women from entering unless they were brave enough to elbow their way through.[11] Similarly when women were first admitted to Cornell University and the University of Michigan in the early 1870s, they were treated by the men as pauper students, isolated and occasionally harassed. At Cornell, in 1872, when the senior class voted on the coed issue, only 15, three of whom were women, voted in favor, the remaining 37 were opposed. The college historian noted that "the first Cornellians were themselves extremely sensitive to mockery on the part of their school friends who had gone to the old eastern colleges. They wanted Cornell to rival [the men-only colleges of] Harvard, Yale, and Princeton socially. The sharpest shafts in the older colleges' quiver was the sneer that Cornell was a ladies' seminary." This historian further observed that the eighteen-year old boys were actively unreceptive of any of the refining influences of womanhood that educators approved of, nor did they like the fact that the women did well in their studies and sometimes outperformed the men.[12] These sentiments help to explain why at some campuses, the men made their derision of the girls evident in their mockery or disruption of the girl's May Day festivals, as discussed in Chapter 13.

The combination of the increasing numbers of women in colleges and society's collective anxiety about them served to reinforce the traditional views of womanhood circa 1900—views that a pretty May Day fête also reinforced. But what of the girls themselves? How did they perceive their college education and role in society?

The first generation of women who graduated from college in significant numbers—that of the 1870s and 1880s—were serious, middle-class women or farmers' daughters from modest backgrounds, eager to obtain an education in order to be able to teach school, one of the few professions open to women outside the home. Many of these women worked in the summer to earn money for college, and a high proportion of these early graduates never married.

By 1893, however, Lida Rose McCabe could begin her book, *The American Girl at College*, with the bold assertion that the higher education of women had ceased to be a "conundrum," a rarity.[13] By the turn of the century greater numbers of affluent young women entered both the coeducational and women's colleges, with little or no thought of an eventual career.

The May Queen as either Venus or a sea goddess in the pageant, "Deep Sea Caverns," performed at Chatham in 1927. The pageant also featured dancing mermaids combing their hair and looking into mirrors. (Archives, Chatham University, Pittsburgh, Pennsylvania.)

With greater wealth, the college girl became more frivolous and fun-oriented. Teas, campus clubs, athletics, and dramatics all flourished. Moreover, McCabe argued that this "aesthetic culture" as expressed in music and art was "the aroma of scholastic training" and that, without it, education was incomplete.[14]

"Do college girls have a good time, or are they all 'greasy grinds' and 'blue stockings?'" runs the opening sentence of the article, "May-Time at Mount Holyoke" by Grace M. Burt published in the magazine, *St. Nicholas for Boys and Girls*, May 1920. Miss Burt's article described the girls' playful activities, especially the springtime festival. But May Day was just one of the college girl's amusing activities. Sophomores entertained freshmen at colonial teas or sleigh rides; classes chose class songs, colors and mottos. There were sleigh rides in winter and "mountain days" (an unexpected holiday from studies) in the spring, room "spreads" or feasts, fudge-making, all-girl dances, and other student-organized festivities such as the "Freshman Frolic"—"a very pretentious affair"—held at Smith College. The dance was held in the decorated gymnasium. Each sophomore girl was the "cavalier" of a freshman girl, adopting all the behaviors that a young man would.

> She sends her flowers, calls for her, fills her order of dance, introduces her partners, fetches ices and frappes between dances and takes her to supper. The whole method of procedure is apt to impress the freshman ludicrously at first, except that the soph fulfills her duties with so much dignified seri-

ousness.... Every soph sees her partner home, begs for a flower and changes orders for souvenirs, and if the freshman has taken advantage of the opportunity and made the desired hit, there are dates for future meetings and jollifications, and a good-night over the balusters, as lingering and cordial as any the freshie has left behind her.

The author noted that at Vassar College, the sophomores went one step further, "those who fill men's parts at the dances affecting [gym] bloomers, sack-coats disclosing a wide expanse of shirt-front, white lawn ties and buttonhole bouquets."[15] These girls weren't marching for votes for women — they were endorsing the status quo by mimicking traditional male-female roles, and could thus be seen as sexually unthreatening.

And the girls' erudition was shown not to harm them: articles like "Life at a Girls' College," published in *Munsey's Magazine* in 1897, demonstrated that, while serious about their studies, the girls at Smith College were not "grinds." The article depicts in words and sketches the pretty dormitory rooms, the celebration of Ivy Day, and the jolly games and delicious food of the college girls. The author stated outright that the girls' studies did not make them masculine or demanding of equal rights:

they do study, the daughters of "Fair Smith," in a manner that would put the average college man to shame. Yet if any one supposes that these young women are a set of "grinds," that they all wear glasses and masculine collars, and go about continually talking women's rights and political economy, he is vastly mistaken.... the Smith girl] blends work and fun in such happy proportions that to her life is always interesting. She is neither a bookworm nor an idler, but keen intellectual competition and wholesome physical activity combine to bring out all that is best in her.[16]

Foremost in the minds of college girls themselves as well as their parents was the fear that intellectual achievement was not compatible with beauty. Beauty, fitness and dressing well (though not necessarily expensively) went hand-in-hand. In 1893 Lila McCabe sternly reminded college girls that

[n]o girl can afford to neglect her toilet [sic] in or out of college. It is not only a personal but a public duty to present at all times the most pleasing and attractive appearance.... Brain-workers are proverbially inclined to run down at the heels. Intellect and artistic dressing have rarely if ever been synonymous. A well-dressed woman, however, is always an art-educator.[17]

Fear of being considered a "grind," with stereotyped features of a narrow chest, pinched brow, scanty hair pulled back over thick glasses, and a petticoat too long for the skirt, haunts many of the novels of college life, for popular literature as well as factual articles also explored the life of the college girl, often with ambivalence; since it is assumed that no woman will continue working after she marries, many stories deal with a girl's dilemma of whether to choose love or dedicate herself to her work: there was no middle ground.

However, the fun of college life appeared in series novels aimed at young readers that feature the adventures of a college heroine and her friends through numerous volumes. These series included Margaret Warde's Betty Wales stories (*Betty Wales, Freshman; Betty Wales, Sophomore*, etc.) published in 1905 and after, as well as Jessie Graham Flower's Grace Harlowe series (*Grace Harlowe's First Year at Overton College, Second Year*, etc.) that followed Grace from her high school years (four volumes) through college (seven volumes), overseas (six volumes) and out west (ten volumes). Finally, Jean Webster's extremely popular epistolary novel *Daddy-Long-Legs* (1912) (made into a play and eventually two movies, one starring Fred Astaire and Leslie Caron) and her less well-known *When Patty Goes to College* (1903) even more engagingly depicted the fun and good times of the college experience. Shirley Marchalonis observes that these early novels emphasize the excitement of self-discovery and the expansion of a girl's talents when she enters college, though as the twentieth-century progressed, this excitement was suppressed.[18]

Wholesome and genial, books and stories like these made college seem unthreatening, a place where the biggest conflict lay in who would win or lose the important basketball game. The four years of study in the green world could be a verdant source of friendship, pride, academic challenges and achievement. And, by 1900, they were also expected to be personally pleasurable.

Thus we have the College Girl of 1900: more numerous than ever before, more fun-loving; generally uninterested in the suffrage question; sometimes dreaming of a career, yet mostly happily looking forward to marriage; perceived with some anxiety as being too forward by parents and young men; generally happy to celebrate their status of girlhood. And the relationship of the College Girl to May Day? When we examine the nature and imagery of the May Day festivals and pageants, we will see that, while the participants might perceive the festivities as both an artistic outlet and a bonding experience, forging ties between the girls and their class and college, overall the May Day was culturally conservative: preserving — promulgating, in fact — a stereotype of girlish beauty and feminine accomplishments.

11. Origins of the College May Day Pageant

> The May Fête brings all the elements of the University together in a wholesome sort of activity and jollity. It shows us the kind of beauty and charm that have not much place in our everyday lives. Along with the lightness and merriment, there is a regard for tradition that is a wholesome thing for us. We have none too much reverence for tradition. There is a pleasure in reviving the old, when that old had for its motive a real instinct of simple enjoyment and an impulse that was a response to natural conditions. Why should it be any more a natural impulse for young Greeks or young English to go out and dance on the green in the springtime, than for young Kansans?
> — From *The Jayhawker Yearbook*, The University of Kansas, 1912[1]

The stage is now set for the May Day pageant of Anycollege, Anytown, circa 1910. There is a perception among participants and spectators alike that the festival is a pretty one, well-suited to girlhood. There is a common desire to see the College Girl acting like a traditional girl. Female physical education instructors at women's colleges are eagerly promulgating the aesthetic and symbolic principles of the American Pageant Association and teaching the folk dances recommended by the leaders of the Playground Association. Middle-class Americans share a common image of Merrie May Day in Merrie Old England, and are happy to use invoke this image to celebrate their Anglo-American heritage while also incorporating the benign and non-threatening folk dances of the immigrants. It is now time to examine the various ways in which the college May Day festival originated.

Part II of this book details the May Day celebrations held at 80 colleges and universities from across the U.S., forming a large, though non-scientifically determined sample. To collect this information I surmised that any women's college extant at the turn of the century or shortly thereafter would have had a May Day celebration and made inquiries accordingly. This theory proved to be quite strong: five of the so-called "Seven Sisters" (Barnard, Bryn Mawr, Mount Holyoke, Smith, and Wellesley, but not — according to their archivists — Radcliffe or Vassar) and virtually all of the principal women's colleges of the South in the early decades of the century (Agnes Scott, Converse, Goucher, Randolph-Macon, Sophie Newcomb, Westhampton, Baylor, Hollins, Hood, Meredith, Sweet Briar, Salem, Tennessee and Wesleyan) celebrated May Day. Internet searches also revealed many other institutions that were then, or are now, co-educational, and that had also sponsored the festival. These were not exclusively small, private colleges: many of the women's adjunct colleges of the big land-grant universities of the West also celebrated May Day. A surprising number of the colleges in the respondent group had strong affiliations with conservative religious sects at the turn of

Brunhilde exhorts the Water Nymphs in a dramatic moment in the May Day pageant of "Sigurd the Volsung," Wilson College, 1929. (Photograph courtesy Elizabeth Boyd '33 Archives, Hankey Center, Wilson College.)

the century. While the respondent group was not rigorously selected, it is nevertheless diverse in terms of size of student body, location and school ethos. Other highlights of the sample group are that:

- The 80 institutions are located in 33 states, including nine respondents from Pennsylvania, seven from Ohio, six from Virginia, and four each from Massachusetts, New York, South Carolina and Iowa.
- 25 of the 80 institutions are still institutions for women only or women predominately.
- Almost 25 percent of the institutions were founded by strict religious groups: six by Presbyterians, three by Baptists, fourth by Methodists, two by Quakers, one by evangelical Lutherans, one by Mennonites, and two (one in Maine and one in Kentucky) by abolitionists. At least sixteen of the colleges still have strong religious affiliations.
- Many of the colleges that celebrated May Day are still small: 18 of them have current enrollments of fewer than 1,000 students, while another 21 have enrollments between 1,000 and 1,999. By contrast, 12 of the respondents have current enrollments in excess of 20,000—however, enrollment figures for the state-supported schools must be treated carefully, as these schools grew at an exponential fashion during the twentieth century. At the turn of the century, even the land-grant universities—and the women's adjunct colleges thereof—were still comparatively small.

As shown in Table 1, the majority — 57 — of the college May Day festivals originated between 1901 and 1920.

Table 1. Breakdown of Origination

Decade	First May Day Festivals at Respondent Colleges
1870 to 1880	1
1881 to 1890	0
1891 to 1900	8
1901 to 1910	30
1911 to 1920	27
1921 to 1930	9
After 1930	4
N/A	1
Total	**80**

As noted in Chapter 4, the first May Day festival held at an accredited college (as opposed to a ladies' academy or finishing school) was given in 1875 by the women of Earlham College. Two girl students, influenced by a romantic illustration and a brief article that appeared in *Harper's Weekly* of May 23, 1874, convinced the matron that the girls should celebrate May Day.

Earlham's first festival was a simple one: the Queen had to borrow a white dress and flowers were scanty as it was a cold spring. The janitor made a throne out of packing boxes and the girls draped it with shawls and rugs. After the maids of honor escorted the fourteen-year old Queen to her throne, the girls marched around it to the music of a mouth harp, waving short sticks with handkerchiefs tied to them. One of the festival's two originators gave a talk on May Day in Old England and the Queen sang a song. The men of the college were not permitted to view the festivities, though they were so permitted the next time the festival was held, three years later, and eventually they participated in them. Earlham's May Day festivals steadily grew more elaborate, with the first winding of the maypole (performed to a sedate march suitable for Quaker maidens) occurring in 1882.[2] In the late 1880s, gypsies were added to the festivities, and a raven-haired Gypsy Queen was crowned as well as the May Queen, eventually rivaling her in popularity. In 1896 the girls performed a pantomime to the reading of Tennyson's poem cycle, "The May Queen," following this, with no apparent sensation of anachronism, with a minuet danced by girls dressed in colonial costume.[3] Within a few more years the festival depicted an elaborate enactment of a visit of Queen Elizabeth I to an English village, and this pageant, now incorporating the men, continued every four years until 1993.

Thus went the first college May Day. The festival soon spread. With May Day and Merrie England in the air, so to speak, the festival began at some colleges because a young woman was inspired by reading about it. Thus, for example, in 1894 a girl at Rockford College in Illinois conceived of the festival "from reading stories about May Day celebrations in Merry Old England, which we copied, so far as we could."[4] Rockford's celebration was unique in its deliberate references both to John Ruskin and to certain facets of the Whitelands College May Day festival, including the presentation to the retiring Rockford Queen of a wreath of violets and the gift to the new Queen of a cross of hawthorn.

The influential May Day festival of another Quaker-founded college for women, Bryn Mawr, began in 1900, when a group of students met at the house of a young alumna to discuss how to raise funds to build a Students' Building. As Mrs. Evangeline Walker Andrews watched the students in their white dresses walk away over the green grass, "there came to her *suddenly and quite complete* the idea of an Elizabethan May Day, a country festival with dances and plays, with shepherds and shoe-makers, and a procession to accompany the oxen that brought in the great central Maypole" (emphasis added).[5] The fact that the vision of May Day could appear to this alumna as "complete" confirms just how strong the holiday's image was. Later, in a 1915 bulletin of the American Pageant Association, Mrs. Andrews added that the festival had begun

> first, because the student community wished to give some sort of entertainment which would express the community as a whole; and secondly, because the setting — an English landscape with Jacobean architecture — suggested the Elizabethan period. Also, it seemed natural and suitable the young, English-speaking students should express themselves in an historic revival of a festival that might be considered theirs, both as a literary and a racial heritage.[6]

The idea was enthusiastically received and the resulting pageant was a representation of "erudition in an entrancing form," as the college history puts it. All 300 women of Bryn Mawr participated and at the conclusion, when all joined hands in a great circle winding in toward the center, both participants and spectators were apparently moved by the sensation of just how much such unity of spirit and enthusiasm could do.[7] Thus the Bryn Mawr May Day festival earned a stamp of approval as representing or even encouraging desirable moral values. This thought was suggested again in 1936 by novelist Christopher Morley (who had seen the 1908 production and was urging readers to attend the even more elaborate '36 event), who wrote that he didn't know "of any other 'project' (this being the master-word of education nowadays) that brings together a whole college body, past and present, in such unity of zeal."[8] Even as late as 1943, educators could point to the intellectual benefits that the May Day festival brought:

> Behind the beauty and the color of Salem [College]'s traditional May-day there is a great variety of work and talent that reflect the more scholastic endeavors of the college. The writing of the pageants, the designing of costumes, the creation of dances, the scoring and playing and singing of the music, the landscaping of May Dell — all represent the serious study of the arts, which is the continuous activity of the college. May-day ... is in keeping with the best of old Salem: that is, the artistic expression of the love of beauty in the heart of mankind.[9]

Contemporary observers and participants also praised the woman-centric nature of the May Day pageant. For example, two women writing in 1916 about the University of Berkeley's *Partheneia* observed that it was a pageant in which all the women of the university had an opportunity to share,

> and which, though produced entirely by women, has always been successful in an artistic and financial way. It is rich in youth and happiness, replete with blending colors and harmonious with music of voice and instrument. The dancing groups flitting across the sward joying in the very movement of the dance, are pleasing sights in a commercial world.[10]

Once initiated at prestigious Eastern colleges, the idea of a May Day festival spread rapidly, transmitted by articles in popular magazines and picked up upon by eager young students. As we have seen, the college girl and her "stunts" and festivals, including May Day, was prime fodder for articles in popular journals and books. For example, the editor of a series on "Festivals in American Colleges for Women," published in *The Century* magazine in 1895, noted, "In all parts of the country is to be noticed of late years an increase of interest in gay and beautiful pageants, of one sort or another, on land or water. Women have in these a great part, and this new tendency in our rather hard and strained American life is surely one to be cultivated at school, in our homes, and in our communities."[11] The series of articles, each apparently written by a college girl, covered celebrations at Bryn Mawr, Smith, Mount Holyoke, Vassar, Wellesley, and Wells, and included a pretty picture of Vassar girls dancing around the maypole (despite the assertion of its archivist that Vassar didn't celebrate May Day; perhaps this was an isolated event).

Some May Day festivals had their origins in spring festivals with different names such as Ivy Day or Tree Day, when the seniors celebrated their forthcoming graduation by ceremonially planting vegetation. These festivals also incorporated dances and drills, including the maypole dance, and often featured the crowning of a Queen. Thus at the Women's College of Western Reserve University (now Case Western Reserve University), the sophomores celebrated Tree Day beginning in 1894; while the seniors began in 1911 to hold a May Day pageant. The two festivals continued side-by-side until the mid–1930s, when they were combined under the May Day name.

While emulation of Eastern women's colleges — Bryn Mawr and Wellesley seemed to have been particularly influential — could be one impetus to creating a May Day festival, college rivalry could provide another stimulant. For example, the Newcomb College May Day festival of 1914 was the idea of one young woman who, over the Christmas holidays, had been asked by a friend who attended nearby Agnes Scott College what special festivities the Newcomb juniors performed in honor of their graduating seniors. As one alumna reminisced, "The inevitable answer of 'Nothing' became a humiliating challenge to [the young woman] and ruined her holidays until she conceived [of] the idea of May Day." Upon the girl's return to school after the holidays she soon had the entire junior class "working as an inspired unit." The program, the costumes and the preparation of the Maypole were all done in secret. "The queen and maids were selected for their college spirit and service on the campus from among those seniors who had not held major offices. So that no one could know in advance who would be in the court the juniors voted by secret ballot just before the celebration began."[12]

At some institutions, student clubs or organizations — such as the YWCA or a debate, literary or athletics club — initiated May Day festivals, often to raise money for a building that the women would benefit from such as a gymnasium. The profits made from May Day at Iowa State University, for example, went to purchasing equipment for women's sports like tennis and basketball. At the coeducational University of Colorado, it was the Women's League that sponsored the first May Day in 1912, with the express purpose to raise funds for a women's building (presumably housing/recreational). Two thousand spectators viewed an elaborate procession, some folk dances and the maypole dance. Later that day the men presented the operetta *The Haymakers*. The event was successful, as the paper reported that "Queen's Crown Costs Visitors over $1,000.00" and went on with the subtitle "Large Sum Added to Fund for $75,000 Women's Building, the Dream of Every Colorado Co-Ed." One author wrote that for months everyone had been hearing about the plans: "Every co-ed, every alumna, in fact every woman in the state who has heard of the plan is becoming more enthused every day. No election in years has aroused any more interest than that of the May Queen and her sixteen maids of honor."[13]

Women physical education instructors, many of whom were themselves graduates of Eastern women's colleges or of Columbia University's Teachers College, also initiated many May Day celebrations, using the festival as a means of showcasing the year's work in dance and light gymnastics. At Iowa State University, for example, the first May Day festival was held in 1907 under the direction of Miss Winifred Tilden, the instructor in physical culture, a 1903 graduate of Mount Holyoke College, where she had experienced May Day. Miss Tilden came to Iowa State in 1904, and directed many of the subsequent celebrations until at least 1923.[14]

And, in several notable cases, college administrators were themselves initiators or active sponsors of May Day. Bryn Mawr College's May Day was actively encouraged and supported by its second president, M. Carey Thomas, a woman who believed that academic work alone would not produce a cultivated and educated woman: that she needed to be exposed to an environment that reinforced high ideals of beauty and moral values and that encouraged groups of women to work together. Thomas discouraged student hazing and encouraged the adoption of supportive customs such as giving lanterns to entering freshmen to light their steps through the intricacies of college life. She apparently also had a personal love of plays and pageantry and was willing to sacrifice student study time to their performance because they fitted in with her scheme of awakening a love of beauty and order in the students. Even today, Bryn Mawr students annually elect two Traditions Mistresses who are charged with the performance and continuation of the college's numerous traditions large and small, including May Day.

Bryn Mawr's festival was not alone in having a strong sponsor: May Day at the University of Maryland was initiated in 1923 by the then newly appointed dean of women, Adele Stamp. One year after her eventual retirement in 1960, the festival folded. And the story of Westhampton College (formerly the women's college of the University of Richmond) represents another example of the deliberate embrace of tradition. That college, which had a conservative Baptist affiliation, opened in 1914. Its historian notes that the first dean had not only to oversee academic standards, but "the development of a cohesive group life for a new and tradition-less college. As the students initiated activities, Dean Keller evaluated each in terms of its potential to unite the classes and provide an outlet for the students' creativity."[15] As a consequence of the dean's initiatives, Westhampton's first May Day was celebrated in 1914, with the winding of the maypole added in 1915. In 1916 the girls celebrated May Day with various aesthetic dances, and by 1922 there was a complete pageant that combined spring characters with dances symbolizing the Purification of Water and other similar themes.

The history of the springtide pageant of University of California at Berkeley shows the girls' springtime pageant as not only having a strong sponsor, but being inaugurated as a woman's event deliberately different from the athletic activities of the men who barely tolerated their presence on campus. In 1912 Professor Lucy Sprague, at that time dean of women, organized a student-written masque with interpretative music and dancing titled *Partheneia* (meaning "the Spirit of Young Womanhood" or "Maiden-Song"). Sprague wanted the college women to present an annual pageant that would represent their highest ideals, allow expression of their creative and artistic talents and uniting them in their work on a common project. "As a group, [women] were tolerated in a man's college," Sprague wrote. "I wanted them to create something that would give them standing in their own eyes and in the eyes of the community."[16] The *Partheneia*, held for many years in the spring, was not a typical May Day festival in that no Queen was crowned. The pageant themes are nevertheless similar to those of other colleges.

The first *Partheneia* masque was titled the *Masque of Maidenhood*, "a rhythmic dramatic masque of great historic women and what they cared for and fought for. At the end, these women in the play [including Joan of Arc on a white charger, Iphigenia (carrying a genuine amphora lent by the museum), and Héloise in her nun's gown with an ancient crucifix] appeared in a long procession and left an offering on an altar of hope," wrote Sprague.[17] Subsequent productions included *The Awakening of Every Maid* (1913), *The Dream of Derdra, a*

Celtic Masque (1914), *The Queen's Masque* (1915), and *Aranyani of the Jasmine Vine* (1916). These themes centered on the transition from girlhood to womanhood and the achievement of love, and incorporated extensive symbolism with a close connection with natural world and imaginative world of fays and sprites. The girls were apparently very conscious of how unique their festival was compared to the rest of the activities of the university. As two women graduates wrote in 1916:

> In an institution in which the activities are largely conducted by men the dominating interest being athletics, women have little opportunity for the portrayal of ideals. The Partheneia is the one event of the year wholly devoted to women in which their ideas find untrammeled vent in the writing, managing, costuming and producing of the masque—the concrete presentation of their ideals. As the Athletic Rally is the spontaneous outburst of virile college manhood, so the Partheneia is the naïve revelation of the spirit of womanhood.[18]

The Berkeley women were not alone in creating their special pageant in defiance of the men. Though women were admitted to DePauw University in 1867, partly as a result of the dearth of male students due to the Civil War, they found themselves, according to the university's history, "in separate—some might say subordinate—campus roles at the close of World War I." Excluded from membership in journalism clubs, debate teams, and scholastic honorary groups, women founded their own versions of these and other activities, celebrating May Day for the first time in 1910. The university's website notes that "[w]ith Old Gold Day in its early years chiefly oriented toward male participation in class scraps and interclass football games, May Day became the premier campus event for women." It was not the only one, however; the on-line history also notes that, beginning in 1923, the college yearbook annually featured a special section on "campus beauties." This section consisted of a handful of photographs of glamorously posed coeds selected by vote of the male student body or by a well-known artist or other supposed expert on female beauty and charm. In 1931, for example, Broadway producer Florenz Ziegfield made the final selection among this bevy of beauties. And, as at many other colleges, DePauw's students also elected other Queens: The Old Gold Day Queen, who was crowned at halftime during the homecoming football game, the Dad's Day Queen, crowned in November, and various Prom Queens, who with their escorts led the grand marches that opened dances.[19]

College administrators of the period actively encouraged the creation of college traditions, whether those that they urged upon the students, or those that the students created for themselves. These administrators, whether consciously or not, saw in the development of school and individual class traditions a means to encourage solidarity and to create loyalty to the school, as well as to create a brand image for their college. Thus, for example, the newspaper of Westminster College in Salt Lake City, Utah proudly reported that the play performed at the 1922 pageant was so well done that "[a]n honored Princeton graduate said the play would have done credit to any American college."[20]

Faculty, administrators, and alumnae approved of the teamwork necessary to produce a successful pageant, and approved as well of the additional learning that the pageants bestowed upon the participants. Thus, for example, on May 1, 1911, the University of Minnesota's Alumni *Weekly* noted approvingly the May Fête did more than just bring students together, it made them actually work together whole-heartedly.[21] And, in 1942, the historian of Mary Baldwin College noted that

> the romance of the past and the realities of today have been artistically combined in the cooperative work of students and faculty [in May Day]. In spite of the satisfaction of the final beautiful display,

Five maypoles grace the sward at Mills College in 1947. The setting of this spectacle in the beautiful campus grounds illustrates one of the principles of the American Pageant Association: that the physical setting should act almost as a character in the pageant. (Special Collections, F. W. Olin Library, Mills College.)

perhaps the chief significance of the pageant lies in the fact that it is a laboratory in which the student can see and participate in the process of artistic creation.[22]

College May Day pageants were enormous theatrical productions, attracting thousands of spectators, including wealthy alumnae, to the college campus, and reinforcing the belief that this was a good institution to which to send their daughters. "By the 1920s, the Carleton College May Fête was 'considered the most beautiful and impressive event of its kind in the northwest,'" the college historians noted, adding that "although it occasioned many 'postponed picnics, broken dates, and sarcastic remarks by the he-men of the College on the general practicability and great everyday usefulness of aesthetic dancing,' it was anticipated with excitement and pleasure by most students."

The festivals were serious affairs: faculty, administration and alumnae placed great value on the festival and expressed their support in many concrete ways. For example at Carleton College in 1921 an island in the campus' lake was chosen for a stage setting and a rustic bridge was built for those taking part to cross over. This location, set in a natural amphitheater, was used for the next forty years, attracting more outside visitors to the College than any other event of the year. In 1924 the college hired the Minneapolis Symphony Orchestra for 500 dollars to perform the difficult Wagnerian orchestration accompanying the May Day presentation of *Sigurd, the Volsung*. Because of the great interest of the local Scandinavian population in this theme, the college spent much time and money to ensure that the costumes and scenic effects were historically correct, while the finale of this extravaganza was a snowflake ballet danced by 125 girls in fluffy white costumes.[23]

In another example of administrative support of the girls May Day pageant, in 1921 the administration of the University of Colorado erected seats for 5,000 on campus for the festivity, while in 1923 it imported 500 small pine trees to form a small forest as a backdrop to the natural amphitheatre. That same year, a stone bridge 130 feet long built by university engineers and containing ten tons of stone "made a graceful entryway for the dancers from the meadow beyond."[24]

A final stated reason for administrators to support the May Day festival was their belief that it created solidarity in each successive class of students. Within a few years of the inception of May Day at Scripps College in Claremont California, for example, the way in which the freshmen and the sophomores interacted had changed dramatically: May Day was now held explicitly to encourage the development of class spirit in the freshmen and sophomores. By 1947 the student handbook stated:

> It is recognized that Sophomore "hazing" connected with Freshman May Fete tends to result in certain desirable ends, which, it is agreed, should not be ignored nor neglected. These ends are: increased familiarity among members of both classes, development of class spirit in both classes, and, especially in the Freshman Class, unity and cooperation in working toward a common goal.[25]

The Scripps freshmen wrote a lengthy play or skit, often incorporating song parodies, in the four weeks prior to the event, keeping the theme secret. In the week immediately prior to May Day, the sophomores "investigated" it, attempting to discover the theme of the play, while the freshmen planted clues, including false scripts and props. After the presentation of the actual freshman play on May Day, the sophomores presented a parody of it, incorporating the clues, both real and false, that they had discovered. They then hosted a breakfast for the freshmen. The college administration apparently felt that these activities created a desirable rivalry between the two classes, strengthening each class in its own class spirit.

As the accounts of the 80 institutions' May Day festivals contained in Part II attest, the college May Day was no small affair. Immediately after one year's performance, planning began for the next; student competitions were sometimes held to determine the theme of the pageant or to write the script. The selection and crowning of the Queen, the folk and aesthetic dances to be performed, and the theme pageant itself were topics of anxious debate among faculty and students. Within a few years of inception at any given college, the May Day festival settled into an event with five standardized components, discussed in detail in the next chapter.

12. "The Play's the Thing"— College May Day Pageant Themes

The Pageant of "Every Girl"
Spring has come to I.S.C's [Iowa State College's] campus attended by her court maidens of Love, Memorie [sic] and Sleep. To Every Girl she brings dreams; to Alma Mater, the realization that a ruler of the season—a May Queen—must be found. In choosing a girl worthy of wearing the crown, Alma Mater finds herself in doubt, and in her dilemma she seeks the aid of the Spirit of Memorie, who will recall the past, and the Spirit of Love, whose presence will reveal the girl worthy of Queenship.

Memorie urges Father Time to allow her to bring back to Every Girl Doll Days, High School Days, and College Days....

The dream is ended. Love, with the Spirits of Joy, Friendliness, Fair Play, Culture, Perseverance, Scholarship, Judgment, and Leadership, qualities which determine a Queen, greet the May Queen as she steps from among her classmates.
— From the 1926 May Fête Program,
Iowa State College (now Iowa State University)[1]

College May Day pageants were spectacles that entertained thousands every spring. While the folk dances performed as part of the college May Day celebration reflected the hygienic philosophies of Dr. Gulick, Elizabeth Burchenal and the Playground Association of America, the elaborate pageants that formed the entertainment of the Queen expressed the artistic and symbolic ideals of the American Pageant Association. Indeed, many of the earliest pageants were educational events: spectators could expect to be instructed and uplifted as well as entertained.

Festival organizers were not troubled by concepts of logic and consistency, leading to some strange juxtapositions of themes and dances. The Elmira College May Day program of 1928 noted that "The May Dances varied in the different sections of England. Since there were no set rules for the festivities, they changed according to the place and the people who took part. But, however they changed, the festivities were always joyous and sportive." Accordingly, that year at Elmira a Robin Hood pageant, complete with a tilting contest, a ribbon dance, a clown dance, a morris dance and the maypole dance, was followed by a series of aesthetic dances depicting the Greek myth of Echo and Narcissus.

Art songs or madrigals could also be interspersed throughout the festival. It is difficult to generalize how music was provided for in these fêtes: sometimes photographs show a pianist or violinists, or musicians are credited in the printed program. Gramophone recordings for the folk dances and drills are certainly a strong possibility: during his trips to the United States in 1915 and 1916, Cecil Sharp oversaw recordings of English country and morris dances by

The following photographs portray the sequence of a typical college May Day festival: the printed program, the general procession, the procession of the Queen and Robin Hood, the crowning of the Queen, the folk dances, the maypole dance and the pageant given in her honor. Top: *Here is the charming program cover for the elaborate Bryn Mawr College 1936 May Day pageant. Titania and Bottom, Robin Hood, a dancing bear, maypole dancers, hobby horses, tumblers, St. George slaying the dragon and Sir Walter Raleigh make an appearance. (Bryn Mawr College Library.)* Bottom: *Oxen dragging in the maypole followed by Shepherdesses with sheep at Bryn Maw College's May Day festival of 1910. Note the long procession still trailing off at the far right of the shot. (Bryn Mawr College Library.)*

12. "The Play's the Thing" 109

Top: *It's a Mad, Mad, Merry May Day as the Queen is crowned at the Meredith College spring Court, 1968. (Archives, Meredith College.)* Bottom: *Students dancing the English country dance "Sellenger's Round" in several concentric circles at the 1977 Earlham College May Day. (Friends Collection, Earlham College, Richmond, Indiana.)*

The author's May Queen and housemate, Elizabeth Lawrence, and her Robin Hood, John Bean, marching in procession at the 1977 Earlham College May Day. (Friends Collection, Earlham College, Richmond, Indiana.)

both the Victor Gramophone Company and the Columbia Gramophone Company.[2] By 1924, more than 100 dance tunes had been recorded by the Victor Military Band, all under Elizabeth Burchenal's direction, plus thirty English morris, longsword, and country dances recorded under the direction of Sharp. "These records are played by full military band, and give all the pauses, accents and peculiarities of the dances as Miss Burchenal and Mr. Sharp use them," noted a pamphlet issued by the Victor Gramophone Company.[3] These recordings certainly contributed to the popularity of folk dances in the school and college curriculum.

Current events rarely touched the festival. Some pageants, especially those held during wartime, expressed ideals of a melting-pot American spirit, but none addressed the sometimes violent protests of workers and socialists that also occurred on May First. I have discovered only one pageant that made even mild reference to the efforts of suffragists to obtain the vote. Instead, most pageants incorporated some type of love story or romance: whether Greek, fairy tale, or invented. The descriptions of programs held at the 80 respondent colleges show that May Day was a conservative holiday that reinforced the dominant image of Girlhood, not one that celebrated female emancipation or workers' rights.

The college May Day pageant represents an example of a mutable tradition: the event itself occurred every year or every four years, but the components of the event could vary widely from year to year. The pageant and the festival could be combined with alumnae homecoming events, with father-daughter or mother-daughter teas, or with sports exhibitions by members of the college's women's athletic association.

While there are some variations among colleges and even over time within the same institution, the typical May Day fête had five main components. The first component was the procession of the costumed participants. In keeping both with the ideals of the American Pageant Association and the spirit of the spring season, May Day festivals usually took place outside and were often located in a particularly beautiful spot on campus: a grassy dell, a hill-

12. "The Play's the Thing" 111

Top: *Dancing around the maypole in the 1950s. This photograph captures the speed and the enthusiasm of the girls as they dance the grand chain that weaves the ribbons down the pole. The Queen and her Court sit in state in the shade of a splendid tree near the stream. (Photograph courtesy C. Elizabeth Boyd '33 Archives, Hankey Center, Wilson College.)* Bottom: *Spear carriers salute the Queen in this Greek-inspired May Day pageant at Judson College in the 1920s. Girl dancers with garlands of flowers over their shoulders echo the "Daisy Chain" popular at commencements. Note the positioning of the actors in front of a building with vaguely Grecian architectural features — again emphasizing the importance the college's landscape and buildings played in the drama. (Archives, Judson College.)*

May Day Procession, University of Colorado at Boulder, 1914. While this looks like a stereo shot, it is not. The Seniors wear academic caps and gowns, the juniors swing flower-filled baskets, and the sophomores and freshmen are distinguished by their flowers. (Collection of the author.)

side, and, in one case, on an island located in the center of a small lake. In fact, abiding with the principles of the American Pageant Association, the physical campus itself became a participant in the festival. Photographs show Grecian dancers posed in front of buildings with Grecian features, or dainty shepherdesses posed in front of Tudor- or Gothic-style buildings. Thus, for the spectators, a charming part of the event was the long, winding procession of the girls (and, more rarely, the men) in their pretty dresses or unusual costumes. The procession was often performed to music or singing, and, if held at dusk, Japanese lanterns added to the picture.

Thus, for example, at the University of Colorado at Boulder in May 1914 the procession was lengthy and elaborate (as shown in the photograph above). As a band played, all the girls in the University processed, walking four abreast, each class headed by its own marshal, the seniors wearing their academic caps and gowns, the juniors swinging flower-filled baskets, the sophomores all in white save for their rose and lilac hoops and hairbows, and the freshmen crowned with smilax and white flowers.

> At a signal from the marshals the line divided, swung to opposite sides, and the sophomores hoops made an arch through which the freshmen passed. And then, in a second, the music ceased, and the whole moving, colorful column stood frozen while the camera-man clicked his shutter. The picture would have been a charming one if it could have caught the flash and glint of sunlit color and mingling costumes.[4]

Other photographs taken this day show aesthetic dances of sunbeams and snowflakes.

The second main component of the festival was the crowning of the Queen or, even more dramatically, the her selection from among the crowd, as discussed in Chapter 15. On occasion the Queen, Robin Hood, or the president of the college would give a brief speech. After the crowning came the presentation of the folk or aesthetic dances, which concluded with the winding of the maypole, the fourth key component of the festival, and the icon of the holiday.

The fifth component of the May Day festival was the play or pageant produced for the Queen's entertainment. Favorite plays included *The Weavers' Play* (the comic tale of Pyramus and Thisbe) from Shakespeare's *A Midsummer Night's Dream*, selections from *As You Like It*, and Alfred Noyes' popular Robin Hood poem and play of 1913, *Sherwood*. At Bryn Mawr and Earlham Colleges, spectators could visit several venues at which different medieval plays were performed in turn, such as *The Deluge, The Old Wives' Tale* (1595), *Gammer Gurtons Nedel* (1575), or *The Play of Saint George and the Dragon* (a mummer's play).

But most pageant producers took the opportunity to write original pageants. May Day pageants of the 1920s and the early 1930s — the heyday of the pageant — frequently retold Greek myths, Japanese or Oriental romances, or the stories of Mother Goose, *Alice in Wonderland* and *Peter Pan*. Some colleges celebrated the various centennials of the births or deaths of Shakespeare, Goethe, François Villon or Milton with pageants in their honor. Later, in the 1940s and 1950s, modern themes such as the *Wizard of Oz*, or the tales of Johnny Appleseed or Bobo [sic] Baggins alternated with the standard Robin Hood or Elizabethan Merrie May Day themes. Colleges might also celebrate their important anniversaries with an historical pageant. The lists of pageant titles for Wilson, Agnes Scott and Muskingum Colleges in Part II are representative of the kinds of pageants offered.

These May Day pageants show that their crafters and directors were deeply influenced by the ideals and techniques of the American Pageant Association: symbolism, the use of masses of color in costumes, and the effect of dance, especially aesthetic or interpretive dance. One such example is the 1920 program, *The Spirit of Grinnell College*, a pageant that included dances set to music by Gounod, Elgar, Saint Saens, Grieg, and Beethoven as well as to the Grinnell College anthem. The prologue opens with the Spirit of the Prairie, who summons the gentle breezes, butterflies and flowers (various dancers) to make the prairie beautiful for man. Indian women perform their daily tasks and only reluctantly leave when they see a prairie schooner approaching, "indicating that the white man is about to begin his life upon the free and open Prairie."

The first episode then showed the dedication of the altar.

> The Spirit of Education, who later becomes the Spirit of Grinnell, enters ... she is inspired to bring to this place The Iowa Band, who founded Iowa College. The Priestesses — Religion, Music, Poetry, History, Science and Philosophy — enter with lighted torches, and the Iowa Band follow, bringing the Altar of Truth.

The Spirit of Education oversees the erection of the altar and instructs the band to take the light of truth out into the world, which they do, accompanied by the Blindfolded Youth, "who is eagerly groping for light for his lamp." The Spirit of Grinnell removes his blindfold and lights the lamp, a symbolic action followed by a religious ceremonial dance set to music of Saint Saens.

Episode three addresses Grinnell's part in the Great War, depicting the spirits of War, accompanied by Lust, Greed and Anarchy, "who bring a heavy chain. They threaten to put out the Altar fire, but are prevented from doing this by the Spirit of Grinnell and her helpers." The Spirit of Grinnell realizes that she cannot serve humanity by keeping her sons at home, and bids them "go forth to fight." After a dance of the Peace Maidens, Humanity and Poverty are released from the chains.

The final episode depicts the hope for the future of Grinnell, and involves the expression of peace and plenty as shown by the dances of the Grain and Fruit Maidens, the Priestesses, and the Spirit of Grinnell, all followed by the singing of the college anthem.[5]

Not all pageants were quite so high-minded. Perhaps because the College of Wooster was coeducational, many of their "Color Day" May Day programs tended towards the humorous. In their presentation of the program, "Historic Wooster," given in 1916, they depicted the accomplishments of the Medical Department from 1883 to 1890 thus:

> The germs of tuberculosis (brown), typhoid fever (blue), measles (small red dots), and small pox (large red dots), attack three victims. Two succumb but are resuscitated by the doctors after much effort.[6]

After other funny skits and "stunts" came the more serious depiction of the "Future of Wooster," which included a visit of Alma Mater, the entrance of the Youth of the Future, and the approach of the Nine Muses and other notables. This pageant was followed by a rose wreath drill, the maypole dance, a grand parade and the dedication of several new buildings.

Romance, the progress of science, fairy tales, myths, and the college's own history were favored pageant topics. The values expressed in the pageants are traditional: the search for love, with the Queen representing the best and fairest of maidenhood; a pageant of the college spirit; or a pageant demonstrating patriotic values of love of country or of truth, or, especially in the 1916–1920 period, with the May Queen personifying Liberty or Columbia welcoming the immigrants to the new land.

Of the hundreds of pageant titles and themes noted in Part II, only a handful addressed modern political issues. One such was the 1937 sophomore May Day masque titled *Now and—When?* held at Pembroke College, the women's college of Brown University. After the coronation, the maypole and folk dances, and the tumbling exercises, the sophomores entered the field and danced "with staccato and angular movements as they presented five phases of present-day civilization: political, domestic, recreational, economic and religious." Their pageant depicted the inhabitants of the world who were sick of conflict and corruption and disheartened by their inability to make the world a better place in which to live. A girl playing a dictator wore gloves with red ribbons attached to each finger and to girls playing ten subordinates. "By clever maneuvers she brought the whole group under her power."

While the masque explored issues of control, political or domestic, the newspaper coverage of the event seems more comfortable describing costumes rather than actions.

> White kerchiefs, worn by the girls in the domestic dilemma, served as bridal veils as they mated, aprons as they washed and ironed, and capes as they went their way to Reno [to obtain a divorce]. A sit-down strike was the feature of the economic strife between capital and labor. The capitalists wore top hats of cardboard and the laborers, in overalls and kerchiefs, sat on the grass until their demands were met.

The conclusion of this masque was "The Vision," in which all took part. This scene represented "the unclassifiable philosophers in whose minds the barriers between the preceding phases have never existed. Upon them will fall the singular honor of uniting the world in the universal petition to the Divinity to create a utopia out of chaos." The pageant concluded with a more typical pageant finale in which a yellow rose was unveiled as the choice of the sophomore class flower and presented to the dean. Music for this, the first "modern" masque ever presented at Brown, was adapted from Gershwin, Ornstein, Moussorgsky and Ravel.[7]

The 1945 May Day pageant of Bucknell University is another of the scant handful of examples of political commentary. Previous pageants had included the much more typical Milton's *Comus* (1919), Maeterlinck's *The Blue Bird* (1932), *A Festival of the Nations* (1935), and a *Physical Education Review from Ancient Times to the Present* (1939). There was no celebration from 1942 to 1944. May Day resumed in 1945 with a pageant titled *Under Three Flags*, with a theme that expressed ideas given by the university's president in his 1941 baccalaureate address: the American flag as a symbol "of the last remaining bulwark against nihilism, anarchy and tyranny," the Christian flag as a symbol of human brotherhood and "high and noble standards of personal conduct," and the Bucknell flag, "a symbol of our loyalty to wisdom, to truth, to beauty." After hymns, the pledge of allegiance, brief descent into a lighter mood with a cowgirl dance routine and a football practice dance routine, the maypole was wound: "a symbol of beauty, the result of absolute co-operation."[8] After this uplifting event,

Bucknell University's May Day pageants returned to more standard topics such as *An English Country Faire* (1947), *Alice in Wonderland* (1955), and *A Salute to Broadway* (1961).

While the May Day pageants may well have been empowering for the young women who wrote them or acted in them, they were not statements of modern feminist values. There is only one pageant out of the hundreds mentioned in Part II that even mildly addresses the suffrage movement: *My Wife Is a Suffragette!*— the 1911 performance by the Fairies of Freya, the secret society that produced the May fêtes for the May Queen of Hollins College. This play, however, is less a feminist polemic than a knock-about vaudeville act. It centers on the antics of Mr. Parry Sighte (parasite) of New York, who is wearing uncomfortable slippers because someone has given his regular shoes away to "some loidy," and who keeps groaning that his wife, Yura Sighte, is at the polls. After fourteen pages of silly jokes, the characters bring various pairs of shoes and sandals to Mr. Parry Sighte, who rejects them all. In marches Mrs. Yura Sighte carrying a banner with "Votes for Women" on it. She announces that:

> I don't know a thing about your shoes. I should think any man ought to be able to look after his own shoes, but they ain't; and if they ain't, they certainly ain't able to look after the government. So I'm for votes for women. I want the women to run the country instead of the men.

(One presumes that at this point the girl audience would burst into loud applause.) Mrs. Yura Sighte then sticks out her foot, shod with Parry Sighte's boot, and they discover that some scamp has exchanged their shoes. As in the Cinderella story, they recognize each other by their footwear and Mrs. Yura Sighte drags her husband off the stage by his neck while the cast sings the song "His Wife Is a Suffragette":

> Oh, his wife is a suffragette,
> And he's unhappy here, you bet,
> For now you see again they've met,
> And his wife is a suffragette!
> Now though you see, my gentle friends,
> Your sympathy condoles,
> He hopes that she's in Mexico,
> But she's got him at the Polls.

But after this somewhat confusing peep into suffragist politics, the audience was immediately brought back to more standard college life: this rousing ditty was immediately followed by a "Squelch Song," which gave advice to a Fairy of Freya on how to squelch any girl who tried to find out if she were indeed a member of the secret society, after which all participants performed the maypole dance.[9] A presumably amusing spectacle, though filled with non sequiturs and now-incomprehensible inside jokes, this topic of votes for women was not repeated at Hollins College, nor have I discovered it or any other even mildly feminist topic portrayed at any other college.

A much more typical statement about womanhood appears in the 1915 pageant given by the girls of what was then Iowa State College (now Iowa State University): a *Pageant of American Women*. The Queen for that year is shown seated in front of a large arch of flowers (probably red, white and blue), in a long gown with broad red and white stripes and a wide sash of white stars on a blue background over her shoulder.

This pageant was divided into seven acts, each with several scenes. The first act showed Hiawatha's wooing of Minnehaha and the arrival of white men. The second scene showed the

Puritans, with John Alden's wooing of Priscilla. After other historical scenes of a similar romantic nature came that of "Foreign Immigration," described thus in the program:

> Opportunity leads the immigrants to Miss America, who is attended by Freedom, Refinement, Learning, Industry, Health and Happiness. Led by Opportunity, the races — English, Irish, German, Swedish, Polish, Italian, Japanese and Chinese — are blended into one by the Virginia Reel, our own real American folk dance.

In the final scene, "America welcomes the women of today."[10] No further description of this action is provided, and here it is useful to observe that, while some of the May Day pageant programs preserved in college archives include the full text of the pageant, most do not. Photographs and student newspaper articles sometimes fill in the gaps and describe the symbolic actions or dances in greater detail, but, much, alas, is left to the imagination.

Another typical example of the expression of womanhood is seen in the pageant written by the future distinguished anthropologist Margaret Mead, given on May Day 1920 at the Methodist-founded DePauw University. The Women's Athletic Association gave a May Fête described as a "Co-ed Gala" (meaning that it was given by the women "coeds," not that the event included men). The gala began with numerous track and field demonstrations and competitions and concluded with two pageants, the first of which, "The Choice of American Girlhood," was written by Mead, class of 1923. With the epigraph, "We kneel to thee, Spirit of Girlhood; and offer to thee Rich gifts from Time's storehouse; choose; thine they shall be," the pageant depicted the Four Hours of the Afternoon (Play, Mirth, Dress, and Beauty), the Four Hours of Night (Luxury, Ambition, Wealth, with the Dollar Bill Jesters, and Power), and the Four Hours of Morning (Art, Music, Intellect, and Service (described as "The Cross attended by an Old English procession"). The pageant's epilogue declaims, "The Spirit of American Girlhood, guided by the Spirit of DePauw, chooses the gift of the twelfth hour — Service Beneath the Cross." This inspirational pageant was followed by a professionally written play, *The Yellow Jacket*, a Chinese tale.[11]

Many May Day festivals were disrupted in 1917 and 1918, when young men were finally called up. The girls turned their attention to Red Cross activities, knitting and making bandages. For example, in 1917 the usual events at Iowa State University were superseded by a "Red Cross Day." In a hollow square formed by the college's male cadets, the Queen was crowned and girls performed various aesthetic dances. Subsequently, "the spectators wandered from booth to booth inspecting the display of surgical dressings and knitting, and buying Red Cross memberships."[12] One year later, in 1918, the physical education instructor and a student wrote a patriotic pageant, *The Gift*, in which Alma Mater, with her followers, the black-gowned "Senioritas" (the college term) hold court on the steps of Agricultural Hall. Queen Indifference leads displays of frivolity and nearly wins over the College Maiden, until the healthful, wholesome pleasures of tennis, golf, and other sports, accompanied by the virtues of Thrift and Service, claim her heart, and she chooses "to be of aid and service to her country during the summer."[13]

As with other pageants inspired by the precepts of the American Pageant Association, the May Day pageant was often unabashedly didactic: patriotism, duty, democracy and the value of work were common themes, particularly during wartime. Thus the 1945 program at Berea College included a procession of villagers, junior- and senior-friendship chains, a dance around the maypole, a minuet, and a pageant titled "A Democracy Calls for Intelligence at Work," with the symbols of the precision of building, the pounding of hammers, the turning of wheels, the rhythm of movement and the building of machines. The demonstration of

"The World Runs on Wheels" was illustrated by the English country dance "Sellenger's Round" (a dance can be performed with many concentric slipping circles, each moving a different direction). This was followed by a military drill in honor of the army and a sailors' hornpipe in honor of the navy, as well as other folk dances. The program included an unidentified quotation: "Important as it is to organize and direct the industry of the world, it is more important to organize and direct the leisure of the world."[14]

While the college May Day festivals never addressed labor or socialist issues, they did, especially in wartime, make political statements about the melting-pot nature of Americanness and patriotism, even as they retained the central images of the crowning of the Queen and the maypole dance. This was evidenced by a change in theme for many pageants during both world wars. For example at Mount Holyoke College in 1918 the maypoles were decked with red, white and blue streamers and the May Queen entered the field mounted on a white horse, personifying Liberty "in a costume of red and white, with a blue bodice adorned with silver stars" and attended by American, English and French officers (presumably girls dressed as soldiers). The usual folk songs were abandoned in favor of the "Marseillaise," "Rule Britannia" and "The Star Spangled Banner," and the student audience busied itself with sewing and knitting for the Red Cross.[15] In 1946, during World War II, the Dramatic Club of the same college performed the pageant "A Fantasy of Nations" in which a minstrel strives to find the Spirit of Beauty and Harmony. He travels to many Allied lands and their people perform various folk dances for him. But it is not until the minstrel returns to the United States that the May Queen is revealed as the Spirit of Beauty, whereupon "all the nations join in the rejoicing."[16]

Mount Holyoke College was not alone in portraying a theme of liberty and brotherhood. The versatility and the imaginative scope of the May Day performance can be demonstrated by a program of May 1920, titled *The Spirit of Americanization*, the second pageant offered by the women of New Hampshire College under the direction of Miss Bartlett, director of women's physical education. When reading the following summary, it is important to remember that in this period Americans were struggling with the problem of how to assimilate the enormous numbers of immigrants arriving daily from the old world. This unusual program becomes another example of the moral and political message that the simple springtide festival could convey.

The complicated prelude to this program begins with Liberty falling asleep and dreaming that she is the guardian of the melting pot, helpfully defined as "America" in the program, indicating that this term was still relatively novel. There is a "low rumbling" in the melting pot and Trouble steps out, followed by her supporters. Liberty calls for the army and navy, who compel Trouble to retreat. The army and the navy present a "March of Victory," but, as the program details, "Liberty's troubles are not yet over":

> From the Melting Pot come discordant sounds. Again the cover is lifted and out come Love, Christianity, Health, Education, Culture, Science, Poetry, Art, Genius, Pleasure, Rest, Recreation, Music, Industry and Success. They are pursued by High Cost of Living leading a motley crew made up of Poverty, Dishonesty, Ignorance, Political Jealousy, Immorality, Laziness, Gluttony, Crime and Disease.
>
> Suddenly Love, Christianity, Health and Education with one impulse turn and squarely face H.C.L. [sic].... Slowly but relentlessly the four advance — the others watching in the distance. Step by step H.C.L. retreats, her supporters growling and showing reluctance to give in. Finally they are pushed back to the Melting Pot; but the others who have taken courage at the success of their leaders rush to its edge and refuse to let them in, so they are driven away as outcasts.

After this complicated prelude, the actual program begins "one year later." It is spring and Liberty holds a festival to welcome the new America, crowning Love as the Queen of the Festival. After the coronation, the Lord of the May (played by a woman) and a Court Lady dance the Minuet. This is followed by fifteen folk dances, such as the English "Rufty Tufty," the Danish "Seven Jumps" and the Hungarian "Czardas." The festivities concluded with the grand finale of the maypole dance, performed by Liberty, Love/May Queen and all of the virtues and vices named above, twenty-six women in all. A total of 186 young women participated in this spectacle.[17]

After the initial burst of May Day enthusiasm in the first few decades of the last century, some colleges mounted the elaborate pageants only once every four years in order to give, theoretically at least, every graduate a chance to participate. One of the most elaborate and long-lived festivals was that of my own alma mater, Earlham College. The entire faculty, staff and student body participated in this event, which received favorable press coverage for years. The premise of this long-lived pageant was that the college was transformed into an English village celebrating its May Day with the crowning of a May Queen.* Queen Elizabeth I, a role traditionally played by the wife of the president of the college, and her court made a surprise visit to view the rustic festivities. As per traditional, the Queen appeared in a gilded sedan chair, carried, in my year at least, by the perspiring male faculty of the history department, all dressed warmly as Beefeaters.

In 1977, the year in which I participated and taught much of the dancing to the students as well as being a member of the "Tudor Tooters," a recorder ensemble, the list of participants covers ten pages of the program, in small type. Even a partial listing of the characters involved in the grand procession is breathtaking: there were close to 1,600 costumed participants. The court of Queen Elizabeth was comprised of 157 faculty members and wives including, in part: halberdiers, pages, an alchemist, a scribe, court falconers with falcons, ladies of quality, townswomen in festive attire, aldermen, puppeteers, and distinguished foreign visitors such as the Queen of the Nile (the sole female African American faculty member, as I recall). The court of the May Queen, including Robin Hood and his merry men, trainbearers, and attendants, and totaling twenty-one persons, marched next. Then came 125 musicians including two groups of madrigal singers as well as divers recorder players, village waits, and Oriana's Merry Minstrels. These were followed by 149 dancers: among them country dancers, shepherdesses (without sheep), chimney sweeps, country lasses, gypsies, and two teams of morris dancers (men's and mixed). Next came a large crowd of approximately 1,020 revelers. These included, in part, stilt-walkers, whifflers, pages on horseback, more gypsies, gypsies with children, tumblers, villagers (321 of these alone), shepherdesses with real sheep, swineherds, fishmongers, butchers, and water carriers. Finally came the Children's Revels with their own Little May Queen and Robin Hood, jesters, maypole dancers and so on: a total of 122 children.

After this lengthy procession and the obeisance to Good Queen Bess, Robin Hood crowned the May Queen, and various gypsies, shepherdesses, country lasses, and children performed the maypole dance around six maypoles. This was followed by the spectacle of all the participants dancing the English country dances "Gathering Peascods" and "Sellenger's Round" in three huge concentric circles around the perimeter of the maypoles. An equestrian quadrille and various antics and short plays, including *The Deluge* presented by members of the Earlham College School of Religion, were performed at intervals during the remainder of the afternoon.

One of my housemates in 1977 — we stuffed the ballot boxes.

It is obvious from these descriptions that May Day pageants were incredibly hard work, involving huge numbers of undergraduates, faculty and staff, and absorbing much of the students' free time during the presentation year. Their very ambitiousness led to their downfall, even if the crowning of the May Queen continued for some years later.

As we will see in Chapter 18, many colleges ceased to hold the elaborate May Day pageants in the 1930s and 1940s. With each annual success, the pressure to produce a bigger and better pageant grew more daunting. In addition, during this period, the Physical Education curriculum and philosophy turned away from its emphasis on folk and aesthetic dance and towards competitive and team sports for girls, a change that contributed to a decline in interest in a dance-based spring performance.

Information on the discontinuance of the pageant is harder to obtain than that of the crowning of the Queen and of celebrating May Day, for the coronation and some simplified festivities often continued for years after the pageant vanished. From the available information, it would appear that many pageants ceased in the Depression years, while of those remaining, another large group ceased in the 1960s. While Chapter 18 describes the May Day festivals still held at some colleges today, none of these respondents produce a large-scale pageant or drama on the lines of their predecessors.

13. Corydon in Arcadia — Men and May Day

> The undergraduate college man [at the University of California at Berkeley] scorns the [girls' pageant] *Partheneia* and would attend only under compulsion, yet he manifests enough interest to climb in the oaks, and sit there during one long afternoon of the final dress rehearsal. The idealism and the allegory seem to frighten man away, his idea of a worthwhile presentation being a well-matched football game.
> — Jean Q. Watson and Frances L. Brown, "The Partheneia of the University of California," *Overland Monthly*, May 1916[1]

Men and May Day — like oil and water, the two elements are difficult to mingle. By 1900 the festival's image in the U.S. had become so bound to a celebration of girlhood that there were relatively limited roles for men to play. And, just as the College Girl was not a modern teenager in period attire, so the College Man of 1900 was a different creature from the young man of today: perhaps more brash, certainly less well-supervised, and, in many cases, overtly scornful of the coeds and their picturesque activities.

The comments of men toward May Day are not well-recorded. In many cases young men had a limited involvement in either the college or the urban May Day. Their roles ranged from being forbidden to view the girls' festivities, to being allowed to be passive (yet often appreciative) spectators; to some participation, either relatively limited as in being Escort to the Queen or, more rarely, actively involved in plays, skits and dancing; to — when older and richer — funding a college or urban parade or festival; or to — when young and testosterone-driven — engaging in May Day spoofs, pranks or scraps.

A handful of the earliest May Day festivals were off-limits to the college men. In the 1880s and the 1890s at both women's and coeducational institutions, men — even fathers, brothers or male faculty — were not permitted to view any of the maidens' play-acting or festivities. This restriction was not limited to May Day. In her analysis of 1893, *The American Girl at College*, Lida Rose McCabe observed that at Vassar, which had a very active student dramatics club, not only were men forbidden to watch the plays, masculine costumes were outlawed: "that is, legitimate trousers are eschewed; coats and vests are permissible, but the divided skirt marks the limit of realism!"[2] Photographs of the Vassar actresses show those girls playing male roles, sporting the slicked-back hair of the masher of the 1890s complete with false mustaches and a man's vest and coat worn over a long black skirt.

Thus at Earlham College's first May Day in 1875, the fourteen-year-old Queen recalled, "The boys were not allowed in, but, as they say, it 'leaked through the lines' and at supper that night, many questions were asked. The next day I received a beautiful basket of oranges, bananas, apples and pears from [two young men] with their compliments — which was greatly appreciated and gave me joy supreme." By 1886, the festival had grown larger and the men were permitted to view the festivities. Men participated at Earlham — a very community-oriented college — for the first time in either 1902 or 1906.[3] Thereafter Robin Hood and his Merry Men appeared without fail, and male students participated in the dancing, the plays and other aspects of Earlham's Elizabethan pageant, held every four years until 1993.

Men participated in a positive fashion in a handful of other colleges' May Day festivals. For instance, a committee of men (ages unknown) dyed and stenciled the 700 historical costumes for the 1921 pageant given by the women of the University of Colorado. And men participated in the long-running festivals at Kent State University and the College of Wooster, both located in Ohio. But in these latter two cases, while the festivals retained their May Day Queen as well as folk dances and the maypole dance, they bore different names: for many years the spring festival was called "Campus Day" at Kent State, and at the College of Wooster the festival originated as "Color Day" in 1905. In both cases men participated by giving military marching drills, or being involved in plays and skits or song-competitions, and in both cases, the annual festival continued until the early 1970s. Perhaps this titular disassociation from the girlish May Day enabled men at these large institutions to participate without fear of loss of status.

At some colleges, especially Southern women's colleges, the men's role in May Day was to appear as woman's protector and admirer, a sort of background for the girls to shine against. At many of these May Day festivals, military cadets from nearby men's colleges performed marching drills before the Queen. At some of the colleges, while a girl took the role of "Prince" or "King" (see Chapter 15) to crown the Queen, it was critical for all participants — especially the Queen — to have a male escort at the evening cotillion. In the 1940s and 1950s this man was usually the Queen's fiancé, as many of these young women married immediately after graduation, often wearing their May Queen dresses as wedding gowns.

An important role for older men and wealthier men was to act as patron or benefactor of the festival. For example, the purpose of the first May Day Fête at Bryn Mawr was to raise funds for a students' building. Evangeline Walker Andrews, the young alumna chairman of the building committee and the individual who had the initial inspiration, wrote to John D. Rockefeller, who had previously given generously to Vassar College, asking for a donation. The president of Bryn Mawr, M. Carey Thomas, then spent a day with Rockefeller's agent and argued so persuasively that the latter gave a conditional gift of $250,000 for a resident hall and power plant if Thomas could raise matching funds for a library in six months — a formidable goal that she achieved.[4]

Politicians, men's clubs or businesses participated in the urban May Day in the sense of sponsoring floats, window-displays, or donations of food or money in order to garner votes or good will. And, while it was typically the college-educated women of the settlement houses or the women's civic clubs who organized the pageants, games and refreshments for the children and the community, men such as Luther Halsey Gulick, Theodore Roosevelt, Herbert Hoover, and others were key leaders of the Playground Association or the Child Health Association, both of which organizations firmly championed the celebration of May Day.

A handful of male May Day Kings appear in the accounts of the 80 respondent institutions, though these tended to be burlesque figures, rather than consorts. The May King was not, however, a version of a Yuletide Lord of Misrule, found in England under various names from the mid–1450s onwards. In the hierarchical structure of fifteenth-century England, the Lord of Misrule was usually chosen from the younger and/or lower strata of society — a boy or a servant — to enjoy a day of parodying the behaviors of his superiors and commanding them to play pranks and games. By contrast, the typical college May King enjoyed no such power, but was more often abused; his existence was a way to mock the election of the Queen.

Thus, in 1922, when Albright College first celebrated May Day, the students elected a King as well as a Queen. Over the years, the Queen was nominated by the students based on her popularity and beauty. As for the King, however, the honor was apparently a punishment. As an article in the college alumni magazine noted in 2001:

> Like the queen, the king was also nominated by his classmates, but for a different reason. Usually the person selected had made himself unpopular, or rather, popular in a peculiar way, such as being known as the campus jokester. Until the evening of the affair, the victim was kept unaware of his fate; then at the proper time he was captured, placed on a crude throne and paraded through the town. During his trip through town, the king was showered with both abuse and garbage. He was then brought back to Sylvan Lake, at that time a shallow pond immediately behind Selwyn Hall, and thrown in. Then all the participants jumped in and a royal water battle ensued, while the ladies cheered the men on from the windows of their residence hallitory [sic]. Albright's neighbors did not always appreciate the "Crowning of the May King," because their garbage buckets often suffered considerable damage. They learned to keep their garbage receptacles off the streets on May Day.[5]

There are, however, a few examples of a benign May King: one is found today at Grove City College, Grove City, Pennsylvania. The custom of electing a Spring King (the festival is not always held in May, so it is called Spring Court) started in the mid–1970s as a joke, but in 2002 the chair of Parents' Weekend decided to formalize the role. Typically six senior men are nominated, and their photographs are mounted on collection jars for the charity of their choice. The winner of the most donations, who will be named Spring King, also presents the contents of the other men's jars to his charity. Dressed in their formal gowns, the women of the Spring Court appear at the Friday night band concert that opens the weekend, and when the winner's name is announced, the Queen drapes a sash with the words "Spring King" over his shoulders. It is notable, however, that the King does not (as yet) appear in the formal, posed pictures of the Grove City Queen and her Court.

Occasionally men engaged in fairly benign May Day parodies: for example, at Ursinus College sometime prior to 1945, the men on campus started a "slightly irreverent" parody a week or so after each year's production. In May of 1946, the women's pageant was an adaptation of *A Midsummer Night's Dream*, titled *Spring Fantasy*. A week later the men crowned "the lovely" George McNeal as Queen of the May. "In gowns à Schiaparelli with a touch of Dali surrealism the 'stronger' sex gave their all in behalf of the cause," reported the yearbook writer. "Shrouded in secrecy until the very end, 'Queenie' made her appearance and *Spring Fandancy* ended to the thunder of applause and laughter of the appreciative audience. Never in the college's history had more pulchritude been on parade in one evening."[6]

However, despite the benign involvement of the men in some college and urban May Day festivals, a perhaps more predictable involvement of the young men was to mock the girls' celebration by participating in a disruptive way. This seems to have been particularly true at institutions that had been founded for men only, and to which the women had been later, and reluctantly, admitted.

Helen Lefkowitz argues that in the nineteenth and early twentieth centuries the purpose of a college education was to knock the corners off a boy, and to turn him into a man fit to compete in the rough-and-tumble world of business. Part of this education lay in competitive sports: Lefokwitz notes that men's college athletics came into being in the 1870s, when students started their teams and set rules. Interclass rivalries gave way to intercollegiate competitions, calling forth intense fighting spirit and loyalty to the college among students.[7] If the College Girls were skipping around in Grecian draperies depicting the birth of spring, the College Men were flocking to intramural sports, where they howled their college "yells," such as this of DePauw University, first heard on November 1, 1890: "Zip Rah Hoo! D.P.U. Rip Saw! Boom Baw! DePauw! Ah-h-h- there!!!"[8]

Unlike college girls, whose lives were highly regulated and controlled, college "men," even those as young as fourteen or fifteen, were left to their own devices when out of the classroom: each student found his own boarding house, clubs, and activities. Due perhaps to this lack of adult supervision, college men were often rowdy and wild and there are many references in both fact and fiction to their destructive habits in both the college and the town. As one female commentator primly noted in a 1901 *Cosmopolitan* article that defended the woman's college, "There is no case on record where students from a girls' college have spent the night in the town lockup, as the result of reckless misbehavior. They have never been known playfully to smash mirrors in restaurants, make bonfires of farmhouse gates, steal the signs from the village shops or swap the tombstones in the near-by churchyards."[9]

Each alternating pair of classes were deemed "brothers": the freshmen and the juniors were thus allied against the sophomores and the seniors. Each man was required to develop an intense loyalty first to his class and then to his college, placing both of these above any personal claims or considerations. Thus, in Joy Lichtenstein's 1901 novel of life at the University of California at Berkeley, *For the Blue-and-Gold; A Tale of Life at the University of California*, when the freshman hope for the football team tries to quit as he is falling behind in his school and boardinghouse work, the entire college is outraged. His fellow students consider that James "showed lack of proper college spirit in not promptly responding, no matter how great the sacrifice of his personal affairs this would entail. And, if the college man recognizes an unpardonable crime, it is this 'lack of college spirit.'" A friend scolds him, saying, "There is no sacrifice that you shouldn't make in order to stay with the game.... The college'll help you if you need it, but it won't excuse you if you throw it down.'" Chastened, James stays on the team and vows to study harder.[10]

This rough-and-tumble environment with its focus on male physicality and an English public school, military or chivalric mentality engendered numerous college "scraps," as they were popularly termed. Lichtenstein opened his 1901 novel with a vivid description of the freshman scrap against the sophomores: a bare-knuckle fistfight that continued until all the members of the losing class were hog-tied and piled upon each other like logs of wood. This annual event occurred apparently without comment or reprimand from the administration. The only possible reason for sanctifying this violent behavior is that offered by a fictional student who notes that the freshmen are actually improved by the scrap: "It makes them acquainted, just as soldiers, fighting side by side, get acquainted in standing up at the outset against a common enemy, the separate atoms of stranger freshmen form into something like a united whole. It gives class spirit."[11]

Contemporary observer Lichtenstein claimed that the freshmen scrap was both common to and beneficial to all men's colleges: "Their clashes produce no ill-will, although for the time the participants are in deadly earnest.... Seemingly queer things [traditions], indeed, but not so queer when one realizes that these customs exist simply to furnish an escape valve for the overflowing spirits of youth."[12]

Given this context, the story of the University of Kansas and its "Maypole Scrap," at first so strange, becomes comprehensible. At this institution the men initiated the May Day activities and continued them for thirteen years. However, their effort was not an exercise in aesthetic daintiness. The tradition of the "Maypole Scrap" began at midnight on April 30, 1891, when the juniors (the graduating class of 1892) planted a forty-foot long pole in front of the main building, leaving two men to guard it. The pole was wrapped in the class colors and bore a banner with the figures "'92" on it. Little happened until after classes started at nine in the morning, when the entire class of '92 rushed out to find the pole fallen, chopped down by the sophomores who had left the guards bound hand and foot. The rest of the day was a wild free-for-all fist-fight between the juniors and their brother class, the freshmen, versus the sophomores and the seniors. Clothes, heads, and college property all suffered.

The Maypole Scrap at the University of Kansas (KU) continued every May Day from 1891 to 1904. Photographs show scores of young men engaged in wild fisticuffs, with stunned victims sprawled bloody and disheveled on the ground. Over the years, local reporters noted with dismay the various sophistications added to the tradition of the battle over the maypole. In 1892, sophomores hurled snakes, liquefied hydrogen disulfide and firebrands at the maypole defenders, while in 1899 they tossed flaming bales of hay at them. In the scrap of 1901, the freshmen imbedded a steel pole covered with sticky tar in concrete. It took "a talented lad from the high grass country" with a lasso to pull down the pole.

One wag noted in the 1903 yearbook that the junior prom (a girl-boy dance) had been termed the best social function for mixing up the students, but the "May-pole Scrap is undoubtedly the best barbaric function for bringing the students together. In fact, we believe the students get in closer touch, one with another, at the May-pole Scrap than at the Prom."[13]

The college historian adds that while KU women "kept to the sidelines," they were more than spectators, sewing class flags and providing coffee and sandwiches to their classmates. In the scrap of 1900, "a daring band of 'freshman lassies' as the Kansas University Weekly called them, even succeeded in liberating some of their captured male classmates. And the KU chancellors were initially permissive to these battles, considering them productive of gentlemanly conduct and class spirit.[14]

By 1903, the scrap was limited to the freshmen and sophomores, as the upper-classmen had finally acceded to the chancellor's request to tone down the proceedings and not get involved. But unwary professors who wandered too near the pole were still dragged up to it and forced to tip their hats to it, or risk having their faces smeared in the noxious and sticky mixtures with which it was covered. In the course of the 1904 scrap two freshmen were seriously injured, and the chancellor finally put a halt to the tradition. When the freshmen raised the maypole the next spring, the sophomores refused to fight. That afternoon, the freshmen organized a funeral procession, marched through the town and finally, with ceremony, "buried the sophomore class."[15]

The University of Kansas' May Day story does not end with the demise of its maypole scrap. After four years, possibly to allow for a turnover of the college population, the women of the University finally held their own old English May Day pageant in 1908. Explicitly modeled on those held at Bryn Mawr and other eastern colleges, the pageant was organized by the local chapter of the YWCA, and included the May Queen riding in on a white pony, maypole dancers, the play of *Pyramus and Thisbe*, and various folk dances as well as a milkmaid drill, performed around a cow. A few years later, the 1912 yearbook noted that the Fête "came into being in answer to a long felt need for an out-of-door play-festival, which should be a traditional part of University life."[16]

By 1913, young men from various fraternities at the University of Kansas were involved in presenting the three plays including all the women's parts, thereby effectively sidelining them, while the girls performed the folk and aesthetic dances. Not everyone was thrilled with

College men "getting in touch with each other" at the University of Kansas Maypole Scrap: on May 1 from 1891 to 1904, the freshmen and the juniors took on the sophomores and seniors in a day-long, bare-knuckle fist-fight for ownership of the maypole. (University Archives, Spencer Research Library, University of Kansas Libraries.)

the event. According to a retrospective article published in 1966 in the student newspaper, "Some alumni accustomed to the sometimes brutal contests of the [18]90's sniffed audibly at 'Lord Fauntleroys who would tolerate such events as Ring Around the Rosy,'" although at least one future alumnus recalled his pleasure at seeing the pretty, white-gowned girls dancing near the famous lilac hedge. As at many large, coed institutions, the event did not last long, however, vanishing around 1921.[17]

The Berkeley men's scorn of the girls' pageant *Partheneia* has already been described. But college men sometimes did more than just sneer at the girls: they could be intrusive or even destructive. The college historian of Miami University in Ohio wrote about the evolution in the 1930s of a men's violent burlesque of the long-standing women's May Day festival:

> In burlesque of [the women's Crowning of the May Queen] ritual the Miami men, on the last night of April, held their Crowning of the April King. It was a wholly native and spontaneous tradition, which expressed the restlessness in the spring night and recalled the years when Miami was a man's abode. Their travesty of the May Day began robustly, and within a few years it grew bawdy. It ended in a raucous parade up High Street, with rolls of toilet paper arching into the trees; some of those streamers defied the reach of the grounds department for days afterward.[18]

This historian of 1958 used the words "ribald," "bawdy" and "robust" to describe the men's burlesque, and attributed it to a desire to return to the good old days when there were no women on campus. To the president's relief, the men's burlesque ended in the late 1930s, due to several rainy springs that forced the women's celebration indoors and out of sight.

Even all-women's colleges could experience their share of masculine Dis-Maying. For example, while the men of Haverford College had earlier participated in acceptable ways in nearby Bryn Mawr College's May Day, there is evidence that by 1953 they began to participate in a more active and disruptive fashion. In her study of the college's many traditions, Virginia Briscoe reported that in 1961 someone — probably a group of Haverfordians — had managed to put up and weave the freshman maypole during the night before May Day. (If they had woven the ribbons all the way down the pole — especially if they made mistakes — it would take considerable time and effort to un-weave it, hence the disruption.) In 1963 one group of men succeeded in removing two poles from the security office where they were kept the night before May Day while another group chained closed the parking lot entrances to keep the security guards from interfering. She reports that "at four A.M. they set off fireworks in front of Pembroke [Hall] to create a diversion while they removed the poles from the other side of the campus. One pole was retrieved [by the women,] who engaged in a water-fight to get it back."[19]

In 1964 the Haverfordians again stole four maypoles and were otherwise disruptive; the consequences were such that they engaged in no activity for the next two years. Several other pranks followed in subsequent years or, as Briscoe noted, were later attributed to the men without a sense of when such legends had occurred.[20]

Wellesley College's May Day also attracted the disruptive attention of students at nearby men's colleges. One of the principal events of the festival was (and still is) the seniors' hoop-rolling race, held early in the morning after the ritual scrubbing of several favorite campus statues. The seniors' little sisters camp out overnight to ensure that their big sisters get a good starting spot, and the seniors respond by arriving with breakfast in hand for their supporters. During the 1930s through the 1950s much attention was paid to the winner of the race, as victory was supposed to ensure that she would be the first of her class to marry: later the first to have a baby; much later, the first to obtain her PhD; and later still, the first to become a CEO. Photographers eagerly took pictures of the winner and her boyfriend or fiancé. The 1939 hoop-rolling remains an historic event for it was then that Ned (alias "Peggy") Read, Harvard Class of 1940, president of the Harvard *Lampoon* and a track star, "smashed Wellesley tradition ... when he bounded daintily over the tape and became the first man ever to win Wellesley's May Day hoop-rolling," according to the student newspaper account. In a paper of 1994, a Wellesley student described the deed in more detail, citing the contemporary accounts:

> Partially on a dare from his friends, Ned joined the line of seniors at 7:25 am, five minutes before the race began. When seniors who had been waiting for some time voiced complaints, he quietly claimed his little sister was saving his place. After winning the race, he was awarded the bridal bouquet by the class president, who was eyeing the winner doubtfully. "Peggy" pointed to a young man on the sidelines as her fiancé, as photographers clicked away. But suddenly, the wig of red curls slipped and "indignant Wellesley maidens rushed upon the Harvard junior in a body with cries of 'She's a man! And 'Throw him in the lake!'.... President McAfee proclaimed in the chapel service after this historic hooprolling, "I think you have made history this morning. Never before have Wellesley women banded together for such a purpose [of tossing a man into the lake]."[21]

In retaliation for this outrage, early the next morning some Wellesley students draped a Wellesley cap and gown on the statue of John Harvard in the town of Cambridge. The entire episode was recounted in the "Ballad of a Bold, Bad Man," a song that remained in Wellesley's stepsinging songbook until at least 1994. For many years after this event it was part of the tradition to have a male imposter run the race, only to be discovered at the end and thrown in the lake. In 1994, senior Arlene Cohen wrote that "There seems to have been competition among various schools [to participate], since many men considered it an honor. The name of the imposter was always written up in the newspapers, alongside the name of the winner."[22] Eventually the winner herself also ended up in the lake beside the imposter.

With little direct information from male informants, it only possible to surmise at why the men might mock the girls' celebration. One evident reason, in the late nineteenth century and the early part of the twentieth, was that they resented the presence — and often the superior academic performance — of the women on campus; indeed, that they rejected the whole idea of education for women. For example, in a story titled "In Maytime," written by Anne Maynard Kidder, Bryn Mawr class of 1903, the reader is invited to laugh at the terribly correct young man-about-town Timothy who particularly detests and disapproves of college girls:

> They represented to his mind a mixture of spectacled phenomena of learning, and of cheering, basket-ball playing New Women. In either capacity he found them peculiarly objectionable. He often said of them, with a fervent horror he might have expressed towards wild Indians: "I sincerely trust it will never be my misfortune to meet one."

Given his strong opinions, his friends find it amusing to arrange for Timothy to absent-mindedly board one of the specially laid-on trains bound for Bryn Mawr College's May Day fête. While at first horrified and embarrassed to find himself amid a group of costumed college girls, Timothy is soon swept into the romance of the day, finally joining in an ecstatic dance with two flower girls — the spirit of Old England has somehow taken possession of him.

The jest of the slight plot of this story is that one "Brynmawrtyr" has asked Eleanor to guard her from a young man whom she does not want to see for fear that he will "pop the question." Eleanor by mistake thinks that Timothy is this suitor and stays with him all afternoon in order to keep him from finding her friend. As he leaves the campus, Timothy overhears two girls talking about Eleanor's ghastly ordeal that day with a "boring stick"— that is, himself — and he hastily departs, presumably having learned a lesson about self-conceit as well as about the College Girl.[23]

This story, written by a woman and told from the woman's point of view, exults over the initial disdain and the ensuing change of heart that the young man exhibits towards the college girls and their festival. For, whether they wished to admit it or not, many men enjoyed watching the festivities or even participating in them. One romantic young man wrote about his first view of the University of Kansas girls' May Day festival:

> Up the hill we hurried ... then the sight of the pretty girls and the smell of the lilacs and that glorious view out over the valley! Good Methodist that I was and with a girl that I liked pretty well at Washburn, I didn't even go to visit Washburn and Baker University as I had originally intended, but decided right then to go to K.U.[24]

Similarly, in 1908, when the girls of the gymnasium classes of Indiana University presented *Merry May-Day as in Merrie England*, members of every woman's club in the city were invited to attend. According to the student newspaper, "many plans are being laid by the men to secure one of these coveted invitations" to view this exhibition of grace and beauty.[25] Even the Berkeley men who publicly scoffed at the girls' *Pageant of Maidenhood* climbed trees in order to have a view of the dress rehearsal. One final, perhaps forever un-provable theory for some college men's disdain for May Day was that they were, in fact, drawn to the prettiness of the girls and their special spectacle and, in the words of the Bard, "did protest too much."

14. Maypole Dances and Drills

Come Lasses and Lads
Come lasses and lads, take leave of your dads,
Away to the May-pole hie;
Where every fair has a sweetheart there,
And the fiddler's standing by.
For Willy shall dance with Jane,
And Johnny has got his Joan,
To trip it, trip it, trip it, trip it, trip it up and down.
To trip it, trip it, trip it, trip it, trip it up and down.
 — Anonymous, *Pills to Purge Melancholy*, 1740

While May Day celebrations are more rare today than 100 years ago, the maypole decked with ribbons remains the icon of the holiday, taking its place beside the Christmas tree, the Thanksgiving turkey and the Valentine's Day cupid and heart. Indeed, for many years, the maypole has been viewed as an icon of childish innocence and even cleanliness, used, for example, in a 1903 Pears Soap advertisement and in a 1945 Lifesavers ad (the children dance around the pole whose streamers are attached to the candies). Modern images of maypole dancers tend to depict very young children or, more often, rabbits, bears or other animals.

A highlight of the May Day celebration, the maypole dance could take place after the ceremony of crowning the Queen and before the pageant, as a finale to the pageant itself, or in the case of the urban children's festival, as a principal entertainment. Because of its importance as an icon, and because there are so many erroneous beliefs about the maypole and its dance today, it is interesting to examine the origins of the dance as well as its actual components.

As noted in Chapter 1, maypoles decked with flowers and greens became popular in England between 1350–1400. Neither decked with ribbons, nor painted or carved to represent a phallus, these poles served as a focal point of the May-tide celebrations. While nineteenth-century folklorists asserted confidently that dances occurred around or in front of the pole, there is little evidence as to what these dances were. The dance with plaited ribbons, however, has a briefer history.

The Origins of the Plaited Maypole Dance in England

Contrary to what many today believe, the origins of the plaited maypole dance are by no means shrouded in the mists of antiquity; it was, instead, the property of nineteenth-century romantics. Only one picture of a maypole dressed with ribbons exists prior to the 1830s — an engraving of a now-lost painting by Canaletto of the Rotundo House and garden at the

Depending on the skill of the dancers and the preference of their instructor, maypole dances could feature robust skipping or dainty footwork, as here at Mills College in 1914. (Special Collections, F.W. Olin Library, Mills College.)

Ranelegh pleasure gardens as they appeared at the Jubilee Ball held on the occasion of the birthday of His Royal Highness the Prince of Wales on May 24, 1751. There, in front of well-dressed spectators, eight costumed characters hold ribbons in their left hands and dance counter-clockwise around a pole. Unfortunately, the problem with this picture, as Roy Judge observes, is its isolation — there are no other descriptions of a maypole with ribbons for another eighty years. He concurs with Violet Alford's theory that it is possible that these were trained comedians or professional dancers engaged in a special performance for the Jubilee.[1]

Judge traces the plaited maypole dance in England to an 1836 production of J.R. Haines's romantic medieval drama *Richard Plantagenet* at the Victoria Theatre in London. Both the morris and the maypole dances in this production were choreographed by a professional dancing master to deliberately re-create a time that was simultaneously picturesque and ancient as well as being peculiarly English in character.

The maypole spectacle proved immensely popular and appeared subsequently in many other theatrical productions. By 1840, according to Judge, the maypole dance had left the stage and could be found in a variety of pleasure gardens, festivals, May Queen fêtes and other venues. The dance was initially spread by dancing masters who were proud to include the dance in their repertoire. Finally, in 1884, John Curwen and Sons published the first printed instructions for the dance. From that time on, as Judge notes, there could have been no difficulty for any interested person in finding out how to perform the dance, whether by word of mouth, by personal contact and example or by the printed word.[2] It is not yet known when these instructions, or the slightly later ones arranged by A.L. Cowley (1891) made their way to the U.S. However, given the relative simplicity of most of the versions of the dance it is perhaps not even necessary that such a book travel over the water: once she has heard about the idea of a maypole dance with ribbons that are plaited, a competent dance teacher can easily invent several simple figures. At any rate, numerous books by American and a handful of English writers documenting some version of the dance were readily available to physical education instructors from about 1909 on. These instructions are summarized at the end of this chapter.

It is not clear when the plaited maypole dance came to the American stage, but I theorize that it was prior to 1867, when it appeared as a humorous act (as opposed to a dainty novelty) in a parody of the popular show, *The Black Crook* (1866)—a romantic, quasi-ballet and variety show, including some apparent nudity, all loosely connected by plot. *The Black Crook Burlesque* (1867) was written by G.W. Griffin with Edwin Christy for Christy's Minstrels. In it, the maypole dance was performed by white men in black face pretending to be white women dancing in French ballet style.

> The ladies who compose the Grand Ballet are dressed in white gauze dresses, reaching nearly to the knee; without hoops. The waists are red or blue satin, abundantly stuffed to form immense bosoms — large heavy shoes — white stockings, stuffed, to form "big limbs" — fashionable lady's wig, with tremendous waterfall — green wreaths upon the head.

The performers danced several burlesques such as a village hornpipe and the entertainment concluded with the maypole dance, with the following stage directions:

> MAN brings on May Pole and holds it on stage — it has six strings of different colored muslin hanging from the top. Each Ballet Girl takes one, and they all dance MAY POLE DANCE. They finally get entangled in the muslin, winding up the man's head, etc., and all run off with the May Pole.[3]

This brevity of these instructions suggest that the simple honors and a basic plaiting of ribbons were already familiar to both the actors and the spectators: had they not been, the dance would have been presented as a pretty feature, not a burlesque.

Maypole Dance Choreography in the Early Twentieth Century

Comparisons of the instructions for the maypole dance found in folk and fancy dance manuals available to early twentieth-century American dance educators prove that — far from being codified — the dance varied as called for by the skills or age of the performers, the nature of the performance, and the creativity of the instructor. In fact, part of the dance's universal charm and usefulness was that it adapted (and still adapts) itself easily to all kinds of music and choreography. Its other charm for both spectators and participants alike was, as famous folk-dance collector Elizabeth Burchenal wrote in 1909, that "every movement of the dance should be free and joyous, expressive of the sunshine and new life that comes with spring."[4] This expressiveness was an integral part of the dance: "Girls vibrating with joy and life take their places [around the pole]," gushed one spectator, adding: "Now bowing and now winding in and out until the May Pole stands woven as if by magic hands."[5] Often, the dance instructions, such as those in an article in the *Ladies Home Journal* in 1911, explicitly require the dancers to skip to, from, or around the pole smiling and bobbing their heads as they make "merry with laughter, while drinking in new life in high glee, as in the old days of 'Merrie England.'"[6]

The ribbons that decked the pole could be in the colors chosen by the May Queen, the college or school colors, or any pretty springtime colors. A minimum of two colors of rib-

Because the maypole dance never features a "star" performer, and because it requires teamwork and symmetry to execute at all, it remains an emblem of unity and harmony, as shown by these women dancing around one of five maypoles at Mills College in 1947. (Special Collections, F.W. Olin Library, Mills College.)

bons is necessary for effect, with four also being pretty; however, as the colors multiply, the challenges for the choreographer and the dancers increase if they attempt to make complex color patterns. Dancers can weave the ribbons singly, or in pairs, trios, or quartettes. There must be an even number of dancers and it seems generally agreed that the dance, to appear effective, requires a minimum of 12 dancers, with 18 and 24 dancers also common; one documented *tour de force* employed 120 dancers, not all of whom, however, held ribbons.

There are basically two types of maypole dances, or, more accurately, plaiting patterns: the closed plait, in which the ribbons are tightly wound in various patterns around the pole, and the open plait, in which the ribbons form a sort of conical tent outward from the pole and the pattern is made by the outer ribbons winding over the inner ribbons. There are numerous variations of these two basic concepts, many of which have been codified with a name such as the Single Plait (a closed plait formed by dancers performing a grand chain, or grand right-and-left) or the Gypsy's Tent (an open plait formed by half of the dancers looping their ribbons around the ribbons held by stationary partners and neighbors).

Though the maypole dance was a highlight of any May Day program, it was rarely a complicated dance: that is, most of the early directions for the dance — and especially those intended for school children — incorporate only one or two of the simpler plaiting figures, or the performers might plait the ribbons but not take the risk of un-plaiting them. (The performance of any plaiting figure is risky; it is riskier yet to un-plait what the dancers have woven; and a dance with multiple plaitings and un-plaitings is the riskiest of all.) The younger the intended performer, the simpler the dance, and the choreographers adhere to this principle.

As E.B. Willard noted in 1907: "Although well known, [the maypole] drill, or dance, is always beautiful. It is not in the least difficult *provided* that entire attention and obedience are given by those who present it. In no other drill is slight inattention or carelessness so fatal to success; for a single false move in the winding will throw the whole dance into confusion. Should this occur it is wisest to order 'halt,' deliberately retrace the false move and start again."[7]

Thus, most versions of the dance were easy, accommodating, as Jennette E. Carpenter Lincoln, creator of some of the most complex maypole drills, observed; not just the strong, graceful, and pretty, but "the entire [physical education] class without selection or discrimination."[8] In fact, the focal point of most maypole dances was the introductory "honors." These were often quite lengthy: the girls would curtsey to the pole, to partners, to the May Queen, and to the audience. They then might skip, march or polka (or in one case dance with a springy, cakewalk step) around the pole or in toward the pole and back. After taking the streamers, the most commonly referenced figure was to have all the dancers skip in one direction around the pole (literally, winding it), or to have half of them skip in one direction in an inner circle and the other half skip the other way to form "barber's pole" stripes: then reverse to unwind the ribbons. The third most commonly referenced figure was a simple grand chain (dancers passing alternate right and left shoulders), a figure that produces a true woven pattern around the pole. Finally, the exercise could be choreographed to fit the storyline of any May Day pageant, in that after the final plaiting, the girls either could exeunt, laughing merrily, or they could sink to the ground in respectful silence, awaiting the next act of the festivities.

The choreographers recommended many different tunes and meters for the dance, from a waltz such as "The Beautiful Blue Danube," a march such as "British Grenadiers," to a polka, a mazurka, or any jolly tune including, for example, the English country dance tunes "Portsmouth" or "Sellenger's Round." Several versions used the tune then called "Bluff King Hal" (known today as "Staines Morris").[9] Another popular tune was the song "Come Lasses and Lads."

In summation, the charm of the maypole dance was that it was a pretty spectacle easily adapted to the numbers and skills of the available performers. While the streamer-decked maypole became the quintessential symbol of May Day and Merrie England, the dance itself was infinitely flexible; in fact, none of the sources that I have examined indicate that any of the writers believed that his or her version represented the one single correct version of the dance. I have found directions for maypole dances in fifteen dance manuals—four imports from England and the remainder by Americans—that were available in the U.S. in the early part of the century. The details of each version demonstrate the dance's flexibility. It is also important to remember that many of the authors of these dance manuals were aware of each other: for example, Elizabeth Burchenal and Mary Woods Hinman were both students of Melvin Ballou Gilbert in the late 1890s; from 1902 to 1905 Burchenal taught dance at the influential Teachers College of Columbia University, thereby influencing other dance teachers; and from 1905 to approximately 1915, Burchenal taught folk dance—including the maypole dance—to public school teachers and students in New York City, where, in the later years, Dr. Crampton, a folk dance manual compiler, was a health inspector.

Trade rivalry among publishers may also explain the numerous versions of the dance: dance and physical education for children and young people were popular topics in the early part of the century. In Chicago, the A.L. Flanagan Company published both Mari Ruef Hofer's folk dance books as well as a handful of the maypole dance pamphlets discussed below. In New York the G.L. Schirmer Company published the numerous books of Elizabeth Burchenal, while the A.S. Barnes Company ultimately virtually cornered the market on books on physical education, folk and natural dance, tap, clog, singing and playground games, and so forth.

The earliest printed version of the dance that I have located is that of A.L. Cowley, who described the maypole dance in *The Maypole Dance for School Concerts*, published in London in 1891 by J. Curwen & Sons. Cowley arranged the tune "Come Lasses and Lads," set to original words, for piano and simple chorus. Verses of the song are interspersed with traditional tunes such as "The White Cockade," "Linden Hall," "Fisher's Hornpipe," and "Oh, Dear, What Can the Matter Be?" Terse dance instructions are printed at the bottom of the page, and there are no illustrations. Cowley recommends that one group of children sing while the others dance. During the verses the children dance simple honors (bow and curtsey, skip around the pole, etc.). During the interludes the children dance the single plait and unplait, then a single plait for couples and unplait, and finally another single plait. The interlude music can thus run *ad lib.* until the dancers succeed in the windings. One striking feature of this choreography is the association of different tunes to different sections of the dance: some, but by no means all, of the later choreographers would employ this concept.

Englishman Ardern Holt's book of 1907, *How to Dance the Revived Ancient Dances* (London: Horace Coz), was clearly addressed to adults. Holt, an admirer of the "airs and graces" school of English country dance — one that stressed pointed toes, romantic postures, and elaborate costumes — did not recommend any particular music or footwork, and his finale is both unique and somewhat inexplicable: dancers take a ring that depends from each streamer, place it in their mouth and join hands for a slipping circle left and right. They then form a final, unspecified, tableau around the pole and exeunt.

In 1907 Grace T. Kimmins published her *Guild of Play Book of Festival and Dance* (London: J. Curwen & Sons., Ltd.) with dances arranged by M.H. Woolnoth. The Guild of Play, like the Guild of the Poor Little Brave Things, was a London-based institution where poor children could go in the afternoons and evenings to play, sing songs, and learn crafts and dances. Kimmins set her maypole dance to the tune and words of "Staines Morris." She did not describe which plaiting figure to use or how to perform it in her book, but instead recommended the reader to the "useful little book entitled 'Maypole Exercises'" also published by J. Curwen & Sons.

In that same year, 1907, E.M. Willard produced *The Favorite Book of Drills* for the T.S. Denison publishing company of Chicago. These drills are suitable for very young children. Miss Willard suggests a polka step, but does not recommend a specific tune. The curtain rises on a tableau of the children in a circle around the pole. Ribbons are not taken into late in the dance, and then only a single plait is performed.

Jennette E. Carpenter Lincoln, then director of the Women's Gymnasium of the University of Illinois, wrote two important books on May Day festivals, the first of which also appeared in 1907. Her vision of the festival and its attendant dances and drills was both elaborate and unique, and her influential books — still found in academic and public libraries — were cited by many other writers. In her 1907 book, *May-Pole Possibilities with Dances and Drills for Modern Pastime,* Lincoln wrote that the dance had first been performed by 24 young women at the university in May of 1898. Each year thereafter more women participated until the so-called *Grande Maypole* incorporated four concentric circles of dancers, "one hundred and twenty young women moving in concerted figures and steps." (Only the inner circle of 24 held ribbons; the remainder, some carrying staves with pennants of the school colors, danced simple figures around the perimeters.) This *tour de force* was preceded and closed by the "Pennant March" and other marching drills, as well as a milkmaid's maypole set to a "lively

A Grande Maypole Dance, 1919. While it is difficult to be certain, there are at least 80 dancers involved, attired variously as shepherdesses, Highland lassies, milkmaids, and so on. (Photograph courtesy C. Elizabeth Boyd '33 Archives, Hankey Center, Wilson College.)

two-step," a peasants' maypole dance for 56 dancers (24 around the pole with streamers, 16 crossing and re-crossing in a double quadrille formation with the eight on the outside holding longer streamers crossing on the sides; the remainder of the dancers in circles or quadrilles along the perimeter), the "Sir Roger de Coverley" (the "Virginia Reel"), a Japanese lantern drill, and a an aesthetic dance choreographed by Melvin Ballou Gilbert and set to the "Faust Waltz." This was performed in a cross formation with the pole as the focal point.

Lincoln in fact included several different maypole dances in her book: the milkmaids' maypole, the peasants' maypole dance for fifty-six dancers, and so on. One of her dances incorporates a figure found elsewhere only in the famous dancing master Melvin Ballou Gilbert's repertoire and very possibly devised by him: a double quadrille formation (eight couples, two on each side of a square), where heads and sides cross alternately to weave the ribbons.

Lincoln's second work, *The Festival Book; May-Day Pastime and the May-Pole*, (1913) is dedicated to "All those who are interested in fresh air, sunshine, and the development of play and the child spirit as a means of bettering the health of our women and children of America." It continues the work of her first, providing elaborate instructions for the construction of props such as a hobby-horse, a fanciful description of an old English May Day, an extensive bibliography, citing many of the antiquarian authors of the mid-nineteenth century, and more dances and drills, including the unusual formation of the "Queen's Coach." The accompanying photograph of this drill shows about forty girls in the long white dresses of the late 1890s marching two abreast, with the Queen suspended on their shoulders in the middle of the procession. Girls behind the Queen hold a canopy of flowers over her head, while the four girls on the corners of the "coach" twirl pink-trimmed parasols to represent wheels and a "leader pony" prances in front, attached to the "coach" by a long wreath of flowers.

In 1908 the John Church Company published an artistic version of the maypole dance in a book titled *Dance Songs of the Nations*, with words by Margaret E. Lacey, music by Eduardo Marzo, and choreography by Oscar Duryea, a professional dancing master. The dance, in 6/8 time, is performed for the King and Queen of the May, and is quite brief.

In 1909 Elizabeth Burchenal published the first of her many books: *Folk-Dances and Singing Games* (New York: G. Schirmer, Inc., 1909, 1933). She set her maypole dance to the tune of "Bluff King Hal," as "Staines Morris" was known then, and, again, the dance is quite

Girls helping the Queen ascend into "The Queen's Coach" formation at the University of Illinois in 1909. The "leader pony" prances to the left but is not in the shot. The girls twirling parasols held low are the "wheels." (Photograph, 0002991.tif, courtesy the University of Illinois at Urbana-Champaign Archives.)

simple and suitable for schoolchildren. It bears marked similarities to Grace Kimmin's dance, though it is far more clearly worded and described.

The 1909 edition of Burchenal's book is illustrated with photographs of schoolgirls performing the dance. In one photograph, eighteen girls dressed in white blouses and dark skirts and stockings are plaiting the ribbons in a park. Spectators line the periphery of the performance space. A second photograph shows twenty-six girls, all in white dresses and black stockings, following their leader to dance away from the woven maypole. Spectators and approximately seven, already-wound maypoles are visible in the background. A third, panoramic, shot, is clearly that of one of the great celebrations in Central Park: almost twenty different rings of children are dancing around maypoles, with a row of spectators down one side of the field.

In 1910 Walter Shaw published *Maypole Dances* (London: J. Curwen & Sons, Ltd.). The book is illustrated with photographs of children in smocks and shepherdess or tricorn hats. Shaw appears to have both devised and named the Spider's Web plait that first appears in this book, the open plait that was later named the Gypsy's Tent, as well as several other unusual plaits. As in Crowley's choreography, each figure is danced to a different strain of music, and Shaw suggests that the use of steps — polka, skipping, waltz, or other — is at the discretion of the dance teacher. Shaw's work, simplified, is still for sale today.

In 1911 the A. Flanagan Company of Chicago published a slim pamphlet titled *Maypole Exercise and Dance for any Equal Number of Boys and Girls*, apparently adapted from a dance by one A. Alexander, whose original work I have not found. The children enter and salute the pole to a march, salute to the audience to a mazurka, and perform the main part of the dance to the tune "British Grenadiers": hopping twice on one foot for one bar, then changing feet.

In 1913 the G. Schirmer Company published *Gilbert Dances*, a posthumous, two-volume collection of the classical or aesthetic dances composed by Melvin Ballou Gilbert, who had died the year before. His maypole dance, with its lengthy description of the procession of the Queen, Robin Hood, the Jack-o'-the-Green, and so on, appears to be written for older children or adults, since it references a procession through the drawing room. The first part of the dance, basically a contra dance arranged around the maypole, is designed for twelve couples; the plaiting figures are for eight couples, in double quadrille formation, crossing heads and sides to weave the plait. The suggested music is the "Blumen-Polka" by C.M. Ziehrer.

In 1915 Mary Wood Hinman, another other important folk dance collector and teacher who taught at Hull House, a settlement house in Chicago, published *Ring Dances and Singing Games* (New York: A.S. Barnes Company), volume three in her five-volume series of folk dance books. She described an elaborate maypole dance, with four distinctive weaving figures, each set to a different tune (most of which are composed, rather than folk tunes). She indicated that she had collected the dance in Leicestershire in 1909. From photographs and other internal information in this book as well as her other works, it is possible that she observed a performance of either the girls of the Guild of Play or Mary Neal's Espérance Society dancers.

In 1916 Dr. C. Ward Crampton, director of physical training, New York City Schools, published the second of his extremely popular books on folk dance, appropriately titled, *The Second Folk Dance Book* (A.S. Barnes Company). Several ladies, in particular a Miss Emily O'Keefe, then inspector of athletics for girls (the position formerly held by Elizabeth Burchenal), assisted him in this effort. Crampton's maypole dance is set to "Bluff King Hal" and, in fact, is a less-well presented version of Burchenal's version of the dance first published in 1909. Such re-use of material in the early folk dance manuals was common.

In 1916 Nina B. Lamkin published her *Dances, Drills and Story-Plays for Every Day and Holidays* (Chicago: T.S. Denison & Co.). Her maypole drill is set to a waltz of the reader's choosing and is suitable even for very little children. The accompanying photograph shows four- or five-year-old girls skipping around the maypole while small boys holding the ribbons kneel on the ground. As no instruction is given as to when the children pick up the ribbons it is possible that they do not take them at all. There is none of the risky plaiting.

In 1924, Lyle Wilson Holden published *Dances and Plays for Sunny Days* (Chicago: A. Flanagan Company). He included a long May Day play, complete with suggested games like an egg-and-spoon race, any of the folk dances from Mari Ruef Hofer's collections (also published by the A. Flanagan Company—surely not a coincidence), as well as a maypole dance for 24 children who perform to an unspecified waltz.

This survey shows that the maypole dance was perceived in the nineteenth and most of the twentieth century as being one that the dance instructor could modify at will to suit the abilities of the performers and the needs of the performance. Not a single choreographer makes a claim that his or her dance is the original, or even the best version of the dance. No choreographer makes any claims for the great antiquity of the dance (other than an occasional, vague reference to Merrie England), nor does he or she ascribe any particular significance or meaning to the pole or to the windings or unwindings of the ribbons.

Indeed, no documentation of the dance prior to the last two decades includes any of the statements below that can now be found in recently published children's books on the topic of holidays and festivals, and in books, instructional materials and Websites written by and for Pagans, Wiccans, and elementary school teachers. There is absolutely no basis in the historical record prior to the last few decades for any of the following fantasies: (1) that when the children change direction in the plaiting, unwinding the ribbons, this action symbolizes the lengthening of the days (found in *Celebrations*, a 1997 Unicef-sponsored publication), or

(2) that the pole is the God (the phallus), the Goddess (the vagina) is represented by the wreath on top of the maypole (found in Yasmine Galenorn, *Dancing with the Sun*, 1999).[10] Other romantic claims made on Web sites that appear and vanish frequently include (3) that the maidens of each English village had a distinctive plaiting pattern and that if no ribbons were broken during the dance, it symbolized good luck; (4) that dancers should build the weaving upon the pole year after year, it being bad luck to unplait the ribbons; (5) that the maypole represents the center of the world, and that plaiting the ribbons is an attempt to put nature awry back on course; that (6) successful plaiting means a successful harvest, or that (7) the men should take the red ribbons and the women the white and that the plaiting of the ribbons (men going under the women's ribbons first) symbolizes either the divine marriage or the passage down the birth canal. While modern participants are free to interpret the maypole in this neo-Freudian/neo-Pagan light if they please, statements like these have no place in any historically based discussion of the maypole.

The maypole dance has by no means vanished, as will be shown in Chapter 18. I have seen recent photographs of maypole dancers performing on St. Thomas, U.S. Virgin Islands (black children), on a small island off the coast of Maine (white children), and in Hawaii (women elementary school teachers wearing traditional muu-muus and incorporating elements of the hula into the dance, set to the song *Nani Wale Na Pua*.[11] While no longer performed as frequently as it was in the past, the maypole dance remains an attractive springtime spectacle.

15. Crowning the College May Queen

> Who shall be Queen of the Maye?
> Not the prettiest one, not the wittiest one,
> Nor she with the gowne most gaye.
> But she who is pleasantest all the daye thru,
> With the pleasantest things to say and to do
> She shall be Queene of the Maye.
> —1923 May Day *Program*, University of Maryland[1]

Who's to be Queen of the May? What are the criteria for her selection and who employ them, what is her role, and what are her sensations on the big day itself? Exploring these questions reveals that from the 1830s until the mid–1960s, recipients of the honor were pleased and proud to be chosen May Queen. After the late-1960s, however, the position abruptly ceased to have positive meaning in all but a few cases.

How to choose the Queen? There was no uniformity in the way the colleges selected and honored their Queens. Each one developed its own set of customs and traditions surrounding the details both of the election and coronation, and which class, club, or sorority the Queen was to be chosen from. At some colleges the festival was given by the juniors in honor of their graduating seniors; or by the sophomores in honor of the juniors. At some women's colleges, the roles of Queen and current or future class president were intermingled, with the one being or becoming the other: for example in the early 1900s at Bryn Mawr College, the senior class president was automatically that year's Queen. This class orientation, though different at every school, doubtless contributed to feelings of solidarity within the individual classes of a college, as well as engendering special feelings toward the college and its traditions as a whole.

In the earliest days of the May Day festival the Queen was sometimes the youngest girl in the class, as when fourteen-year old Tennessee Tomlinson was elected Earlham College's first May Queen in 1875. But youth was rarely the most important criterion. An article of 1916 in the *Ladies Home Journal* echoed John Ruskin's ideals and suggested that the Queen be chosen because "she 'helped everyone' and 'liked everyone.'"[2] Even children's fiction could allude to Ruskin's ideals. In *Dimple Dallas*, a saccharine children's novel of 1900, the schoolteacher decides to have a "real May party, with a May-pole and a May-queen and all that." She suggests that the little girls vote for May Queen in two weeks time, in order to have time to consider the matter carefully, and coaches the students on how to make their choice: "'I do not think we shall want to select the prettiest, nor the wealthiest, but the one who shows the most loving disposition or the most conscientious work, or some quality of mind or heart to commend her.'" Tellingly, the selfish, dislikable girl, who not only casts two votes for her-

Crowning the Queen of the May in 1910. This photograph appears in Jennette Carpenter Lincoln's The Festival Book, 1912, 1918. (Courtesy the University of Illinois at Urbana Champaign Archives.)

self in the first ballot, but who also votes for herself in the final ballot, is displaced, and little Dimple wins the honor.[3]

Some colleges transformed Ruskin's ideal of worth and service into one in which the Queen was a girl who best embodied the spirit of the college. For example at Wilson College, one of the handful of women's colleges that continues to crown a May Queen, the entire student body voted and still votes for the woman who best represents the qualities of a Wilson woman, choosing from six senior representatives selected by the senior class. The Queen's Court is then made up of the remaining senior representatives as well as representatives from the underclasses. Similarly, at Carleton College in the 1950s, May Day honored the twelve senior women (the May court) who, in the eyes of their peers, had contributed the most to the college.[4]

In another example of the importance placed upon the role, in 1931 at Rockford College it was noted that "[a]s May Day grew in importance, so the May Queen came to embody our ideals of loyalty, sincerity, and versatility."[5] By 1962 the Rockford College student handbook described the May Queen thus:

> [She] must be a member of the senior class, and must have attended Rockford College for at least three years. She must represent academic interest and accomplishment. As well as being a constructive thinker for the welfare of the college, she must have more extensive interests; fundamentally considerate and dignified, she must be loyal to these ideals, and open-minded in her convictions.[6]

At Penn State University, strong feelings were expressed about the candidates and especially that their qualifications should be based on positive attributes, not just beauty. An alumni article from 1937 opined that it would be inappropriate "[f]or some pashy bisquit [*sic*] to fall into a spot like that just 'cause she happened to be born beautiful but dumb. No, indeed girls, this department certainly agrees that by all means May Queen should be elected for 'suitability, interest, and past activities.'"[7] And at Meredith College in 1938, a newspaper article noted that of the thirteen Queens elected under the tenure of one member of the physical education department, only four also held the title of college Beauty Queen, though all were seniors and all were chosen by a popular vote of the students. "Popularity has played a large part in all [Meredith College] elections as well as charms, grace, and beauty."[8]

In a few cases the selection criteria were less high-minded. To select the Queen at the first May Day festival in 1938 at the University of Tennessee, a list of about fifty junior girls making high grades in their sophomore physical education classes was compiled. The intramural council then picked four candidates from this list, and the Queen was selected by the faculty of the Physical Education department on the basis of her physical education work.[9] In a more unusual twist, at the coeducational University of Denver from 1911 to at least 1921, the selection of the Queen was made by the winner of a four-mile relay race of the male representatives of each class.[10]

All these high ideals, good grades, charitable works and impressive qualifications pale, however, before the more common attribute of beauty. Photographs from all colleges over the entire range of study rarely depict May Queens who are only just tolerably pretty — most of them are lovely by any period's standard of white female beauty.

Lois Banner has suggested that nineteenth-century America long had a cult of beauty; each community had its noted Beauties, the details of whose charms and costumes were written about in papers, and whom men flocked to see when they made public appearances. Banner directly ascribes the beginnings of beauty competitions like the Miss America pageant, first held in 1921,* to the nineteenth-century May Day coronations, Ring Tournaments, and other pageants and spectacles at which beauty was celebrated and rewarded. She notes that these spectacles were so popular that in the long history of May Day or Queen of Beauty festivals, she found only one recorded instance of a protest against the idea of an action that violated the Victorian prohibition against a lady displaying herself in public. Banner notes that the Queen could also serve as a symbol of democracy and social mobility, since, theoretically at least, any girl could be elected. But the Queen's image, as well as the sheer fact of her existence, also forcefully announced the way white women were supposed to look, as well as reinforcing the centrality of physical beauty in women's lives.[11]

Thus year after year, in college town after college town, the local newspapers published pictures of the May Queen and her court, and included descriptions of the Queen's ideals and aspirations, her social background and, sometimes, her beauty tips. Some Queens achieved national recognition; for example, May Queens at the University of Denver automatically went on to compete in the Miss Colorado beauty pageant. In the late 1930s, the *New York Times* current events section ran the photograph of one Randolph-Macon Woman's College Queen, resulting both in a proposal of marriage from a doctor in Chicago as well as an invitation from the Metro-Goldwyn-Mayer movie studio to come to New York to have her photograph taken for a possible movie career. (She declined both offers.) And Norma Collier,

---

*As with college May Day pageants, the Miss America contest has been until recently dominated by white Anglo-Saxon Protestants. The first Miss America contest was won by a petite, fifteen-year old blonde. In 1945 the first Jewish Miss America was crowned. African American contestants began appearing in the contest in the 1970s, but the first African American Miss America was not crowned until 1984 (though she was soon thereafter forced to relinquish her crown when Penthouse magazine published nude photographs of her taken before her victory). The crown went to the runner-up, also an African American.

The symbolic Gifts formerly given to the Wilson College May Queen. In 1952 the Freshmen class gave her the Footstool, the Sophomores the World (the globe), the Juniors the Scepter and the Seniors the Crown. (Photograph courtesy C. Elizabeth Boyd '33 Archives, Hankey Center, Wilson College.)

the Wilson College May Queen of 1960, appeared shortly after her coronation on *Glamour Magazine*'s list of Ten Best Dressed College Girls. As we will see in Chapter 16, it was this emphasis on beauty — even if the Queen had other admirable attributes — that caused the festival to lose its value in the eyes of college women (termed "women" now in the late-1960s, no longer "girls").

Beauty might not (theoretically) be critical to being selected a May Queen, but an unmarried state was also important. While prior to the 1950s, most women who married prior to matriculation dropped out of college (having obtained the coveted "M.R.S." degree), a few women in the post–World War II era chose to continue their education. At Winthrop University, most of the May Queens were campus leaders, and it was not surprising when the seniors elected their class president as May Queen in 1949. However, shortly before the event it was revealed that the young woman had recently married. "When the news became public," the report went, the woman resigned as Queen. "There was no rule against a Queen being married (probably no one had considered the possibility) but public opinion was against it." The Maid of Honor was elevated to Queen, and the married class president directed the pageant.[12]

The process of electing the May Queen varied from college to college. Secrecy was often a key component of the process. In the early years, the identity of the Queen was often not announced until the moment of the crowning, and the suspense of the announcement was an important part of the whole celebration. For example, at Mount Holyoke College in the early 1920s, the entire student body voted for the Queen and the results were not revealed until the final moment, creating great excitement and drama as in this account from 1920: "Sometimes she rides into the midst of the pageant grounds in her chariot, drawn by her lovely attendants; again upon a huge mushroom is she crowned, or sometimes upon a rustic throne."[13]

As the college class from which the Queen was selected varied, so did the constituency of the voters. In 1923 at the coeducational University of Colorado, the program noted that the selection of the Queen and the (girl) King was made by a board

> composed of one representative from each of the ten sororities and an equal number of independent women. These were elected by secret ballot, and all ballots cast by them were secret. No nominations were made at their meetings, but each girl submitted the names of three girls who she believed best represented the spirit of the rating sheet which was compiled as a standard for judging collegiate representation.... The Queen is a senior girl who was given the highest rating by the electing board. The King is a junior girl with the highest rating.[14]

The details provided in 1929 by the chairman of the committee at Elmira College, at that time a women's college, shows just how much effort could go into maintaining the secrecy of the election. Two weeks before May Day, the freshwomen voted for the prettiest sophomore girl. The names of the three highest nominees were kept secret until a subsequent meeting at which the girls voted for the Queen. These ballots were kept hidden until three days before the festivities, at which time the chairman of the festival counted and then destroyed the ballots. She then sent a telegram to the May Queen's mother, asking her to come to the exercises but to keep her arrival a secret. At that point only the chairman, the college president, and the May Queen's mother knew the identity of the lucky girl. "It was difficult to keep silent," wrote the chairman, "when everyone, including newspaper reporters, was after us."

On the morning of the festivities, the chairman took the photograph and biography of the May Queen to the newspaper to be published in the evening edition. At the scene of the festivities, the senior Queen with her junior attendants led the coronation procession, followed by the junior Queen with her sophomore attendants. This court grouped itself around the throne prior to the announcement of the new Queen. Girls dressed as guards then went about the crowd, pausing thrillingly in front of each of the three nominees. Finally the chosen one was revealed, led to a pavilion where she was given a purple and white cloak, and crowned.[15]

The Queen was not the only elected participant at many May Day festivals. Many colleges, especially the Southern women's colleges, added additional roles to the May Court. From the 1930s through the late 1950s, for example, the Judson College May Queen was accompanied by a "Prince," a role played by a female classmate. Early photographs show the Prince garbed in a tuxedo with a top hat; later ones show her in a costume of the Revolutionary War complete with knee breeches or a Regency-style cutaway coat and trousers. (In this era, girls did not wear trousers for any reason save sports and acting; indeed, at many of the Southern women's colleges, students were not permitted to wear shorts or trousers on the street until the mid–1960s. "Breeches" roles were therefore a thrilling part of the May Day experience.) The Judson College Queen was also accompanied by one or two Pages, also girls in boy's costume. Similarly, a girl Prince (Robin) Hood appeared to crown the Queen at Hood College, while at Converse College, after the first few years at least, the president of the Women's Athletic Association was always named King and she always crowned the Queen.[16]

As the festival grew more elaborate, the roles of Trumpeters, Jesters, Scepter-Bearer, Crown-Bearer, Page-Boy, Flower-Girl, Train-Bearer, and others were added along with the

The Judson College May Queen and her "King," 1952 or 1953. (Judson College Archives.)

May Court. In many cases the May Court was composed of the girls who had been runners-up for the position of Queen.

At the Southern colleges in particular, the Queen had a male escort whose role during the coronation was usually minor. In one or two cases, the tradition was to have the girl's father or a significant male member of her family escort her down the aisle to be crowned. At most of the Southern colleges, however, the escort was the Queen's boyfriend or fiancé. In the 1950s and 1960s the pressure to marry right after graduation — "Girls feel hopeless if they haven't a marriage at least in sight by commencement time," the *New York Times* stated firmly in 1955[17] — was such that many May Queens used their coronation gowns as wedding gowns a few weeks after the festival.

Indeed, at many colleges, especially those in the South, the coronation ceremony echoed that of a formal wedding: the elaborately gowned May Court (with or without escorts) processed down a long cloth of white laid over the grass, then stood on either side of a long aisle. They were followed by the Jester, the Crown-Bearer, the Scepter-Bearer, the Flower-Girl(s), the Pages and the Queen, the latter dressed in an elaborate white dress that could well serve as a wedding gown. All save the Crown-Bearer and the retiring Queen might then kneel while the retiring Queen crowned the new Queen. Thus the description of the 1932 coronation at Sweet Briar College:

> The heralds were dressed in white satin, had ruffs about their necks and carried white trumpets. The ladies of the court were all dressed in green and yellow chiffon with matching sandals and short shirred chiffon jackets with puffed sleeves. After the heralds came the flower girls, dressed in yellow and green, carrying bouquets of roses. After them came the ladies of the court, carrying bouquets of spring flowers. They were followed by the Honor Girls: the Scepter bearer, and Maid of Honor, the Crown bearer. As the Maid of Honor took her place with the others, the May Queen approached her court. She was dressed in white satin with a matching jacket. Her satin train with a wide inset of lace down the center was attached to her shoulders and was carried by her page. The page was dressed in a white satin costume similar to the heralds.' As she passed between the lines of her court they curtseyed in her honor. The May Queen, carrying a large bouquet of white orchids, reached her throne. Her court then took their places about their Queen. She received her crown, scepter and garland and then greeted them with words of welcome. Then followed the dancing about the May Pole and a pageant in her honor.[18]

Once crowned, the Queen's role was not onerous. In many cases her duty was to declare a holiday or half-holiday. In general, however, the role of the Queen was to be the focal point of the pageant that followed the crowning, and, with her escort, to lead the cotillion at the dance that took place after dinner.

Reactions of the May Queens

There are still many college May Queens alive today and, because most of them were elected prior to 1967, most of them remember the event with pride and pleasure. Their comments show the profound change in women's views of their bodies and their roles in society that emerged in the 1960s.

It is apparent that from 1830 through the early 1960s, participants maintained a traditional view of their femininity and regarded their election as Queen as a positive and meaningful event. The Nineteenth Amendment that gave women the right to vote did little to change their traditional roles in society as mothers and homemakers, as, during the 1930s and 1940s, the organizations that once had made up the woman's movement shrank or folded. And while the bulging biceps of Rosie the Riveter briefly empowered women to work in defense-related industries during World War II, historian Nancy Woloch points out that even before the war was over, the government moved rapidly to coax women back to the kitchen. Women's war-work was to be temporary and women were not to replace men in the labor force, crowd the market, force wages down, and destroy family life.[19]

Woloch observes that the domestic ideology that permeated the 1950s incorporated a backlash against women and the fear of female competition that had followed the war. She argues that women themselves, stressed by growing up in the Depression or in wartime, found domesticity and the role of traditional femininity comforting and safe. The traditional cultural roles continued to be stressed in popular literature as well as in the college classroom and the stated aspirations of students, and thus the May Queen retained her power during the 1940s and 1950s. Thus, a typical response to the event was like the one scribbled by the former owner of a yearbook over the photo of the 1955 Sweet Briar Queen: "May Day is always the best part of May. The Queen was so lovely, and the girls in their hoops [skirts] looked like enchanted dolls."[20]

Maintenance of traditional gender roles was stronger in the South through the nineteenth and most of the twentieth centuries. In her study of the Southern Belle, Christie Ann Farnham argues that the South had a leadership role in establishing colleges for women due to its cultural emphasis on conventional gender ideology, specifically, its focus on gentility. Higher education was available only to the wealthy, and only to the white, which meant that it did not threaten the status quo, particularly with regard to the black population. She argues that the ideal of "being a lady" remained relevant in the South far longer that in the North, principally because the model was useful in maintaining a biracial society. And while the image of the Southern Belle, as epitomized by the May Queen, was the female counterpart of the male cult of chivalry, it was also a way in which women could exercise some control over the courting process.[21] Farnham's arguments help to explain not only why the custom of May Day was so strong at southern women's colleges, but why some of the colleges that experienced the most controversy over giving up the custom were Southern: Randolph-Macon Woman's College,* Meredith College, and Sweet Briar College.

---

*In July 2007, Randolph-Macon Woman's College changed its name to Randolph College when it rather suddenly and amid much controversy began to admit men. I continue to use the old name in this work, as the May Day tradition was a part of the college's past.

In an article published in a 2002 issue of the Randolph-Macon Woman's College (R-MWC) alumnae magazine, "To Be the Queen; Evolution to Extinction ... Tradition Dies a Natural Death in a Changing World," Molly Roper Jenkins captured memories of some of the at-least 33 still-living R-MWC May Queens. She notes that the Queens from the 1940s until the mid-sixties "used words like 'honor,' astonishment,' 'exciting,' 'beautiful tradition,' and 'a private source of pride' to describe the experience." For example, the R-MWC May Queen of 1945 wrote that:

> The honor embodied all the fine values and virtues one could aspire to. I was trying to shape my character to those ideals, so being elected gave validation to the person I wanted to be.... Since then, the experience has fortified my confidence, and it has helped me meet the difficult challenges.

The Randolph-Macon Woman's College Queen of 1962, Nora Kizer Bell, former president of both Wellesley and Hollins Colleges, was proud to note that her selection meant something additional to beauty. "It shattered the stereotype applied to women at the time (and Southern women in particular). Could a Southern blonde May Queen also be Phi Beta Kappa? Absolutely," she wrote. And several of the May Queens whom Jenkins interviewed were proud to be the daughters or granddaughters of former Queens, as the alumnae tradition of attending R-MWC was so strong.[22]

May Queens of other colleges from the 1940s to the early or even the mid–1960s had similarly positive memories of the experience, from the excitement and honor of being elected by their peers, to the beauty and romance of the day. I interviewed several May Queens of the 1950s and 1960s from Wilson, Earlham and Grove City Colleges. As with the R-MWC Queens, most of their reactions are positive, stressing the honor of the position and their pride and pleasure in being chosen as a leader and an exemplar by their classmates.

At Sweet Briar College, the festival organizers and the Queens developed a habit of documenting each year's dance and crowning ceremony, resulting in numerous notebooks filled with descriptions of how to run the committees and the events. The Queens placed a high importance on their role, as shown in this letter written in the spring of 1961 by the retiring Queen to her unknown successor:

> Dear Queenie,
> Many, many, many Congratulations, Sweet Briar May Queen 1962! I am so happy proud and excited for you, our fifty-sixth Queen of the May! This is such a thrilling event — how I wish I were back at Sweet Briar to see you now. This new position is one of the highest honors your classmates and schoolmates can bestow upon you — their loveliest and most charming representative! Congratulations!
> With this honor also comes a responsibility to those who have elected you — to exemplify the qualities in all you do whether at Sweet Briar or away. The title of Sweet Briar May Queen is now yours; not just 'til you graduate, nor just for May Day Weekend — but always.[23]

But, just a few years after the retiring Sweet Briar Queen wrote these words, women no longer enjoyed the tradition as they once had done. For example, the Wilson College May Queen of 1966 noted that while it was a special honor to be chosen, and that being a May Queen was fun, she felt uncomfortable with the focus on beauty, rather than brains and what one accomplished with them.[24] Other contemporaries agreed. Thus, for example, writing twelve years after her own 1965 coronation as R-MWC May Queen, Dr. Carolyn Wilkerson Bell, now the Sarah Duvall Adams Professor of English at that college, wrote:

> Although I was not aware of it at the time, the election of the May Queen and her court supplied a focus for the students' competitiveness about their appearance, and for their socially-induced narcissism, as well: since most of them applied eyeliner, slept on giant rollers, dieted furiously, or did

whatever the current fashion dictated they must in order to achieve the right look, they were not only choosing the fairest one among them; they were also vicariously rewarding their own efforts to deserve the label "beautiful." Certainly the May Queen was admired and envied, but she bore a tremendous responsibility, too, for she represented the ideal result of that adolescent and post-adolescent preoccupation with mirrors, clothes, makeup, and jewelry which even today afflicts many women, afflicts them because of society's constant commentary on their faces, bodies, and garments.[25]

By 1969, the next-to-the-last Queen elected, and the last to be presented in full regalia at Randolph-Macon Woman's College, felt that the tradition was ridiculous. "I certainly was not part of the beauty culture, was pre-occupied with my major, and, to make matters even more difficult, I was in competition with my roommate for the honor," she wrote. The last R-MWC Queen was elected amid contention about the tradition in 1970, and did not wear the customary long white gown. Several of her friends had husbands in Vietnam; her own fiancé was in training. She wrote: "How ridiculous would it have been for our May Court to have proceeded in full-length gowns in courtly, archaic procession while our contemporaries were rebelling on campuses all over America and our classmates' loved ones were fighting in Viet Nam?"[26]

By the mid-to-late sixties, the May Queen no longer wanted to sit passively on a pedestal nor did she want her whole life to be dominated by the pursuit, or the loss, of physical beauty. Twelve years after her coronation, Carolyn Wilkerson Bell expressed her frustration and anger at *still* being identified as a May Queen by friends, acquaintances, and students, even after she had achieved much more significant milestones in life: "I am angry," she wrote," angry that. By ... countless [people] I have been valued so highly and honored so memorably for the ephemeral look of my face at twenty-one.[27]

Bell further argues that the beauty pageant aspect of the southern colleges' May Day was something that both subverted and supported the prevailing gender ideology of the period and of the region. It subverted the gender ideology by affirming that intellectual women could be popular and physically attractive; it supported that ideology by confirming that "beauty — physical attractiveness leading inexorably to marriage and domesticity — was a southern white woman's most important attribute and thus should be the goal of her striving." Her experience of the pageant was that it created divisive competition among the women for the prize of nomination to the May Court since, "as one alumna put it, all students 'may never have achieved the title but [all] were taught by society to aspire to it.'" Bell argues that the parietal rules and customs at R-WMC (and other Southern colleges) as well as the cultural emphasis on beauty and social skills — including May Court — worked to reinforce the objectification and subordination of women.[28]

By the end of the 1960s, the May Queen was tottering on her throne: as we will see in Chapter 16, the Vietnam War protests, the women's liberation movement, the black power movement, and the May 4, 1970 killings of four students on the campus of Kent State University by the National Guard after a protest of the U.S. invasion of Cambodia would finish off the celebration at most colleges.

16. The May Queen Unthroned

A Student Debate Over Whether to Continue with Meredith College's Springs [May Day] Court

"I think the presentation of the court with the dancing, singing, and May Pole is quite out of date and unnecessary. I also think it reduces the role of women that Meredith [College] is supposedly trying to produce."

"I think it would be taking away part of the uniqueness of Meredith itself to do away with, or even lessen the significance and excitement of Springs Court. I really feel a minority is being catered to if Springs Court is abolished."
— Two Student Comments, "A Student Questionnaire on Whether to Maintain Springs Court (May Day)," Meredith College, 1975[1]

The May Day festival and the crowning of the May Queen died at different times and with greater or lesser controversy at all but eight of the 80 colleges and universities in the respondent group. Some colleges maintained the May Day festival for only a handful of years; others maintained it for decades. Certain characteristics of these colleges, as well as the profound social changes of the 1960s, contributed to supporting or undermining the festival.

Data problems blur some of the conclusions. In many cases the college archivists could not find information as to when the pageant or the coronation (the coronation frequently continued for decades after the big pageant folded) ceased to exist; in others they could see that pictures of the pageant or the coronation were in one yearbook but not the subsequent one, thus providing an endpoint; in a few cases there was sufficient controversy or dismay over losing either the pageant or the crowning that they could provide additional documentation surrounding the demise of May Day.

Despite these data issues, Table 2 shows that while 23 of the 80 respondent colleges ceased crowning a May Queen in the fifty-year period between 1900 and 1950, 40 of them, or 50 percent of the total, canceled the festivities in the 1960s and 1970s; indeed, 24 colleges held their last May Day in just the four springs of 1967 to 1970, inclusive.

Table 2. Colleges That Ceased Crowning the May Queen

1900 to 1920	3
1921 to 1930	8
1931 to 1940	7
1941 to 1950	5
1951 to 1960	7
1961 to 1970	34
1971 to 1980	6

1981 to 1990	1
1991 to 2000	2
Continues festivities	8
Total	**81***

Because this is not a robust data set, it is difficult to make firm, statistical conclusions; nevertheless, three general observations may be made as to why May Day survived longer at some institutions than others: the presence of a strong supporter (advocate); the number of students (size); and the absence of men (gender).

Anecdotal information suggests that the maintenance or discontinuance of May Day and, in particular, the elaborate pageant, often depended for continuity of leadership on the presence of a May Day advocate — whether the college's president, the dean of women, or the head of the Physical Education department. At Earlham College, for example, Professor Edwin Trueblood first experienced May Day as a student in 1888, began directing the Elizabethan pageant in 1906, and continued as its director throughout his career as president until his retirement. In 1941 he was named director emeritus of the festival. His long-time assistant, Clara Comstock, the head of the physical education department, then succeeded him as director.

There are numerous other examples of long-lived enthusiastic supporters of the May Day tradition. For example, May Day at the University of Maryland was instituted in 1923 by Adele Stamp, dean of women, and continued with her enthusiastic support until one year after her retirement in 1960. The loss of the Dean's guidance, as well as controversy over how to choose the Queen, were the two factors cited in the discontinuance of the festival.

In yet another example, the change in the presidency — as well as sheer exhaustion — killed both the pageant and the crowning at Skidmore College after its 1957 production of a pageant honoring the departing college president's thirty-second and final May Day. The thirteen-scene play began with Lucy Skidmore's birth and her life as connected to the Civil War and other major events in history, depicted the founding of the college, and culminated in two final scenes honoring the retiring president. One professor "recalled that the effort in 1957 simply exhausted the community and, aware that they could never top that memorable performance, she reported, 'We just threw in the towel.'"[2]

While the presence of an advocate was certainly helpful, the size of the student body also appears to have made a big difference in how long May Day was continued: at smaller institutions the ties between students and faculty are presumed to have been stronger, and it was more meaningful to the participants to maintain the communal holiday. It is often true that smaller, private Eastern colleges often have prettier campuses than the large, land-grant universities of the Midwest and West, and the landscape may have played a small role in the continuation of the festivity. In her study of Bryn Mawr's numerous traditions, Virginia Briscoe also suggests that the space in which the event takes place has an effect on the quality and tone of the event: an athletic stadium versus a bosky glen or the chapel steps, for example, each venue reflecting a different value image. Bryn Mawr's lush and romantic campus is more conducive to a celebration of spring and femininity than the far-flung, utilitarian buildings and flat, straight sidewalks of a large agricultural school.[3]

Thus, an examination of the duration of the coronation ceremony by current undergrad-

---

*Wells College, a women's college that just recently began admitting men, is counted twice: it discontinued the May Day festivities in 1967 after 46 years of observances, but reinstated them in 1986 and still continues them.

"*Queen rose of the rosebud garden of girls*" *(Tennyson)—the Wilson College May Queen of 1928. (Photograph courtesy C. Elizabeth Boyd '33 Archives, Hankey Center, Wilson College.)*

uate enrollment figures (a far-from-ideal measure since many of these institutions had significant increases in enrollment as the century wore on) shows that, in general, smaller colleges maintained the custom longer than did large universities. Of the 72 institutions that ceased celebrating May Day, 33 have current enrollment (ca. 2006) of 2,000 or fewer, and these celebrated the festival on average for 54 years, with a range of 26 to 89 years. By contrast, there are 21 institutions with current enrollment of more than 10,000 undergraduates, and their average celebration lasted for 30 years, with a much-wider range of duration from 3 to 70 years. All of the colleges that still celebrate May Day have a current enrollment of 2,400 or fewer students, and, using the year 2006 as an "end-date," these eight colleges have celebrated May Day for an average of 96 years, with a range of 82 to 107 years—a formidable tradition.

Table 3 Duration of Ceremony According to Enrollment

Current Enrollment	Number of Respondents	Average Duration of May Day Festival	Range of Duration
Fewer than 1,000	14	54 years	26 to 89 years
1,000 to 2,000	19	52 years	12 to 119 years
2,001 to 10,000	17	44 years	3 to 67 years
More than 10,000	21*	30 years	3 to 70 years
Total	71		

Thus for example, while the Scripps College librarian speculated that the demise of Scripps' May Day could be attributed in part to the Vietnam War, which made the festival seem irrelevant and superficial, other factors included "a change in curriculum at Scripps which de-emphasized the bonding experience of all freshmen; a shift in faculty-staff attitudes/lifestyles away from their nurturing role in the community; and an increase in the student body from 250 to nearly 400."[4]

In another example, the current coordinator of the Grove City College May Day and Parents' Day weekend attributes the college's small size as well as the long tenures of former coordinators as reasons for the longevity of the May Day tradition. One coordinator held the post for 40 years, her successor held it for approximately 30 years, and the current coordina-

*University of Charleston did not supply a beginning date for the tradition, so it is excluded from this analysis.

tor has served since 1999. The first two coordinators were faculty in the Physical Education (PE) department, and all girls taking PE were required to participate in the dance portions of the pageant. A final reason for this college's maintenance of the tradition is its conservative, religion-grounded ethos; as of 2005, the girls still live under parietal rules, and all fraternities and sororities are located on campus.[5]

The third general observation is that the presence of men, or the arrival of men on a formerly all-women's campus, caused the coronation to vanish. At large, co-ed universities it was sometimes the case that the girls' event was overshadowed and eventually taken over by the focus on men's athletics, particularly on football and its related activities. The concept of an annual alumni reunion — "Homecoming" — tied to an important fall football game began in the 1910 to 1925 period, the time frame, in fact, when many May Day festivals were also inaugurated. The concept of Homecoming officially began at the University of Missouri in 1911, an event that the university claims formed a model for other universities. Homecoming events typically included a parade, the football game against the traditional school rival, a dinner-dance, song or house-decoration competitions among the fraternity and sorority houses, and, frequently, the selection and crowning of the Homecoming King and Queen. Homecoming weekend was often the biggest social event of the fall school calendar, and formed a counterpoise not to the girls' May Day festival, but to a coeducational spring carnival. As the men's intercollegiate sports became more important, the women's traditions and activities seem to have diminished, as theorized by Virginia Briscoe. The data confirm her theory that, regardless of the size of the college, coeducational settings tend to foster rowdier, less sentimental traditions than those that appear at women's colleges. "When the opposite sex is present, and actively engaged in some aspect of the event, there is more spontaneity and less structure, and in co-educational colleges the events more closely resemble those at men's colleges than at women's." Briscoe concluded that "[t]he presence of traditions at women's colleges, then, cannot be attributed simply to a greater commitment to education, but rather to the dynamics of women in groups."[6]

Twenty-five institutions in the respondent group are still women's colleges, or admit only a few men,* and five of these still celebrate May Day, and have done so for almost 100 years, on average. At the remaining 20 women's colleges, the average duration of the tradition was 56 years, with a range of 26 to 89 years. By contrast, only three of the 55 coeducational colleges still celebrate May Day; of the 52 remaining respondents (tradition start date unavailable for one respondent), the average duration of the tradition was only 38 years with a range of 3 to 119 years. It is apparent that college women find it easier and more meaningful to maintain their own traditions in the absence of the opposite gender.

At several formerly all-women's colleges, the appearance of men quickly threatened May Day. Elmira College's discontinuance of May Day in 1967 was attributed to the anticipated advent of the men in 1969 as well as to war protests. The Valdosta State University historian noted in 2001,

> "The coming of men to campus [in 1950; prior to this event the institution was called the Georgia State Women's College] made immediate and lasting changes at Valdosta State. The elaborate costumed festivals came to an end early in the 1950s with more co-ed events taking their place. Dances and beauty contests took the place of the May queens and Christmas festivals. Within a few years, most of the extracurricular activities were led by men. In fact, by 1956, men on campus outnum-

---

*Wells College, one of the colleges that still celebrates May Day, began admitting men in the fall of 2005; the extent to which this will impact the women's traditions is unknown.

bered the women. Greek organizations were formed, with fraternities leading the way, and inter-collegiate athletics became a part of campus life when the Rebels, an all-male basketball team, was formed.[7]

The historian speculates that since May Day already had the key elements of beauty pageant activities, fraternity activities, and sports, it was able to last a little longer than the college's other annual tradition: the old English Christmas festival.

While these three factors — size, gender and advocacy — could affect the existence of May Day at any point in the century, several more specific reasons for dethroning the May Queen emerged in the mid-to late-1960s. The sixties were a decade of rapid and profound change: at the beginning of the decade, college women still lived under parietal hours and, in some schools, were forbidden to wear trousers or shorts on the street. By 1969, students were calling policemen "pigs," breaking into the president's office, and reveling in discarding the standards and traditions of the past. Thus, for many students, the election and crowning of the May Queen had just become too old-fashioned. At Newcomb College, for example, the festival ceased in 1962 at the request of the students. Several years later the Dean wrote to an alumna,

> Student interest in the event had steadily diminished for several years until the point was reached that it seemed useless to continue a ceremony which had lost meaning for the participants. I cannot tell you how much I personally regret the situation, but at the same time I, and other members of the Faculty, could not bear longer to witness a performance which had become a mockery of a fine tradition. It is my earnest hope that this tradition may be revived and restored to its rightful place in Newcomb's lore, but it is not something I wish to force on the student body. Please be assured, however, that we are attempting to accomplish this and through quiet persuasion.[8]

"Quiet persuasion" was ineffective; Newcomb's May Day festival was not revived.

At Skidmore College, while the change in presidency and community exhaustion caused by the 1957 pageant were two reasons to end May Day, the students also had tired of the event. Even by the early-1950s, some students were less interested in watching their classmates crown the Queen and more interested in having weekends free to spend at nearby men's colleges. The college historian writes that "[b]y the mid–1950's, the Skidmore *News* was asking, 'Is Tradition a Burden?' and noting that Founder's Weekend, as the festival was now called, was competing with house party weekends at 'various Ivy League institutions.'"[9]

As the sixties progressed, May Day became controversial and even acrimonious: May Day was perceived to be too "white" for students of color to participate in, and indeed it was, in part because not many black women were admitted to colleges until the second half of the century. I have in fact identified only four African American May Queens. In 1954 a young African American woman from Georgia, "the first of her race to be so honored," was crowned May Queen at Case Western Reserve University, possibly making her the first so-crowned in the nation. The article that announced her coronation added that "The queen ... is selected on the basis of scholarship, leadership and beauty."[10] In 1967, the Duke University women elected their first African American May Queen — the young woman was also the first black woman to attend the university — while the last two May Queens of Berea College, those of 1973 and 1974, were African American. In addition, there was one Korean-born Queen at the College of Wooster.

The two most frequently cited reasons for canceling May Day in the Sixties and Seventies were, however, the feeling that it was inappropriate to celebrate during the Vietnam War and the increasingly strongly held feeling that beauty pageants and their ilk were demeaning to women. In 1972 at Wellesley College, for example, there were two different protests of the college's May Day hoop-rolling tradition: one a demonstration of twelve students lying on the ground near the finishing line (the chapel) with crosses above their heads symbolizing those who had died in Vietnam. The second was two seniors who carried signs that read "Hoop-rolling Is a Sexist Tradition" and "Stop Running." Neither protest affected that year's hoop-rolling race, although 1972 did mark the first time the winner was thrown into the lake along with the now-traditional male imposter, indicating the relative decline in the perceived importance of the role.[11] After the Kent State Massacre of May 4, 1970, in which four students protesting the U.S. invasion of Cambodia were shot and killed by the National Guard, many colleges changed their calendars, shortening the spring term so that students were either not on campus or were too busy with final exams to stage either a protest or a festival.

May Day's emphasis on beauty created tension at some colleges, mirroring the 1968 drama about the "sexploitation" of the Miss American contest. Carolyn Wilkerson Bell argues that at Randolph-Macon Woman's College, a college founded on the premise that a woman's education, while equal to that of a man's, should preserve her charm and grace, the tensions that this emphasis created led to a parallel tradition from at least 1943 on of May Day parodies, known as the "DisMay Court." These spoofs sometimes featured male faculty dressed as students competing for the honor using cross-dressing to parody the physicality and the conventions of gender.[12] However, DisMay presentations did not always mock the stereotypes; they were supported in, for example, a 1943 parody of "As Time Goes By" that portrayed the R-MWC Queen lamenting that she was not engaged by Graduation and May Day: "the fundamental things in life have passed me by."[13]

While the beauty pageant aspect of R-MWC's May Day created tension among the students, the celebration actually ended in acrimony and controversy more focused around the Vietnam War and the issues of racial integration. Thus, as Bell relates, in the spring of 1970 the Randolph-Macon Woman's College Queen and her court were elected as usual; however, after the election, a dozen court nominees announced that they had allowed their names to be placed in nomination with the "understanding that if they were elected, they would withdraw, would try to persuade the rest of the court to withdraw with them, and would make a collective public statement about their actions." They apparently felt that this group action would make a more public statement than their individual protests. Bell writes that "[s]everal of the nominated students who secretly planned to withdraw had spoken out the year before in behalf of African American employees, and one, Dianne Oliphant '72, was an African American student who had been elected to the previous year's May court, the first and only black student to be so honored."[14]

Four of the dissident nominees were indeed elected, spoke out against the event, and resigned from the court, citing concerns about the divisiveness of beauty competitions and the inappropriateness of the event during wartime. Bell reports that the ensuing debate divided the student body. As a result, there was no formal presentation of the Queen in 1970, though the rest of the weekend's events occurred as planned. The festival ceased after that date. It is interesting to note, however, that by 1984, some of these issues had been forgotten; a student paper written at that time and formerly published on the college's Web site suggests (inaccurately) that the reason for the holiday's discontinuance was the combination of too many activities during that weekend and a change in the academic calendar that inhibited a girl's social life: "After all, nobody wanted to host a date during exams."[15]

Controversy over the festival raged at Meredith College as well where, by 1972, the event was called Springs Court, and was held on Parents' Weekend. A Queen, a senior, was still crowned. In 1975, however, a change in the academic calendar, moving Parents' Weekend from May to mid–April, meant that the dance classes were not ready to perform, and the weather was felt to be unreliable. While organizers still planned to present the Queen and her court at the parents' banquet, they sent out a questionnaire to the students requesting their input into "the continuation and relevance of such a tradition on the campus of a women's college in the 1970's." 173 respondents voted yes; 33 voted no. The "yes" respondents were almost equally divided, however, as to whether to have a traditional May Day celebration with all students participating in the maypole dancing, one in which the modern dance classes performed after the crowning, or a simpler event in which the Queen was presented at the parents' banquet. Respondent comments were illuminating: most called for the retention of tradition, while a few added that the choice of the Queen should be made on the basis of service rather than beauty. It is apparent from the comments that a small but vocal minority of feminists on the Student Council was arguing against the tradition that was, in fact, generally supported, or at least tolerated, by the majority. Some of the more extreme responses to the poll included those cited in the epigraph to this chapter. However, despite the support of the polls, and over the subsequent objections of a student who pointed out that this support should not be ignored, the Student Life Committee voted to end Springs Court in the fall of 1975.[16]

As it initiated the first college May Day, it may be appropriate to detail the demise of the last of the big college pageants and coronations: that held every four years at Earlham College from 1875 to 1993. Here we see combined faculty fatigue, a lack of student interest and perceptions of social inappropriateness. From the 1950s on, the nationally acknowledged success of this massive Elizabethan pageant — costuming, rehearsals, assigning parts and other details — was achieved only with increasing effort, much of it provided by the unpaid labor of faculty wives. In the mid-fifties there was discussion about whether to continue with the festival, but the faculty and most students were still enthusiastic about continuing. By the late 1960s, however, campus activists were openly questioning the continuation of the tradition.

In 1969, Earlham College's black students preferred assimilation and apparently participated in May Day, although there were Vietnam War protestors who criticized it. An ad in the school paper asked, "'How can you hear madrigals on Saturday and maim children on Sunday?'" By the 1973 celebration, however, a *New York Times* article cited the wife of the President of the college who noted that in 1969 and 1965, respectively, faculty had wondered if the event could continue: "'But people are beginning to have fun again,'" she added hopefully. More gloomily, the president noted that a change in faculty-student relationships, with each group growing more aloof, was adversely affecting the long-standing Quaker sense of community at the college, causing May Day to be more difficult to maintain.[17]

In 1973 nearly all of Earlham's black students, who made up about 6 percent of the college's 1,200 students, pointedly shunned the May Day festivities, contending that the Old English theme of a village's revelry during a visit by Queen Elizabeth was a purely white cultural activity. They suggested a multicultural medieval day as an alternative. There were white students, too, who, as the *New York Times* reported, "complained that they had been coerced into participating, and started planning a Prune Day — with a prune Queen, class prunes, and edible prunes 'hopefully coming in from all over the world'" in satiric retaliation. The same article noted approvingly, however, that the

> mock-Elizabethan pageantry, in a day of declining student participation in almost all campus activities [elsewhere], was an affirmation of a much-desired but fast-disappearing quality that students can now seem to find only at the smallest colleges — a sense of community. That Quaker phrase is used here to mean whole-hearted, mutual involvement within the student body."[18]

Despite this endorsement, however, the celebration of 1973 was marred and the college historian notes that there was notable alienation: one opponent sprinkled thumbtacks around the maypoles for the benefit of the barefooted dancers.* He continues:

> "[B]y 1981, criticism had changed from focusing on the event as a waste of time to emphasizing what critics saw as its exclusive aspects.... By the 1989 observance, the whole multicultural arsenal of analysis was being turned on May Day. It was a "disgusting display of status" that created "a stratification between classes." Its pageantry was a "mockery of the values we try to achieve," while the roles contributed to the "stereotyping and degradation of persons."[19]

By 1993, the last time the event was held at Earlham College, a compromise was suggested of calling the event simply "May Day." While most participants took the traditional English roles, and the morris dances and maypole dances still took place, multi-cultural villages represented other cultures. The compromise was not successful. The loss of faculty wife labor, the change in political popularity and, finally a change in the academic calendar to move up graduation from June to May, had caused there to be, as the college historian concluded, "not enough May for May Day."[20]

The data show that May Day survived longest in colleges that were relatively small, generally all-women's, and frequently geographically isolated as well. In these institutions a springtide festival that is meaningful to a community's sense of history, as well as an individual's own participation in it, can survive longer. While Earlham College, for example, is a coeducational institution, it is located in a small town in Indiana. Furthermore, from inception it has prided itself on its Quaker sense of community. Earlham's longtime maintenance of Big May Day, held every four years from 1875 through 1993 (making it the last of the big pageants), is thus no surprise.

It is possible that the controversy over whether or not to abandon the old tradition proved more valuable to participants at the time than the sheer fact of May Day's existence or nonexistence. The last Randolph-Macon Woman's College Queen wrote later that the discussions prompted by her controversial 1970 election were "'one of the axes of change that propelled us into a more valuable assessment of who we are as women in relation to each other.'" This woman's grandmother had been the R-MWC May Queen of 1911 and was thrilled to share this honor with her granddaughter. "But it was a tradition 'borne out of another time and different circumstances,'" the latter wrote, "and its time to end had come."[21] While the May Queen was an important part of that college's history, she had no place in its future.

---

*Fearing another episode of sabotage, guards were placed around the maypoles on the night before May Day in 1977.

MAY DAY FESTIVALS OF TODAY

17. May Day as Labor Day, Loyalty Day, Law Day, Child Health Day, and Lei Day

> *The Worker's Maypole*
> World Workers, whatever may bind ye,
> This day let your work be undone:
> Cast the clouds of the winter behind ye,
> And come forth and be glad in the sun....
>
> Let the winds lift your banners from far lands
> With a message of strife and of hope:
> Raise the Maypole aloft with its garlands
> That gathers your cause in its scope....
> — Walter Crane, verses to accompany his drawing
> published in *Justice* on April 13, 1894

The May Day festivals of urban children and college girls flourished in a dream world apparently untouched by the sometimes violent worker demonstrations and marches that for more than 100 years have also been held on May First, as this day is celebrated as Labor Day in most countries save the United States. In response to the co-opting of this date by first the Marxists and then by the might of the former Soviet Union, in America we have also celebrated May First as Law Day and as Loyalty Day — both still official U.S. holidays — while the state of Hawaii and some cities that have large Hawaiian populations, such as Las Vegas, celebrate the day as Lei Day. Finally, for a brief time in the late 1920s and early 1930s, May First was also celebrated as Child Health Day. With only a handful of exceptions, however, neither the urban children's nor the college girls' May Day festivals acknowledged any of these alternative celebrations.

May Day as Labor Day

For many people, May Day conjures up images of worker strikes; mass demonstrations by students, nurses, and soldiers; and parades celebrating the armed might of the former USSR. The first of May has been celebrated as a day for workers in most of Europe since before the turn of the last century, and has been regarded with unease during that time in the United States, which celebrates Labor Day on the first Monday in September. Yet, while May Day is celebrated as Labor Day in many European countries, it is possible that many have forgotten that the original impetus for the holiday came from dramatic events that occurred in the U.S. in the 1880s.

17. May Day as Labor Day, Loyalty Day, Law Day, Child Health Day, and Lei Day

The last third of the nineteenth century saw the beginnings—often violent—of the union movement when men who worked twelve to eighteen hours a day, six days a week, for pitiful wages began to organize themselves in trade unions. In the spring of 1872, a young man named Peter McGuire and 100,000 workers went on strike and marched through the streets of New York City, demanding a decrease in the long working day. McGuire continued his organization work, and on September 5, 1882, the first official Labor Day parade was held in New York City. An elaborate and apparently orderly parade, "the German Bricklayers marched in their white aprons, with uplifted arms clasping white trowels with blue trim; the Newark Manufacturing Jewelers marched four abreast wearing derby hats and dark suits with boutonnieres, and bearing canes held against their shoulders." Workers carried banners that read: "Labor Creates All Wealth," and "Eight Hours for Work, Eight Hours for Rest, Eight Hours for Recreation!" The holiday caught on, and by 1894, thirty states had Labor Day holidays.[1]

On May 1, 1886, the American Federation of Labor declared a national strike to demand an eight-hour workday and 350,000 workers across the country responded. The city of Chicago was virtually paralyzed. On May 3, police fired randomly into crowds of striking workers, killing four and wounding many more. Then next day, when the police attempted to disperse a peaceful rally in Haymarket Square, a bomb was tossed in their midst, wounding nearly 70 officers and killing several of them. The police again fired randomly into the crowd and later arrested eight revolutionary labor leaders, seven of whom had not even been present at the time of the bombing. The "Chicago Eight" were tried purely on the basis of their political beliefs and all eight were sentenced to death: four were eventually executed.

The Workers' Maypole, by Walter Crane. This illustration and poem appeared in the 1894 issue of *Justice* and the May 1902 issue of *The Comrade*, an illustrated Socialist monthly. The workers, both men and women, dance around a maypole with streamers bearing slogans like "Eight hours a day" and "Leisure for all." (The Working Class Movement Library.)

News of the unfair trial galvanized labor groups around the world. In 1889, the Socialist International declared May 1 a day of worker demonstrations and rallies. In 1890 the leaders of the American Federation of Labor, headed by Samuel Gompers, organized a strike of the Carpenters' Union, in support of the eight-hour day. By 1891, the Socialist International added to the demand for the eight-hour day a general demand to improve working conditions. May Day demonstrations were increasingly becoming demonstrations of power, with open street-fighting with the police and military taking place in major cities. In Russia, Lenin and Engels supported the May Day demonstrations, calling them an example of class solidarity. Workers were called upon to support various slogans: "International Working Class Solidarity; Universal Suffrage; War Against War; Against Colonial Oppression; the Right to the Streets; Freeing of Political Prisoners; the Right to Political and Economic Organization of the Working Class."[2]

By the late 1880s, several U.S. states had named May First as Labor Day, even though others were celebrating it in September. Finally, in 1894, President Grover Cleveland signed an act declaring a national labor holiday on the first Monday in September, but demonstrations on May First in the U.S. continued in various locations for many years. Americans increasingly feared May First as a day of labor, Bolshevist, or Communist riots. In 1931, the editor of *Good Housekeeping Magazine* wrote: "In many countries—and in several cities of our own—May Day is a day of anxiety. There is a tightening of police belts as the men go out to patrol the streets, for on this day, the forces of [Bolshevik] disorder ... rises to haunt organized society with the specter of disaster."[3] He then urged all readers to join in the Child Health Day activities also planned for May First.

In an attempt to diffuse the Red threat, various U.S. constituencies lobbied successfully to name May First as, variously, Child Health Day, Loyalty Day, and Law Day. These new holidays had mixed success in their diverse goals. During the 1950s, for example, the huge Loyalty Day parade in New York City distracted attention away from the Communist Party march on the same day. By the mid–1960s, however, the association of such parades with support for the American war in Vietnam led to a drastic decline in public participation across the land.[4]

May First is still celebrated as Labor Day in many European countries, and May 1 of 2007 saw "hundreds of thousands" march in major U.S. cities in support of immigrant rights.[5] The holiday continues to evolve.

May Day as Loyalty Day

The origins of May Day as Loyalty Day are somewhat obscure. Loyalty Day appears to have developed as a direct weapon against the Communist threat, especially as it was expressed through not just worker strikes and parades, but parades of the military might of the former Soviet Union. One source states that Loyalty Day originally began as "Americanization Day" in 1921 to counter the Communists' May First celebration of the Russian Revolution. While occasional observances of Loyalty Day were held in the 1920s and 1930s, it was not until 1947 that the United States Veterans of Foreign Wars declared May Day as Loyalty Day. The Red Scare of the era led to enthusiastic support of the holiday by civic organizations, schools, churches, and the armed forces. Finally in 1958 Congress enacted Public Law 529 proclaiming Loyalty Day a permanent fixture on the nation's calendar. The still extant law requests the president to issue a proclamation calling on government officials to display the flag of the United States on all government buildings on Loyalty Day, and inviting the people of the

United States to observe Loyalty Day with appropriate ceremonies in schools and other suitable places.

While Loyalty Day was celebrated with parades, speeches, sermons on loyalty, and flag-waving during the 1950s, the ramifications of the unpopular Vietnam War seriously affected the popularity of this political holiday. While some scattered local celebrations are apparently still found today, the holiday, save for the president's annual proclamation, is essentially moribund.[6]

May Day as Law Day

In 1958, the American Bar Association urged President Dwight D. Eisenhower to institute Law Day on May 1. Like Loyalty day, Law Day was conceived of as an anticommunist cold war initiative. Its avowed purpose — both educational and patriotic — was "'to foster respect for law; to increase public understanding of the place of law in American life; to point up the contrast between freedom under law in the United States and governmental tyranny under Communism.'" In 1961 Congress formally designated May 1 as Law Day, and President John F. Kennedy asked all Americans to display the flag and observe the occasion with suitable ceremonies.[7]

Since the 1960s, however, observances of Law Day appear to be sponsored principally by state and local bar associations and schools that conduct lectures or educational programs on the rule of law in a constitutional democracy. In 2004, for example, the Mississippi Bar Association conducted a state-wide art contest for grades 1 through 12 on the theme of "In Pursuit of Peace," challenging students to consider "how our nation's system of government and its democratic ideals help to pursue and promote peace, both at home and abroad."[8]

May Day as Child Health Day

Since May Day for most Americans was a celebration of youth and community spirit, it was consequently a holiday to which it was easy to add other attributes. One example of this was the short-lived celebration of May Day as Child Health Day.

As health conditions for urban children at the turn of the century were deplorable at best and deadly at worst, one of the major goals of the Progressive movement was the reform of health-related conditions affecting urban children. Even after the passage of the Pure Food and Drug Act of 1906, community standards governing sanitation and tuberculin-free milk were lax or non-existent. Infant mortality was a serious problem, but reformers found it difficult to measure their progress because few cities kept birth records. The European relief work of World War I, and the shocking fact that one-third of the American men who were drafted had had to be rejected for health reasons, accelerated health reform movements, but the early organizations were weak and fragmented. In 1923, under the leadership of Herbert Hoover, the American Child Health Association was formed from an amalgamation of several relief agencies. One year later, the Association proclaimed that May Day would be known as Child Health Day. Within three years Child Health Day was being celebrated in every state plus the territory of Hawaii, and in 1928 President Coolidge made Child Health Day an official observance.[9]

The intense publicity given to the inauguration of Child Health Day revealed to the nation the shocking facts that 41 out of 86 larger cities surveyed had no full-time health official, that half the cities had no reliable child birth or mortality records, that vaccinations were required in only 37 cities, that pasteurization of milk was required in only 8 cities and that there was no health instruction in 21 cities. An editorialist for a fortnightly paper, *The Independent*, was impressed by the first announcement of May Day as a day devoted to child health. He wrote in April of 1924 that it was "a shock to our complacency" to read the grim facts about infant death rates, impurities in water and milk, and incompetent administration of public health. He further observed that he found the recent spate of "Days"—such as "Father's Day"—to be "duds," but nevertheless concluded his article in a burst of sentiment averring that he will attend the May Day event not just because the question of child health will benefit future citizens, but more particularly

> because of an old fashioned and frankly sentimental feeling we entertain toward children, that they are innocent and lovely beings ... that about them, trailing their clouds of glory, is really an intimation of immortality, a spiritual quality which we have lost; that, in short, of such is the Kingdom of heaven. Whether or not the May Day celebration results in great benefit to the children, it will make us adults, if we give our minds to it, better and kinder men and women.[10]

The American Child Health Association (ACHA) encouraged local women's clubs and health organizations in rural and urban communities to work both to improve local health conditions and to sponsor annual observances on May 1 as a way of educating the public to the importance of obtaining proper immunizations, of drinking milk only from tuberculin-tested cows, of sleeping in fresh air, of obtaining frequent physicals, and other health-related topics.

The connection of Child Health Day to May Day was a natural one, given that the vision that its founders had was of the child, "sound in body, mind, and spirit, expressing unconsciously in the freedom of play its physical and spiritual joy."[11] Its other connection was that the event—like the holiday—was perceived to be a community-based event, one that could galvanize local men's and women's clubs, churches, the Grange, Merchants' Associations, schools, doctors, elected officials, and other dignitaries to illustrate and address issues of importance to the local community.

In 1929, the association published a pamphlet that described a variety of plays, pageants, and other Child Health Day activities that a community could sponsor. One recommended May Day pageant was a fairly standard *Pageant of the Nations* featuring folk dances from all nations, the crowning of the Queen, and the winding of the maypole. This type of entertainment was particularly recommended for an urban festival, as children from many different schools could then present the dances of the different nations. Also recommended was a Robin Hood play, in which Robin chooses the May Queen from among the girls who, once again, perform the folk dances of many nations.

Other recommended entertainments could be so-called "health" plays that clearly were inspired by the precepts of the American Pageant Association. An example of such a play is *Baby's Godmothers*, in which the spirits of Purity, Air, Nourishment, Sleep, Knowledge and Love (clad according to aesthetic principles in, respectively, white, light blue, dark red, gray, green, and rose) instruct a young mother on how to care for baby and frighten away the Witch of Ill-Health. Another such recommended exercise was a play titled *The Road to Wellville*, in which children representing different countries would describe each country's achievements in the arena of child health: for example, the child representing Switzerland declares that "Sunlight and rest have cured many ills. Let the sun reach your skin and get your body well tanned. Open the windows in homes and schools so health-giving ultra-violet rays may enter." (Upon which other children demonstrate giving baby a sunbath, playing in the sun with very little on.) The pageant was to culminate with a child who represented the state that the play was given in, and who summarized that state's health-related strengths and weaknesses. After this entertainment, the participants conclude by singing the rousing song, "We're All Marching to Wellville," set to the tune of "Marching Through Georgia."[12]

The pamphlet also suggested a variety of parades and "health floats" that could be used in a May Day parade, such as "The May Queen Enthroned":

> The child taking this part [as Queen]] should personify health. She may be surrounded by a guard of honor composed of children who have been selected because they have no physical defects or have had all defects corrected and have shown a reasonable observance of health habits, together with good school records — or other agreed conditions. The Queen's costume may be of flowing white material, with the word "Health" either on her crown or on a colored sash across her breast. Streamers or garlands springing from the throne may be held by the guard of honor.[13]

Accompanying floats in this instructive parade demonstrated the benefits of fresh air or long hours of sleep or pure milk. The pamphlet writers suggested that as part of this May Day parade, for example, the local Dairymen's Association might sponsor a procession of tuberculin-tested cows, led by a boy in overalls. The cows were to bear placards reading "I have been tested," or "I give safe milk." Other parades, for example, that held in 1928 in Jefferson City, Missouri, featured children who had reached certain health standards. "Thirty floats and 150 cars carried the 1329 'six-point' children and 138 'nine-pointers,' children who had reached a certain standard of health."[14]

Child Health Day parades of this type were often sponsored by different local businesses, who were encouraged to create window displays and advertising that carried a health message. Thus, for example, in Oklahoma in 1928, there was a parade of children from five schools, each dressed in costume and carrying slogans to represent some health principle. That same year at a parade in Berea, Kentucky, the Berea Telephone Company "boasted of the [school] health nurse" and advocated health, happiness, and a high school, and incidentally, displayed a convenient telephone calling for a doctor in an emergency."[15]

Different types of festivities were recommended for small communities, rural counties, and cities. For example, rural celebrations tended to be less complex and the ACHA suggested that most appropriate activities would be a county play day, competitive health pageants at the county seat, special health conferences for babies and young children, health plays performed in the schools or playgrounds, or a child health parade with floats. An appropriate song for rural children might include the inspiring ditty written for a May Day Celebration for rural schools and communities in West Virginia in 1928: "Let Every Family Own a Cow," sung to the tune of "Yankee Doodle."[16]

Child Health Day could also be celebrated by a "Play Day on May Day"— a day of games and competitions in basketball, volleyball, relay races and other sports. It was felt that rather than contributing to inter-school rivalry, a well-organized Play Day could help young people from different schools mingle, thereby building community spirit.[17]

By May of 1929, the ACHA reported that every state, backed by community organizations, schools and national organizations, had plans for some type of celebration that would lead to improved health for children.[18] Each of the subsequent years featured a different health-related theme: for example, recognizing that the current focus on team sports was directed to the star athletes and not following out "its original idea of building sound bodies for all children and all young people, whether in school or in college," the theme of May Day of 1929 was a call to return to the principles of earlier days. The slogans for the year were "A Team for Everyone and Everyone on a Team," and "Playing for the Sake of the Game Rather Than for the Sake of a Particular School or a Particular Team."[19]

While Child Health Day was primarily a community-based celebration, at least one college observed the day. In 1943, Berea College's May Day program was "May day — health day; Young America at Play." The phrase, "Oh America, because you build for mankind, we build for you," appeared twice on the program, which was more devoted to physical education demonstrations than in prior years' performances, though there was still the crowning of the Queen and a few folk dances.

The American Child Health Association was successful in its efforts to improve children's hygiene and health instruction. Within a few years of its inception, the Girl Scouts, Boy Scouts, and other child welfare organizations were sponsoring health educational programs. Smallpox and diphtheria were conquered, unsafe milk was no longer the chief cause of deaths among infants, and the overall infant mortality rate had declined by 70 percent. In 1935 the ACHA turned its work over to state and local health officials and disbanded.[20] However, National Child Health Day was still celebrated on May 1 every year until 1960, when it was moved to the first Monday in October. Over the years, the topics for National Child Health Day have run the gamut from prenatal care to adolescent health issues, and have included the effects of day care on child development, strategies to prevent childhood injury, and the importance of immunization.

May Day as Lei Day

In the late 1920s the poet Don Blandings observed that his beloved Hawaiian people had abandoned the custom of giving leis (garlands of flowers) to each other in favor of giving them to the tourists that flocked to the island. Blanding suggested that as part of an annual celebration to honor their Hawaiian traditions, the people should place the garlands around their own necks and foreheads. A local columnist picked up the idea and suggested that the appropriate day would be May Day, a day not only traditionally connected with flowers, but also a time of year at which the lei-making flowers in Hawaii are at their peak. A local musician wrote the lyrics and tune to the famous song, "May Day is Lei Day in Hawai'i," and the first Lei Day was celebrated quietly in downtown Honolulu in 1927. The first Queen was elected in 1928.

Today, many schools, churches, and communities in Hawaii gather on Lei Day to celebrate with hula dancing, the election of a Queen and/or King, feasting, lei-making competitions, and other events. (Interestingly, in several accounts of local festivals, the role of Queen rotates among a young girl, a mature woman, and an older woman, so that on at least one occasion the new Queen was crowned by her granddaughter, the retiring Queen.) The Honolulu Department of Parks and Recreation sponsors one of the largest festivals, whose theme is that of unique leis each representing the eight islands that form the state of Hawaii. A Queen is selected along with eight Princesses who represent the eight islands.

Lei Day in general has only a tenuous connection with the English May Day — the emphasis is on the leis, the celebration of Hawaiian culture, and the crowning of the Queen and King and their court. One Web site, however, shows photographs of the teachers of an elementary school performing the maypole dance in 1983 and again 1989: "[a] beautiful weaving of love and *aloha* with the song *Nani Wale Na Pua*." Clad in traditional muumuus, the dancers appear to be incorporating some movements of the hula into the maypole dance.[21]

Cinco de Mayo

Not every holiday in early May has an English May Day connection. Some western states celebrate the Mexican holiday of Cinco de Mayo (the Fifth of May). Not the Mexican Independence Day (which is September 16), Cinco de Mayo commemorates the victory of the Mexicans over the French army at the battle of Puebla in 1862. In Mexico it is considered a regional holiday, celebrated most vigorously in the state of Puebla. Celebrating Cinco de Mayo has becoming increasingly popular along the border of the U.S. and Mexico, and in those parts of the U.S. that have a high population of people with a Mexican heritage. The holiday celebrates Mexican food, music, dance, costumes, and customs, and, apart from being held in early May, has (as yet) no stated or hidden connection to the English May Day.

18. Celebrating an Old English May Day Today

> *The Crowner's Speech*
> Kind friends, we have met this lovely day,
> To welcome again the spring.
> The birds are singing a joyous lay,
> And the trees their fragrance bring.
> Nature has on her robe of green,
> She smiles all through the day.
> The pretty blossoms with the buds between,
> Now blush in their old-fashioned way.
> The fairies are calling for someone to reign,
> Over all of the springtime array.
> So we must now hasten our laurels to gain,
> And crown — — — our Queen of May.
> — Bishop Henry C. Sorensen, ca. late 1930s, Mendon, Utah[1]

The elaborate May Day pageant has vanished, and the May Queen has retired, at least in most communities. But an old English May Day is far from dead. Rather than being produced as a major pageant by a large institution, the festival now tends to be celebrated in the United States by small groups of people in a more spontaneous way, in a fashion perhaps closer to that of 1830 than that of 1930. Today, May Day is celebrated by a handful of colleges that seem to share certain characteristics, by some elementary and high schools, by Pagans and Wiccans, by folk dancers and Revelers, and, in a few, relatively rare cases, by small communities.

Regardless of the form or content of the festivities, these diverse groups appear to share a common appreciation of the value of tradition. Participants, organizers and spectators speak about how pleasant — indeed, how moving — it is to engage in an annual observance with some components that change every year and some that remain the same. Colleges and schools with their transient, "sojourner" populations are consciously aware of the value of the May Day tradition in binding students to the institution's community and to the circle of alumnae or alumni. For these communities, ever-changing in their constituency, the celebration is often a rite of passage, as one age-group moves up through or out of the community. Folk dancers and Revelers similarly enjoy the annual tradition, and derive great pleasure from their own performances. And Pagans and Wiccans embrace May Day as an expression of personal faith, even as the components of the tradition varies from circle to circle.

Colleges That Celebrate May Day Today

Eight of the 80 respondent colleges celebrate May Day in some fashion today, and these eight have certain similarities: all but three are women's colleges, all are small (ranging from 300 to 1,300 students), and most are located in small towns. Seven of the eight colleges crown a Queen and two of the coed colleges also crown a King; three still showcase the maypole dance; and at most of them some portion of the day is given over to traditional spring fling or fun-fest activities such as face-painting, ice-cream sundae making, games, movies, and so on. The festival thus celebrates the end of the school year, the welcome arrival of spring, and a sense of shared community among students, faculty, and alumnae or alumni.

In alphabetical order, then, Bluffton University, founded by the General Conference of the Mennonite Church in 1899 and located in the small town of Bluffton, Ohio, began celebrating May Day in 1910. The coeducational university is still affiliated with the Mennonite Church and offers a faith-based educational experience. Each year eight first-year men and eight first-year women are chosen from the approximately 1,100 students to dance around the maypole in colorful, "Germanic" costumes (pale blue and pink lederhosen or skirts — one might well argue that this college's traditions are more German than English). A King and Queen are elected, and there are games, sports, and fun-fair events. As the university's Web site notes, the celebration "represents the end of a school year for students, the beginning of a new chapter for seniors and the remembrance of times past for alumni. The tradition weaves together past, present and future around the May Pole in a never-ending circle."[2]

Brenau University in Gainsville, Georgia, was established in 1878 as the Georgia Baptist Female Seminary; its Women's College currently enrolls approximately 600 students. May Day began in the 1920s as a Spring Festival highlighting the various states from which the students were drawn. Gradually the event added a Queen, a Prince, a Princess and the winding of the maypole as well as a pageant. The students still vote on the Queen and court members; on one recent occasion one of the male students enrolled in the coed weekend program was voted May Prince. May Day used to be held on the first weekend of May, but after Brenau changed to the semester system, it was moved to April so it would not conflict with graduation.

As noted earlier, Bryn Mawr College, a women's college with 1,200 students located near Philadelphia, Pennsylvania, first celebrated its elaborate and famous Elizabethan May Day in the spring of 1900 and then every few years thereafter until 1936. While a Little May Day (celebrated with more informal festivities that still included traditional songs and the maypole dance) continued to be held each year for the next twenty years, it was not until the 1970s that May Day became again a more elaborate function. For example, May Day 2002 was celebrated with events that began at 5:45 in the morning with the sophomores distributing May Baskets to the seniors and awakening them with the song attributed to Henry VIII, "The Hunt is Up." (The hunt is up, the hunt is up, / And it is well nigh day, / And Harry our king, is gone a-hunting / To bring his deer to bay!) Other events throughout the day until midnight included (in part) the singing of the Magdalen Hymn to the sun from the top of Rockefeller Tower (the hymn had been sent to Bryn Mawr in 1903 from Magdalen College, Oxford), a Greek play, a strawberry breakfast, morris dancing, Scottish dancing, hair-braiding, maypole dancing, the crowning of two May Queens and their delivery of humorous speeches, the senior hoop race, various musical performances, and student glee clubs singing funny songs. The festival is organized by the two, annually elected Traditions Mistresses.

Each year the participating students race to weave the five maypoles: one for each class

"Hey hey, ho ho, the patriarchy has got to go!" The "May Hole" Celebration at Bryn Mawr College, 2006. This tradition was created by the women sometime after the mid–1980s and is meant to symbolize how they assist each other to "rise above the bonds of the patriarchy." (Photograph credit: Paola Rogueras. Bryn Mawr College Library.)

plus one for the graduate students. "The seniors pretty much win every year," observes a former Traditions Mistress on her Web site, "but it is suspected that their pole is fatter, thus using up the ribbon more quickly." A modern contribution to the day is the May Hole dance (created sometime in the 1980s), as described by this same individual:

> A feminist rebuttal to the phallocentric [sic— see Chapter 1] Maypole, the May Hole centers around the ability to women to help each other rise above the bonds of the patriarchy. To begin, everyone participating is bound together in a big circle using toilet paper, which represents the bonds of the patriarchy. One woman begins to free people, and they begin to free more people, soon everyone is free and chanting "Hey, hey, ho, ho, the patriarchy has got to go!" Once everyone is free, they rush to a [silk] parachute in the center of the circle and grab hold of it. When it is stretched open, there are hundreds of flower petals in the center of it, which then fly over the crowd. There is usually much dancing and celebrating. It's definitely something that's ONLY done at Bryn Mawr.[3]

As the evening progresses, the movie *The Philadelphia Story*, starring Bryn Mawr alumna Katharine Hepburn, is shown. The college's May Day traditionally concludes with a final Step Sing called "Giving Up the Steps," at which each class moves up to a new position on the steps of the library as the seniors, still singing their class song, march away from the steps and, symbolically, away from the college. The Traditions Mistress cited above observes that this last Step Sing is very emotional:

> This moment is impossible to describe. It is an incredible clash of emotion with love for the seniors and the realization that they will soon be gone and the excitement of the juniors in assuming the

senior role.... All four [major Bryn Mawr] traditions (Parade Night, Lantern Night, Hell Week, and May Day) ultimately culminate in this moment. It is the passing of time and the handing of the torch from one group of leaders to another. The emotions that are felt during it exemplify the highs and lows that one experiences in all of life. It is the birth of something new and the death of something old, extreme joy and extreme pain, the making and the loss of friends, but ultimately, the understanding that life goes on."[4]

Converse College, a college of 500 women located in Spartanburg, South Carolina, began celebrating its May Day in 1910, and the college still honors the May Queen and her Court. The event focuses on celebrating scholarship, leadership, and service to the college. The students select four girls each from the freshmen, sophomore, and junior classes and five from the senior class. The Queen is then chosen from the five women elected from the senior class.

The Converse May Day celebration begins after the general campus awards ceremony. The girls, dressed in their Sunday best, are escorted to the outdoor amphitheater by their fathers or a significant older male member of their family. Something is read about each girl in the Court and her contribution to the college, and the President of the college crowns the Queen with a crown that has been used for decades. The event is brief, and attended mostly by the families of the girls.

Coeducational Grove City College, in northwestern Pennsylvania, began celebrating May Day in 1916. As early as 1925, it began the tradition of the Returning Queens: every four years all former May Queens are invited to return to campus to be treated as "Queen for a day," and to walk in the procession. In 2004, 19 former Queens, the oldest from 1938, returned out of 67 invitations sent.

Grove City College still celebrates the coronation of the May Queen as part of Parent's Weekend, yet now the term Spring Queen is used because the event is not always in May. While not every girl is interested in being a Queen, the role is generally considered an honor and only a conflict with another very significant activity would prevent her from accepting it. The 2004 Queen, for example, passed up a chance to compete at a national water polo tournament in order to participate in May Day. And not everyone who would like to dance may; the dance coordinators must turn away all but about 80 dancers who participate in the student-choreographed dances.

The custom of electing a Grove City College Spring King started in the mid–1970s as a joke, but in 2002 the Chair of Parents' Weekend decided to formalize the role. The students nominate six senior men, and their photographs are mounted on collection jars for the charity of their choice. The winner of the most donations, who will be named Spring King, also presents the contents of the other men's jars to his charity. Dressed in formal gowns, the Court appears at the Friday night band concert, and when the King's name is announced, the Queen drapes a sash with the words "Spring King" over his shoulders.

Simmons College, a women's college of 1,300 students located in Boston, Massachusetts, first celebrated May Day in 1912 when the sophomores hung May baskets on the doors of the seniors. While the May Queen ceased to be elected in the 1970s, Simmons' sophomores still celebrate May Day in honor of the seniors. The event consists of the maypole dance, the ceremonial planting of a class tree or flower, and the popular strawberry shortcake breakfast.

Wells College, a women's college of 430 students located in Aurora, New York, celebrated its first May Day in 1922. In the 1950's May Day became encompassed with Father's Day weekend and was held on Sunday afternoon, but by 1960, the event moved back to Sunday, and folk dances and madrigals replaced the freshman play. Controversy about May Day began in 1963 and the student body voted whether or not to maintain the tradition: one-half voted yes, one-quarter no, and the remainder were indifferent. While the event lived on during Father's Day weekend for a few years, no May Queen was elected in 1967, and the event disappeared from the college calendar for the next decade.

However, as the college historian observed, with the "non-observance of May Day and the lack of activities to enjoy during the late seventies, students complained about nothing to do on campus." The event was revived in 1979 as students performed literary and music programs with nature and springtime themes. In 1986, May Day reappeared fully on the calendar with the pageant. The historian adds:

> Though May Day does not hold the same significance it once did, the freshman class still gathers around the may pole and does the may dance. Wearing white dresses and dancing to music, provided by the renaissance music class, spectators enjoy the dawning of spring. Members of the may pole dance their freshman year are eligible for the May Queen position. Today, the May Queen, still elected by the student body, is a member of the senior class.[5]

In September 2005, Wells College accepted 33 men, to the dismay of many students and alumnae. A *New York Times* article of September 2005 indicated that the women had enjoyed the camaraderie of their campus sisters and "their playful traditions," like the maypole dance and kissing the feet of the statue of Minerva before examinations, and the advent of even a few men had already made a difference in campus life: the article noted that women were waking up early to put on makeup, for example.[6] It will be interesting to see if the women succeed in maintaining the May Day tradition.

Wilson College, a women's college of 300 traditional students and 400 continuing education students located in Chambersburg, Pennsylvania, first celebrated May Day in 1902 as a pageant given by the juniors to honor their seniors. In about 1966 the plays were dropped and the event turned into a one day festival, more like a fun fair or carnival, with entertainment by a local musical group, face-painting, games, and so on. The Queen is still crowned and members of a modern dance group perform the maypole dance. From the mid–1960s through at least 2002, the name of the festival was sometimes "Mayhem," though as time passed it became more commonly called "Spring Fling."

Though there is no official language addressing the requirements for electing the Wilson College May Queen, the procedure has been for the student body to vote for the woman who "best represents the qualities of a Wilson woman" as well as her attendant from six senior representatives chosen by the senior class. The Court is made up of the remaining senior representatives and representatives from the other classes. Every four years Queen Bess (Elizabeth I) is also crowned. She is chosen from among four senior representatives by the entire student body for her dual attributes of studiousness — and red hair. No other Elizabethan pageantry is involved. In 2005, the event included the presentation of the May Court, a maypole dance, a dog show, an equestrian drill team performance, various student fund-raising booths, and a semi-formal dinner and dance.

Some other colleges celebrate a tiny portion of the traditional May Day: the women of the all-women Wellesley College still engage in their May Day hoop-rolling contests, while the first-year students of Chatham University (the undergraduate college is still women-only) put flowers before the doors of their favorite seniors on May morning. Some colleges celebrate the spring intermittently: for example, in 1998 the music and dance students at the coeducational University of Oregon put on an outdoor "Spring Revels," that included Renaissance music and entertainment, the teaching of court and country dances, and the maypole dance.[7] It is not known whether this event was ever repeated. There are other colleges and universi-

18. Celebrating an Old English May Day Today   169

A Modern May Queen and her Court, Grove City College May Day, 2006. (Photograph credit: Davor/Grove City College.)

ties at which, at a minimum, the maypole dance is performed, often by members of a folk dance club rather than the student body at large (the spring festivities of Swarthmore College in Philadelphia that usually include morris and maypole dancing is an example of this). It is evident, however, that the tradition of celebrating May Day remains strongest at smaller, women's colleges.

Elementary Schools (K–12)

Some schools for children from kindergarten through twelfth grade use some aspect of the English May Day — usually the maypole dance but occasionally another English ceremonial dance or song — to mark the end of the school year. Given the state of the current public education system, with its under-budgeted funding for the arts, as well as the challenges of presenting a custom so apparently "white" to ethnically diverse urban children, it is perhaps not surprising that the examples that I have unearthed so far have tended to come from independent (private) schools or from small schools located in small towns. Both of these types of schools tend to pride themselves on maintaining school and class traditions, and the maypole dance is often performed by a specific class, representing a rite of passage for the children.

For example, the coeducational and ethnically diverse independent school that my children attend uses the annual maypole dance as a rite of passage for pairs of kindergarteners and eighth-graders, who will soon enter the Lower and Upper Schools, respectively. The children, who have been paired as reading buddies all year, perform a brief maypole dance to the morris dance tune of "Country Gardens." The dance has been performed since 1917 when the school was actually two independent girls' academies, which merged to form the present-day Winchester Thurston School in Pittsburgh, Pennsylvania. The school began admitting boys in the late 1970s, and boys participate in the dance.

As another example, Shady Hill School, an independent K–8 school located in Cambridge, Massachusetts, has been celebrating May Day as a culmination of the year's training in folk dancing since the school's origin in 1915. At some point John Langstaff, founder of the Boston Revels and a former music teacher at the school, taught the children the "Padstow May Song" and some other English traditional songs and dances. The day culminates with the maypole dance performed by the graduating eighth-grade children.[8]

Waldorf schools, dedicated to the teaching principles of Rudolf Steiner, are well-known for their commitment to celebrating nature in all her seasons. Waldorf schools from Cape Cod to San Francisco celebrate the May with processions through halls decorated with flowering branches, skits about the battle between Lady Spring and King Winter, and the maypole dance.[9]

Finally, as another example of a rite of passage, seniors at the Portales High School in New Mexico have been dancing the maypole dance since 1929 as part of their graduation ceremony. The celebration began as a simple winding of one pole, when ordinary social dancing was prohibited at the school due to some board members' religious observances. A decade later the maypole waltz was choreographed and the event became an evening social. In 1966 a new physical education instructor, Barbara George, joined the faculty and, during her twenty-five years as maypole dance instructor, choreographed the dance and ran the event strictly. The boys wear tuxedos and the girls wear huge hoopskirts in pastel colors. Rehearsals begin nine weeks before the big night, and student participants must have passing grades and attend all rehearsals. Couples waltz around two maypoles until all are standing near a streamer. Then the girls take the ribbons and weave the maypole: in 2003, for example, to the rather mournful Jim Croce song, "Time in a Bottle."[10]

It is apparent from accounts like these that the origination and/or the maintenance of the tradition at some of these institutions was due to the involvement of a key individual who had connections with the world of English folklore and music. However, the May Day tradition could not have continued with mere tacit acquiescence from school administrators, parents, and alumnae or alumni; active involvement from these individuals is also required to maintain a school tradition.

Finally, numerous Web sites devised for or by teachers offer classroom activities, songs, crafts projects, and "histories" of May Day. Most of the latter range from sweetly misinformed to wildly and thoroughly inaccurate. Most of these instructional sites offer a broad offering of spring-tide customs and traditions from many times and places across Europe, treating them all as evidence of a sort of pan-European, ur–May Day celebration: a salmagundi of historical nonsense. However, the crafts, snacks, songs (such as, "Here We Go Round the Maypole Tree" sung to the tune of "Here We Go Round the Mulberry Bush"), and other activities provide evidence that the springtime holiday is still important in many school calendars, especially for younger children.[11]

Folk Dancers and Revelers

Folk dancers, in particular morris dancers, remain (not surprisingly) enthusiastic supporters of May Day. The Cotswold morris that Cecil Sharp first collected and advanced as the archetypical form of the dance, was during the late-nineteenth century, at least, performed in the spring in England, typically on or around Whitsun (the forty-ninth day after Easter Sunday, also known as Pentecost). In the United States today, numerous Cotswold morris teams (as well as sword dance teams, molly dance teams, or Northwest clog morris teams) report that they "dance the sun up" on the first of May or on other or additional days in May. As the San Francisco Bay Area's collective morris sides' Web site puts it: "We start by waking the sun and bringing it back for a whole year! (Besides being a great deal of fun, is this dedication or what?! You may have noticed that it works, too.)"[12]

Some of these events involve simply one or more morris sides gathering together to dance at sunrise, and spectators are few, and usually related to the performers, but other events can be quite elaborate, incorporating maypole dances, songs, participatory dancing (often the English country dance "Sellenger's Round"), traditional music, mummer's plays, and even vendors selling crafts or food. Some of these events have been occurring for twenty-five years or more in a given community and are often sponsored over that time by the same morris teams.

It should be noted here that many, perhaps most, morris dancers are aware of the modern research into the origins of the morris: specifically, as discussed in Chapter 2, that it was developed as a court display dance in the mid–1400s. In their announcements to the public, however, they tend to reiterate nineteenth-century folklorists' assertions about ancient pagan fertility rites: assertions particularly invoked for the dance "Bean-Setting," with its apparent imitation of planting, and certain Cotswold morris customs, such as sharing pieces of a cake impaled on a sword carried among the crowd. These are presented either as evidence of fertility rituals whose origins are lost in those famous mists of time or as a ritualistic expression of the Eucharist. The claims are outdated and inaccurate, but they make good copy: "It's hooey," accurately notes the Syracuse, New York–based Bassett Street Hounds' Web site, "but we can't seem to stop ourselves."[13]

Dancing the sun up tends to be a relatively informal event organized by the folk dancers themselves. On a more formal basis is Revels, Inc., a non-profit performing arts company founded in 1971 by award-winning author and musician John Langstaff to promote the understanding and appreciation of traditional folk music, dance, and rituals from around the world. From a modest start in Cambridge, Massachusetts, more than thirty years ago, Revels, Inc., has grown into a national, year-round organization that provides opportunities for communal celebration through fully staged and costumed seasonal performances that blend traditional music, dance, drama, and ritual. Children and adult volunteers drawn from the community as well as many professional actors, musicians, artists, directors and "bearers of tradition" from various cultures engage the audience in participating in the festivities. Different Revels productions are performed annually in twelve cities across the country, and, in addition, many smaller Revels-inspired productions are performed in various small towns throughout the nation.

While Christmas Revels are more common, several cities, notably Washington, D.C., sponsor May Revels. The Washington Revels May Celebration incorporates singers, a "noisy" band, mummers, the Padstow 'Oss, jugglers, the maypole dance, the crowning of a May Queen, dancers, craftspeople, and food vendors.[14]

In an even more community-oriented fashion, since 1975 In the Heart of the Beast Puppet and Mask Theatre in Minneapolis, Minnesota, has been holding an elaborate festival on the first Sunday in May, involving a community band, mask- and puppet-making workshops open to the public, a twelve-block parade, a short play, morris dancing, and other political and arts events. The event is conceived of as a testament to community, and while there is a different theme each year, the overall stated purpose of the festival is to celebrate the return of spring, the commitment to community, and the celebration of every person's creative potential.[15]

In the cases of the folk dancers and the Revelers, the May Day festival is a combination of a spectacle for the public, as well as a source of satisfaction and fun for the participants. Some participants have detailed knowledge of the background of the customs that they are re-enacting while others simply enjoy the romance of the springtime festivities. Regardless, it is apparent that participants are often deeply moved by their involvement in May Day customs, and by their belief that they are connected over the years with prior participants in a long chain of tradition.

Pagans and Wiccans

May First is also Beltane, one of the four quarterly festivals of the Celtic year (though not, traditionally, the greatest of them). In the United States, modern Pagans and Wiccans now celebrate Beltane with a variety of customs, including the maypole dance, the crowning of the Lord and Lady (primal spirits of fertility), summer blessings, drumming, the crowning of a sky-clad (naked) May Queen, the custom of hand-fasting (a trial marriage lasting a year and a day), and, on occasion, more orgiastic celebrations of sexuality. Textbooks such as Marian Singer's *The Everything Wicca and Witchcraft Book*, or Denise Zimmerman and Katherine A. Gleason's *The Complete Idiot's Guide to Wicca and Witchcraft*, as well as numerous websites, some sponsored by groups, some by individuals, provide numerous and inconsistent details on the Beltane festival. Most of these represent cross-cultural gleanings of customs collected in many countries and many time periods; some represent individual beliefs and ideas. These can range from drumming circles to Irish step-dancing to American Indian practices involving feathers and smudge sticks. It is rare to find any sort of verifiable source for these customs: all are presented as incontrovertibly old and Pagan, regardless of when or whence they came. While the customs are charming, and undoubtedly satisfying to participants, few of the claims made in these books and websites as to the antiquity or the meaning of any of them should be taken at face value.

For example, some Pagan/Wiccan sources describe May Day as a post–Freudian sexual holiday and their proponents seem to celebrate it in an exuberant fashion not seen since Puritan extremist Stubbs' famous diatribe against the maypole. Thus Yasmine Galenorn's *Dancing with the Sun* informs us that the maypole is a representation of the divine marriage between the Lord and Lady of the Greenwood:

> The Maypole represents the phallus of the God. The wreath atop represents the vagina of the Goddess. As the Maypole is danced, the ribbons wind around the pole and the wreath lowers [*sic*: I have read this statement that the wreath lowers as the ribbons are wound in several sources, though none explains exactly how this mechanism would work], symbolizing the Divine Marriage, the sexual union of God and Goddess.[16]

Other websites — now vanished over the course of my research — provided further imaginative details such as that there should be eight dancers, one for each sabbat of the year, paired into four couples; that dancers should choose ribbons symbolizing the virtue or destiny that they wish for in the coming year (or, alternatively, that men should take red ribbons and women white); and that the weaving represents the passage down the birth canal. Many books and sites point out correctly that these Beltane customs are rich in pagan symbolism, but Ronald Hutton reminds us that these are not *ancient pagan* but *modern* symbols and beliefs.[17] There is no evidence that a plaited maypole dance was popular in England prior to

Dancing around five maypoles in Mendon, Utah, in 2006. This community has celebrated May Day continuously since its pioneer days in 1863. (Photograph credit: Karole Sarensen.)

1836, well after the days of the Druids. The cost of wasting precious fabric to streamers in the days before the invention of power looms would alone prohibit a plaited maypole dance. Researchers and elementary school teachers must be very wary about using any information — especially Internet-based information — from any Pagan/Wiccan site when searching for May Day materials.

Small Communities

Some small communities in the U.S. hold, or have held, a May Day celebration, one that typically focuses on children or teenagers performing the maypole dance. I have seen photographs of young children dancing the maypole dance in communities as far apart as St. Thomas, the U.S. Virgin Islands (black children), and a small island off Acadia National Park in Maine (white children). In Hastings, Minnesota, for example, little girls performed the maypole dance for about ten years during the 1990s in front of City Hall, until the greater popularity of the town's "Rivertown Days" festival caused this tradition to end.[18] And in 2007, the town of Geyserville, California, celebrated its community May Day as it has since 1925. Activities included a climbing wall, a clown, an egg-toss competition, music and food as well as the crowning of the Queen and the third-grade maypole dance.[19]

Some historical re-creation communities, such as Westville, "Georgia's Working 1850 Town," offer a May Day with the maypole dance performed by local children in period clothing, a tournament of games, and the crowning of the "Queen of Love and Beauty." These events are obviously a formal part of a deliberate re-enactment.[20]

Other communities mount a May Day festival that may continue as a long tradition or may disappear after a year of two. While the town of Fremont, Oregon, located near Seattle, celebrates the summer solstice with an elaborate parade, they also celebrate a "Beltane May Day" in which participants dressed in white and wove the maypole. In 1999 the town had a Green Man, described as a "male nature spirit, like the Greek Pan." This particular year, the Green Man chose his May Queen—and also asked her to marry him. (She said yes.) Organizers of this event were apparently not familiar with the history of May Day: one organizer is quoted as saying that the festival reminded him "of ancient times when things were simpler," while another felt that it had to do "with mating." These individuals concluded, however, that the festival "delivered the maximum amount of fun for the least amount of effort": it was simply fun, as well as pretty, with all the white clothes, flowers, and ribbons.[21] As another example of such a community event, in 2002, the town of Fairfax in Marin County, California celebrated its tenth annual May Day festival, a family-friendly one that involved crafts, food, music performances, and the annual maypole dance with the "Queen of the Fairy Godmothers."[22]

Some churches, especially Catholic churches, also still sponsor May Queens who place a crown of flowers on the statue of Mary. While the Catholic May Queens are usually children, in the spring of 2005 members of St. Hedwig Church, a worship site for Christ the Light of the World parish in Duquesne, Pennsylvania, selected a one-hundred year old great-grandmother as May Queen: a symbol, for this parish, of the mother of Jesus.[23]

Many of the above festivals were created self-consciously, as it were. Each had one or more moving spirits who learned enough about some May Day customs and the dances to be able to persuade others to join in. It is rare to find a community that celebrates May Day apparently independently of the work of folk enthusiasts. One such rarity is the May Day festival that has been held continuously since 1863 in Mendon, Utah, located in northern Utah's Cache Valley. All eleventh-grade girls in this town of about 1,750 are eligible to be entered into the drawing for Queen, and the festival also honors its former May Queens, who dance around a pole of their own. This festival owes its longevity to at least two stabilizing factors: one is the continuous involvement of the Sorensens, the family of the first May Queen; the second is the longtime involvement of the community itself, many of whom members of the Church of Jesus Christ of Latter-Day Saints.

Finally, the popularity of the May Day festival spawned at least two recipes. One Grange cookbook from the 1950s provided a recipe for a May Queen cake: basically a white cake with an orange or lemon curd filling. And, in the wacky Edwardian world of humorist P.G. Wodehouse, hero Frederick Altamont Cornwallis Twistleton, fifth Earl of Ickenham, has the following to say about the concoction, "May Queen," in *Uncle Fred in the Springtime*. As he tells a young companion, one sip of this drink will raise the spirits of anyone who has lost his last shilling on a slow horse:

> Do we by any chance know a beverage called May Queen? Its full name is, "Tomorrow'll be of all the year the maddest, merriest day, for I'm to be the Queen of the May, mother, the Queen of the May." A clumsy title, generally shortened for purposes of ordinary conversation. Its foundation is any good dry champagne, to which is added liqueur brandy, armagnac, kummel, yellow chartreuse, and old stout, to taste. It is a good many years since I tried it myself but I can thoroughly recommend it to alleviate the deepest despondency.[24]

It is clear that there are many ways of celebrating May Day. It is unlikely, though not impossible as shown by the recent popularity of Renaissance Faires and Festivals, that a community will once again sponsor a huge Elizabethan pageant of the type seen in 1900. But there is still room for a community-based rite of spring that features some combination of the maypole dance, the selection of a Queen or King of the May, flowers, song and dance.

Conclusion: "The Merriest Day of All the Glad New Year!"

Staines Morris
Come ye young men come along,
With your music, dance, and song.
Bring your lasses in your hands,
For 'tis that which love commands.
Then to the maypole haste away, for 'tis now our holiday.
Then to the maypole haste away, for 'tis now our holiday.
— From Robert Cox's play *Acteon and Diana* (1656)*

This discussion of the celebration of Merrie May Day in America reveals the richness of the traditions and the complexity of the agendas that lay (and lie) behind this apparently innocuous holiday. A pretty spectacle, a happy, springtime festival, a part of American cultural and political history, this study of May Day helps us to better understand the dynamics and emotions of an earlier time.

I hope that this survey also inspires readers to examine their assumptions about the nature of tradition. Thanks to the well-publicized work of the nineteenth-century folklorists, many laypeople today still think of a traditional dance, song, or ritual as a relatively unchanging thing, a jewel preserved from the ravages of time by simple peasants incapable of understanding the treasure they guard. This jewel can, so to speak, be prised out of its setting and recreated elsewhere. If a school or community is interested in portraying the traditional spectacles of the Padstow 'Oss or the Castleton Garland, for example, their leaders can consult reference sources and pictures to reproduce those aspects of the events that they wish to show. They will then refer to this as a "traditional" English custom or dance. In this sense, traditions represent a grab bag of performance practices that can be used at will. The recreation of Merrie May Day, with its "traditional" morris dancers, Robin Hood, Maid Marian, Jack-in-the-Green, sword dancers, mummers' plays, folk dances of many nations, and so on, represents this aspect of the word *tradition*: culture as artifact; indeed, culture as unchanging artifact.

While this definition is not precisely inaccurate, it is incomplete. It is certainly useful in a performance or pedagogical sense to think of some cultural items as artifacts: this permits the existence of folk festivals or of colorful books with titles like *Holidays Around the World*,

---

*The play featured dancing around the maypole, which had recently been proclaimed both heathen and sensual. In 1855, W. Chappell, in his Popular Music of the Olden Time, *set these words to an old tune, now known as "Staines Morris." The song appeared frequently in college May Day programs.*

that give children and adults a sense of the cultural diversities and similarities among different peoples, for every culture has some colorful holidays that are entertaining to observe or to participate in. But this simple definition ignores the fact that the cultural artifact — the dance, the song, the custom — has itself been changing within the context of the originating culture; that it is changing even now, as new performers and spectators add their input to the event.

In recent years the study of folklore has moved away from this static view of tradition as a cultural fossil of an earlier (and better) period, preserved in rural areas, preferably by poor and elderly inhabitants. We now see tradition as a river, a continuum of experience. Traditions are always in flux and calendar customs in particular provide an excellent example of a fixed custom with a variable content: "We *always* celebrate May Day with the crowning of a King or Queen and the maypole dance, but this year we will *also*...."

In 1983 Eric Hobsbawm and his colleagues published an important work titled *The Invention of Tradition*. Hobsbawm argued convincingly that invented traditions self-consciously invoked the values of the past to legitimize the present. One essay in the study examined, for example, the invention of the modern kilt — that garment romantically associated with the ancient Highlandman running down to battle through the heather — that can be traced back to a pragmatic English Quaker industrialist in 1727. Hobsbawm's theory is useful because it forces historians examine more closely social constructs that they may have taken for granted. But what Hobsbawm did not address was *why* a tradition is invented; why it satisfies a need of the time. The Highlandman became a romantic figure to the English at the turn of the eighteenth century only after all military threat from the Scots was removed, and many of them deported. Similarly, the celebration of Merrie May Day in Merrie England became an important holiday in late nineteenth-century America as its middle class became increasingly concerned about the influx of immigrants. The college girls' May Day grew more popular in the late 1890s and early 1900s in part because of society's concerns about the nature of the New Girl. It remained popular, especially in the conservative, patriarchal South, because after the suffrage amendment was passed, the feminist movement collapsed. And May Day dwindled and vanished, for the most part, in the late 1960s because of the profound social upheavals of that period: in particular, women's new views of themselves and their roles in society.

Merrie May Day is indeed an invented tradition, but it is no less valid than the May Day customs of earlier centuries, that are themselves invented though we have fewer details on how and why. It is tempting to think that if a tradition is invented, it is somehow tainted and not really authentic; that there were more "real" traditions back in the golden past. If the May Day celebration of 1906 or 2006 is considered to be invented, one might yet find the "real" May Day by going back to the Middle Ages, or to those even more romantic Druids or Romans. But not only is this not historically possible, it is irrelevant. As Nissenbaum concludes, "it will not do to think there is a usable line, whether historical or aesthetic, dividing invented traditions from real ones."[1] Or, as Richard Handler and Jocelyn Linekin point out more fully: "Genuine and spurious — terms that have been used to distinguish objective reality from hocus-pocus — are inappropriate when applied to social phenomena, which never exist apart from our interpretations of them."[2]

The story of May Day in America also shows us that traditions last only as long as do their supporting economic, social, and even political substructures. The elaborate urban May Day pageants vanished when playgrounds were no longer organized with playground directors and when funds from local business sponsors dried up due to the Depression and, later,

World War II. The college pageants began to buckle under their own weight and vanished at different times at different colleges: affected also by the change in leadership as the first wave of enthusiasts retired, by women's colleges going coeducational, and by sheer fatigue and increasing lack of interest. Most dramatically, the selection and crowning of the May Queen collapsed almost everywhere between 1967 and 1975 due to the profound social changes of the period.

Tradition is by no means dead or disvalued; even in the modern world traditions are perceived to have value. The recent introduction in many elementary schools of the Indian holiday of Dewali or the creation in 1966 of Kwanzaa, the African American celebration, shows that modern people still crave symbolism, celebration, and continuity.

Thus in 2007, Bryn Mawr's official Web site stated that the college's many traditions, big and small, are more than just colorful spectacles that divert participants from the intensity of study, "they are ceremonial enactments of common values that help create a sense of community," a community that lasts beyond the four years of undergraduate study.[3] Participants speak more emotionally about the experience. A Bryn Mawr Traditions Mistress of 1997–1998 writes on her Web site:

> Traditions are really hard to explain and even harder to understand if you haven't been through them yourself. But they establish a sense of community that lasts beyond the confines of the four-year college experience. Women who attended Bryn Mawr in the '30s had the same traditions as I did, as we share that experience with every woman who attends Bryn Mawr from here on out.[4]

This woman is, in fact, correct in her belief that many fellow alumnae from the early 1930s *valued* the May Day experience as she did, but incorrect in stating that the event was *held* in the same fashion at that time — and that is exactly the point.

Bryn Mawr College may have some of the most elaborate of existing college traditions, but it is not alone in perceiving their value. In 2005, the official Web site of Wellesley College, for example, acknowledges that the college is now a different place, "encompassing a diversity of cultures, backgrounds, and viewpoints unknown to the generations of women that came before" than it was when its traditions were first celebrated. But, "in transcending these differences, our traditions are one of the major bonds uniting us and shaping our common identity, spirit and pride as Wellesley women."[5] As another example of the use of tradition, a spokesperson for the co-educational, agricultural Utah State University wrote firmly that "Tradition at a university brings involvement, and involvement increases retention.... Ag [agricultural] Colleges have always been founded on traditions and we're still establishing new traditions."[6]

The celebration of May Day, in whatever form, at colleges and universities (the principal focus of this work) served, and still serves in some cases, five main purposes. First, it was a public ritual to mark both the ending of each academic year as well as to mark the transition of a group: a farewell, for example, to the seniors who would depart the campus in a few weeks or a welcome to the freshmen who performed the May Day skits as they entered the academic world. Second, it effectively demonstrated that, while smart, the girls remained pretty, talented, and non-threatening to the status quo. Third, it was a symbolic communication that demonstrated to outsiders as well as to the college community itself the erudition and the quality of the school and the students. Fourth, the celebration of May Day helped to form a *communitas*: both to separate the college that celebrated May Day from those that did not, as well as to shape the image of a particular college class ("The performance that *our* class gave was the prettiest ever seen!"). Finally, May Day was undoubtedly a private source

The 1920 Elmira College May Queen and Court, dressed as Greek nymphs. Note that the Guards all have fashionably bobbed hair, whereas most of the Court still sport a "woman's crowning glory," and all the girls save the Queen wear the headache band popular with the flappers of the time. (Elmira College Archives.)

of pleasure (perhaps, on occasion, of pain); a memory that each alumna could return to happily or use as a marker to remind her of events before, during, or after the festival.

Celebrating May Day satisfied and still satisfies a basic need to experience a repeated, calendar-based celebration, that offers us a sense — even if it is illusory — of permanence and continuity. There is comfort in the repeated annual patterns of activity and celebration that contribute to our feelings of belonging within a culture or a community, and to our need to feel a part of its long history. J.A. Widdowson argues that some dim awareness of the long history of such customs and a sense of being a part of their continuity certainly contributes to the participants' involvement in and enjoyment of these events.[7] Community celebrations can also be a substantial source of local and personal pride,

May Day is an unusual festival in the American calendar. It is not a public holiday celebrated with parades, fireworks and speeches such as the Fourth of July, Memorial Day, Veterans' Day or Labor Day. It is not a private or family-oriented holiday such as Mothers' Day, Valentine's Day or many celebrations of Christmas or Thanksgiving. It is not a religious holiday, such as Yom Kippur, Easter or Ramadan. May Day is a *community* holiday, best celebrated in small, closely connected groups such as schools, Pagan circles, small towns or neighborhoods or folk dance clubs. It requires a community with a modicum of organization to organize and practice the maypole dance, but beyond that, it is a "feel good" holiday that bears none of the emotional baggage or gift-giving requirements of many other holidays.

Does May Day still have something to offer us today? Of course — almost all the same benefits as noted above. Certainly for many communities the festival offers the pleasures and comfort of an annual ritual as well as a celebration of the community and its values. In some communities the tradition can be a rite of passage for one age group or another. Participants and spectators can enjoy the prettiness of the event, which welcomes in the verdant spring after a long, cold winter.

Finally, for many of us the festival represents an ideal of a mythical past — a time in which we believe that people were kinder, happier, less commercial, and more in tune with Nature. Indeed, as we become an ever more urbanized society, our yearning for a Golden Age seems to increase. The Now is degenerate and the Then was much better. This sense of nostalgia for a past that we never experienced (that, actually, *no one* ever experienced) may in fact be a critical factor in the sustaining of what we call "traditional customs." We long for a connection to the past, to tradition, even if that tradition is an illusion. We hang on to outdated images of the past because we need them.[8]

For, as Washington Irving rhapsodized in 1822:

> I always experience, wherever I may be placed, a delightful expansion of the heart at the return of May. It is said that birds about this time will become restless in their cages, as if instinct with the season, conscious of the revelry that is going on in the groves, and impatient to break from their bondage, and join in the jubilee of the year. In like manner I have felt myself excited, even in the midst of the metropolis, when the windows, which had been churlishly closed all winter, were again thrown open to receive the balmy breath of May; when the sweets of the country were breathed into the town, and flowers were cried about the streets. I have considered the treasure of flowers thus poured in, as so many missives from nature inviting us forth to enjoy the virgin beauty of the year, before its freshness is exhaled by the heats of sunny summer.
>
> One can readily imagine what a gay scene it must have been in jolly old London, when the doors were decorated with flowering branches, when every hat was decked with hawthorn, and Robin Hood, Friar Tuck, Maid Marian, the morrice dancers, and all the other fantastic masks and revelers, were performing their antics about the May-pole in every part of the city.[10]

One can, indeed.

Part II: The College Festivals*

The admissions statistics listed for these 80 colleges comes from Internet information circa 2005 and are provided to give a sense of the relative size of the institution.

The Colleges

Agnes Scott College, Decatur, Georgia

Founded in 1889 as Decatur Female Seminary by reform-minded Presbyterians, the seminary was renamed Agnes Scott Institute in 1890, and chartered as a college in 1906. It currently enrolls approximately 820 women.

The first May Day was held in the spring of 1903, but it was a very simple affair and was not repeated. In 1912 (or possibly 1913; there is some confusion about this), the YWCA sponsored a more elaborate event as a moneymaking scheme, serving chicken salad, sandwiches and lemonade for a "consideration." The Queen was crowned, and the different classes came dressed as various "bucolic groups" with "fudge-aprons" over their dresses. At the second May Day, in 1914, one of the girls taught the others the maypole dance. "How we gazed at her in awe," wrote an alumna,

> because she was the first girl we had ever seen who had taken *dancing lessons*! She was dressed, as to feet, in high-top white shoes almost to her knees. [Another girl] was to dance in the Morris Dance but as she didn't find her belt for her costume she appeared at the last minute, out of breath, with two brown stockings tied together to make a belt.

At about this time, the alumna remembered, Miss Isabel Randolph of the physical education department

> suggested a plan that had been used at some Eastern college, Barnard maybe — that of taking some mythological characters, using them as a basis of the May Day performance. The students were not only to write the scenarios, but to plan the costumes and dances with the aid of the Physical Education department. This particular plan was followed for years until both students and audience wearied of the sameness of the themes. And so they began to select subjects from a broader field, various legends and traditions, the work of planning and costuming still being largely the work of the students. The student community was notified several months ahead that the scenarios in the competition would be due before the Christmas vacation and the results passed upon by a committee of faculty and students. The plan was followed ever since, except in 1940, known as Alumnae Year, and the year of the Semi-Centennial Celebration when a student committee wrote a special scenario titled, *The Heritage of Woman*.

A list of the college programs shows the following titles. The pageants or plays were all written or adapted by students. In several instances a student wrote the play for two May Days in succession.

1911	May 1st celebration, "but no may pole dances in the rain."
1912–1916	No mention in the college yearbook
1917	Masque: *The Homage of Time to Shakespeare*
1918	*The Crowning of Flora*
1919	*Psyche and Eros*
1920	N/A
1921	*Pandora*
1922	*Pipes of Pan*

1923	*Maize Moon*
1924	*Psyche and Eros*
1925	*Sherwood Forest*
1926	*The Triumph of Spring*
1927	*Endymion*
1928	*The Dawn of Delight*
1929	*Paris and the Gold Apple*
1930	*Virgil, the Immortal Bard*
1931	*Auburn Dell* ("Replica of the original English May Day laid in time of Robin Hood and his Merry Men")
1932	*Spring in Many Lands*
1933	*The Dance of the Hours*
1934	*Le Fête du Maie*
1935	*Peter Pan*
1936	*Down an English Lane*
1937	*Comus*, by J. Milton (adapted)
1938	*A Midsummer's Night's Dream*, by W. Shakespeare (adapted)
1938	*Orpheus and Eurydice*
1940	*Heritage of Woman* (Script written by an Alumnae Committee)
1941	*On an English Green*
1942	*American*
1943	*The Four Seasons*
1944	*The Making of the Rainbow*
1945	*The Creation*
1946	*Festival to Beauty*
1947	*May Day Revels*
1948	*A May Day Legend*
1949	*An Irish May Day*
1950	*The Net—A Sea Legend*
1951	*The Adventure of Prince Abdul-Kader*
1952	*Chess and Joy Fantasy*
1952	*Flower Fantasy*
1954	*A Knyght Ther Was* (Chaucer)
1955	*Mountain May Day*
1956	*A Harlequinade*
1957	*Nezumi No Yomeivi* ("The Marriage of a Mouse")
1958	Fine Arts Festival replaced May Day
1959	*Orpheus*
1960	*Electra*
1961	Combined with Arts Festival

As early as 1958 there had been some indication that something needed to be done to relieve the pressure of the crowded calendar of spring activities. The Queen did not appear in 1958, the first year that May Day was combined with a Fine Arts Festival. Queens were crowned again in 1959 and 1960, but the ceremony was dropped after 1960.[1]

Albright College, Reading, Pennsylvania

Founded in 1856 and affiliated with the United Methodist Church, Albright currently enrolls approximately 740 men and 980 women.

The May Day tradition began in 1922 on the campus of the Schuylkill Seminary, a coeducational normal school. In 1928, when the seminary merged with Albright College, the festival continued.

Both a May Queen and a May King were named: the former nominated by the students based on her popularity and beauty; the latter as a symbol of derision. There was a procession through campus, followed by music and dancing. The Queen was crowned and sat on a decorated throne, but the King was paraded through town and showered with abuse and garbage, as described in Chapter 13.

In the late forties it was noted that the junior women, dressed in crepe paper due to wartime restrictions, danced around the maypole. The May Day tradition ended in 1962.[2]

Auburn University, Auburn Alabama

Chartered in 1856 as the East Alabama Male College and designated a land-grant college in 1872, Auburn currently enrolls 22,000 graduate and undergraduate students.

While there are hints of an earlier celebration, the archivist states that with the sources available he can confirm that in 1937 a May Day program was held at Auburn University, sponsored by the Sphinx, an honors organization comprised of senior women. He writes:

> The Sphinx were first organized in 1935. On May 5, 1937 there is a front page story reporting the success of that year's program, which it describes as "a revival of an annual college affair … it is planned that the women's Student Government Association will continue to present such a pageant on each succeeding May Day." No mention of the pageant was made in the 1941 paper, but the 1942 pageant witnessed the crowning of a Queen and a performance by the Auburn Players.
>
> The 1945 program had a performance by over 80 coeds, including "the traditional May Club Dance," with the coeds "carrying flags of the allied nations," "flag-bearers of the United Nations."
>
> The 1948 and subsequent yearbooks did not mention the pageant on the Sphinx page (unlike the previous years), so apparently that was the last year. 1948 was the first year the Student *Handbook* was published, and nowhere is a May Day event mentioned in its calendar. When it was celebrated before 1937 is unknown. I went through the school paper back to 1915 (the earliest available issue) and found no mention of it.
>
> Why it was stopped isn't known, though I might speculate that the dramatic influx of servicemen in the student population may have been a factor, or perhaps the communist connotations of the holiday combined with the political climate of the period may have contributed. Or maybe they just felt like doing something else instead (like studying for finals?).[3]

Bates College, Lewiston, Maine

The first coeducational college in New England, Bates College was founded by Maine abolitionists as a private liberal arts college in 1855. It currently enrolls approximately 870 men and 890 women.

The first May Festival was held in 1910; it was sponsored by the Girls' Athletic Association with the crowning of the Queen and the weaving of the maypole "in the old English way." The archivist writes that "they seem to have held it through 1916 and then there was an absence of 5 years; perhaps due in part to World War I (it may have seemed inappropriate). There was one held in 1921 and again in 1927 (this one was put on by the YWCA). I could find no mention of it beyond 1927."[4]

A student newspaper account provides more details of the 1916 celebration, when approximately 400 students and townspeople attended the ceremony. The music consisted of cornet, violin, and piano. The procession was led by the herald, followed by the crown bearer, the pages (black gowns and white capes), and finally the Queen "carried in her chair of state all gay with pink and white drapings." The Queen was followed by the Goddess of Liberty with her train bearers and the court jester. After the crowning came the songs and dances. Thirteen sophomores danced the Polka Française, "in which arm draperies were used effectively." Nearly all the freshmen girls danced the English folk dance, "London Bridge." "Their white costumes were especially pleasing, a feature being the butterfly wings, dotted with gold spots, just peeping over their shoulders." After other songs and dances the maypole, with its pink and white streamers, was wound. "The prize marching was of much interest. Each class designed its own figures and at the end of the march sang an original song, the words and music for the song being composed by members of the class. The marching was of a high order and being given without music was all the more difficult." The student newspaper account of the day commended Miss Bell, the director of physical hygiene, for the success of the affair "into the preparation for which she put much time and study."[5]

Newspaper accounts show that, in general, the early celebrations at Bates College were quite modest, involving songs, aesthetic dances, and the competitive marching drills. The 1927 event, presented by 125 members of the YWCA, was more elaborate. After an afternoon of tennis tournaments, archery contests and soccer games, all held under the auspices of the Women's Athletic Association, came the festival pageant:

> At sunrise, six little village maidens come to the edge of the village green. There they were surprised and delighted to see the Sun maidens in their morning dance and the joyous entrance of the Dawn Wind. Dawn Wind ushered in the Spirits of Spring and the Water nymphs who danced around the old well in their ritual of the purification of the water. The village maidens washed their pretty faces in the dew and peeped at their reflections in the well to see who was the most beautiful. Surprised by the woodland folk, the maidens accepted their help in choosing a Queen. A jester ran to the village and informed the villagers of the presence of their Queen. They, with the dancers, formed a triumphant procession which escorted the Queen to her throne. In her honor the Milk maids [sic] and Robin Hood's men, the Garland dancers and Hobby Horse Riders performed. The animals of the wood were there too, and enjoyed, as did the Queen and her subjects, the pleasure of a memorable May Festival.[6]

Berea College, Berea, Kentucky

Founded by abolitionists in 1855 as a college and a community committed to interracial education, though African Americans were prohibited from attending by Kentucky law from 1904 to 1950. Berea currently enrolls approximately 1,500 students.

K. Helen McKinstry, director of the college women's physical education and health department, organized the first May Day festival, held in 1935. She specifically devised it as a method of demonstrating the improved physical health, posture, and grace of the girls who had completed their physical education courses. The college women, as well as girls from the Junior High and the Academy, processed in, crowned the Queen, and then performed several songs and fourteen folk dances, concluding with the winding of the maypole. Over the next years, slightly more elaborate pageantry — though less ambitious in scope than that of other colleges, perhaps because of Berea College's emphasis on thrift and simple living — as well as gymnastic demonstrations were added. Men did not participate, though they were spectators. (The college did not permit mixed dancing at all until the 1940s when Navy battalions were stationed at the college for training.) Photographs show the girls dancing or forming gymnastic pyramids on a lawn behind which are the student-maintained gardens planted with corn. The pageants ran until 1955, though May Day continued through the seventies with a crowning and an indoor spring formal dance, with no other pageantry associated with it.

The last two May Queens, in 1973 and 1974, were African Americans. During this time there was also a Black Student Union Queen, likewise elected in the spring. It is possible that the addition of this event may have caused the May Queen to seem superfluous. Today the students still elect a Homecoming Queen (a tradition founded in the mid–1950s) and a Miss Black Student Union.[7]

Bluffton University, Bluffton, Ohio

Founded by the General Conference of the Mennonite Church in 1899, offering 1,110 coed students an educational experience, "rooted in learning, faith, and respect."

According to the college's Web site, the May Day tradition dates to 1910, and continues to feature the maypole dance, performed by sixteen first-year students, eight men and eight women, dressed in colorful, Germanic-style costumes.

> At Bluffton the May Day celebration represents the end of a school year for students, the beginning of a new chapter for seniors and the remembrance of times past for alumni. The tradition weaves together past, present and future around the May Pole in a never-ending circle.[8]

Brenau University, Gainsville, Georgia

Established in 1878 as the Georgia Baptist Female Seminary, the university maintains four divisions, one of which is the Women's College, with 607 students.

The college's Web site notes that May Day is still celebrated today and features a program presented by the junior class in honor of the seniors. The celebration features the "presentation of the May Court, crowning of the May Queen and the wrapping of the May Pole. The Queen is joined by the Princess and Prince (a girl); all are elected by the student body."[9] May Day is held as part of an alumnae reunion weekend.

The director of alumni affairs, who has been involved with the event for many years, adds that

> Our May Day tradition began as a "Spring Festival" highlighting the states that were represented by the student body during the 1920s. This evolved into the May Day celebration complete with a queen, a prince, a princess and the wrapping of the May Pole, skits and plays (some were major productions with costumes) and a front campus for of parents and alumnae. The students vote on the queen and court members. Several years ago, one of the male students who was enrolled in our Evening and Weekend College (which is co-ed), was voted May Prince. I believe that this was the only time a male was involved. Fathers, brothers, uncles, boyfriends escort the court members to their seats."[10]

May Day used to be held on the first weekend of May, but after Brenau changed to the semester system, the event was moved to April so it would not conflict with graduation. The college continues to treasure its tradition; in 2003, to coincide with the college's 125th anniversary, a senior student prepared a video highlighting former queens and their gowns, and many of the gowns were displayed on campus. In the video, titled *May Day: A Lasting Tradition at Brenau University*, the narrator states that "the women of Brenau believe this is one of the best traditions of all the ones they still participate in. May Day is always mentioned to prospective students because it means that much to the students who have experienced the tradition."[11]

Brown University, Providence, Rhode Island

Seventh oldest college in America, currently enrolling 5,700 undergraduates.

The YWCA of the Women's College of Brown first celebrated May Day on May 15, 1901. In 1912, the event was held at dusk: the seniors performed the maypole dance, the juniors and sophomores executed difficult fancy dances, while the freshman displayed folk dances. These were followed by a picnic dinner and a "faculty stunt," at which various professors and the dean "were represented with affecting likeness."

In 1914 the custom began for the freshmen to present their senior sisters with May baskets. In 1918, the sophomore masque, presented by that class since 1907, became part of May Day, and the freshmen that year knelt, in their costumes, before the academically gowned seniors to give each her basket. In 1942 the celebrations of Spring Day and May Day were combined. In 1993, the college historian wrote, "[I]n the fall of 1943 a Harvest Queen was crowned, for the benefit of seniors who were graduating in October or February under the accelerated system and would miss the traditional May Day. May Day festivities became part of the Mother-Daughter weekend in the 1940s and were last held in 1967."[12]

Bryn Mawr College, Philadelphia, Pennsylvania

A women's college founded by Quakers in 1885, Bryn Mawr currently enrolls 1,200 undergraduates.

Of all the women's colleges, Bryn Mawr College originated and still maintains the most elaborate college traditions and rituals, as demonstrated by the annual election of two Traditions Mistresses, who are responsible for planning the events and instructing their fellow students in their duties. The four "Big" traditions include Lantern night (when the freshmen receive lanterns, symbols of wisdom), Parade Night, Hell Week (when freshmen must carry out the frivolous requests of upper-classwomen) and May Day (symbolizing in part the end of the seniors' college life). There are as well many lesser traditions, some incorporating ritual gift-giving. Bryn Mawr's traditions are so numerous, complex and long-lived that they formed the topic of folklorist Virginia Wolf Briscoe's Ph.D. thesis. Bryn Mawr still celebrates May Day with a full day of programming and speeches given by the two May Queens.

May Day began in 1900 with an elaborate Elizabethan festival, which grew steadily more complicated and erudite. With Little May Day (much briefer and more informal celebration) held on the off-years beginning circa 1903, the Bryn Mawr "Big" May Day was held in 1900, 1906, 1910, 1914, 1920, 1924, 1928, 1932, and 1936 — the last of the Big May Days, and an extraordinary production. A total of 14,000 invitations were sent out for the event, which involved more plays, animals, and costumes than before. However, the size of the event had begun to exhaust the school, and the time required for rehearsals, costume- and paper flower-making, and other organizational matters was overwhelming. Briscoe noted that "[f]rom 1939 until a middle-sized May Day was proposed in December, 1950, the question of Big May Day was debated within the college community, and, as the years passed, interest in putting it on declined."[13]

By the time that Briscoe did her field work, from 1977 to 1981, the May Day tradition had taken the form that it follows today as described in Chapter 18, although the "May Hole" celebration seems to have been added in the early to mid–1980s.

Bucknell University, Lewisburg, Pennsylvania

Founded in 1846 by a group of Baptists, the college was opened to women in 1883. Bucknell now enrolls 3,350 undergraduates.

Bucknell's May Day celebration began in 1915. In the early 1930s,

President Homer Rainey established the celebration as "Spring Festival," a broader day of programming for the women of the university that included the May Queen and her Court. The Spring Festival continued until at least 1969, after the discontinuation of the May Day portion of the programming.

Programs included Milton's *Comus* (1919), Maeterlinck's *The Blue Bird* (1932), *A Festival of the Nations* (1935), *A Physical Education Review from Ancient Times to the Present* (1939), *An English Country Faire* (1947), *Alice in Wonderland* (1955) and *A Salute to Broadway* (1961). There were no celebrations from 1942 to 1944, but May Day resumed in 1945 with a pageant titled *Under Three Flags*, that expressed ideas given by the university's president in his 1941 baccalaureate address: the American flag as a symbol "of the last remaining bulwark against nihilism, anarchy and tyranny," the Christian flag as a symbol of human brotherhood and "high and noble standards of personal conduct," and the Bucknell flag, "a symbol of our loyalty to wisdom, to truth, to beauty." After hymns, the pledge of allegiance, a cow girl dance routine and a football practice dance routine, the maypole was wound: "a symbol of beauty, the result of absolute co-operation."[14]

The last May Queen was crowned in 1964 at a presentation of "Ye Olde Maye Daye." The Spring Festival continued, and in 1970 the name was changed to Spring Convocation Weekend. This springtime weekend continues to this day and is currently called Parents' Weekend. As mothers of students had been initially honored during Spring Festival, parents have been an integral part of the weekend celebration throughout its evolution.

Carleton College, Northfield, Minnesota

A private, liberal arts college founded in 1866 by the Minnesota Conference of Congregational Churches as a preparatory school; the first graduating college class was that of 1874 with one man and one woman. Carleton currently enrolls approximately 920 men and 1,010 women.

The Carleton College May Fête had its origins in an ice cream social that was a highlight of the spring season at the end of the nineteenth century. In 1907 the social became a May Day festival, featuring a maypole dance, and in 1909, the first Carleton May Queen, a senior, was crowned. The Queen was selected by secret ballot at a regular Wednesday evening devotional meeting of the YWCA which, together with the YMCA, sponsored the fête honoring the 35 members of the senior class. Marches, the maypole dance, and the mystery surrounding the identity of the Queen made the fête a popular and successful way of raising money, so in 1911, the YWCA added a performance of *As You Like It*. The subsequent year, the Queen was escorted from the women's hall to her throne under the trees by a long line of girls dressed in white and carrying wreaths of flowers. After the crowning and some folk dances and gymnastic drills, six women members of an advanced oratory class presented *Ingomar, the Barbarian*. This was followed by a Venetian dance given by twenty-four girls who carried arches, hoops and garlands of flowers.

In 1915, with the advent of the first full-time physical education instructor at the college, for the first time a theme, "The Story of the Crocus," was portrayed by aesthetic dancing and pantomime. Three years later, the pageant was moved to the shores of a beautiful nearby lake and the gate receipts of more than $200 were donated to the Red Cross. Later, larger receipts were accumulated in a fund for a women's gymnasium. "By the 1920s, May Fête was 'considered the most beautiful and impressive event of its kind in the northwest,'" the college historians noted, adding that "although it occasioned many 'postponed picnics, broken dates, and sarcastic remarks by the he-men of the College on the general practicability and great everyday usefulness of aesthetic dancing,' it was anticipated with excitement and pleasure by most students." May Day attracted more visitors to the college than any other event.

In 1921 the island in the lake on campus was chosen for a stage setting and a rustic bridge was built for those taking part to cross over, and this location, set in a natural amphitheater, was used for the next forty years. In 1924 the Minneapolis Symphony Orchestra performed the difficult Wagnerian orchestration accompanying the presentation of *Sigurd, the Volsung*. Because of the great interest of the Scandinavian population of the area in this theme, the college spent much time and money to ensure that the costumes and scenic effects were historically correct. The finale of this event was a snowflake ballet danced by 125 girls in fluffy white costumes. From 1933 on, a horse show was added to the attractions. By the mid–1930s, May Day was an elaborate festivity, though it was unchanged in being held "to honor 'the twelve senior women [the May court] who, in the eyes of their classmates, have contributed the most to Carleton.'"

Sample program titles include:

1909	First May Day festival with crowning and maypole dance.
1910	Fête held indoors, which cramped the sophomores' military drill that was offered after the crowning and the maypole dance.
1911	*As You Like It*
1912	*Ingomar, the Barbarian*
1913	After the crowning the juniors gave a club drill, the seniors gave a marching drill and the freshmen gave a Venetian dance. A Japanese operetta followed.
1914	*Snow-White*
1915	*The Story of the Crocus*
1916	*Ceres and Proserpina*
1917	*Cinderella*
1918	*The Prince of Spring*
1919	*Story of Oenone*
1920	*A Tale of Ancient Rome*
1935	*Peter Pan*
1946	*We Hold These Truths*
1957	*A Mere Meanwhile*, from *Songs of the Pogo*, by Walt Kelly

For fifteen years after World War II, the May Fête still occupied a prominent place in the College calendar, and both men and women performed in productions such as *The Frantic Physician* and *The Mikado*. Toward the end of the 1950s, however, student interest in the event was waning. The college historians write that "[i]n 1959 the May Fête court was introduced to the women's breakfast not as 'ideal Carleton women,' but as those 'selected on the basis of service, but not necessarily office; that have made tangible contributions in those areas in which they are gifted.'"[15]

By 1959 the students had evidently begun to tire of the event, as two students wrote up a summary of a poll from which they received 150 return questionnaires: all in favor save for 10 that were negative and another 13 negative toward the idea of a Fine Arts Weekend.[16] The traditional May Fête ended after the spring of 1963, though an event by the same name, now involving a concert of student bands, continues.

Case Western Reserve University, Cleveland, Ohio

The university in its present form is the result of the 1967 federation of Case Institute of Technology (founded in 1880 as the Case School of Applied Science) and Western Reserve University (founded in 1826 as Western Reserve College). The two institutions had shared adjacent campuses since the late nineteenth century, and were involved in cooperative efforts for many years.

In 1888, women ceased to be admitted to the Adelbert College of Western Reserve University, and instead were admitted to the newly established Women's College of WRU, renamed the Flora Stone Mather College in 1931. The girls were very active in dramatic presentations; and in the spring of 1894 the sophomores (the class of 1896) gave a Tree Day presentation, ceremoniously planting a maple tree. The custom of the increasingly-elaborate sophomore class Tree Day continued for many years; in 1897 the first photograph of a maypole dance in honor of Tree Day appears in the college yearbook. In the spring of 1900 the sophomores, by then numbering in the low forties, added a pageant to the ceremony. These pageants often featured the Spirit of the Sophomore Class searching for Truth or Beauty while being hindered or helped by the spirits of the other three classes.

At about the same time the seniors were also offering a Class Day play, typically held in mid–June. In 1909 the play was a pageant of Robin Hood; in 1911 there appeared for the first time the "May Games of Ye Senior Class," complete with archery contests, two sides of girl morris dancers, the pageant *The Downfall of Robert, Earl of Huntingdon*, by Anthony Mundy (1597), a minuet performed by "powdered-hair dancers," and a maypole dance performed with lights in the early evening.[17] While many pageants appear to have been written by the students, the 1914 senior May Day pageant, *The Awakening of Princess Da*isy, was explicitly based on a similar pageant performed at Sweet Briar College.[18]

Thereafter until the mid–1930s, the seniors performed a May Day pageant while the sophomores performed a Tree Day pageant. The first mention of the crowning of a May Queen appears in 1914. "Sing-outs"—competitive, inter-class, song parody contests—also began to be part of May Day in the 1920s.

Records are sketchy for the decade of the 1920s, but resume again in 1937 when a "Country Fair" May Day pageant was performed by the sophomores, who had apparently dropped the tradition of Tree Day. Program information is complete from that time until the last apparent mention of May Day, in 1969. Plays included *Alice in Wonderland, Cinderella, The Wizard of Oz*, various Gilbert and Sullivan parodies, and the periodic reappearance of Robin Hood. Reflecting the popularity of the L'il Abner comic strip, the theme of the 1940 celebration was "Daisy Mae Queen of May Day." Girls were invited to nominate a (girl) "L'il Abner" who, dressed in overalls, then crowned the Queen. In 1943 the Queen, now wearing overalls herself, was crowned as Rosie the Riveter. The program was curtailed "in the interest of wartime economy" and was also combined with the traditional announcing of student honors and Step Night.[19]

In 1949 the men of Adelbert College of WRU joined in the girls' festivities with their "Campus Day" activities. A 26-mile relay race conveying the greetings of the headmaster of the Western Reserve Academy preparatory school in Hudson, Ohio, to the University President was one of the men's contributions: other athletic events, including a tug-of-war, also became part of the day.[20]

In 1954 a young African American woman from Georgia, "the first of her race to be so honored," was crowned Queen, possibly making her the first so crowned in the nation. The article that announced her coronation added that "The queen ... is selected on the basis of scholarship, leadership and beauty."[21]

By 1960, the pageant and the skit were produced by the freshmen, which may account for an apparent decline thereafter in quality and interest. The May Day chairman's report of 1964 states that although the Queen was crowned, the event had deteriorated. The chairman wrote that May Day

> faced unusual problems this year.... Enthusiasm was greatly lacking on the part of the Mather students, and participation was feared to be at an all time low. The previous year the Adelbert men had been asked to join in the program in an effort to increase interest; but participation did not increase significantly, and the skits were not of a high quality nor in proper taste.
>
> Desperate to fill up time on the program, the chair had asked various sororities to sing song parodies; but these groups also dropped out. The chair concluded that there was just too much going on: Stunt Night, spring vacation, Greek Week, the Spring Formal and Derby Day were competing for students' attention.[22]

In 1965 the Queen was crowned and the men held their traditional relay race, but there does not seem to have been a skit or pageant. The year 1966 saw the theme of "Rites of Spring," while 1968 had no Queen listed in the program for what was not only Parents' Weekend, but the inauguration of a new University President. In 1969, while the weekend was called May Day weekend, there was no mention of a Queen. The event seems to have died after that date.

Chatham University, Pittsburgh Pennsylvania

A private, liberal arts university for women chartered in 1869 as Pennsylvania College for Women, Chatham currently enrolls approximately 530 undergraduate women.

May Day celebrations began circa 1908 and were held annually until 1920, after which they were held every two to three years until 1930. Elaborate pageants began in 1912 with *Virful Cu Dor (The Peak of Yearning, a Roumanian Folk Tale)* (1912); *Paskennodan (The City of Smoke Vapor or The City of Mist)* in 1915; *A Mid-Summer Night's Dream* in 1916 — this pageant was given both in the afternoon and the evening and attracted twelve thousand spectators; *Victory through Conflict* (1920); *The Birth of May Day* (1923); *A Day in Fairyland* (1925); *Deep Sea Caverns* (1927); and *Persephone* (1929). After a hiatus from 1930 to 1934, the pageant was resumed with an original play, *The Two Queens*, in 1935. The last pageant, an Elizabethan drama written by a professor in the Drama Department, was held in 1947. A waning of student interest, as well as a change in the Arts Course curriculum which produced plays involving fewer students and serving a more clearly academic purpose, caused the demise of the event. Today May Day is celebrated simply by the freshwomen placing flowers outside the doors of the senior women.[23]

Three Grecian Graces in an aesthetic pose with their basket of gleanings in the 1920 pageant, "Victory through Conflict." (Archives, Chatham University, Pittsburgh, Pennsylvania.)

Colby College, Waterville, Maine

Chartered in 1813 as the twelfth oldest independent liberal arts college in the U.S., in 1871, Colby became the first formerly all-male college in New England to admit women. Colby now enrolls approximately 1,820 students.

In 1910 the 143 girls of the Women's Division of Colby presented their first Ivy Day exercises with a Cornish May dance in which all the girls participated, a milk maid's dance around the maypole by the seniors, and various musical selections. After addresses and the formal presentation and acceptance of the trowel, the class ivy was planted. This was followed by a garland dance performed by the sophomores, a Dutch dance by the freshmen, and then the maypole dance. The evening concluded at dusk with the junior "stunt," which was a drill with Japanese lanterns. Prizes were awarded to the two best classes for their dancing.

The 1911 Ivy Day followed the pattern of its predecessor, but in 1912 there was a Robin Hood pageant and the crowning of the Queen, followed by a "Dancing-Match" in which the various classes, dressed as lords and ladies, fools, and village folk, competed. The maypole, in the senior class colors of green and white, was wound. In 1913 the pageant invoked King Winter dragged from his throne by seven fairies, farmer "boys" and a fancy dance by the juniors. 1914 saw the pageant *In Mother Nature's Garden*, with the dances of the Spring Maidens, the Summer Nymphs, the Autumn Sprites and the Snow Babies. These dances were followed by dances of milkmaids and their swains, a procession of characters from *Mother Goose* and *Alice in Wonderland*, and an umbrella dance for six girls, who were overtaken by Showers, who in turn were quickly chased away by Rainbow, Night, and the Spirit of Sleep.

The Ivy Day pageants continued to grow more elaborate: that of 1918 included dances by the four classes representing the spirits of Italy, France, England and America. In 1921 the exercises concluded with an evening performance of *The Merchant of Venice*, while in 1925 the girls performed *As You Like It*.

The last mention of Ivy Day was in 1929, when the student newspaper noted that the exercises would differ radically from those of the prior two years and return to the format of a pageant in the afternoon and a Shakespeare play in the evening. The various classes sang songs, and the freshmen danced "Mallebroke." At this time there were 365 men and 240 women students at the college.[24]

College of Wooster, Wooster, Ohio

Founded in 1866 as an independent college, affiliated with the Presbyterian Church. The college currently enrolls approximately 850 men and 950 women students.

In 1899, the girls of the women's residence hall celebrated May Day with a simple ceremony, crowning a junior girl as May Queen. The first formal May Day celebration was known as Color Day and was held on May 1, 1905. Still a simple celebration, students were expected to wear the school colors all day long and there was a special evening church service. In 1911 the first Queen was crowned. In 1917, the war affected the pageantry, and rather than presenting a pageant of the Reformation period, as had been planned, the girls temporarily took over Color Day with the crowning, a rose wreath drill, the winding of the maypole, an operetta, *The Garden of Japan*, and a special folk dance, while forty-eight men of the Wooster Battalion executed a military drill. Theme-oriented pageants, including an old English May Day, continued from 1918 onward, and a formal dance was added in 1933.[25] In 1940, a play given on the Friday night was added, turning the event into a weekend of festivities.

The pageants of Color Day, written and put on by the students under faculty direction, become increasingly elaborate. Themes included fairy tales, an old English May Day, *Canterbury Tales*, Milton's *L'Allegro*, a celebration of Virgil's birthday two thousand years prior, and one celebrating the one-hundredth anniversary of Goethe's death. This pageant, held in 1932, was possibly the college's greatest Color Day, for Lou Henry Hoover (the president's wife) attended, and at the end of the pageant accepted a honorary L.H.D. "That day the Queen of the May, Elma Sage, had the honor at the end of the ceremony of handing her own armful of roses to the mistress of the White House."[26]

In 1945 the Color Day was patriotic in nature. "The ceremony on that afternoon began with the review of Naval cadets by [the retiring college president] and the naval Officer in charge, and with the hoisting of the national ensign by the color guard. After the crowning there followed a precision drill with a review of the Cadet Regiment by the May Queen."[27]

In my review of the College of Wooster's photographs and programs, I concluded that the war caused a diminution of the festivities, and perhaps a decline in the complexity and the quality of the pageants, as post-war pageants appear to have been closer to student-led skits and burlesque than the more ambitious faculty-managed undertakings of prior years. The 1946 Color Day program contains a note from the manager that this was the first post-war Color Day that the college had had, and they had tried, "as nearly as possible, a pre-war set-up, but with the lack of experience in this type of program within the student body, the going has been tough."[28]

Perhaps because of the Color Day orientation of the May Day festival, the Wooster men participated more fully in the annual event than was evidenced at most other coed colleges. A 1915 photo shows both girls and men performing a gun drill, termed a "Military Parade Senior Stunt." And from at least 1917 through the early 1940s, photographs show men performing the maypole dance with the women. The earliest picture of this dance, from 1917, shows the girls in Kate Greenaway smocks and picture hats and the men, bare-headed, in white flannels.

From the earliest years, the Queen's court had six escorts (regardless of the number of women in the court). In 1928 they wore white trousers and dark blazers and carried white boaters and black canes. Their fashions changed with the times, so that by 1969, one of the last events, the five escorts wore gray slacks and what appear to be navy blazers over gray turtlenecks, while the sixth escort, the Queen's escort, wore a suit and tie.

Photographs of the procession of the Queen consistently mirror that of a formal wedding: she walked down a long white carpet laid on the grass, preceded by her court and two little flower girls, and followed by a little boy who carried her crown on a pillow and two more little boys to hold up her long train. The court progressed between the six escorts, who were lined in pairs close the throne, and the women of the court paused between the escorts as the Queen proceeded to be crowned. In the crowning, all the participants knelt save the crown-bearer and the retiring Queen, who crowned the new Queen. Year after year, the formal photographs of the event invariably pose the Queen and her court, her pages, and her escorts formally seated on a tiered platform, with two girls dressed as trumpeters standing at the lower ends of the pyramid.

From the 1920s on, much publicity was given to the Queen, who was elected in late February or early March. Her major, her career goals, and her civic, artistic and sports accomplishments were often the subject of local newspaper articles, alumnae bulletins or even contained within the program. In the spring of what was probably 1931, a paper ran an article titled, "What Becomes of May Queens? Here's Answer." The writer noted that of the twenty prior Wooster College Queens, more than half had married and "all the remainder except the two who have part in tomorrow's ceremonies are teaching."[29]

From the early 1950s onward, the event became less elaborate: the Queen was crowned at about eleven in the morning, followed by a brief pageant or skit and some dancing and gymnastics demonstrations or a military drill. After a luncheon, parents and friends would view a variety of athletic competitions. By the late fifties, a mother-daughter tea was added to the day, which concluded with a formal dance.

The 1958 Color Day pageant depicted six scenes showing the history of the town and the college: "in 1852 the coming of the first passenger train; 1870 the coming of the first students to the College, when the College of Wooster opened its doors; 1908 the Centennial of Wooster; 1920 scenes from the 'roaring twenties'; 1950 a town's 'crash night'; and Color Day 1958.[30]

In 1959, the senior and junior men nominated the six junior girls, who were then voted upon by the entire student body. The winner was a young Korean woman, the first foreign-born Queen of the college. At this time the senior women performed the maypole dance.

The last Wooster Color Day appears to have been held in 1969, when the event took place in the gym, rather than the football field, undoubtedly due to bad weather.

Columbia College, Columbia, South Carolina

A private, liberal arts women's college founded by Methodists in 1854 "to educate young women for fruitful service to church, state and nation." The college currently enrolls 1,500 women.

Columbia College's May Day began in 1909 as a contest sponsored by the staff of the college yearbook to raise funds. According to a local newspaper account in 1967 that summarized the history of the festival, "[c]andidates were nominated by classes, and the votes cost one cent each. The maid of honor was chosen by the Queen. Around 1920, the charge for voting was removed and the Queen was elected by the student body ballot. The runner-up was the maid of honor." There is some evidence of associated pageantry, but no information on this is available.

The exercises were canceled during 1943 and 1944 and the Queens of those years were crowned at the Junior-Senior prom. The 1967 newspaper article revealed that many prior Queens came to the celebration that year, wearing or carrying their gowns.

"Many of the Queens wear their May Day gowns as wedding dresses," the writer noted. Several of the Queens interviewed said that they were married within a few weeks of May Day. "Commenting on the rapid changing of fashion, [the Queen of 1962] looked down at her white lace dress and said, 'Five years ago it was pretty.'"[31]

The crowning of the May Queen continued until 1995, when the celebration was discontinued due to "changing times," as per the archivist.

Converse College, Spartanburg, South Carolina

A private, liberal arts, women's college founded in 1889. The current undergraduate population numbers 500 women, with an additional 100 commuting students, a graduate program, and an older student program.

The first celebration took place on May 21, 1910, under the auspices of the athletic association. It was organized by Miss May Riser, class of 1912. The local newspaper noted, "So delighted was every one, including college authorities, students and visiting public, that it may be taken as a settled matter that, as President Pell put in impromptu verse, 'As surely as there's another May, So surely we will keep this day.' The announcement from him brought enthusiastic applause from every quarter."

Despite this support, there was no festival in 1911. In 1912 Miss Riser again organized the festivity, with the assistance of Miss Josephine MacDonald, director of physical education. Proceeds of $125 were contributed to the endowment fund.

The festival took place again in 1915, with various dances and pantomimes. In 1916 a performance of *Twelfth Night* was included. There were no festivities during 1917–20 as the athletic association "expended its energies on activities aiding the war." In 1921 the pageant returned with Greek dances, Mother Goose frolics and the maypole dance.

> From that day to this, the May Day pageant has been a much-heralded annual event at Converse. The beauty and high quality of the performances have lured many alumnae and friends of the college back to the campus and drawn thousands of spectators from Spartanburg and neighboring counties.

Sample programs include *Battling the Boll Weevil* (1923) featuring the "uncanny" characters of Fire, Moisture, and Lamentation; *Princess Briar Rose* (1925); *The Twelve Dancing Princesses* (1928); a dance drama based on *A Midsummer Night's Dream* (1929); and a pageant, *Merrie England* (1926). In 1930, a four-act dance drama based on Alfred Noyes' play *Sherwood* drew more than 3,000 spectators. The pageant of 1932, long considered one of the most beautiful, was a *Plantation May Fair in Colonial Carolina*, set circa 1785.

Converse College maintained several special traditions with regard to the selection and crowning of the Queen. The Queen's identity was kept a secret, until she appeared at the end of the May Day procession, always to the Triumphal March from *Aida*. "The audience watched

The Converse College May Court in the late 1940s or early 1950s. The "King" sits on the Queen's left, almost hidden under the splendor of her gown and train. (Archives and Special Collections, Converse college, Spartanburg, South Carolina.)

eagerly as the seniors in the May court came one by one down the hill into the amphitheater, leaving the May queen to appear at the very last." Since 1926 the student body had been instructed to elect the girl who "best represented the spirit of Converse." After the first few years of May Day, "the president of the athletic association was always king and she always crowned the Queen. A member of the athletic association was always in charge of the celebration, receiving assistance and direction from the physical education department."[32]

Converse College still honors the May Queen and her Court. The event focuses on celebrating scholarship, leadership, and service to the college. The students select four representatives from the freshmen, sophomore, and junior classes, and five from the senior class. The Queen is then chosen from the five candidates from the senior class.

The May Day festival begins after the general campus awards ceremony. At the ceremony, held in an outdoor amphitheater on the grass, the girls used to wear white dresses; now they wear their Sunday best. They are escorted by their father or a significant older male member of their family. The archivist talks about the history of Converse or of May Day. Members of the School of Music or younger groups of performers from Spartanburg perform. Something is read about each girl in the Court and her contribution to the college, and the President crowns the Queen with a crown that has been used for decades. The event is quite brief, and attended mostly by the women's families.[33]

DePauw University, Greencastle, Indiana

Founded by Methodists in 1837 as Indiana Asbury College, an ecumenical, liberal arts institution, with forty men students aged 13 to 28. The university currently enrolls 2,300 students.

Though women were admitted to DePauw University in 1867, partly as a result of the lack of male students due to the Civil War, the college's Web site notes that they found themselves "in separate — some might say subordinate — campus roles at the close of World War I." Excluded from membership in the men's journalism clubs, debate teams, and scholastic honorary groups, women founded their own versions of these and other activities, celebrating May Day for the first time in 1910. The university's on-line history notes:

> With Old Gold Day in its early years chiefly oriented toward male participation in class scraps and interclass football games, May Day became the premier campus event for women. Held in early May the festivities usually began with a lantern parade on Friday evening — sometimes complemented by an unofficial "pajama parade" of male students to the women's dormitories after hours. The next day the Y.W.C.A. served an early morning breakfast on the East College lawn, which was followed by a women's tennis tournament or field day and a student-written and directed pageant. (In 1920 Margaret Mead, later the distinguished anthropologist, wrote the day's pageant, entitled "The Choice of American Girlhood.") The climactic events took place in the Dells behind Longden Hall, where gaily dressed coeds danced and sang, the seniors winding the Maypole, juniors forming a daisy chain, and the Queen of the May accepting her crown in the midst of her court. A play performed first in Meharry hall and later in the theatre in Speech hall concluded the day's events. Sometime in the 1930s May Day was combined with Mothers' Day and survived in that form down to recent times [approximately 1977].

This history also notes that beginning in 1923 the college yearbook annually featured a special section on 'campus beauties,' consisting of a half dozen photographs of glamorously posed coeds selected by vote of the male student body or by a well-known artist or other supposed expert on female beauty and charm. In 1931, for example, Broadway producer Florenz Ziegfield made the final selection. DePauw's students also elected other Queens: The Old Gold Day Queen, who was crowned at halftime during the homecoming football game, the Dad's Day Queen, crowned in November, and various Prom Queens, who with their escorts led the grand marches that opened dances.[34]

Duke University, Durham, North Carolina

With a long history dating back to Methodist and Quaker founders in 1838, the institution was named Trinity College in 1859. While women students were admitted as early as 1878, in 1894, the Duke family offered the college three $100,000 endowments, one of which was contingent upon accepting women "on an equal footing" with men. In 1924, upon even larger gifts of the Duke family, the college achieved university status and took the Duke name. It currently enrolls approximately 6,300 undergraduate and 4,300 graduate students.

May Day apparently began in 1920, as the 1931 program announced it as the eleventh annual May Day celebration, given in honor of alumnae homecoming. The program noted that the women now had an auditorium, gymnasium, an administration building and "West Duke" all their own. After tea came the pageant (*The Dance of the Day*) and the crowning of the Queen. A modern version of *The Taming of the Shrew* was presented in the evening. The archivist writes:

> We have several folders of photographs of the May Day celebrations here and a file of programs, news clippings, and tickets. The tickets are to the 1937 celebration and have "17th May Day Pageant" on them, so it would appear the festival began in 1920 when this school was still named Trinity College. In an article about the Pageant in our alumni magazine for June 1924, the author writes that "for the past several years the young women students have been staging a very enjoyable and elaborate May Day Celebration...." This magazine, the *Duke Alumni Register*, covered the festival almost yearly up through 1947, including the years during World War II. I've not found any document that

tells just when the last celebration was held, but it seems to have died out about 1950 or so. As late as 1967, however, a May Queen was still being elected. That year, the woman was Wilhelmina Reuben, one of the first African-American students to enroll here. Elizabeth Dole, Class of 1958, was also a May Queen. It appears that by the 1950s, the May Queen was being named by her fellow women students in recognition of accomplishments and service to the university community.[35]

Earlham College, Richmond, Indiana

A coeducational college founded by Quakers in 1847, Earlham currently enrolls 1,170 students.

The college held an increasingly elaborate Elizabethan pageant held approximately every four years from 1875 to 1993. The first Queen, Tennessee Tomlinson, was, at the age of fourteen, the youngest girl in her class. From 1880 to 1891 the same coronation gown was used by the various Queens, regardless of their size. At this time, the May Day observances were under the auspices and management of the Girls' Phoenix Literary Society. The first maypole dance was in 1882. In 1886 girls with dark hair portrayed gypsies, crowning their own Queen, and until 1902 almost as much was made of the Gypsy Queen as of the Queen of the May herself.

In 1886 the festival became more elaborate. The Queen was crowned and then given a scepter by a girl who proclaimed: "In the name of these thy subjects I crown thee Queen of the May, investing Your Majesty with the authority of a sovereign, and promising the loving obedience of thy people." The Queen then gave a speech, describing old English May customs and relating the story of King Henry VIII and his young Queen Catherine of Aragon going out in the May. She concluded:

> You today are performing a duty which we all owe in keeping up the beautiful customs which remind us, as the year goes round, of the occasions which they celebrate, and revive in us the feelings and sentiments which called them into life. I thank you for the part in it which you have given me. My efforts will be to rule wisely and well in my brief reign, without tyranny or despotism, but with the welfare of good subjects at heart. May the day be one full of enjoyment and happiness to you, and may your lives be full of May Days.

After this speech, the Maids of Honor took the oath of allegiance. The nine Gypsies, all "pronounced brunettes" in full gypsy costume and "considered by many the most attractive and unique feature of the occasion" gave the Queen flowers. Songs, recitations and the maypole dance followed, in which the girls, the smallest in the class, "stepped lightly and gracefully round and round with feet that would have liked, perhaps, a quicker time and different motion, but which followed their Quaker tendencies in the slower movement of a march." After this drill, the Queen rose and recited Herrick's poem "Come, Corinna, let's go a-Maying" [36]

In 1891 the festival was moved to a more central location to provide more room for spectators. The year 1902 marked the last festival to be handled entirely by the women. Finally, in 1902, a newspaper article reported that the exercises "were made a general college feature to an extent which had not previously been the case. In other words, in the Faculty language of today, it was made an 'approved gathering.'" Admission was charged for first time, proceeds of which went toward equipping the gymnasium and the students' parlor.[37]

By 1911 it was noted that in the weeks before the event one could hear the sound of several pianos being played at the same time. "Every afternoon from 4 until 6 o'clock, and every evening from 7 until 9 some rehearsal in full swing. For the last two weeks, the college students and professors have realized that the day for the spectacular May Day celebration is not far off and hard work must be done." Three big casts rehearsed three times a week for the past month "until they have now almost reached the state of perfection."[38]

By 1929 so many spectators were attending the event that it had to be moved to a large, flat field to accommodate the more than 3,000 visitors.[39] This year also marked the first appearance of "Queen Elizabeth," a role traditionally played by the wife of the president of the college.

By 1937 there were five maypoles and the students also danced the English folk dances "Sellenger's Round" and "Gathering Peascods." There were still gypsies who crowned their own Queen.

As related in Chapter 6, Earlham's Big May Day, held every four years, ended after the 1993 celebration.

Elmira College, Elmira, New York

Founded in 1855 as a college for women and the first in the U.S. to offer a Bachelor of Arts degree commensurate to those offered to men. The college admitted men in 1969, and currently enrolls 1,200 students.

May Day at Elmira College was introduced by Dean Anstice Harris and the first Queen was crowned in 1902. The freshmen elected a Queen from among the sophomore girls, and the Queen was then *de facto* president of her class during her junior year. Festivities in the early years were held on campus and included dancing around the maypole and an outdoor theatrical or dance entertainment, often performed by the college's modern dance group, Orchesis. Sample pageant themes included *Echo and Narcissus, An Old English May Festival, Cupid and Psyche, Cinderella, Alice in Wonderland,* and *Pictures at an Exhibition.*

Around 1910, when the audience became too large to be accommodated on campus, the festivities were moved to a local state park, where they were held until 1942, when transportation difficulties associated with the war temporarily prevented them from occurring. May Day was held at this park at least once after the war, but when the college expanded its grounds in 1961, the festivities returned to campus. The last May Queen was crowned in 1967, "in the midst of Vietnam War protests and on the eve of coeducation."[40]

For some years after this May Day was replaced by Spring Weekend, which according to librarian and researcher Julia Schult was "mostly an outdoor party on a Saturday, with beer and rock bands." Concern about drinking caused the administration to ban Spring Weekend in 1997 and to instruct the Student Activities Board to rename and completely revise the event. They did so by picking the name "May Days" for the new festival, "apparently without any knowledge of the history of that phrase at Elmira College." The event includes a ball and an alcohol-free carnival. However, Schult reported in the year 2000 that some student clubs staged a small event, called The Old Elmira May Fest, featuring a local morris team, a maypole, a bagpiper, and a student choral group singing the college's own May Song.[41]

Goucher College, Baltimore, Maryland

Founded in 1885 as a private liberal arts college, Goucher currently enrolls 334 men and 840 women.

The girls first observed May Day at sunrise in 1920. According to the college history:

> the veiled Queen, in a chariot of yellow, drawn by two nymphs, was borne across the campus to her throne. After a moment of suspense the veil was withdrawn and the choice of May Queen [a senior] was disclosed…. To the music of violins the nymphs danced before her, pages crowned her with a wreath of wild flowers, the chorus sang in her honor, and then the chariot bore her away.[42]

The first Queen later wrote:

it was an almost impossible hour of the day for city girls ... and almost equally difficult for the [residence] hall girls to crawl out of bed.... The enterprising fire chief of [the girls' hall] planned a fire drill for that very time and had her charges march out on the hockey field, so several [women] who hadn't planned to attend the coronation found themselves there after all![43]

The dramatics club organized the voting for Queen, though nominations and voting were open to the whole college. "There was a big box with a guardian in the basement of Goucher Hall for about a week, and every passer-by was hailed and urged to cast her vote for one senior for May Queen."[44]

The second year's festivities were rained out. The year after that, the Queen was red-haired — noted as an unusual attribute in the college's history. The "taboos of the Titian Tints were respected. Not only were pink roses and red streamers barred from any part of the ceremonies, but a vigilant Board of Censors, stationed at the entrance, removed all vestiges of offending colors from the audience."[45]

After perhaps a brief hiatus, when the college purchased a new campus in 1925, the festival resumed in more elaborate form. The women staged the pageant, *The Green Spring Lady*, based on themes connected with Maryland history. It had been intended that the pageant be continuous from season to season in a four-year cycle, but "somehow the sober spectacle of Margaret Brent and her struggles for civil liberty seemed to the students out of harmony with the joyous abandon of a May fête, and after two years the plan was given up, though, in honor of the tercentenary of the founding of Maryland, 'A Vision of Maryland' was given in 1934." In other years Greek and Norse mythology, English and Irish fairs and revels, and occasionally plays such as *Pandora's Box* and Alfred Noyes' *Robin Hood in Sherwood Forest* were presented. The identity of the Queen was always a closely guarded secret, and the festivities were presented to her and her court included a formal program, games, fortune telling and puppet shows that "filled the time before the picnic supper and the return in buses to the College."[46] The selection and crowning of a Queen continued as part of May Fair until some time in the 1960s.

Grinnell College, Grinnell, Iowa

Founded in 1846 as a private liberal arts and science college, Grinnell currently enrolls approximately 610 men and 690 women.

For many years the college sponsored a May Music Festival, which began at the turn of the last century and continued well into the 1950s. The festival featured visiting orchestras and singers, often lasting for two or three days. Its programs make no mention of the May Pageant, which often occurred around the same time of the month.

The May Pageant began simply in 1909 with a crowning, a garland drill and a maypole dance, with the ribbons in the college colors of scarlet and black. The student newspaper of that year noted that "this festivity is two centuries old but just as beautiful as ever, and many colleges make it an annual affair, as Grinnell may in the future."[47] Miss Anderson, the physical education instructor, directed this and apparently all subsequent programs. In 1910 the event became more elaborate: to music provided by the college band, spectators viewed a flower dance, the maypole dance, a figure march, several songs, a Dutch dance, the "Norwegian Mountain Dance" and a Swedish folk dance.

Subsequent programs included a *Pageant of the Spirit of May* (1914), *The Spirit of Grinnell* (1920), *The Quest for the Moon Goddess* (1924), and *In Golden Days; A Festival to Apollo* (1936). The last pageant, that of 1937, was titled simply a *Dance Recital*. It was still under the direction of Miss Anderson.

Grove City College, Grove City, Pennsylvania

A liberal arts, Christian college founded in 1876, Grove City College now enrolls approximately 2,300 students.

While there is sketchy information that the girls of Grove City College (GCC) celebrated May Day as early as 1905 (a photograph of that date shows men and women sedately winding the maypole), the college officially dates its celebration from the first elaborate coronation held in 1916, directed by the dean of women. The titles, roles and costumes of court members were Elizabethan in style. Beginning in 1920, the first pageant of dances was presented in honor of the Queen. During the next six years, a full symphony orchestra accompanied the pageants and added to the festivities. A heavily-jeweled crown was rented each year for the May Queen until 1937; at that time President Weir Ketler and his wife purchased a crown for the May Queen, their daughter Eleanor. This crown has been worn by each succeeding Queen since then.

Like Whitelands College, Grove City also enjoys the tradition of the Returning Queens: every four years all former May Queens are invited to return to campus to be treated as "Queen for a day," and to walk in the procession. The tradition was extant as early as 1925. In 2004, the eighteenth anniversary of this tradition, 19 former Queens, the oldest from 1938, returned out of 67 invitations sent.

In 1957 the day's activities were expanded further when the Recognition Convocation (awards ceremony) was established. That year Greek Sing, now titled All-College Sing, was added, which offers student groups an opportunity to display their musical talents.

The college continued with pageants, plays and dances until the 1980s, when the focus turned to modern dance. The weekend-long event, now Parents' Weekend, sees a host of musical, dance, dramatic activities, a business competition and a Recognition Convocation to give academic awards. The Spring Queen is crowned on Saturday during the Spring Pageant. Since 2003, the Spring King, chosen by popular vote, is recognized on Friday evening after the Band Concert when the Spring Queen puts the Spring King's sash over his shoulder.

The College's May Pageant themes include:

1917	N/A. The girl with the second-most votes was named the Goddess of Liberty
1918	N/A. The president's wife was named the Goddess Columbia. Folk dances were performed as well as a pantomime of women's involvement in war, featuring Joan of Arc.
1922	*A Young Woman's Choice between Education or Homemaking*
1923	*A Triumph of Beauty*
1924	*Fairy Tales*
1925	*An Hour in Demeter's Garden*
1926	*The History of the College*
1928	*The Call of the Sea*
1929	Milton's *Comus*
1930	*The Masque of the Two Strangers*
1931	*Old English May Festival*
1933	*The Founding of Grove City*
1934	*Japanese Star Legend*
1935	*The First Movement of Schubert's Unfinished Symphony*
1936	*Greek Games*
1937	*International Dance Festival*
1938	*Spring Through the Ages*
1939	*A Child's Fantasy*
1940	*Alice in Wonderland*

1941	*Ida and Marpessa*
1942	*The History of Physical Education*
1944	*Pierrot and the Singing Arrow*
1943 and 1945	The Queen was crowned but the Pageant was canceled probably due to the war.
1946	*May Day Festival* (traditional English festival)
1947	*My Diary*
1948	*Americans 1948*
1949	*Sing, Gypsy, Sing*
1950	*Waltz Dream*
1951	*A Historical Tribute to Grove City College*
1954	*International Friendship*
1961	*New York*
1962	*Dance Americana*
1964	*Husband Hunting* (GCC girls in search of a husband)
1969	*The American Way*
1970	*Food for Thought*
1981	*The Enchanted Jewels*

Grove City College still celebrates the coronation of the May Queen as part of Parent's Weekend, yet now the term Spring Queen is used because the event is not always in May, but occasionally in the last weekend in April. The coordinator states that pulling together the event is a lot of work.

In late January or early February, the students vote among ten candidates for the senior Queen and her Ladies-in-Waiting as well as a Junior Queen. Freshmen girls take the role of the four Heralds, while the Bearer of the Sceptre and the Bearer of the Crown are sophomores and the Marshall of the Day and the Coronation Officer are juniors. The positions are assigned by votes:

1st Freshman — Bearer of the Sceptre
2nd and 3rd Freshmen — Heralds
1st Sophomore — Bearer of the Crown
2nd and 3rd Sophomores — Heralds
1st Junior — Junior Queen
2nd Junior — Coronation Officer
3rd Junior — Marshall of the Day
1st Senior — Senior Queen
2nd–5th Seniors — Ladies in Waiting

While not every girl is interested in being a Queen, the role is generally considered an honor and only a conflict with another very significant activity would prevent her from accepting it. The 2004 Queen, for example, passed up a chance to compete in a national water polo tournament in order to participate in May Day. And not everyone who would like to dance may; the dance coordinators must turn away all but about 80 dancers who participate in the student-choreographed dances.

The current coordinator of the event attributes the college's small size as well as the long tenures of former coordinators as reasons for the longevity of the May Day tradition. From 1927 to 1966, Esther Post served as coordinator; from approximately 1968 to 1998 Cindy Walters served; from 1999 to the present, Carol Yeager. Post and Walters were in the Physical Education Department. (According to the May Queen of 1952, all girls taking PE had to participate in the dance portions of the pageant.) A final reason for this college's maintenance of the tradition is its conservative nature; as of 2005 the girls still live under parietal rules, and all fraternities and sororities are located on campus.[48]

Hollins University, Roanoke, Virginia

Founded in 1842, and Virginia's first chartered women's college, Hollins received college standing in 1913. It now enrolls approximately 812 women undergraduate students and 280 coed graduate students.

The Roanoke Female Seminary, one of Hollins University's precursors, existed, though it did not flourish, from 1820 to 1841. Little information about the Seminary survives, though a letter from a student, the niece of the headmaster, notes in 1838 "a delightful party here on the 1st day of May, which day is generally celebrated with great rejoicings in nearly all female schools."[49]

Much later, an alumna remembered:

> Long before 1903, the coming of the May had been celebrated at Hollins, but no one had felt responsible for its always being done. In 1902, just before May 1, a group of representative girls met to revive the May Day custom which seemed about to die out. These girls, the next year, 1903, became the charter members of the secret society of the Fairies of Freya.[50]

The 1902 event, a simple affair, involved a half-holiday, a procession of the participants, the maypole dance, and the crowning of the Queen by a girl who represented a Bishop "of the 'diocese of youth and beauty.'... It is impossible to picture the grace, beauty, and gladness of the entire scene — expressive of the association between the May-time of the year and the May-time of youth — both so full of promise.[51]

In 1903 the Fairies of Freya devised an elaborate and lengthy pageant, involving Robin Hood, morris dancers, mummers, and a maypole dance. The image of the Freya bird was placed over the Queen's throne. Initially 13 in number, the secret society grew to a total of 39, after which membership was limited. Often the characters of the Fairies of Freya were masked, as befitting a secret society; the photograph of the 1913 Queen, for example, shows her two attendants in long white gowns and white half masks.[52]

Other pageants included *Alice in Wonderland* (1904), *A Hollins History — A Masque* (1905), *A Flower Fantasy* (1906), *Mother Goose* (1907), and, in 1911, a most unusual topic: *My Wife Is a Suffragette*. In 1909 the celebration was honored by the first singing of the school song, *The Green and the Gold*, written by Phoebe Hunter, who was also crowned Queen that year. In the following year Miss Hunter wrote the song by which the May Queens were subsequently welcomed as they processed: "She Comes, She Comes, Our Radiant Queen."[53]

The patriotic production of 1914 was attended by Vice-President Thomas R. Marshall and Mr. and Mrs. Sinclair Lewis.[54] After the 1916 celebration of Shakespeare's tercentenary, festivities were interrupted by the war and not resumed until 1921. The event varied over the years. At some point the members of Freya introduced a "Nixie-Pixie May Day" for the faculty's children. In 1935 some imaginative playing with headgear in a play production [of the] class of 1935 led to the custom of choosing as Queen the girl under the most ridiculous hat."[55] However, by the 1940s, "pictures of athletes outweighed even the May Day and beauty sections of the *Spinsters* [the student newspaper] ... for at Hollins, as elsewhere, the sports program was extensive, and riding was by now inseparable from the college."[56] In the 1950s, the faculty committees, rather than the Fairies of Freya, sponsored May Day, adding a riding show and an informal cotillion to the festivities. May Day disappeared from the campus in 1970, not returning until 1994, when two students revived the festival, including the traditional daisy chain and the court, for one year.[57]

Hood College, Frederick, Maryland

Founded in 1893 as an independent, comprehensive college for women, Hood College currently enrolls approximately 560 women and 38 men.

The archivist notes that information from the early years is spotty. In 1908 a group of students with two chaperones went on a May Day picnic. College yearbooks show that in 1913 the annual May Fête of the School of Art was held at an outdoor venue. This was in the form of an outing, probably a picnic rather than a formal pageant, and was repeated in 1914. In 1915 the YWCA sponsored the fête held on the evening of May 1. It included the crowning, a maypole dance, a vocal solo, the dancing of the minuet, and a Japanese play. "After the conclusion of the program the people went to tables decorated to represent different nationalities and there were served dainties characteristic of that nation. The subdued lights from the Japanese lanterns threw an enchanting glow over the entire scene."[58] A similar event occurred in 1916.

In 1917 the festival became more elaborate. After the procession and the crowning two girls recited "The Pageant Story," a long poem written by a senior. The story begins with the words of "Prince Hood" (a neat juxtaposition of Robin with the college name and principles) as "he" crowns the Queen of May:

> Come, let me crown thee Queen of May,
> Wear thou this garland of early flowers,
> Wakened to life by soft spring showers.
> Flower of womanhood, lovely to see,
> Ideals of honor and sweet purity,
> Has Prince Hood given thee, fairer than day.

The Queen then responded:

> Beautiful wreath of virtue, the crown,
> May I prove worthy, increase they renown;
> Noble Prince Hood, may I ever bear
> Thy laurels unsullied, pure and fair,
> And here in my court do I welcome you all,
> May everyone join in the gay festival.

After further springtide speeches came a variety of folk dances and songs and the play, *The Gooseherd and the Goblin*. The maypole dance concluded the festivities.[59]

May Day was celebrated again in 1918 and in 1919, with the reappearance of Prince Hood (always played by a girl) and the Queen and their courts. The college yearbook reported that "this year, contrary to the usual custom of giving the proceeds of the May fête to Miss Gerhard, the Hood Girls' Missionary in Japan, the money was sent for the rebuilding of North Japan College which was recently destroyed by fire and where Miss Gerhard is a teacher."[60]

The year 1920 saw another pageant, but in 1921, the girls had an afternoon ramble in the mountains instead. In 1923 rope-jumping was added as an attraction, continuing as a feature of the day until 1932. In 1923 a dinner-dance was also added to the event, and in 1933 an elaborate horse show, which continued until at least 1959, formed part of the festivities. Mother and Daughter and Father and Daughter banquets were added during this period, possibly continuing into the 1960s. The last pageant was apparently held in 1958, and it was noted that it was in a different form than the past: the theme was "Roman Holiday" and the girls performed *Menaechmi*, a comedy by Plautus.

The archivist's official list of May Queens show that there was a crowning almost continuously (the gaps probably reflect lack of documentation) from at least 1915 through 1965. During this period a Prince or Princess Hood was also part of the court as well as a Maid of Honor.

From 1927 through 1942 there was also a "Best Man" (also played by a girl) and from 1927 through 1958 a Jester. In 1966 there was no mention of a May Queen or court, but in 1967 the last Queen was crowned. By 1968, a college newspaper article mentions May Day as a tradition of the past.[61]

Indiana University, Bloomington, Indiana

Founded in 1820, Indiana University currently enrolls approximately 13,000 men and 14,800 women students.

The university's archivist notes that information in the early years is spotty. In 1904 the women of the university gave a big May festival under the auspices of the YWCA, yet a program from 1905 calls that year's festival the First Annual. A program from 1924 calls that year's festival the Third Annual, and there is also an undated program for a May Music Festival that the archivist is tentatively dating 1897.[62]

Some of the confusion may lie in the fact that in the early years, the May festival was musical, and involved citizens of Bloomington as well as students. In 1905 the May festival was purely musical in nature, with orchestral pieces and songs performed under the baton of Adolph Hahn. "He is a thorough musician and handles his men perfectly," noted the newspaper. "The rendition of the program will please the most critical ears."[63] A large chorus, soloists and an orchestra performed in three indoor concerts held over two days. Indeed, after the event, the newspaper reviewer felt that it had stamped Bloomington as a musical city.

In 1906, the chorus was opened to the university as well as the city, and it was noted that the trainer of the chorus was "a man of experience and means business. He will make any one interested sing and improve his voice."[64]

There was no mention of any May Day activity in 1907, but in 1908, the girls of the gymnasium classes of Indiana University presented *Merry May-Day as in Merrie England*, including the winding of the maypole in the school colors of cream and crimson. The program was to begin with an example of the regular gymnasium work done by the girls every week, and "will consist in swinging Indian clubs and handling dumb bells with all the vigor and skill of their brothers." This was to be followed by folk dances: "Dainty maids in the picturesque garb of the English peasants or the flaxen-haired Norwegian, will dance the complex, but graceful folk dances of long ago." The grand finale was a maypole dance performed by twenty-four girls "in dazzling white with green wreaths entwined in their hair," who wound the maypole decked with streamers of cream and crimson. Members of every woman's club in Bloomington were invited to attend, but only a few men were invited to "witness this exhibition of grace and beauty, and many plans are being laid by the men to secure one of these coveted invitations."[65]

Details of the events held between 1908 and 1922 are not available, though a newspaper article of 1922 writes of the "customary ceremony" accompanying the crowning. All classes took part in the maypole dancing, while each class also performed different folk dances. At dusk, a dance drama was given on the meadow. More than 90 women participated. The residence house presidents made nominations, and ten girls were voted upon for the honor of being Queen, with the one with the most votes the winner and the next highest three her maids of honor.[66]

In 1924 the Department of Physical Education presented the Third Annual May Festival. After the procession and the crowning of the Queen, the girls performed six folk dances and then twelve "natural" (interpretive) dances to the music of piano, harps, and violins.

In 1925, the program depicted the story of Proserpina, with various natural dances and an augmented group of musicians, and in 1926 the pageant was that of *Sylvia, or a Nymph of Diana*, also with dances.

By 1927, the event was called a "Dance Drama" and was presented by the Classes in Natural Dancing, and in 1928 it was called a "Dance Festival." Large formal festivals seem to have ceased after 1930.[67]

Iowa State University, Ames, Iowa

Founded in 1858 as a public, land-grant institution. The university now enrolls 27, 400 students.

The Women's Athletic Association held the university's first May Day festival in 1907 in honor of the women in the senior class, or, as they called themselves, the "senioritas." The activities included the crowning of the Queen, who was "the most accomplished senior woman," the maypole dance, and a picnic. Profits paid for equipment for women's sports. This first event, and many of the subsequent celebrations until at least until 1923, were under the direction of Winifred Tilden, the instructor in physical culture, a 1903 graduate of Mount Holyoke College, where she had experienced May Day. Miss Tilden came to Iowa State in 1904.[68]

By 1912 the celebration included a pageant: *The Vision of Youth*. In 1913 the pageant was titled, *Columbia, Queen of the May*, and depicted the spirit of America (Columbia), who welcomed the State Flower, as well as peasant girls who performed folk dances from many nations. By 1914 the minutes from a meeting of the Board of Deans indicated that due to the increased number of women students in the college and the increasing importance of the event, a business manager needed to be appointed to oversee the event. The pageant of 1914 was a dance pantomime titled *Spring-Time*. The year 1915 saw the *Pageant of American Women*, and 1916 a Shakespearean May Day, with excerpts from *As You Like It*.

In 1917 the usual events were superseded by a "Red Cross Day." In a square formed by the college's cadets, the Queen was crowned and girls performed various aesthetic dances. Subsequently, "the spectators wandered from booth to booth inspecting the display of surgical dressings and knitting, and buying Red Cross memberships."[69] In 1918, Miss Tilden and a student wrote a patriotic pageant, *Her Gift*, in which Alma Mater, with her followers, the black-gowned Senioritas (*sic*), held court on the steps of Agricultural Hall. Queen Indifference led displays of frivolity and nearly won over the College Maiden, until the healthful, wholesome pleasures of tennis, golf, and other sports, accompanied by Thrift and Service, claimed her heart and she "chose to be of aid and service to her country during the summer."[70] The 1921 pageant was a similarly earnest spectacle of History, which included the Spirit of Iowa State College (as it was then) calling American Vision "to behold her achievements."[71]

In 1922, VEISHEA, named after the five original colleges of the university (veterinary science, engineering, industrial studies, home economics, and agriculture), combined several of the divisional celebrations (including May Day) into one centralized event. VEISHEA continued to hold a May Day Fête as part of its celebrations until 1933, when it was seen as outdated and was not drawing much of a crowd. In 1938 the title of May Queen was changed to Queen of VEISHA and then later VEISHA Queen of Queens. VEISHEA is now considered the largest student-run celebration in the United States.[72]

James Madison University, Harrisonburg, Virginia

Founded in 1909 as the state Normal and Industrial School, with 150 women. Men came to the campus as day students in 1946. The university currently enrolls approximately 5,600 men and 8,000 women.

Early celebrations involved a May Breakfast at which the girls, dressed in bright new spring dresses, feasted on strawberries under the apple blossoms in the school orchard. In 1913, after a procession of the girls bearing green garlands, the senior maypole dance and the singing of the class song and various May Day songs, the senior class president was crowned the first Queen.

In the period 1913 to 1923, every senior class president was also crowned Queen. From 1924 on, however, the Queens were elected by the student body, then numbering 640 women. During the early years the Athletic Association chose a different theme for the festival: Elizabethan England, Robin Hood, Peter Pan, and so on. In 1935, when the Social Committee of Student Government took over the organization of the event, an evening dance with men was added to the festivities. Known as a "girl-break" dance, it was one "at which many a boy had his first acquaintance with feminine 'stags' lining the walls, dances from which many a young man emerged nearly breathless as his date tried to give him a 'rush' by having all of her acquaintances dance with him."[73]

The war years featured patriotic themes; in 1943 the Queen carried red, white and blue carnations and the program honored the Allied Nations. In 1953, Alumni Homecoming was moved from March to May Day to add to the celebration that now included a parade through town with student floats. In 1955 May Day expanded to an all-day affair, with caroling before breakfast, music between classes, and the festooned fronts of dorms and sorority houses vying for decorating honors.

In 1946 the college began to admit men, and while the election of the Queen and her court continued into the sixties, according to the college historian, "it seemed more an outmoded vestige of the all-girls school than a reflection of the 1960s." The tradition ended in 1971.[74]

Judson College, Marion, Alabama

Founded 1838 by members of Siloam Baptist Church. The college is still a women's college remaining true to the tradition of Christian guidance and affiliated with the Alabama Baptist Convention. The college currently enrolls approximately 280 women and 6 men.

The first May Day fête was held in 1893, "a simple and decorous affair." One of the girls of the Conversational Club was crowned Queen, after which the women "took our tea by a little table out on the lawn just at sunset and had a little programme in the parlor."[75] At subsequent events, the cadets at Marion Institute were invited to attend and act as escorts.

The festivities grew more elaborate over the years, especially in the 1930s under the direction of Aileen Moody, physical education instructor. Such pageants included *May Day in England, 1585* (1935), *Physical Education Through the Ages* (1933), *A Ceremonial Day in Ancient Mayapan* (1936), and *The Festival of the Eighth Moon* (1937), while later themes included *Billy the Kid, Judson Spirit*, and *The Israelites' Flight from Egypt*. On at least one occasion the cadets drilled as part of the entertainment.

From the 1930s through the late 1950s, the Judson May Queen was accompanied by a "Prince," a role played by a female classmate. Early photographs show the Prince garbed in a tuxedo with a top hat; later ones show her in a costume of the Revolutionary War complete with knee breeches or a Regency-style cutaway coat and trousers. (Note that in this era, girls did not wear trousers for any reason save sports and acting. At many of the Southern women's

The 1950 Judson College May Queen, "King" and Court. (Judson College Archives.)

colleges, the girls were not permitted to wear shorts or trousers on the street until the mid-sixties.) The Queen was also accompanied by one or two pages, girls also in boy's costume. The custom of girls acting as part of the Queen's court was not added until 1942.[76]

In 1966, concurrently with the installation of the new college president, the college's successful defense against the desire of the Alabama Baptist Convention to make it accept men, and the permitting of the girls to wear sports clothes (i.e., shorts) off-campus when riding bicycles, May Day changed its name to "J" Day and moved from May to March. A talent program replaced the previous pageant-type performance and the event was held in the Alumnae Auditorium rather than on the lawns.[77] J-Day Queens were elected until 1967.

Kansas State University, Manhattan, Kansas

Founded in 1863 as a land-grant institution, Kansas State University currently enrolls approximately 8,500 men and 7,500 women.

May Day Festivals were held from 1910 through at least 1929. The YWCA sponsored the first festival, and the senior class was given the honor of electing the Queen. While 3,000 tickets to the event were sold, many more people attended, as there was no enclosure to keep non-paying spectators out. "The program consisted of band music, the rendering of 'Pyramus and Thisbe,' a May-pole dance, a tug of war between the Juniors and Seniors, and a baseball game between the girls of the Eurodelphian and Ionian societies. The proceeds went to the Cascade fund."[78] According to the student newspaper, the event was considered the most successful student function ever celebrated at the college.

In 1911, both "Christian associations" (the YMCA and the YWCA) sponsored the festival. Admission was ten cents with proceeds earmarked for two religious conferences. In 1912 the

May Queen was crowned by the state governor's wife and there was apparently a competition among the different societies (clubs or early forms of sororities) for the dancing. "The Ionian Society butterfly drill was awarded the prize as the best stunt of the May Festival program given on the college campus last Saturday. The Milkmaid's Dance given by the Eurodelphian Society won second place."[79]

In 1916 the event was judged to be "one of the most successful and pretentious [sic] events of the kind presented by students of the College. Approximately 300 persons participated and the attendance was estimated at 2500," while receipts were more than $500. The net proceeds of $400 were divided between the YWCA and the YMCA.[80]

The event continued annually for a while. In 1918 there were nearly 5,000 spectators including many soldiers from the nearby training camp. A cinematographer took moving pictures of the event for the Pathé News. In 1921 five hundred dancers took part in the fête. In 1922 the pageant was presented under the auspices of the YWCA, with the cooperation of the Women's Athletic Department, the Music Department and the Applied Arts Department. "Six hundred women students participated in the fête 'Ad Astra per Aspera.' Miss Osceola Burr, author of the pageant, won a $25 prize for submitting the best manuscript."[81] The last pageant was that of 1929, with a theme centering around the neglected statue of a dancer, in the forest on the edge of a village.[82]

Kent State University, Kent, Ohio

Founded in 1910 as Kent State Normal School with a mission to train teachers. In 1912 the college's president established 20 Kent Normal School Extension Centers throughout northeast Ohio. The university currently enrolls 22,000 students.

In 1914, to mark the enrollment of 1,600 students in Kent's extension classes, President McGilvrey declared that Saturday, May 16 would be "Extension Day." All extension students, many of whom had never been on campus before, were invited to attend. After an address by a faculty member of the University of Chicago on the topic of "Theoretical and Practical Education," the third- through eighth-grade girls danced many folk dances, while the older girls performed a milkmaids' drill, the "Faust Waltz" and the "Peasant's Floral Arch." The program culminated with 84 girls of the Normal school, dressed in flowing white gowns, who performed the "Grande Maypole Dance" and Pennant Drill. Miss Ruth V. Atkinson, Kent State's first physical education instructor, who had joined the faculty in 1913 at the beginning of the fall quarter, directed the dances.[83] The fact that the program so closely mirrors that recommended by Jennette Carpenter Lincoln in her books on maypole dances and drills suggests that Miss Atkinson used them as a direct source.

In 1918 the event was renamed "Homecoming Day," since alumnae returned for it, until a fall Homecoming Day celebrated in the fall in conjunction with a football game was held in 1929. Thereafter the spring festival was called "Campus Day." After this time, a "songfest" competition and an elaborate parade became part of the event.[84]

Campus Day, with the involvement of the sororities and fraternities, continued well into the 1970s. The judges who selected the Queen were, at various times, prominent individuals in the community, making the event more similar to a standard beauty pageant, rather than a vote by the students. In 1960, for example, the "Campus Day Queen" was serenaded by the "Merrymen of Kent" and then crowned. Members of Orchesis, the modern dance group, then performed the maypole dance. In 1966, there were thirty-six songfest entries and fifty-seven parade units. While the Campus Queen was crowned, 1966 marked the first year that the maypole dance was not performed. However, a brief history of Campus Day contained in the 1966 program noted that the festivities began with the celebration of the "K-Girl."

This history further reported that in 1923 the large concrete "K" on the university's front lawn was dedicated by the Delta Upsilon social fraternity. Since then, "each year a K-Girl is selected and during the ceremony she paints the 'K' and is serenaded by the brothers. The annual event has become the traditional opening of Campus Day." The program gave the name of the 1966 K-Girl, noted that she was the pin-mate of a fraternity brother, and added that this was the first year that the maypole dance was not performed.[85] The celebration was large enough in the 1960s that the weekend could feature name entertainment, including at various times, the Kingston Trio, Steve Lawrence and Eydie Gorme, the Philadelphia Orchestra conducted by Eugene Ormandy, Sergio Mendes, and Blood, Sweat and Tears. By 1972, however, it seems that both the May Queen and the K-Girl had disappeared, and the event was simply a weekend of fun activities.

Lebanon Valley College, Anville, Pennsylvania

Founded in 1866 and associated with the Methodist Church, Lebanon Valley College currently enrolls approximately 1,530 undergraduates.

In 1912 Miss May Belle Adams directed the first May Day pageant at the college. The event was described as being similar to Homecoming: there was a May Day Court with the winner being crowned as Queen. The tradition of maypole dancing and an evening dance were staples of the celebration. Pageants were held every year until the mid–1960s, and the college's on-line "Traditions" page states that it was discontinued at that time "because of its association with communist beliefs."[86]

Mary Baldwin College, Staunton, Virginia

Founded in 1842 as the Augusta Female Seminary. Mary Julia Baldwin, who later served as principal for thirty-five years and for whom the school was later named, was among the first pupils. In 1916 it achieved junior college status; in 1923 it received accreditation as a standard, four-year liberal arts college. Mary Baldwin College currently enrolls 2,250 women.

The college archivist writes that the first May Day was held in 1848, when the school was the Augusta Female Seminary, and that there were others held at least in 1866 and 1867, but that documentation of these early events is scarce. The first elaborate celebration was held in 1914 and the last in 1968, after which the event was canceled because of "lack of interest."[87]

In 1942, the college historian wrote:

> The May Day pageants are interesting and significant both in theme and in manner of production. The art and physical education directors cooperate in the production with the assistance of students who help with the music and the dances. Students also assist the art director in the planning of costumes. In 1934, students were asked to suggest themes and a plan for the pageant, and an idea worked out by two students was accepted. This pageant suggested by Van Loon's *Geography*, just published, consisted of two parts presenting humanity in conflict (Van Loon's "So These are the people who live in the world we live in") and the forces of nature ("So this is the world we live in"), with a final accord between Humanity and nature and a dance of peace. Among the other themes of the pageants have been Mother Goose (1930) and Alice in Wonderland (1932), always varieties in Mary Baldwin; Pandora (1931), with the classic theme and dances; Gareth and Lynette (1933) with medieval background; Virginiana (1935), based on Mary Johnston's poem "Virginia," depicting Queen Elizabeth's dreams of Raleigh's new-found land; Coronation and a real English May Day and Maypole

in 1937 with court and folk dances; Austria in 1860 (1938), with the queen attending a country fair with its variety of peasant dances of the different nationalities of the old Empire; Americana (1939), a panorama of modern America with sports, regional culture, new themes in art and music, surrealism, jazz, etc.; and Fiesta Day in Mexico (1940), with bull fights and Spanish, Indian, and Mexican dances.... Thus the romance of the past and the realities of today have been artistically combined in the cooperative work of students and faculty. In spite of the satisfaction of the final beautiful display, perhaps the chief significance of the pageant lies in the fact that it is a laboratory in which the student can see and participate in the process of artistic creation.[88]

Meredith College, Raleigh, North Carolina

Founded by the Baptist State Convention of North Carolina in 1891, Meredith College is now an independent, comprehensive institution for women, currently enrolling approximately 2,000 women.

Field Day, held beginning around 1906, an exhibition of physical education training, was the forerunner of May Day. The college historian reported:

> It was a lively affair; several activities going on at once in the small court on the teeter ladders, climbing ropes, flying rings, and giant strides made of it almost a three-ring circus. There were gay folk dances; intricate drills with wands, dumbbells, and Indian clubs; and contests in low jumps, high jumps, and chinning the bar. For these classes and for their sports the girls wore blouses and modestly voluminous bloomers.[89]

In 1926, the first year on the "new campus," Field Day gave way to May Day. From that time on various pageants drew in increasing numbers of spectators from town. In 1929, various classes performed folk dances including the "Danish Ace of Diamonds," the "Highland Fling," the "Irish Lilt" and "Irish Reel," the "Alumni Three-Step," the contra dance "Portland Fancy," the "Boscastle Schottische" (English), and "L'Zoronto" (Spanish); these were followed by a dance of the Brownies, a dance of the Flowers and the maypole dance. Other pageants included *Another May Day Greets Us* (1935), a pageant of the earth with dances of butterflies and grasses as well as a colonial quadrille and the maypole dance; *Waltz and Flowers* (1946); *The Seasons* (1958) with various folk and modern dances; a celebration of North Carolina's tercentenary (1963); and *The Sensational Sixties* (1970) that provided a review of the decade in dance form in five movements, "music, space, hippies, fashion, and a dance of mourning." The three movements of the last dance commemorated John F. Kennedy, Martin Luther King, Jr., and Robert Kennedy. Approximately 65 girls participated in the performance. The day also included a horse show, a fashion show presented by the home economics department, and, after the performance, a hootenanny.[90]

By 1972, the May Day event was called Springs Court, and was held on Parents' Weekend. A Queen, a senior, was still crowned. In 1975, however, a change in the calendar, moving Parents' Weekend to mid–April, meant that the dance classes were not ready to perform, and the weather was felt to be unreliable. As described in Chapter 18, this change prompted discussion of whether Springs Court should continue. Some of the more extreme responses to the poll are cited in the epigraph to Chapter 18; five other students wrote as follows:

> I feel qualifications for Spring Queen should be changed. If it is for beauty it should be for beauty — a sex queen. If it is for personality or contribution to Meredith, beauty should not enter into it.
>
> Just because we are a woman's college in the 1970's does not mean we cannot retain those Meredith traditions that bring the college community closer together and endear Meredith to our hearts.
>
> Meredith is based on traditions which make her unique. And I feel that Meredith is beginning to lose some of this [sic] tradition and will continue to do so if we compare ourselves with other col-

leges. We are Meredith and not N.C. State or Chapel Hill. My mother looks forward to coming and seeing everyone perform.

Isn't there some useful, meaningful way in which to direct our efforts? Or shall we remain the silly, pampered maidens of the 19th century? Even Baptists accept more liberation now!

Let's not let everything old and traditional die here! Please!

However, despite the support or at least the apathy reflected in the polls, and over the reasonable objections of a student who pointed out that this support should not be ignored, the Student Life Committee voted to end Spring Court in the fall of 1975.[91]

Miami University, Oxford, Ohio

Founded in 1809, Miami University is Ohio's premier public university, currently enrolling 14,200 undergraduates.

The university's archivist writes:

The first recorded May Day celebration at Miami occurred in 1910, and was given by the freshmen women in honor of the seniors. Florence Van Dyke, president of Miami's YWCA was chosen as the first May Queen. The last celebration of which I could find evidence occurred in 1965, when Alice Carson, an Arts and Science senior, was crowned May Queen.

Initially, the celebration included a May Pole dance, songs, a processional, and a senior dinner. By 1933, a regular celebration routine had evolved in which the CWEN and Mortar Board honorary societies presented their newly elected members to the May Queen. Before 1933, the celebration was generally held in the morning after a May Day breakfast given by the junior women. Beginning in 1933, however, the program moved to the evening after a buffet dinner. Over subsequent years, the celebration included a song contest, which was replaced by a skit performed by the freshman halls. The number of individuals presented to the Queen also increased and, by 1958, included House chairmen, editors of various student publications, and organizational presidents and counselors.[92]

Chapter 13 describes the short-lived men's burlesque with the rowdy election of the April King. The official college history, written in 1958, elaborated on this event, clearly feeling that it was an attempt to return to the days when there were no women on campus.

Mills College, Oakland, California

Founded in 1852 as a private women's college, Mills, a nationally renowned liberal arts college, currently enrolls 950 female undergraduates and offers graduate degrees to women and men.

The archivist writes that information on origin and ending dates of the festival is sketchy. A program from 1909 indicates that a Queen was crowned after which came the performance of Shakespeare's *A Winter's Tale*. The 1915 yearbook indicates that "many years ago," the girls crowned a classmate Queen and in her honor, "the little girls danced upon the lawn and among the trees, sang May songs, and waved their garlands of beautiful flowers. The older girls danced around the Maypole, braided its many colored streams, and then unbraided them again, as if by magic." According to this account, everyone in the school participated in the drills, maypole dancing, and the crowning.

In the fall of 1911, Miss Margaret Andrews became director of the Physical Education Department, and the following year, the seniors with Miss Andrews "worked out the idea of presenting some simple, romantic, or picturesque theme as a background for the dances and

The procession of the Queen and her Court. With the flower-girls, the white carpet and the elaborate gown and embroidered or painted train, this looks very similar to a wedding procession, and in fact, many May Queens used their coronation gowns a few weeks after their vent for their own weddings. (Special Collections, F.W. Olin Library, Mills College.)

songs. Naturally, the dancing became more aesthetic and symbolic and the songs suggestive of the plot or theme."[93] By 1915 the production was given at the lake on campus, a pretty area that added much to the spectators' enjoyment.

1912	*The Passing of Winter and the Coming of Spring*: Symbolized by the Rain Dance and the Dance of the Young Green Things, dances of Nymphs, Butterflies and Fairies and the Children of the Earth dancing in glee around the Maypole.
1913	*The Quest of Youth for Happiness*: A young lad searches for happiness in this world and the land of Myth. Terpsichore attempts to please him by exhibiting the dances of Night, Sleep, the Pleiades and Diana, followed by Aurora and her Children of the Mists. At last the youth returns to this world, where he is met by a band of Maidens, typifying the springtime of life and happiness among the mortals.
1914	*California*: In the beginning the Creatures of Drought rule the Pacific Coast. Mother Nature brings Rain and Sunshine and then the Green Things and Spring Dance. Without warning, the Creatures of Drought reappear and the flowers droop. Mother Nature, brings great Water, and as it advances, "the Fruits of Cultivation appear and triumphantly cast their mantle of flowers about California, while all join to do her homage."
1915	*May Fête at Lake Aliso* (trolls, fairies, gnomes and nixies)
1917	*The Lost Poem*, by Hilda Clute: Evil Migla captures and imprisons the Rose

Girls and their escorts celebrating the end of May Day in 1947 with a nine-piece band. (Special Collections, F.W. Olin Library, Mills College.)

                Maiden and her companions, while a Poet sleeps and elves and fairies dance and play. The wind mischievously blows away the Poet's poem. After many adventures, he finds it again, conquers Migla and frees the Maiden.

1919   *Ariadne of Crete*

No information on subsequent programs was provided, but the archivist notes that photographs show that the crowning of the Queen continued until at least 1951 and possibly after this date.[94]

Mount Holyoke College, South Hadley, Massachusetts

Founded as a female seminary in 1837, and one of the so-called Seven Sisters. The college currently enrolls 2,000 women.

May Day began circa 1898 with a simple crowning of the May Queen. The more elaborate May Fête was inaugurated on the day after President Mary Woolley's formal installation on May 15, 1901. In 1905, Mary Crawford described the procession of the performers in college's Elizabethan May Day festival in her study, *The College Girl of America*:

> Preceding the May [Q]ueen are lordly heralds, and while Robin Hood and his merry men escort the damsel fair, Little John and Fair Maid Marian follow close behind. Beruffed and powdered ladies and gallants of Queen Elizabeth's court are also here, as are morris-men, milkmaids, May-pole dancers, and many other fanciful and grotesque characters.

Crawford adds that, after the crowning, came the maypole dances, "performed by Britanny fisher maidens," a "Rainbow Dance" or the "Daisy Dance," "symbolic of the season, with twelve seniors gowned in yellow to represent the middle of the flower, twenty-four in white for the petals, and twelve in green for the stem." Music was provided by the Mandolin Club.[95]

After 1901 the college sponsored elaborate pageants approximately every two years including topics such as a pageant addressing the life of poet François Villon (1915), a version of Spenser's *The Faerie Queene* (1921), *The Odyssey* (1923) and an adaptation of *The Aeneid* (ca. 1930).

The college had the custom of alternating blonde and brunette Queens in, respectively, even and odd years. The identity of the Queen was always kept a strict secret. By 1947 the criteria for nomination was that the nominee had to be a member of the senior class who was at least five feet, five inches tall, and with the backing of at least twenty-five other students. The whole student body voted, and the six runners-up comprised the Queen's Court. The results of the balloting were kept "a dead secret" until the Queen and her Court were presented.[96] During the war years of 1943–45 the pageant tradition, but not the crowning, was suspended. The last pageant was held in 1949, and, thereafter, the crowning grew less elaborate, with the last crowning occurring in 1967.[97]

Muskingum College, New Concord, Ohio

Founded in 1837 as a private liberal arts and science institution affiliated with the Presbyterian Church, Muskingum College currently enrolls 1,600 students.

The first recorded May Day celebration took place in 1910, but information is sketchy about the early days of the festival. The college year book first made mention of the event in 1922, when it noted that the pageant was held by the Department of Physical Education for Women and that "many weeks are spent by the girls in thorough drill and preparation for the event and much skill and time is consumed in preparing dainty gowns and showy costumes." The procession of the Queen and the crowning opened the event, and the Queen then reviewed the dances and gymnastic drills performed in her honor.

The college archivist notes that in 1944 the celebration began to include a Fine Arts Festival during which the college would invite guest musicians to perform. The festival lasted for a week, concluding on the last day with the May Day celebration. She notes that, no matter what theme was chosen, or whether the event was held indoors or outside, the maypole dance was performed.

In the later years, the Queen and her court all had escorts; frequently their fathers or grandfathers.

The list of pageant themes shows the typical array of student interests (some years are missing) alternating with a more traditional English May Day:

1929	*An Elizabethan May Day*
1931	*East of the Moon and West of the Sun*
1933	*Legend of the Red Flower*
1934	*Story of the May Day*
1936	*Voyage of S.S. Montgomery*
1937	*Centennial Year*
1938	*Folk Festival*
1939	*Memories*
1940	*Dancing on the Green*
1941	*Fanmaiped* [sic]

1945	*Gypsies*
1946	*Wanderings of Donald Duck*
1947	*Alice in Wonderland*
1948	*Hi Ho Come to the Fair*
1949	*Along the Mississippi*
1950	*May Magic*
1951	*America Dances*
1952	*Mother Goose on Parade*
1954	*Spring Safari*
1955	*The Golden Coins* (Robin Hood)
1956	*Adventures of Johnny Appleseed*
1957	*Wizard of Oz*
1958	*Welcome to the World's Fair*
1959	*Once Upon a May Day* (Storybook)
1960	*In the Merry, Merry Month of May* (Mr. Spring in 1890's Park)
1961	*Hue in Harmony* (Rainbow Colors)
1962	*Isle of May* (Visitors to Isle)
1963	*May a l'Ode* [sic]
1964	*Gallery B* (Museum Paintings)
1965	*Go a Maying to a Fun Fair*
1966	*An Elizabethan Carol*
1967	*Spring*
1968	*A Mod May*
1969	*May Day in Disneyland*
1970	*May Day in Camelot*
1971	*Welcome Aboard—Flight #1471*
1972	*Under the Big Top*
1978	*An Almost May Cabaret*

The archivist notes that the festival ceased after the 1978 production, for no documented reason. She suspects that the tradition just seemed too antiquated and the celebration became obsolete.[98]

Newcomb College, Tulane University, New Orleans, Louisiana

Founded in 1886 by Mrs. Josephine Newcomb in memory of her daughter. The first degree-granting women's college founded within a university system. Tulane University now enrolls approximately 2,800 men and 2,900 women.

A modest celebration known only to the nine girls of the class of 1899 was held in the spring of that year, but the first acknowledged May Day was given in the spring of 1914 by the junior class in honor of the seniors. The festival was the idea of one young woman who, over the Christmas holidays, had been asked by a friend who was a student at the nearby Agnes Scott College what special festivities the Newcomb juniors performed in honor of their graduating seniors. "The inevitable answer of 'Nothing' became a humiliating challenge to [the young woman] and ruined her holidays until she conceived the idea of May Day." Upon her return she soon had the entire junior class "working as an inspired unit." The program, the costumes and the preparation of the Maypole were all done in secret. "The Queen and maids were selected for their college spirit and service on the campus from among those seniors who had not held major offices. So that no one could know in advance who would be in the court the juniors voted by secret ballot just before the celebration began."[99]

Thus, in 1914, the seniors, wearing caps and gowns, marched around the campus escorted by nine juniors, who danced around them and finally raised garlands of flowers for the seniors to pass under.

"The first thing in the festival was the killing of Winter. Twelve maids representing flowers were almost crushed by Winter ... but revived and pelted her down with flowers. While they were dancing around her she rose as beautiful Spring and went to chose her Queen [the president of the senior class]." After choosing six girls to be the Court, the juniors danced "many pretty folk dances" around the maypole. The sophomore class gave the Queen a large bouquet of flowers and the seniors sang a song composed in honor of the juniors.

The early pageants had a strong love theme, and the stories tended to involve a male character, accompanied by his dukes, (all roles played by girls) who searched for a worthy bride and her court. Sample programs included:

1915	*A Fairy Tale Play*
1918	*An Old English May Day*
1920	*The Blue Bird*, by Maurice Maeterlinck
1921	*The Land of Oz*
1922	*A Myth Dream*
1923	*One Silver Night*, a romance of the man-in-the-moon who searches for a bride, encountering the Muses, the Vanities, the Pleasures, Wealth, the Spirit of Sleep, and various Lovers of the Ages.
1924	*Symphony of the Sea*
1926	*A Buccaneer Pageant*
1927	*Comus*, adapted from Milton
1934	*A Chinese Pageant* celebrating the legendary wedding of the Emperor of China to a Japanese princess, who was the Queen selected as the most beautiful girl in college
1946	*The Wizard of Oz*
1951	*You Were There*, a pageant of good King Arthur

The festival ceased in 1962, due apparently to lack of student interest and with references to the poor quality of the performances of the last few years.[100]

New Mexico State University, Las Cruces, New Mexico

A land-grant institution founded in 1888 when New Mexico was still a territory. The university currently enrolls 23,000 graduate and undergraduate students.

The archivist writes that:

There is an interesting variety of material on May Day celebrations here at New Mexico State, or as it was known for most of its early existence, New Mexico College of Agriculture & Mechanic Arts (NMCA & MA). Looking at the first student publication, *The Collegian*, the first crowning of a May Queen, Elizabeth Coleman, took place in May 1901. "Queen Elizabeth I," as she was described (a fitting "title," since the 1902 Queen was also named Elizabeth [Newcomb]), was dressed in a satin and ermine robe. She also wore a rhinestone crown. Often, May Day did not take place on May 1, but rather, at a point several days later. The 1901 picture of Elizabeth Coleman in her regalia is a favorite from our University Archives.

A 1925 account from *The Round Up*, the campus newspaper, gives a brief history of the May Queen event. It states that in order to finance a grandstand for Miller Field, students nominated their favorite young ladies for the May Queen position. In order to support their favorite candidate, "the fight was on and the money started to pour into the coffers." In later years, faculty also voted for the May Queen. Like many happenings in the early days of the College, self-supportive events gave rise to new traditions.

The earliest activities at this time in the academic year, however, were presaged by the NMAC Field Day. This first took place in 1893, and was the College's annual track and field meet. It was an important sporting event, with a full recap of events published in the New Mexico Collegian. There are, in fact, later references to the May Queen being named as the Queen of Field Day in *The Round Up*. What is interesting, though, in referring to a later account in *The Round Up* from May 1916, is that the May Day celebration was only commemorated as that name starting in 1915. Up until then, the events in May were referred to as Field Day.

With regard to other auxiliary events, there is also mention of an annual baseball game, the Maypole Dance, and a music program. The 1925 article on the event described that "... after the final strains of the recessional march had died away the hall had been cleared for dancing and the syncopated jazz of an El Paso aggregation of music makers...." Another amusing mention of the Festival is its alternate name, the Kollege Kactus Karnival, which in acronym form would not pass muster from University administration today. The headline of the article announces it has the "biggest amusement of the year."

Along with other events, NMCA & MA commemorated May Day and the crowning of the May Queen. In each edition of the *Swastika* (the yearbook of the College; that is no error, that was its name), the May Queen would be listed. This tradition took place until 1943, when the name of the Queen was the Spring Carnival Queen. The yearbook offers no explanation for the change, but on a campus with a strong military training/ROTC presence during World War II, the notion of "May Day" being celebrated was no longer palatable, especially during the Cold War. If I do find any mention of the reason for the name change, I will let you know about the circumstances. Spring Carnival continued as an event that commemorated the end of the academic year and a good excuse to let off steam before final exams. This continued as a campus tradition until the early 1970s, when this tradition faded into the Spring "Blow Off," an off-campus party.[101]

Oberlin College, Oberlin, Ohio

Founded in 1833 as a coeducational college and the first to accept black students. The College of Arts and Sciences now enrolls 2,600 students while the Conservatory of Music enrolls 500.

The college's earliest festival, held at Baldwin Cottage, the women's residence hall, seems to have been held for the first time on May 6, 1897.[102] At this time *The Oberlin Review* reported that on a "revival of the old English May Day," held on the lawn in front of the women's residence hall. Early festivals were quite small — involving 20 or so participants — and men were involved to some extent: in 1904 and for a few years after, for example, the Queen chose a King and part of the festivities included the men tilting at a quintain or engaging in archery competitions or in presenting Shakespearean plays. The festival continued, growing large enough to warrant bleacher seating, through at least the early 1920s.

After a lengthy hiatus, the archivist reports that some occurrence of selected festivities, such as dawn singing or dancing at dawn, occurred from the early 1970s through possibly the early 1990s.[103] For example, May 2, 2002, was celebrated with "The Big Parade," to bring the community together. It included jugglers, llamas, giant puppets, a variety of live music and other events. It appears, however, that these festivities fall more into the "Spring Carnival" category than into a representation of an English May Day.

Oklahoma State University, Stillwater, Oklahoma

Founded in 1890 as Oklahoma Agricultural & Mechanical College, the university currently enrolls 26,000 students.

May Day at OSU began in 1909, as described by the college historian in 1988:

> Campus-wide excitement and participation recurred in the spring with the May Carnival [in the fall there was a Harvest Carnival]. Started in 1909, the May Carnival, to the delight of college authorities, was held without confetti or paint. The May pole dances highlighted the afternoon and evening events. A parade through the campus and town and a carnival, again with booths, were part of the festivities. All other scheduled college events were suspended for this one special day of noise and laughter. The two deputy sheriffs that were usually assigned to the event, in case of problems, were typically not needed. Prizes were given for the most attractive and most grotesque make-up in the parade. [The town's] churches and businesses participated, many selling food to the revelers. The May Carnival served to raise money to help student organizations pay their bills. The primary sponsors, the Women's Athletic Association and YWCA, cleared about $130 for their hard work in 1910. The May Carnival also marked the end of another college year for the students. Before long, final examinations would be upon them.[104]

The celebration is documented through 1919, but later records are spotty. The 1926 yearbook contains photographs of the maypole dance and the Queen, and that seems to have been the last May Day festival.[105]

Oregon State University, Corvallis, Oregon

Founded as a private academy in 1858, it was named a land-grant college in 1868 and graduated its first class — two men and one woman — in 1870. The university currently enrolls approximately 19,100 students, of whom 15,700 are undergraduates.

The archivist writes:

> While there is an early reference to May Day being held in 1902, the festival appears to have begun in earnest in 1908. The celebrations were called May Pageants in the 1910s and were sponsored by the Department of Physical Education. Men appear to have participated in at least a limited manner — the King listed in the 1914 program was a male, Everett May. The event ceased sometime in the 1920s.[106]

Pennsylvania State University, University Park, Pennsylvania

Founded in 1855 at the request of the Pennsylvania State Agricultural Society and eventually made a land-grant institution, in 1874 Penn State had only 64 undergraduates, but their numbers had increased to 5,000 by the 1930s. Pennsylvania State University now enrolls more than 70,000 undergraduates.

The first May Queen pageant was celebrated on May 20, 1914, at sunset, with the crowning of the Queen. Within five years the celebration featured dancing, plays and performance by the Glee Club. The crowning of the May Queen remained an important part of the festival, and strong feelings were expressed about the candidates. A *Collegian* article from 1937, cited in a recent alumni bulletin article on traditions, opined:

[F]or some pashy bisquit [*sic*] to fall into a spot like that just 'cause she happened to be born beautiful but dumb. No, indeed girls, this department certainly agrees that by all means May Queen should be elected for 'suitability, interest, and past activities." May Day officially ended in 1960, when students instituted Senior Class Day in its place.[107]

Randolph College (formerly Randolph-Macon Woman's College), Lynchburg, Virginia

Founded as a liberal arts college affiliated with the United Methodist Church in 1891, Randolph-Macon Woman's College enrolled approximately 700 women circa 2002. In July 2007, the college rather abruptly, and amid controversy, announced that it was going coed. The name changed at this time.

The first May Day was held on the "chilly rainy dawn" of May 1, 1910, with a senior crowned as queen. That year also saw the popular Halloween Lantern Parade, first held by the class of 1909.[108]

Field Day, an athletic competition, was the first spring tradition for the college; May Day began on May 4, 1909, when "ten or eleven determined girls danced around a Maypole one morning before breakfast." May Day continued as a small event until 1922, when a building was erected on the site of the maypole and the event was moved indoors. In 1930, however, May Day took precedence in college life, dominating spring activities for the next 30 years. "May Queens were named as early as February, and their personalities, finances, and 'beauty secrets' were perennial copy." One May Queen was offered a Hollywood contract on the strength of her looks; she turned it down to stay at the college. Eventually the festival occupied an entire weekend. The crowning of the Queen ended acrimoniously in 1970 as described in Chapter 16, and the last May Weekend was held in 1971.[109]

Rockford College, Rockford, Illinois

Chartered in 1847 as the Rockford Female Seminary. Now a private, liberal arts college enrolling approximately 330 men and 490 women.

The first May Day was celebrated in 1894 when the institution was known as Rockford Female Seminary. Members of the Castalian Society (a literary society) suspended baskets filled with apple blossom from each girl's door along with an invitation to the party. In the afternoon, one girl was elected by popular vote to be Queen. She was led away to be made ready,

> and in due time appeared at the head of the stairs, clad in royal robes of white, bordered with purple and decorated with violets and attended by 14 members of the Castalian society, gowned as ladies-in-waiting, and preceded by a dainty little maid from the preparatory department, bearing the violet crown, who led the way to the throne, draped in white and smothered with a wealth of violets and ferns.... Here she was given a scepter of apple bloom, the crown was placed upon her head, while her subjects chanted the "ancient rhyme":

> Oh, thou dear Queen, from me receive
> This beauteous apple spray;
> A garland for they head we weave,
> Be thou our Queen of May.

The Queen's subjects then passed in front of her and "bending the knee in token of fealty, touched her hand with their lips." Students danced the maypole dance, the Virginia Reel "and other simple measures to the vast delight of the occupants of the carriages which had drawn up along the edge of the campus until all travel along the streets was suspended." Supper followed.

The originator of this festival, Grace Sherman Dorcass, Class of 1895, was also the president of the Castalian Society. She wrote that she had "conceived the idea from reading stories about May Day celebrations in Merry Old England, which we copied, so far as we could."[110]

The Castalians held the festival again in 1895, and began the custom of the retiring Queen leading the procession and exchanging her crown of withered flowers at the foot of the throne for one of forget-me-nots. The custom seems to have gone into abeyance in 1898, 1899 and, possibly, 1900.

Hortense E. Johnson, class of 1904 and May Queen of 1902, later recalled how the students celebrated May Day from 1900 to 1904. There were two college societies, each of which sponsored one of the outstanding events of the school year: the Vesperian Society sponsored the Washington Birthday Party and the Castalian Society sponsored the May Party. Early in May work began on the May "party," including rehearsing the maypole dance with one extra dancer, in case one of these girls was made Queen. The Queen was chosen by secret written ballot on the basis of her beauty, her friendliness and her personality, and her identity was kept secret. The day before the party, which was held on a Saturday, all the girls washed their hair, as the custom was that the Queen's hair was left hanging. Her account continued:

> After the votes were counted the chosen girl was taken to Middle Hall where a long cheesecloth robe covered with bunches of violets was put on her, then the procession was formed, first the May Pole Dancers, then children carrying the wreaths of violets and forget-me-nots, then the queen followed by little train bearers. These children were from the Alumnae and friends of the College who were gathered on campus to see the crowning. The fences, too, were alive with youngsters and neighbors looking on and there was a gala feeling everywhere.
>
> The procession got under way to the music of a string quartette. While the new queen was being made ready the old queen was taken to the throne where she waited the coming of the procession. The May Pole dancers marched to the May Pole, the crown bearers, new queen and attendants went to the throne where the new queen received the crown of violets and in turn placed the forget-me-not wreath on the old queen, after they exchanged places. The May Pole dance followed and then a general reception was held for the queens. Many old girls made it a point to be a College for May Day whether or not they came any other time of year. In later years a Shakespearian play with lovely dances was given following the May Pole Dance.[111]

In 1902 someone conceived of the idea of giving the Queen a small gold cross set with a sprig of hawthorn as a badge of sovereignty of service, conceived of by Ruskin. This account noted further that:

> as the years went by the symbolism of the ceremony has been more and more emphasized. The choice of May-Queen is now determined, not by personal beauty or scholarship alone as it used to be, but by the worth and character of the girl. Ruskin's idea of the sovereignty of the May queen being the sovereignty of service, has come to be the foundation of the May-Party, until today our Queen is a symbol to us of the finest and fairest in character, unselfish, serving all — the symbol, as she stands violet-crowned, of the best in Rockford College.[112]

After the turn of the century, the Kappa Theta sorority took charge of the arrangements, until the mid–twenties when it became an "all-school" event. By 1931–32 it was noted that while at first the Queen had been chosen from any of the four classes, it had grown to be a custom for her to be chosen from the senior class. It was also noted that "As May Day grew in importance, so the May Queen came to embody our ideals of loyalty, sincerity, and versatility."[113]

From the 1920s through at least the early 1960s the students presented pageants and dance performances, such as the following examples: *A May Idyll* (1912); *The Story of the Seasons* (1922); Voltaire's *The Princess of Babylon* (1932); *College Suite* (a modern dance program presented by Orchesis), (1942); *Cinderella* (1952); and *Gingham and Gunsmoke; A Dream of the Golden West* (1962).

Beginning in 1974 a May King was added to the event, which by that time was more like a prom, with dinner and a dance being the primary events of the day. The custom of electing a Queen continued through 1982, after which, according to the college archivist, the tradition died out "without comment due to lack of interest." The festival was revived for one year in 1997 as part of the college's sesquicentennial celebration.

Rollins College, Winter Park, Florida

Founded in 1885 as a private, liberal arts college, Rollins College now enrolls approximately 1,740 students.

May Queens were crowned from at least 1915 through the 1930s, though the archives contain no specific information on the inception and ending dates. A King and Queen were also crowned in the May Court of 1946, but no other information is available.

In 1918 the student newspaper reported that the "Gala Day Will Show War-Time May Spirit; Terpsichorean Features are Promising Program of the Day." Since there were so few men students present, the girls carried off the performance alone. After the "Cossack Revels" of Tchaikovsky, played by the school orchestra, the students processed in to the strains of a war march, "Athalia," by Mendelsohn. After the Queen's coronation, the maypole dance was performed to "La Cinquantain," by Gabriel Marie. A solo dancer performed an "Egyptian Dance," the Glee Club sang two songs, and twenty-four girls performed a "Venetian Flower Dance" with wreaths, arches, and garlands. A duet, "I Know a Bank Where the Wild Thyme Blows," a violin solo, and a "Swallow Dance" followed, after which came the singing of the "Star Spangled Banner." Admission was twenty-five cents. "Do not let this detain you," noted the student paper, "Think of it as helping to win the war, for it is. The proceeds will go to the Y.W.C.A. If you want to miss half of your life and regret the loss for the other half, just stay away from Rollins campus [on May Day]."[114]

The last program available, that from 1938, calls the festival the "First Annual," perhaps suggesting that the celebration had fallen into abeyance in prior years. The program was composed almost entirely of English folk dances, beginning with a morris "call" played by a trumpeter and the singing of the song, "Come Lasses and Lads." The program included the Castleton Garland Processional, noting that this is danced each year in Derbyshire; the morris dance "The Blue-Eyed Stranger"; the country dance "Step Stately"; the Wyresdale "Greensleeves" morris dance; the English morris dance "Rigs O' Marlow" (mistakenly identified as an "Irish stick morris dance from County Cork"); the country dances "Newcastle," "Dargason," "Rufty Tufty," "Nonesuch," and "Gathering Peascods"; the Swedish folk dances "Tretur" and "Oxdansen"; the "Kentucky Mountain Running Set"; and the (English) "Kirkby Malzeard" sword dance. Given this heavy orientation to English dances, one speculates that the director, Helen Rae, may have attended one of the folk dance camps sponsored by what was then the English Folk Dance Society of America (now the Country Dance & Song Society).

Russell Sage College (The Sage Colleges), Troy, New York

Founded in 1916 to prepare young women for careers as typists, dressmakers, and so forth. The college now enrolls approximately 740 women.

The first May Day was held in 1917. A spontaneous event, seen as a break from war work, the before-breakfast celebration was sponsored by someone's chance remark on the "truly sorrowful condition of Emma Willard's statue." (Willard founded the Troy Female Seminary in 1821.) It began with the freshmen thoroughly scrubbing the statue and decorating it and "continued with much capering about in the rain and singing of college songs, and culminated in a very pretty and special breakfast, before which one of the girls was crowned Queen. "This before-breakfast May Day was stopped short of becoming a tradition largely because irate neighbors telephoned to the college to inquire if nothing could be done about that hideous noise that had aroused them in the middle of the night!"[115]

The college archivist believes that the celebration continued in some form for some years, though after a while the ritual scrubbing of the statue (a custom borrowed from Wellesley College) was discontinued as the statue was deteriorating. Student newspaper articles covering the last two May Day festivities, held in 1941 and 1942, respectively, refer to the winding of the maypole in 1941 as a new feature. In 1942, a humorous article refers to the crowning of the "first" Queen of the May.

> A breathless hush fell over the crowd as we were told the qualifications that were taken into consideration for the final selection. There were points allotted for glamour, personality, dress, physical appearance, and a small allotment of grey matter. This was an afterthought, so all we aspirants to this coveted position relaxed and breathed a sigh of relief— there was hope yet.

The punch line of the joke, however, is apparent in the accompanying photograph, which shows a male professor holding a large bouquet of flowers, seated on a small sofa and being crowned with a flower wreath. Two other male professors appear in the photo as members of his court. The student reporter then interviewed the "Queen," who said that she was especially pleased with her throne—"it was one way of giving someone a hot seat."[116] The festival seems to have ceased after this point.

Salem College, Winston-Salem, North Carolina

A private, liberal arts college founded in 1890, Salem College can trace its roots back to 1772 when it was begun as a girls' school founded by Moravians. The college currently enrolls approximately 650 women and 11 men.

In 1920 and 1921 a children's festival was held, including, in 1921, a parade of "kiddie kars," doll carriages, wagons, bicycles, and two camels. In 1922 and 1923 the students held a May Day pageant that included dancers and attendants in Grecian robes of pastel shades. There was then a gap of a few years until 1927 when an elaborate celebration that included a Maid of Honor and the May Court as well as a pageant of the Sleeping Rose was held. The Queen of the 1930 festival, Fritz Fierey, was honored by being the only Salem Queen to be crowned twice—she had been the May Queen in the 1921 children's festival. The celebrations for the next forty-two years from 1927 onwards included a pageant but did not necessarily include a Maypole dance. Sample pageant titles include *When Fairy Tales Come True* (1928), *Merrie England* (1931), *Mother Goose* (1936), *The Gay Nineties* (1940), *Persephone* (1942) and *Ka-Zam* (1965). The last May Day was held in 1969.[117]

Scripps College, Claremont, California

A private, liberal arts college for women founded in 1926 and currently enrolling approximately 780 women.

The first May fête was given by the freshman class in 1929 as a surprise to the faculty and students. The theme of the dance was built around the Greek story of the slaying of the Python, with the second act being a spoof of the faculty, each one being depicted in the form of a Greek character. Subsequent plays given by the freshmen included that of Robin Hood, a Chinese story, an American Indian tale, Alice in Wonderland and others. The festival did not always incorporate maypole dancing, but did involve the crowning of a Queen.

By 1947, the student handbook offered detailed instructions for the fête which was held explicitly to enable the freshmen to display their creativity and originality and to encourage the development of class spirit in the freshmen and sophomores:

> It is recognized that Sophomore "hazing" connected with Freshman May Fête tends to result in certain desirable ends, which, it is agreed, should not be ignored nor neglected. These ends are: increased familiarity among members of both classes, development of class spirit in both classes, and, especially in the Freshman Class, unity and cooperation in working toward a common goal.

In the four weeks prior to May Day, the freshmen would write a play or skit (often lengthy and incorporating song parodies), keeping the theme secret. In the week immediately prior to the event, the sophomores "investigated" (as the action was termed), attempting to discover the theme of the play. The freshmen planted clues, including false scripts and props. Subsequent versions of the student handbook indicated that the administration apparently felt that the investigations created a desirable rivalry between the two classes, strengthening each class in its own class spirit. After the presentation of the actual freshman play on May Day, the sophomores presented a parody of it, incorporating the clues, both real and false, that they had discovered. They then hosted a breakfast. The last fête was held in 1967, and there was no sophomore parody. The event vanished from subsequent student handbooks. In 2003 the college librarian speculated that the demise of the function could be attributed to the Vietnam War, which made the festival seem irrelevant and superficial, "a change in curriculum at Scripps which de-emphasized the bonding experience of all freshmen; a shift in faculty-staff attitudes/lifestyles away from their nurturing role in the community; and an increase in the student body from 250 to nearly 400."[118]

Simmons College, Boston, Massachusetts

Incorporated as a women's college in 1899, Simmons College currently enrolls approximately 1,300 women undergraduates.

In May 1912, the sophomores at Simmons College began the May Day festivities by rising early, hanging May baskets on the seniors' doors and parading through the halls singing traditional college songs to awaken the seniors. The president of the senior class was crowned Queen and the sophomores performed the maypole dance in her honor, after which the festivities ended with a breakfast of strawberry shortcake. The history of this tradition as described on the college's Web site adds that:

> Between 1919 and 1920, May Day was divided into two parts. In order to allow the entire college to participate in the celebration, the freshman class began hanging the "May baskets" on the doors of their sister class (the juniors). This came to be called "Freshman May Day" and in later years was often referred to as the "May Party." The sophomores continued to perform the rest of the activities and even added a skit, usually from Shakespeare, that was performed for the Queen and her court

before the maypole dance took place. This part of the tradition was called "Sophomore May Day" and later came to be called "May Breakfast."

Freshman May Day celebration appears to have ended around 1956 or 1957 and the modern dance club took over responsibility for the maypole dance. The Queen and the "skit" or play performed in her honor vanished sometime in the 1970s, and the college president took over the role of the tree- or flower-planting that the Queen had presided over since the late 1950s or early 1960s. It is unknown when May Day was reinstated, but today the Simmons sophomores celebrate May Day once again in honor of their seniors and the festivities consist of the maypole dance, the planting of a tree or flower, and the strawberry shortcake breakfast.[119]

Skidmore College, Saratoga Springs, New York

Founded in 1903 as an independent liberal arts and sciences college, the college currently enrolls 924 men and 1,325 women.

May Day began sometime prior to 1915, and in 2000, the college historian noted that the second celebration, a boisterous one, was held under the auspices of dean Margaret Calvin, a rigorous disciplinarian who "enforced the rules of the 'refined home.'" May Day 1915 began thus:

> It seems the seniors, equipped with baskets of food, had crept out of Skidmore Hall in the middle of the night, evading the juniors who were chasing them and who found solace in ransacking the senior rooms and decorating the flagpoles and tennis courts with stolen shoes. Meanwhile, despite rain, the seniors walked at about 4 AM to the Geyers (now Saratoga Spa State Park) and caught a trolley to Ballston Lake. By this time the juniors had become so rowdy that an unidentified school employee connected a hose and watered them down, according to the newspapers. Nevertheless, the juniors chased the seniors to Ballston Lake, so the seniors hopped another trolley, leading the juniors to rent three cars for what turned out to be a futile pursuit. But back in Saratoga, other juniors had captured the dean and held her, along with the housekeeper and the two seniors who had come back to campus for a play rehearsal, as "prisoners of war." The dean "graciously admitted [that] the juniors had outwitted the seniors," and she became their honored guest at a luncheon party. At dinner that night, the returning seniors also honored the dean and sang songs of the school as they marched through arches made of wisteria blossoms.[120]

The college historian commented on the dichotomy apparent in the idea of well-bred young women running around town in the middle of the night, being "hosed down" with water, and holding the dean prisoner, while other aspects of the festival — the sentimental school songs, the floral arches — are gracious and lovely. Calvin suffered serious health problems and left the college at the end of 1915. The new dean had very different ideas about the way in which May Day should be celebrated. From 1916 on, May Day was an all-college affair with carefully controlled student participation, starting with a chapel service and a demonstration of the work done by the girls in different departments. The festival also became Founder's Day, to honor Lucy Skidmore Scribner. "The students still could have a break from their 'studious quietude' but the break was to be refined and ladylike, celebrating beauty and art rather than wild predawn larks on the trolley cars," the college historian writes.[121]

In the 1920s, May Day became the major festival of the Skidmore year: in 1926 three grandstands were erected to accommodate an audience of more than 1,000 alumnae and townspeople.

> By the end of the decade, May Day began with a strawberries-and-cream breakfast, proceeded to a special morning chapel service (usually with a guest speaker), followed with a formal luncheon, and featured the opening of an art exhibit and, in mid-afternoon, the pageant with the crowning of the May Queen....

In 1932 May Day/Founder's Day became much more extensive and had to be shifted from the traditional Wednesday observance to Friday-Saturday. Friday afternoon classes were canceled to allow more time for the preparation of what was that year an elaborate medieval pageant featuring milkmaids dancing, miracle plays, and the ringing of bells "to scare away demons." Friday night featured the class song contest, while on Saturday the traditional chapel service and pageant were followed by a community dinner and dance. In 1933 all alumnae, not simply those who lived nearby, were invited to return to Saratoga Springs for the festivities.

Subsequent May Days included participation by more and more of the college's departments' home economics students [who] mounted exhibitions of their work in some years, while in others the science departments presented an open house with laboratory demonstrations. Omnibus, in addition to producing the May Day pageant, began to offer a play in the Little Theater on May Day weekend. The Skidmore horse show became a featured event as well: in 1936 it boasted a trotting race, jumping, a potato race, musical chairs, and an interclass derby, among other contests. May Day festivities were occasionally interrupted by rain, and in some years the pageant was held indoors, in the city's Convention Hall. But rain or shine, the event grew to acquire the elements of an alumnae reunion and a parents' weekend. By the end of the thirties, May Day was the major event of the spring term.[122]

The May Day pageant of 1957 was titled *On a Proud Hill* as a memorable extravaganza performed on two nights for audiences of thousands to honor the departing college president's thirty-second and final May Day. The thirteen-scene play "began with Lucy Skidmore's birth and her life as connected to the Civil War and other major events in history," depicted the founding of the college, and culminated in two final scenes honoring the retiring president.

Smith College, Northampton, Massachusetts

Chartered as a college for women in 1871 and opened in 1875, Smith currently enrolls approximately 2,750 women.

The college began celebrating May Day in 1912 and ceased sometime circa 1963, but the event principally involved the seniors carrying baskets of flowers to the home of the college president and other officials and serenading them. In later years a senior brunch was added to the day. The archivist reports that there seems to have been only one time when the maypole dance and a pageant were held, in 1948, and the last photograph in the archives of May Day is dated 1963. The archivist notes that not only were there other popular events that occurred at the college in early May, but there was an anti–Vietnam War rally on May 2, 1964, and she speculates that the combination of these two factors ended the festival.[123]

Sweet Briar College, Sweet Briar, Virginia

Founded in 1901 by Indiana Fletcher Williams in memory of her daughter, Sweet Briar College opened in 1906 with 51 students. It now enrolls 710 women.

The first May Court was held in 1907 by the original 36 girls of the college. It was a simple affair, not well attended by outsiders as the roads were bad. The girls in their white dresses decked with flowers wended their way in and out of the Boxwood Circle, a special planting on the campus. In 1909 heralds and a pageant of Robin Hood were added to the event, and the Queen made the following speech of welcome to her subjects:

> My faithful subjects and my May Day court, and you friends, all who have crowned and garlanded me with flowers to be your Queen of May, I thank you and I ask your help that I may be a Queen

worthy to wear your rose and your crown. And you, blithe company, who are gathered at our Court of May, I bid you welcome. By virtue of my crown, my garland, and my May Day scepter, I give to you my royal command, "Be merry, I pray you, and fill with gladness all my reign of this May Day."[124]

The festival continued, with the coronation held in the Circle and the pageant in the West Dell. Early sample programs included: *The Awakening of Princess Daffodil* (1912), Milton's *L'Allegro*, which featured various interpretive dances set to classical music by Debussy, Sibelius, Wagner, Mendelssohn, Brahms, Grieg, and Verdi (1918); and *The Pipes of Pan* (1920). In 1927, after a catastrophic fire, the entire festival was moved to the West Dell. It was also at that point that admission, formerly limited, was opened to all visitors.

Prior to 1938, the selection of the Queen appears to have been in the hands of a few girls: perhaps the prior year's Queen and May Court. At that time a student requested that the selection process for May Court be changed, finding the current system unfair, even though, according to her, the school's best-looking girls were being selected. Thus, in February 1948, the girls were elected by their own classes, with freshmen and sophomore pages and junior and senior members of the court. In February 1949 the election of the May Queen was held in the "'presence of general havoc'; and a parade across the stage of upperclassmen who aspired to be Queen of the May. Some of them were quite in jest, as there appeared a person with a [toilet] plunger! The observers shouted as their favorite candidates walked." At this time the elected queen began the custom of running a triumphal lap down the corridor of cheering girls.[125]

By 1958 this custom had solidified: the entire senior class "costumed in 'everything from the new chemise to the Four Horsemen of the Apocalypse,'" paraded into the main hall. "Nominations for May Queen began and after the third ballot the student body lined up outside from Manson to the Refectory arcade. According to Sweet Briar tradition the May Queen and her crown bearer are first known when they run past this line.'"[126]

The archivist noted that very little description of the festival could be found after the early 1940s, as the emphasis was on the dance that followed the crowning.

> Throughout the 1960's there were editorials, articles and letters to the editor in the Sweet Briar News requesting changes in the traditional May Day weekend. The Sophomores, the class who was responsible for organizing the entire event, came in for the most criticism. They were accused of "lacking imagination" (1969), but this apparently was not a problem unique to Sweet Briar. Hollins College, "sisters in Southern womanhood" to Sweet Briar, held a similar "fête de printemps," but in 1969 they questioned the affair "as having more or less gone to pot." (*Sweet Briar News*, May 16, 1969). The major entertainment was now concerts in the dell and formal dances.[127]

The festival was discontinued in 1969 by a vote of the students.

Trinity University, San Antonio, Texas

Founded in 1869 as a liberal arts institution affiliated with the Presbyterian Church, now enrolling approximately 1,200 men and 1,200 women.

Trinity celebrated May Day from 1913 to 1915. There is no further mention of the festivity until 1924 when the event was featured as the "first" May Fest. The 1924 event, presented by students of the Department of Physical Education for Women, was titled *The Quest of Youth, a Masque of May*. It was the story of Pan, elves, sprites, and so on, who assisted a Forest Youth to find his own true love. This pageant was apparently the last presented.[128]

University of California at Berkeley, Berkeley, California

Formed in 1868 by the merger of two institutions with an enrollment of 40 students, the university began admitting women in 1870 with a class of 8 girls.

The first Partheneia masque, titled "The Masque of Maidenhood," was performed in April 1912. Sample pageant titles included: *The Lilies of Mirones* (1921); *The Vision of Marpessa* (1922); *The Merrie Masque of May* (1924); *Mara, A Maid of the Balkans* (1928); with the last pageant being *The Potter's Wheel* (1931).[129]

University of Charleston, Charleston, West Virginia

Founded as the Morris Harvey College in 1888. Currently enrolls approximately 265 men and 590 women.

The first May Queen was crowned on May 16, 1935, as part of the observation of Founder's Day and the forty-seventh anniversary of Morris Harvey College. In the first year, the students paid for the privilege of voting in order to raise funds to buy appropriate costumes, including those of two jesters and a troubadour, played by men. The 1936 event had little newspaper coverage, but in 1937 it was noted that the practice of paying to vote had apparently been dropped, though it was reported that each student voted only once, a practice, as the alumnae news bulletin reporter wryly remarked, that "broke with some major West Virginia traditions." In this year the short-lived practice of crowning a burlesque May King was also dropped.

Over the years, the student body elected the Queen and her court, choosing from candidates representing each class and, during some years, certain sororities. There was no celebration during 1943 due to the war, nor in 1951, as the students were busy portraying themselves during Paramount Picture's month-long filming of a movie about another of the college's customs, Sadie Hawkins Day.[130] The last Queen was elected in 1970.

University of Colorado, Boulder, Colorado

Established in 1876, the university currently enrolls approximately 11,175 men and 10,200 women.

On May 4, 1912, the Women's League sponsored the university's first May Day in order to raise funds for a women's building. Two thousand spectators viewed an elaborate procession, the crowning, folk dances, and the maypole dance. Later that day the men presented the operetta *The Haymakers*. The event was successful, as the paper reported that "Queen's Crown Costs Visitors Over $1,000.00" and went on as subtitle "Large Sum added to Fund for $75,000 Women's Building, the Dream of Every Colorado Co-Ed." Another article was titled: "May Festival is Co-Eds Way to Get Golden Shekels." This author wrote that for months everyone has been hearing about the plans: "Every co-ed, every alumna, in fact every woman in the state who has heard of the plan is becoming more enthused every day. No election in years has aroused any more interest than that of the May Queen and her sixteen maids of honor."[131]

The event of May 1914 was even more elaborate. As a band played, all the girls in the university processed, walking four abreast, each class headed by its own marshal, the seniors wearing their academic caps and gowns, the juniors swinging flower-filled baskets, the sophomores all in white save for their rose and lilac hoops and hairbows, and the freshmen crowned with smilax and white flowers. This provision is captured in the photograph on page 112.

At a signal from the marshals the line divided, swung to opposite sides, and the sophomores hoops made an arch through which the freshmen passed. And then, in a second, the music ceased, and the whole moving, colorful column stood frozen while the camera-man clicked his shutter. The picture would have been a charming one if it could have caught the flash and glint of sunlit color and mingling costumes.[132]

Other photographs taken this day show aesthetic dances of sunbeams and snowflakes.

The May 6, 1916, biennial fête program quoted lines from Alfred Noye's poem, "Song of Sherwood," and featured an Old English Festival rather than the aesthetic dances of prior years. As reported in the student newspaper:

> The freshmen coming first will wear the time-honored green of their station, but the little caps and aprons will have the gay coquettishness appropriate to Irish colleens. They will be followed by the sophomores who have chosen the gay colors of Gypsy wanderers. The juniors in the plaids and caps of Scotch lassies will march next, and after them, the seniors, coming last will be dressed as dainty English shepherdesses.

Each "nation" was preceded by a marshal in full costume. Next came Robin Hood on a black horse followed by sixteen archers dressed in green, then Maid Marian, the Queen of the May. "From the east she will come to meet them, a dainty maid of the forest in white and gold on a white horse, surrounded by her sixteen maidens, scarcely less charming than herself."[133]

The war slightly interrupted the biennial progression of performances as the next one appears to have occurred on May 24, 1919. It featured two girls portraying Oberon and Titania, the "Rulers of the Day," who were entertained by the characters of Fairy land, including Scheherazade "attired in the rich silks and flashing jewels of distant Araby" and followed by the Forty Thieves; the Queen of Hearts, Mother Goose, Simple Simon and the Pieman, and other characters from fairy tales and myths.

The University of Colorado pageant directors were becoming ever more ambitious. The festival of Saturday, May 16, 1921, portrayed the tale of the betrothal of a Chinese Prince and the Sun Princess (with both roles portrayed by girls); a wedding at which many other "rulers" appeared. So many spectators were expected that seats for 5,000 were erected in a natural amphitheater on campus. Seven hundred women participated in the event, and even the men were pressed into service: "A committee of men has been working steadily for the last two weeks, stenciling and dyeing the 700 costumes which will be worn in the Fête, and which will conform to the styles of those worn by the Russians, Egyptians, Byzantines and Persians around the period A.D. 800." These costumes were to be both "modest, historically accurate, and comfortable to dance in." The May Fête was still being sponsored by Women's League, which now had raised a little more than $12,000 from prior fêtes. At this time they hoped to raise up to $15,000 with which to purchase a pipe organ.[134]

In May 1923, the pageant, performed under the auspices of the Women's Self-Government Association, involved even more effort and landscaping: five hundred small pine trees were specially imported to form a small forest in the natural amphitheater "formed by a curve between the rushing waters of Boulder Creek and the high hill of the south shore." A stone bridge 130 feet long built by university engineers and containing ten tons of stone "made a graceful entryway for the dancers from the meadow beyond." At this point, the student paper noted that "Preparation for the Fête, which every two years is the biggest thing in the coeds' life, has been going on for months."[135]

On May 23, 1925, the women offered a "Dance Drama," which featured characters and dances from nursery rhymes. In the program for this year, it was noted that: the selection of the Queen and King made by a board

> composed of one representative from each of the ten sororities and an equal number of independent women. These were elected by secret ballot, and all ballots cast by them were secret. No nomi-

nations were made at their meetings, but each girl submitted the names of three girls who she believed best represented the spirit of the rating sheet which was compiled as a standard for judging collegiate representation.... The Queen is a senior girl who was given the highest rating by the electing board. The King is a junior girl with the highest rating.[136]

The program of May 26, 1927, saw a return to an Old English Festival. The girls performed the Maypole to the "Kreutz Polka" and danced the morris dances "Bobbing Joe" and "Country Gardens." Peasants danced "Portland Fancy" and the Swedish dance "Bleking" set to a Scottish reel, and the sailors danced a hornpipe. After other folk dances, the hobby horses performed a dance set to Haydn's "Minuetto" from *Symphonie Militaire*. At this time, though the name of the "King" (a girl) appeared in the program, that of the Queen was left blank—suggesting that the Queen would be chosen on the day itself.

The festival appears to have vanished in the late 1920s or possibly the early 1930s. An unnamed, undated document from the university archives states that "Success killed the Fête as each year it became more and more elaborate leaving less and less profit."

University of Denver, Denver, Colorado

Established in 1864 as a private institution, the university currently enrolls approximately 1,600 men and 1,830 women.

The first record of May Day, "the most popular of the spring festivities" began in 1911 with a four-mile relay race between representatives of the classes, on the result of which hung the selection of the Queen for the day. The juniors won; the candidates from the defeated classes, including the preparatory school, formed the court of honor. Twenty-four girls from the physical culture class performed the maypole "drill," and members of the YWCA served refreshments, after which came the annual ball game between the university and the School of Mines.[137]

In 1919 the race was followed by various Greek dances, a men's quartette, a song, and the maypole dance. The program includes an extensive list of local patronesses. In 1920 the races were followed by a pantomime ballet by Louis H. Chalif, titled "The Sun," and in 1921 the races were followed by Chalif's pantomime ballet, *The Farmer's Garden Party*. In 1924 the event was called the "Annual May Fête and High School Night Entertainment." No queen is mentioned in the program, which included an Indian pageant, *Kaye Povi*, by Lenore Cohen.

By 1939, May Day was a weekend event, with songs, violin solos and double-piano music played on Friday evening. On Saturday, after the lengthy processional, came the crowning of the Queen and various recognition of school honors. The "School Princesses" (girls representing the university schools of Chappel, Commerce, Engineering, Law, Liberal Arts and Library) were escorted by senior men. After the crowning, each of nineteen different clubs, fraternities and sororities sang a song. Later in the afternoon came a musical, a dance recital and a May Day play. The celebrations of the next few years seem to have been similar to those of 1939, but without the songs.

In 1948 the students "again this year" expressed a desire to hold May Day in the traditional medieval setting, using a Gothic-style college building as background. The event began with songs for chorus, a "Festival Overture" for the college symphony and the procession of the Honorary Parakeets and Phi Epsilon Phis (pep club members), the Mortar Board Society, and other college clubs. The procession included College Princesses from the six colleges of the university, plus the five candidates for Queen. These had been nominated by vote of a selected group of twenty men from all the colleges, and were voted for on a preferential ballot by the undergraduate women. The candidates are variously described as "gentle, poised and gracious," "natural, lovely and warm-hearted," and so on.

The university archivist noted that no programs or yearbook photos appear for the 1950s — it would seem that the tradition was in abeyance for a decade. In 1960 the May Days Committee presented a "May Days Internationale Twilight Sing." Various fraternities and sororities presented songs and dances, followed by a simpler presentation of the candidates for Queen. The year 1964 saw a similar program. In 1966 "May Days" covered a long weekend of events. By this date, is apparent that the different clubs and fraternities were competing for a trophy during the Twilight Sing on Friday evening, at which more than 2,000 spectators watched as each club presented an eight-minute performance. Friday had begun with a "Sunrise Dance" that started at nine in the morning and continued to noon. On the Thursday of this week, a fraternity and a sorority "brought over 150 orphans to the MayFair before it was opened to the public."

In 1969 the theme of May Days was "Bubble Up to Broadway," which was "to reflect the creativity and spirit that sororities, fraternities, and independents can create in working together toward common goals." The May Day Queen, chosen on the Tuesday of this festival week, was to represent the university at the Miss Colorado Beauty Pageant.

In 1970 the theme was "Go Mad in a Mod May." It was noted that in addition to the fun and competition, all proceeds from the event would be donated to the minority scholarship program. There was no mention of a Queen.[138]

University of Idaho, Moscow, Idaho

Founded in 1889 as a land-grant institution, the university now enrolls 12,900 students.

May Day celebrations were held beginning on May 23, 1910, at the urging of Permeal French, dean of women from 1908 to 1936. Students, faculty, and townspeople cleaned the campus, planted shrubs, and gathered together in the afternoon to sing songs and watch the girls wind the maypole. Over the years the event grew larger and ever more popular, and the campus work-day aspect was dropped as the university enlarged its maintenance crews. The college historian notes that Miss French "perhaps influenced social life at the university more than any other person" as she created beloved traditions. The May Fête evolved into a Parents' Weekend sometime in the 1940s, and it would appear that the May Queen vanished upon or shortly after Miss French's retirement.[139]

University of Illinois at Urbana-Champaign, Champaign, Illinois

Founded in 1867 and now enrolls approximately 11,500 men and 13,110 women.

May Day began in 1898. The elaborate festivities including costumed dancers and the winding of the maypole disappeared circa 1931, although a May Queen was crowned at least until 1968. The archivist noted that since that year, a change in the school calendar making May primarily a month of exams and graduation, limited other May celebrations.[140]

University of Kansas, Lawrence, Kansas

Founded in 1866 as a public institution, the university now enrolls approximately 8,500 men and 9,350 women.

The first May day activities were started by the men in 1891 as a day-long fist-fight or "scrap" between the freshmen and the juniors against the seniors and the sophomores for possession of a forty-foot long maypole. Though condemned as hooliganism by local newspapers and commentators, the scrap continued until 1904, when two freshmen were seriously injured and the chancellor put an end to the event, as described in Chapter 13.

It was not until 1908 that the women of the University of Kansas held their own old English May Day pageant, explicitly modeled on those held at Bryn Mawr and other eastern schools. It was organized by the local chapter of the YWCA, and included the May Queen riding in on a white pony, maypole dancers, the play *Pyramus and Thisbe*, and various folk dances as well as a milkmaid drill, performed around a cow.[141] A few years later, a writer in the 1912 yearbook noted that the fête, then called "Spring Kirmess," came into being "in answer to a long felt need for an out-of-door play-festival, which should be a traditional part of University life."[142]

By 1913, young men from various fraternities were giving the three plays (apparently including the women's parts), while the girls performed the folk and aesthetic dances. The fête continued at least until 1921, then faded away.

University of Maryland, College Park Maryland

Founded in 1856 as the Maryland Agricultural College, the institution eventually became a Morrill land-grant college. It currently enrolls 34,933 graduates and undergraduates.

Adele Stamp, the dean of women, established the May Day festival in 1923 as an opportunity to honor and celebrate women and their achievements. The junior girls chose a senior as May Queen, and, according to the 1958 yearbook, the choice was to be made not on beauty alone but upon "citizenship, scholarship and service to the University."

Over the years it became the custom for the junior women to present a play in honor of their seniors while the sophomores performed the maypole dance. While the 1923 May Day festival had seen only 16 performers and an audience of about 50, by 1937, 125 women participated in front of an audience of 2,000.

A typical May Day in the 1940s or 1950s commenced with a welcome address. After the welcome address, a lengthy procession began, lead by two junior ushers. A junior representative of each dorm or sorority followed the ushers. The pages came next, and then the honor guard of senior women made their appearance. Once the honor guard was in place, the Queen and her court processed onto the green. The Queen's procession could be compared to a wedding procession. Her entourage included flower girls, a crown bearer, a book bearer, and a train bearer. The book bearer traditionally presented a first edition *Terrapin* yearbook to the Queen. May Day also included songs, a pageant or play to honor the queen, and the May Pole dance.[143]

The last May Day festival occurred in 1961, at the time of Dean Stamp's retirement and to her regret. The college archivist indicates that another factor in ending the celebration was controversy over how to select the Queen.[144]

Pageant titles from 1923 through 1960 were as follows:

1923	*First Maye Daye*
1924	*Fairy Stories*
1925	*The Man in the Moon*

1926	*Japan*
1927	*Plantation Days*
1928	*Mother Gooseland*
1929	*Neptune, God of the Sea*
1930	*Zinagree the Gypsy*
1931	*Maiobka in Old Russia*
1932	*Harp of the White-Thorn Tree*
1933	*The Spring Maiden*
1934	*A Maryland May Day*
1935	*Rip Van Winkle*
1936	*The Magic Toys*
1937	*Famous Women Past and Present*
1938	*Maryland, A Miniature of America*
1939	*A Modern May Day* (The Machine Age)
1940	No Theme?—Dance and Chorus
1941	No Theme?—Dance and Chorus
1942	*Dance of the Seasons*
1943	*A Spring May Day*
1944	Theme Unknown
1945	*A United Nations May Day*
1946	*Americana May Day*
1947	*May Day Recap*
1948	*Famous Lovers*
1949	*The Golden Apple*
1950	*May Time around the World*
1951	*May Day at the Fair*
1952	*May Day in Wonderland*
1953	*Pygmalion* and *A Jester Dance*
1954	*A Pan-American May Day*
1955	*Plantation Pageant*
1956	*Centennial May Day*
1957	*Flowering Future May Day*
1958	*Sugar N' Spice*
1959	*Legend of May*
1960	*May Day around the World*
1961	Theme Unknown

University of Minnesota, Minneapolis, Minnesota

Founded in 1851 as a land-grant institution, the university currently enrolls approximately 11,500 men and 10,500 women.

The May Fête was first held May 20, 1909 under the auspices of the YWCA. It included the crowning, the maypole dance, a short play, *A Box of Monkeys*, and, after dinner, a concert by the University Band, a Pageant and Tableaux and the May Queens' Response.

There was apparently no event in 1910, but in 1911 there was an all-campus festival, which all students attended in costume, as well as numerous dignitaries, including the governor of the state. This spectacle drew an estimated 3,000 spectators, paying one dollar each, and funds generated by this event were earmarked for the proposed Northrop Memorial Men's building. The program included four plays, each performed two to three times; morris, folk and maypole dancing performed by the girls; food vendors; singers; and the antics of various rabble and peasantry. The event was organized by Eleanor Sheldon Myers who had either seen or participated in Bryn Mawr's festival, where she did graduate work after attending the university.

In 1911, while apparently some of the men students had qualms about appearing in tights, the entire campus was activated. The student newspaper describes the procession, showing how the festival incorporated all participants. After the commandant of the cadets opened the procession, came the heralds, Queen Elizabeth and her champion, the Lord Mayor of the city, the French, German, Spanish and Scandinavian "embassies," the May Queen's heralds, the Queen on a white palfrey, followed by Robin Hood's men, Jacks-in-the Green, the maypole, morris dancers and

> Sir Francis Drake and his crew of pirates, with captive Indians, the Seven Liberal arts, alchemists from the college of Chemistry, mouth doctors from the college of Dentistry, apothecaries from the college of Pharmacy, barristers from the college of Law, plague physicians from the college of Medicine, the Nursing orders, preceded by Hygeia, Goddess of Health, the Spirit of Nursing, the Spirit of Science, saintly women [such as Hilda of Whitby], woman catholic sisters, secular nursing sisters, nursing attendants [Sairy Gamp and Betsy Prig], sisters of Charity, the personel [*sic*] of the Abraham and Isaac play, milk maids and farm hands with cows, strolling singers, person of "The Arraignment of Paris," strolling minstrels, the Nine Muses, Spring group, fairies, witches, shepherdesses with sheep, the Hobby horse knights, heralds, St. George and the Dragon, the Seven Cardinal Virtues, the Seven Deadly Sins, [and a] band of Pirates with a captured princess.

This prodigious event must have exhausted campus resources, for, according to the archivist, there are no records of a subsequent event.[145]

University of Missouri, Columbia, Missouri

Founded in 1839. Women were first permitted to attend beginning in 1867, but it was not until 1868 that the first 22 women actually enrolled. By 1915 there were 700 women enrolled. The University currently enrolls approximately 8,300 men and 9,100 women.

May Day was celebrated at "Mizzou" with a crowning of a Queen chosen from the senior class and a pageant from approximately 1910 until sometime in the 1920s. According to the college's Web site history, "[i]t was an important festival on campus, and it was virtually the only holiday that specifically celebrated women."[146]

University of New Hampshire, Durham, New Hampshire

Founded in 1866 as part of a public university system, the university currently enrolls approximately 4,175 men and 5,800 women.

The women students, under the direction of Helen B. Bartlett, hired in 1918 to head the women's physical education program, presented the first May festival in 1919. The Girls' Council sponsored the festival as a way to advance their goal of bringing the girls of the college together to strengthen the feeling of college spirit. The program included a pageant in which the Queen was crowned. The second festival, that of 1920, was titled "The Spirit of Americanization." Bartlett directed one more pageant, but after she left the university the festival was discontinued until 1931, when the president — believing that the college needed more traditions — revived it. After six more years, however, interest declined. A 2003 article in the university alumni bulletin notes that:

In 1940, the acting head of the P.E. department wrote to the sponsoring committee, saying with considerable tact, "I feel for various reasons that this would be a propitious year for a musical festival." As war approached, women's physical education focused more on fitness then recreation and the May Day festival was allowed to take its place in the pageant of UNH history.[147]

University of Puget Sound, Tacoma, Washington

Founded in 1888 as an independent liberal arts and sciences institution, the university currently enrolls approximately 990 men and 1,530 women.

The university archivist summarized the following information after an exhaustive search of the yearbooks, as no programs exist in the archives. She wrote:

The first mention of a May Day celebration was 1917, although [since] it was already referred to as our "annual Mayday festival" I would say it began about 1915. For May Queen a senior girl on the YWCA cabinet was elected with 2 attendants. There was dancing and a fantasy play was performed.

We continued to have May Day Festivals, with the Queen and Duke chosen from the YWCA and the YMCA. 1926 was the first time it was an all-college event and the Queen and Duke were chosen from the senior class at large by the whole student body. Girls wore white dresses and leaf garlands and children attended the court.

In 1929 the May festival honored the royalty and their mothers. There was a trumpet solo, a maypole dance and solo dancing, a Women's double quartet, Men's Glee club, instrumental numbers, an art exhibit, and informal reception.

In 1930 it became a student musical recital and mothers of all college students were honored. There was a March of the Court, the attendants were called Heralds and Queen's Attendants., a Maypole dance, athletic exhibition, Girls' Tumbling club, Girls' Glee club, and a sailor dance of small children.

In 1932, royalty was selected from the ASB officers on the basis of service to the school and representative of school ideas.

1934 was a big affair—"Duchesses" elected from surrounding high schools as well as from the college's organizations were present. A daisy chain was brought to the Queen and as each duchess approached, she curtsied to the Queen. There was a musical program and a recessional.

There were still Queens up to 1944 and 1945, when they were called "Bond Queen" for the war bond campaign. Homecoming court was becoming more prominent. In the later 1940s the event was much smaller affair. In 1951 it was called the Spring Festival, and still with a Queen, entertainment, dance, departmental open houses. In 1963 the festival honored visiting high school seniors. There was a songfest and carnival booths. In the later '60s only the Queen's portrait [not the Court's] is shown in the [yearbook], with the last one being that of May 1970.

In 1971 there was still a spring weekend, amid lots of student protests. This weekend was filled with the Black Arts Festival Cultural Night. Alex Haley was a speaker, there was a jazz festival, dance, and a carnival. There was no mention of a May Queen or court.[148]

University of Richmond (Westhampton College), Richmond, Virginia

While the first woman to matriculate from what was then Richmond College graduated in 1899 at the top of her class, the Westhampton College for women, affiliated with the Baptist Church, did not open until 1914. The college is now fully merged with the university.

In a 1990 article on the history of the college, the writer noted that a priority for the Dean in 1914 was to "oversee the development of a cohesive group life for a new and traditionless college." Dean Keller evaluated every tradition for its creative and unifying potential.[149]

As a consequence, the first Daisy Chain was prepared by the sophomores for their senior big sisters in 1915, at the occasion of the first graduation ceremony of the new college. In 1926 the Junior-Freshman Wedding, a symbol of union between the two classes, was added to the list of traditions. According to the archivist, the first May Day was celebrated in 1914, with the winding of the maypole added in 1915. In 1916 the girls celebrated May Day with various aesthetic dances, and by 1922 there was a complete pageant that combined spring characters with dances symbolizing the Purification of Water and other similar themes.

Information on May Day and its pageants at Westhampton College is sketchy. In 1939, when the theme was "Fair Day at Nottingham," at which Robin Hood crowned the Queen. In 1941 the theme was that of the Pied Piper.

A Queen was crowned until at least 1973, though by then the May Queen's court was called Spring Court. The Spring Court day included a picnic, a spring concert, an exhibition of student artwork, a dance and other events.[150]

University of South Carolina, Columbia, South Carolina

Founded in 1805, the university now has eight campuses and more than 40,000 students.

Information about May Day is sketchy, but it was apparently celebrated from at least 1940 until its demise in 1969. The university president, "usually dressed in white tie and tails," crowned the Queen.[151]

University of Tennessee, Knoxville, Tennessee

Founded in 1794 as the original campus of the state university system, now enrolling 8,800 men and 9,340 women.

The first reference to a May Day celebration was in 1938 when the festival was presented by the Physical Education Department. After the procession, the Queen was crowned by the president of the college and an octet sang, "Now is the Month of May." A pantomime that included male performers, *Pierrot Passes By*, was performed, incorporating a soprano solo, a flute solo, a clown dance given by students of the physical education classes and a modern dance given by the modern dance club. A few folk dances and a maypole dance performed by 48 girls from the folk dance classes and majors in physical education concluded the performance. Music was provided by the university band and a pianist.

To select the Queen that year, a list of about 50 junior girls "making high grades in their sophomore physical education" classes was compiled. From this list the intra-mural council picked four candidates, "and the Queen was selected by the [Physical Education] department on the basis of her physical education work." It was also noted that the director of the festival had offered a class in "Festivals and Pageants."[161]

The event seems to have been held only for three years, with 1940 the last year listed. The archivist speculates that the popularity of another celebration held in mid–May, called the Alohe Oe, may have led to the discontinuance of May Day.[152]

Ursinus College, Collegeville, Pennsylvania

Located just outside Philadelphia, Ursinus College was founded in 1869 and currently enrolls approximately 1,480 students.

Agnes R. McCann, director of physical training for women, originated Ursinus' May Pageant in May 1919 as a dance showcase. The pageant had several "rules" and was announced as a contest. In 1939–40, for example, a manuscript was to be submitted in an open competition and women students from any class were eligible. During at least the 1941–1959 period, women could choose as an elective a two-semester hour course called Pageantry that gave them training and experience in the management of the May pageant.

The pageant had to include last no more than one and a half hours, include at least 125 performers of whom 20 to 25 were major characters, and was required to be enacted in pantomime with a minimum of action for the Queen. "It was to be divided into episodes and have as few changes of the scenery as possible." By the 1950s, the prize for the winning manuscript was twenty-five dollars. Sample winning themes included: *Mexican Springtime: A Pageant for May Day* (1941); *Maiden America: An Ursinus May Queen* (1943); *Land of Oz* (1944); *May Pole of Merry Mount* (1947); *Disneyland* (1958); and *Visitor from Space* (1960). As described in Chapter 13, sometime prior to 1945, the men on campus started a "slightly irreverent" parody a week or so after each year's production. The May Day pageant ceased in 1962 and the event became known as the Spring Festival.[153]

Valdosta State University, Valdosta, Georgia

Opened in 1913 as the South Georgia State Normal College: a women-only normal college with a two-year course in teacher preparation, with three freshmen and fifteen sub-freshmen (preparatory) students. In 1922 the school became a four-year college and was renamed Georgia State Women's College (GSWC). By that year the undergraduates numbered 402 and the training school enrolled 108 students. In 1950, the college began admitting men, and changed its name to Valdosta State College. The college achieved university status in 1993, and now enrolls approximately 9,000 graduate and undergraduate students.

The girls of the college celebrated an Old English Christmas festival from 1913, with a few breaks during the 1940s, until the last year of GSWC in 1950. The festival recreated various medieval English traditions, though Dickens, ice skaters and rag dolls made their way into the program that otherwise included a Lord of Misrule, a Yule Log, the Boar's Head, a costumed minuet, morris dances, skits, carols, and other revels.

Some time after the inception of the Christmas festival, but certainly by 1922 when it was described as an "old" tradition, the girls began to celebrate May Day, with the crowning of the Queen, a maypole dance, folk dances, and plays. Both festivals were discontinued briefly during World War II. Miss Leonora Ivey of the Physical Education department directed both festivals from 1927 or 1928 until 1950, another reason for their longevity.

The advent of the men changed the girls' community: the last Christmas Fest appears to have been held in 1950, the year that men were admitted. The May Festival lasted a little longer, until the spring of 1956, perhaps because of the focus on the coronation.

The college historian noted in 2001 that

> The coming of men to campus made immediate and lasting changes at Valdosta State. The elaborate costumed festivals came to an end early in the 1950s with more co-ed events taking their place. Dances and beauty contests took the place of the May queens and Christmas festivals. Within a few years, most of the extracurricular activities were male-led. In fact, by 1956, men on campus outnum-

bered the women. Greek organizations were formed, with fraternities leading the way, and inter-collegiate athletics became a part of campus life when the Rebels, an all-male basketball team, was formed.[154]

Wartburg College, Waverly, Iowa

Founded 1852 as an academy and a four-year liberal arts college of the Evangelical Lutheran Church in America, Wartburg College now enrolls approximately 1,800 students.

There were no women on the faculty until 1914. In 1919 the Wartburg Academy (high school) girls presented the first May Festival, directed by Margaret Reu, director of physical education. The festival program lists two parts: Part I included the entrance of the Festal Train, the coronation of the May Queen, and the grand march before the throne of the Queen. Part II contained eighteen dances, a mixture of ranging from aesthetic or interpretive dances to folk dances. They included "Stormy March Winds," "Moonlight," "Brownies," "Fairies," "Awakening of Spring" (solo dance), "Spring Dance," "Spirit of Warmth," "Maypole Dance," "Bohemian Dance," "How Do You Do" (a morris dance), "Gathering Peascods" (English), "Sailors' Hornpipe," "Dutch Klappdans," the "Irish Lilt," the "Ace of Diamonds" (Danish), "Parson's Farewell" (English), "Dance of Happiness," and "Golden Butterfly."[155]

The 1920 program, though it includes a more descriptive story of the pageant, reused the same dances. A pianist is identified by name, and the program included a cello solo.

May programs were probably given throughout the 1920s, and no termination date was provided to me. The last program information provided dates from an account in the college yearbook describing the program of the spring of 1929, at which time a pageant of the history of Wartburg was given. "The Spirit of Wartburg, a Senior chosen by the girls, entered to view the progress of the school." The pageant depicted the boys first, then the Pre–Seminary department in which girls could enter, then the subsequent development of the college and the academy. "All this development was presented through music and dance steps in the Pageant. At the last, the Spirit of Wartburg was crowned with a golden crown to signify the culmination of fifty years of useful activity."[156]

Wellesley College, Boston, Massachusetts

A liberal arts college chartered in 1870, Wellesley now enrolls approximately 2,300 women.

Worn out by studying, the seniors of 1883 initiated a "play-day," involving dressing up as little girls and running out to play on a nice day in May with hoops, jump ropes and other infantile games. It is unclear whether this tradition continued thereafter until the class of 1895 took charge of this student-organized frolic, not yet considered an official tradition. That day too, the statue of the "Backwoodsman" had its first May Day scrubbing and other statues were decorated with hats and feather boas.[157] The senior Hooprolling event later developed into a race from the Hill to the Chapel, the winner popularly destined to be the first bride of the class (later the first to have a baby, later the first to obtain her Ph.D., and later still the first in her class to become CEO, as each of these milestones became more unique).

In 1901 the maypole was plaited and first May Queen, the senior class president, was crowned. The tradition went into temporary abeyance during World War I. In 1918, the girls made surgical dressings: the Junior and Sophomore classes staged a competition in which they made 19,600 dressings in one week. "On May Day, the Seniors spent the afternoon which was usually given over to play and Maypole rites in making dressings. Eighteen thousand seven hundred and twenty were turned out on that one day."[158]

During the 1920s a type of pageant was added to the afternoon program of games and fun, but May Day was competing with Wellesley's Tree Day celebration. Tree Day began in 1877 and by 1889 this festival incorporated elaborate pageantry more typical of other colleges' May Day pageants. In 1949, the college historian noted that:

> The class of '89 in its senior year gave a masque in which tall dryads, robed in green, played their dainty roles; and that same year the freshmen, the class of 1892, gave the first Tree Day dance; a very mild dance of pink and white English maidens around a maypole — but the germ of all the Tree Day dances yet unborn. In its senior year, 1892 celebrated the discovery of America by a sort of kermes of Colonial and Indian dances with tableaux, and ever since, from year to year, the wonder has grown; Zeus, and Venus, and King Arthur have all held court and revel on the Wellesley Campus. Every year the long procession across the green grows longer, more beautiful, more elaborate; the dancing is more exquisitely planned, more complex, more carefully rehearsed. In the spring, Wellesley girls are twirling a-tiptoe in every moment not spent in class; and in class their thoughts sometimes dance. Indeed, the students of late years have begun to ask themselves it if may not be possible to obtain quite as beautiful a result with less expense of effort and time and money; for Tree Day, the crowning delight of the year, would defeat its own end, which is pure recreation, if its beauty became a tyrant."[159]

By the mid–1930s, May Day celebrations had disappeared, save for the seniors' hoop-rolling event, a treasured tradition that continues today. Sophomore "little sisters" rise early or stay out all night to save a place on the starting line for their senior big sisters, who give them their hoops when the race is over. Many of these hoops have been handed down for generations. Arlene Cohen, an alumna of 1994, noted in a student paper on the history of hooprolling, that "May Day, when it was celebrated in all its glory at Wellesley, marked the beginning of the end for seniors. It was the first of the springtime festivals (Tree Day and Float among others) and was the first indication to seniors that this was truly the end of their Wellesley years." She concluded by noting that it was with mixed feelings that she looked forward to her own hoop-rolling experience.[160]

Wells College, Aurora, New York

Founded in 1868 as a private liberal arts institution for women, Wells College currently enrolls 430 women and 7 men.

May Day was first celebrated in 1922 as the coming of spring. In the next and subsequent years the event also became a formal celebration commemorating the birthday of E.B. Morgan, the co-founder and financial supporter of the college. The May Queen, a junior, was elected that day and crowned by her predecessor, after which there was an elaborate pageant. In 1995 the college historian noted that:

> The May Queen wore a special gown for the occasion. Surrounded by her attendants, also in costume, the May Queen and her court rode in the Wells Stagecoach to the ceremony. As well as a pageant, May Day ceremonies consisted of the may pole dance and a play or masque with music. Also, the freshman class would put on a play, and in the evening the Phoenix Society or Kastalia offered a production, most often a choral concert.[161]

In the 1930s, the celebration added other components. In 1932, the Xi chapter of Phi Beta Kappa was formally installed on campus and in that and subsequent years May Day also honored the inductees. During the late 1930s and through the early 1940s, the senior class produced a play such as *Oedipus Rex* (1937) or *Samson Agonistes* (1938). The festivities, however, gradually lessened over time: the sophomores of 1955 claimed to be tone-deaf and refused to participate in the tradition of placing wildflowers at the doors of faculty and friends while singing, and that tradition lapsed.

In the 1950s May Day was blended with Father's Day weekend and was held on Sunday afternoon, but by 1960, the event moved back to Sunday and folk dances and madrigals replaced the freshman play. As described in Chapter 18, controversy about celebrating May Day arose in 1963, and, while one-half the student body voted to keep the festival, the event dropped from the college calendar, only to be revived in 1976 and then, more fully, in 1986.

> Though May Day does not hold the same significance it once did, the freshman class still gathers around the may pole and does the may dance. Wearing white dresses and dancing to music, provided by the renaissance music class, spectators enjoy the dawning of spring. Members of the may pole dance their freshman year are eligible for the May Queen position. Today, the May Queen, still elected by the student body, is a member of the senior class.[162]

A retrospective article in the alumnae bulletin from early 2004 adds that from 1979 onward, various classes participated with more or less enthusiasm in May Day. In spring 2003, the students "were excited to participate despite a rain storm. The Class of 2007 are also enthusiastic and planning a great event for this year."[163] However, in fall of 2005, the college began — amid much dismay from the women — to accept men. A newspaper article indicate that immediately there was a different feel to the campus, with women waking up early to put on makeup. It is uncertain how long the women will maintain their distinctive traditions.[164]

Westminster College, Salt Lake City, Utah

Founded in 1875 as an independent, private, liberal arts college, the only such entity in the state. Westminster College now enrolls 2,500 students.

The earliest record of a May Day celebration at Westminster was in 1918, at a time when instructors and male students were being called up for war. The May festival formed a part of Commencement week. According to the college newspaper:

> The festival took the form of the old English custom, dear to the traditions of many American colleges, the crowning of the May Queen.
> The procession formed at sunset — an hour of special enchantment in the Salt Lake basin; an hour when the sun, radiant in its full orbed splendor, suddenly dips behind a mountain peak and the valley catching the glow, lies in a halo of reflected light.

The Lady of the Coronation, a married woman, with her train bearer and crown bearer, led the procession, followed by ladies and gentlemen in waiting, "spring sprites, the glees clubs, the faculty and student body, and lastly the beautiful white veiled queen ... and the king." After the crowning of the Queen, the glee club sang and the girls danced various dances followed by a performance of *The Mechanic's Play* from *Midsummer's Night's Dream*, followed by the maypole dance, "when movement, color and music were perfectly blended."[165]

The tradition of crowning a Queen continued to be celebrated until at least 1968, changing form as it evolved. The 1954–1955 Student Handbook indicates that the May Queen was crowned at the Spring Formal: a "girls' date dance" with the girls footing the bill. The 1967–1968 Student Handbook references the crowning of King Arthur and his Queen at the springtime "Westminster Faere."[166]

Wilson College, Chambersburg, Pennsylvania

A women's college founded in 1869 by two ministers and given an initial endowment by Sarah Wilson. Wilson College now enrolls approximately 600 women.

The first May Day was celebrated in 1902, and the festival continues today, though the event is now called "Spring Fling" and some non–May Day activities have been added. The pageant was originally given by the juniors to honor their seniors. The Queen had train-bearers, a herald and the twenty members of the Glee Club as attendants. Each class dressed to represent its flowers. The Queen was presented with a crown by the sophomores, a scepter by the juniors and the globe by the freshmen. (Later, by the mid–fifties, the order had changed, and the Queen was presented with "The Footstool from the Freshmen, The World from the Sophomores, the Sceptre from the Juniors and the Crown from the Seniors.")

Good Queen Bess first appeared in 1908, and now arrives every four years. The 1908 pageant was particularly elaborate. The Queen is enthroned and her subjects go to find her the fairest maid to be crowned Queen of the May:

> They form a motley throng, villagers and peasants, milkmaids in colors bright, and shepherds fair, reverend monks and clowns "To bring the smiles to cheeks grown grave with too much seriousness." Gaily they march along to where their chosen May Queen waits with all her festal train. With cheers and happy shouts they greet her. Down the slope she sweeps, right beauteous to behold.
>
> A trumpeter announcement makes to all of her approach. Then come four heralds gorgeously appareled in silver and in blue with silver trumpets and with waving banners. A troop of tiny flower girls next, and following them her majesty the May Queen, a canopy of lowers borne o'er her head by loyal servitors, and with four youthful subjects to support her mantle. The Maid of Honor next, a dainty roguish brown-eyed lass, selected like the queen by common voice. And after her a jester in his parti-colored clothes. A laughing group of village maids, with garlands and with brave attire decked out in honor of the May, serve as the fair attendants on the queen.
>
> Behind the May Queen's Court come those who shall participate in merrie daunce and masque in honor of the day, a strange and varied crew. First come the May-pole dancers, milkmaids and village lads, "Spring in their blood and on their lips the longing kiss.' Next the Morrice dancers all fancifullie attaired [sic]. And following hard upon them masquers, who anon present the Foresters, with Robin Hood and all his merry twain [sic]. More May-pole dancers, village lads and maids from far and near. And then the Chimney Sweeps in sooty doublets swinging high their implements of toil.
>
> Then follows on the populace, with boys and maids all decked in ribbons bright and joining hands and dancing to the scene. The old and young, the serious and the gay joining the long procession and hurry to the games. So pass they in review, as glad a throng as e'er sang welcome to the joyous May.
>
> Ye Order of Ye Revels
>
> Firste. The crowning of the May Queen, with the gifts to her of royal symbols, and the gifts of guilds.
> Seconde. The merrie May-Pole dancing, with circles round and ribboned maze, a pretty sight.
> Thirde. The Chimney Sweeps in their black robes carrying brooms, do a laughing turn in honor of the queen.
> Fourth. The jollie Morrice dancers in their quaint way, make the scene mirthful with their curious dance.
> And last. The gorgeous train in order fair sweeps forth along the stream to where the blithe and joyous Foresters perform their masque.
>
> And thus with joy and song, with dance and interlude, shall Wilson greet the coming of the May and keep high festival within her learned courts.[167]

May Day was held annually at Wilson College; the missing dates below refer to gaps in programs filed in the archives. The court was presented first, the Queen was crowned, and the pageant performed. The programs generally read: "Presented in honor of her Majesty The Queen of the May, that her heart may be as eternally young and joyful as the flowering spring."

1911	*King Rene's Daughter*
1912	*The Hue and Cry after Cupid* (Ben Jonson)
1918	*The Palace of Truth*
1919	*The Spirit of the Present Age, a Pageant*
1924	*The Celebration of a Roman Triumph in the Year 17 A.D. for Queen Bess in Honor of Her Guest, the Queen of the May*
1925	A series of episodes, including "The Story of the Nativity," "The Theft of Persephone by Pluto," "The Winter's Tale," "The Three Musketeers," "The Saving of Rome," "Joan of Arc at the Court of Charles VII," "October 12, 1742 (an Indian pageant)."
1927	*Idylls of the King*
1928	An adaptation of Milton's *Comus*
1929	*Sigurd the Volsung*, adapted from William Morris
1930	*Robin Hood*
1931	*Arthur of Camelot*
1932	*Merrie England Goes A-Maying*, (Queen Bess in attendance), at which the girls performed did the sword dance, morris, maypole and country dances
1935	*Aucassin and Nicolette*
1934	*The Road to Canterbury*
1935	A series of episodes, including "The School of Athens," "A Roman Cycle," "The Age of Chivalry," and "The Elizabethan Cycle"
1937	*American Spring*, an Indian pageant (Queen Bess in attendance)
1937	*The Moon-Princess* (an adaptation of Japanese folk tales)
1938	*The Enchanted Meadow, a Cumberland Idyll* (original pageant). This included dances of Water-Sprites, Tree-Pixies, Grasses, Social Butterflies, Scholars, Dictators and others (performed as unidentified English country dances).
1939	*The Sleeping Princess*
1940	*In the Land That Was England* (Queen Bess in attendance)
1942	*No Malice toward Alice*, an adaptation of Lewis Carroll's classic
1943	*A May Day Carol*: various English country dances, morris dances, songs, and skits
1944	*Mother Goose Goes to Court* (Queen Bess in attendance)
1946	*Peter Pan*
1947	*Bobo and the Magic Cloak*, a student adaptation of Tolkien's *The Hobbit*. No explanation of the name change (Tolkien's permission granted). Included the dance of the spiders, the dance of the dwarves and Bobo, and so on. Proceeds directed to the World Student Service Fund.
1948	*The Wizard of Oz* (Queen Bess in attendance)
1949	*Treasure Island*
1951	*Cinderella*
1952	*The Bell*
1954	*Once Upon a May Day* (an adaptation of *Winnie-the-Pooh*)
1955	*A Magical Day in May*
1956	*A Holiday in Nottingham*, which included the maypole dance (which had been missing from the previous ten or so programs)
1957	*The Wizard of Oz*
1959	*A Dream of Jade*, a Japanese fantasy (the program was printed back to front, in Japanese style)

In 1961 there began the first of several years of a dramatic change in programming. The

May Day festival went on for most of the weekend, and incorporated new events, such as a father-daughter softball game, and a formal prom or dance. The Queen was usually crowned on Saturday afternoon, with the maypole dance following. In the evening, the drama club presented formally enacted plays such as John Synge's *Playboy of the Western World* (1961). By about 1966 the plays were dropped and the event turned into a one day festival, more like a fun fair or carnival, with entertainment by a local group, "The Ten Tones," face-painting, games, and so. The Queen was and is still crowned and members of Orchesis, the modern dance group, performed the maypole dance. From this time through 2002, the name of the festival was sometimes "Mayhem," though as time passed it became more commonly called "Spring Fling."

Though there is no official language addressing the requirements for May Queen, the procedure has been for the student body to vote for the woman who "best represents the qualities of a Wilson woman" and her attendant from six senior representatives chosen by the senior class. The Court is made up of the remaining senior representatives and representatives from the other classes. Members of Orchesis, a student modern dance ensemble, perform the maypole dance. Every four years Queen Bess (Elizabeth I) is also crowned. She is chosen from among four senior representatives by the entire student body for her dual qualities of studiousness and red hair. No other pageantry is involved.[168]

Winthrop University, Rock Hill, South Carolina

Winthrop Training School was founded in 1886 with a class of 26 future teachers. The college admitted minorities in 1964, men in 1972 (somewhat prior to this time, men were permitted to take evening classes, but not to earn a degree). It achieved university status in 1992, and currently enrolls 6,500 students.

There are hints that celebrations occurred in 1919 and 1925 when the college produced several historical pageants during this time, including *The Making of South Carolina: A Historical Pageant* in 1921, and *Old English Pageant: The Visit of Queen Elizabeth to Kenilworth Castle* on May 13, 1913 — these pageant programs are available on-line through the Archives. However, the first official May Day celebration was held in 1929, with an elaborate pageant that showcased springtide customs and dances of many lands. The performance, under the direction of the head of the department of physical education, included a maypole dance performed by 60 modern dance students. This first program attracted 3,000 spectators.

An article in the student newspaper on April 27, 1929, noted that the Puritans had stamped out May Day celebrations. "The American colleges," it continued," have been in large part responsible for the revival of this lovely custom. The reason why set aside one day for laughter, song and dance is not known." The author suggested noted the custom of some Northern colleges for the sophomores to give May baskets to their favorite seniors, and added that "some of the American colleges set aside a whole day for their celebrations. People flock from all over the country-side to witness the festivities, which culminate in the crowning of the May Queen, and the dances in her honor. It is a coveted honor to be chosen Queen of the May."[169]

Seniors organized the May Day event and elected the Queen and her Maid of Honor. To complete the 18-member Court, each class elected four attendants based on the qualifications of beauty, popularity and good academic standing.

While the first program was held on the athletic fields, in the mid–1930s an amphitheater that included a blue-walled lily pond with goldfish and floating blossoms in front of the earthen stage was constructed to showcase the event. In 1963 it was noted that 5,000 spectators attended. From 1946 to 1952, with the financial backing of the Rock Hill Elks Lodge, the Winthrop May

Day Court traveled to the Veterans Hospital in Columbia to entertain hospitalized vets. Sample program titles included: *Spring's Triumph of the Seasons* (1931); *An English May Day* (1933); *Trial by Jury* (1949); *The Firebird* (1954); and *A Midsummer Night's Dream* (1964).

The last May Day celebration was held in the spring of 1970, two years before coeducation arrived. It appears that in the last few years of the event, it got shorter and a few madrigals or one dance replaced the elaborate pageants of the past.[170]

Chapter Notes

Introduction

1. Thomas D, Hamm, *Earlham College: A History, 1847–1997* (Bloomington: Indiana University Press, 1997), p. 321.
2. Stephen Nissenbaum, *The Battle for Christmas* (New York: Alfred A. Knopf, 1997), pp. 315, 317.
3. See, for example, *College Girls: A Century in Fiction*, by Shirley Marchalonis (Rutgers, N.J.: Rutgers University Press, 1995), and also *The Girl's Own: Cultural Histories of the Anglo-American Girl, 1830–1915*, edited by Claudia Nelson and Lynne Vallone (Athens: University of Georgia Press, 1994).

Part I • Chapter 1

1. John Forrest, *The History of Morris Dancing, 1458–1750* (Toronto: University of Toronto Press, 1999), p. 3.
2. "May-Day in 'Merrie England,'" *Harper's Weekly*, May 23, 1874, p. 439.
3. See Stuart Piggott, *The Druids* (New York: Frederick A. Praeger, 1968. Reprint, London and New York: Thames and Hudson, 1975).
4. Ronald Hutton, *The Pagan Religions of the Ancient British Isles* (London: Blackwell, 1991), p. 183.
5. Ronald Hutton, *Stations of the Sun* (Oxford: Oxford University Press, 1996; 2nd ed., 2001), pp. 219, 223.
6. Ibid., p. 225.
7. Ibid., p. 226.
8. John Stow, *A Survey of London*, cited in Forrest, p. 128.
9. Forrest, p. 146.
10. Hutton, *Stations*, p. 227.
11. Ibid., p. 234.
12. Forrest, p. 133.
13. Hutton, *Stations*, p. 229.
14. Ibid., p. 237.
15. Forrest, Chapter 5, passim.
16. Ibid., pp. 29–30.
17. Ibid., pp. 150–151.
18. Hutton, *Stations*, pp. 270–274.
19. Forrest, p. 193.
20. Violet Alford, *Introduction to English Folklore* (Downpatrick, U.K.: G. Bell & Sons, Ltd., 1952), p. 51.
21. See Roy Judge, *The Jack-in-the Green: A May Day Custom* (London: Folklore Society, 1979; 2nd ed., 2000).

Chapter 2

1. Gillian Bennett, "Folklore Studies and the English Rural Myth," *Rural History*, vol. 4, no. 1 (1993): 77–91.
2. Nissenbaum, *The Battle for Christmas*, p. 5.
3. Roy Judge, "May Day and Merrie England," *Folklore*, vol. 102, no. 2 (1991): 133.
4. Roy Judge, "Fact and Fancy in Tennyson's 'May Queen' and Flora Thompson's 'May Day,'" in *Aspects of British Calendar Customs*, edited by Theresa Buckland and Juliette Wood (Sheffield: Sheffield Academic Press, 1993), pp. 171–172.
5. Hutton, *Stations of the Sun*, p. 296.
6. Roy Judge, "'The Old English Morris Dance': Theatrical Morris 1801–1880," *Folk Music Journal*, vol. 7, no. 3 (1997): 324; and Judge, "May Day and Merrie England," p. 132.
7. Washington Irving, "May-Day," in *Bracebridge Hall*, edited by Andrew B. Myers (New York: Library of America, 1991), pp. 245–246.
8. Ibid., p. 215.
9. Judge, "Fact and Fancy," pp. 167–183.
10. Ibid., pp. 133–134.
11. Mark Girouard, *The Return to Camelot: Chivalry and the English Gentleman* (New Haven: Yale University Press, 1981), p. 90.
12. Fiona MacCarthy, *William Morris: A Life for Our Time* (New York: Alfred A. Knopf, 1995), p. 63.
13. Judge, "The Old English Morris Dance," pp. 311–350, passim.
14. Cited in Roy Judge "Tradition and the Plaited Maypole Dance," in *Traditional Dance*, vol. 2, edited by Theresa Buckland (Sheffield: Crewe and Alsager College of Higher Education, 1983), p. 3.
15. Ibid., pp. 1–21. See also Hutton, *Stations of the Sun*, pp. 295–303.
16. Keith Thomas, "The Perception of the Past in Early Modern England," The Creighton Trust Lecture 1983 (London: University of London), p. 22.
17. Roy Judge, "D'Arcy Ferris and the Bidford Morris, " *Folk Music Journal*, vol. 4, no. 5 (1984): 443–480.
18. Alice Brown, "Latter Day Cranford," *Atlantic Monthly*, vol. 77, issue 462 (April 1896): 529.
19. Judge, "May Day and Merrie England," pp. 142–144.
20. Ibid., p. 134.

Chapter 3

1. John Ruskin, *Sesame and Lilies* (1864. Reprint. New York: A.L. Burt Company, n.d.), p. 106.
2. Violet Alford, *Introduction to English Folklore* (Downpatrick, U.K.: G. Bell & Sons, Ltd., 1952), p. 53.
3. Judge, "Tradition and the Plaited Maypole Dance," p. 17.
4. Malcolm Cole, *Whiteland's College May Queen Festival, 1881–1981* (Whitelands College Monographs, 1981), p. 15.
5. Ibid., p. 18.
6. Ruskin to Faunthorpe, 26:4: 1881, Letter 24, Whitelands Archives, cited in Cole, p. 17.
7. J.P. Faunthorpe, "Professor Ruskin's May-Day Festival," *The Girl's Own Paper*, vol. 10, no. 486 (April 20, 1889): 450.

8. Eric S. Robertson, "Mr. Ruskin's 'May-Day,'" *The Living Age*, vol. 170, issue 2194 (July 10, 1886): 119–121.
9. "History of May Party Reveals the Traditions of Rockford College," *The Purple Parrot*, May 17, 1924, p. 3 (courtesy of the Rockford College Archives).
10. Cole, p. 24.
11. For more information on the Whitelands May Day celebration, see http://www.roehampton.ac.uk/whitelands/maymonarch/index.html.
12. Monica Godfrey, *The World of Elsie Jeanette Oxenham and Her Books* (Bath: Girls Gone By Publishers, 2003), pp. 168–170.

Chapter 4

1. Patricia H. Virga, *The American Opera to 1790* (Ann Arbor, MI: UMI Research Press, 1981; 2nd ed., 1982), p. 262.
2. "Editor's Drawer," *Harper's New Monthly Magazine*, vol. 6, issue 36 (May 1853): 850.
3. Nissenbaum, *The Battle for Christmas*, pp. 194–195.
4. Morton's account comes from his work, *New English Canaan or New Canaan* (1637. Reprint. New York: Arno Press, 1972), pp. 132–137. Bradford's account comes from his *History of Plymouth Plantation*, edited by William T. Davis (1908. Reprint. New York: Barnes & Noble, Inc., 1964), p. 238. Spelling modernized.
5. Lester J. Cappon, *The Adams-Jefferson Letters, Vol. 2, 1812–1826* (Chapel Hill: University of North Carolina Press, 1959), pp. 311–322.
6. Charles Francis Adams, Jr., "The May-Pole of Merrymount," *Atlantic Monthly*, vol. 39 (May 1877): 565.
7. Esther Willard Bates, *Pageants and Pageantry* (Boston: Ginn and Company, 1912), p. 162.
8. *Merry Mount, an Opera in Four Acts*, libretto by Richard L. Stokes and music by Howard Hansen (New York: Harms, Inc., 1933).
9. "Symptoms of Insurgency Cured, by Cutting down a May Pole," *The Herald of Liberty* (Washington, Pa.), vol. 1, issue 13 (May 7, 1798): 3.
10. Kate Van Winkle Keller, *Dance and Its Music in America, 1528–1789* (Hillsdale, N.Y.: Pendragon Press, 2007), 303–306.
11. Ewing, *Military Journal*, 44–46 (May 1, 1778), cited in Keller, p. 600.
12. Rollin G. Osterweis, *Romanticism and Nationalism in the Old South* (New Haven: Yale University Press, 1949), p. 216.
13. Ibid., pp. 89, 214.
14. Bertram Wyatt-Brown, *Southern Honor: Ethics and Behavior in the Old South* (Oxford: Oxford University Press, 1982), p. 48.
15. See http://www.geocities.com/marylandjousting/history.html.
16. E.J. Crooks and R.W. Crooks, *The Ring Tournament in the United States* (Richmond: Garrett and Massie, 1936), pp. 1–2.
17. Ibid., p. 7.
18. Ibid., p. 154.
19. Ibid., pp. 152–153.
20. "From the Boston Evening Transcript. May-Day Fair Concluded," *Salem Gazette*, vol. 11, issue 40 (May 17, 1833): 1.
21. Cited in Christie Ann Farnham, *The Education of the Southern Belle: Higher Education and Student Socialization in the Antebellum South* (New York: New York University Press, 1994), pp. 168–170; see also p. 117 for a student's sketches for costumes for the 1841 May Day celebration at Barhamville, which shows girls dressed as flowers and as the months of the year.
22. Ibid., p. 169.
23. Francis J. Niederer, *Hollins College: An Illustrated History* (Charlottesville: University Press of Virginia, 1973; 2nd ed., 1985), p. 1.
24. Boleyne Reeves, *Colburn's Kalendar of Amusements in Town and Country* (London: Henry Colburn, 1840), p. 126, cited in Roy Judge, *The Jack-in-the-Green: A May Day Custom*, p. 69.
25. Samuel Manning Welch, *Home History: Recollections of Buffalo during the Decade from 1830 to 1840, or Fifty Years Since* (Buffalo: P. Paul & Brother, 1890), pp. 384–385.
26. "Editor's Easy Chair," *Harper's New Monthly Magazine*, vol. 8, issue 48 (May 1854): 845.
27. Marion Cumming, "The First May Day Party in San Francisco, May 2nd, 1853," *The Overland Monthly*, vol. 21 (1883): 559–560.
28. Rodney J. Sorensen is one of the organizers of the town of Mendon's annual May Day and he also maintains the history of the community's celebration. Visit www.mendonutah.net for more information about the town's history and practices.
29. Opal Thornburg, *Earlham: The Story of the College 1847–1962* (Richmond, Ind.: Earlham College Press, 1963), pp. 157–160.
30. "May-Day in 'Merrie England,'" *Harper's Weekly*, vol. 18, no. 908 (May 23, 1894): 439.

Chapter 5

1. Jennette E. Carpenter Lincoln, *May-Pole Possibilities with Dances and Drills for Modern Pastime* (Boston: American Gymnasia Co., 1907), pp. 9–10.
2. Ernest Earnest, *The American Eve in Fact and Fiction, 1775–1914* (Champaign: University of Illinois Press, 1974), pp. 210–211.
3. Cited in Thomas Woody, *A History of Women's Education in the United States, Vol. 2* (New York: Octagon Books, 1966), pp. 205–206.
4. Dorothy S. Ainsworth, *The History of Physical Education in Colleges for Women* (New York: A.S. Barnes & Co., 1930), pp. 3–5.
5. McCabe, *The American Girl at College*, p. 22.
6. Ainsworth, p. 29.
7. Sherrie A. Inness, "It Is Pluck, But — Is It Sense?" Athletic Student Culture in Progressive-era Girls' College Fiction," in *The Girls' Own: Cultural Histories of the Anglo-American Girl, 1830–1915*, edited by Claudia Nelson and Lynne Vallone (Athens: University of Georgia Press, 1994), p. 217.
8. Annual report to the president by K. Helen McKinstrey, Director of Women's Physical Education, Berea College, ca. 1935 (Berea College Archives, Record Group 6.32: Physical Education and Health Department), pp. 2–3.
9. Willard, E.M., *The Favorite Books of Drills: Original Drills and Marches for Boys and Girls of All Ages* (Chicago: T.S. Denison & Co., 1907), p. 4.
10. Ida M. Tarbell, "Ida Tarbell Lists Fifty Foremost Women of United States," unidentified newspaper clipping, Earlham College Archives.
11. Gulick, Luther H., "Folk Dancing: Illustrating the Educational, Civic, and Moral Value of Folk Dancing," Pamphlet No. 118 (New York: Russell Sage Foundation, Department of Child Hygiene Department, n.d.), p. 1.
12. Gulick, "Folk Dancing," p. 1.
13. Esther Willard Bates, *The Art of Producing Pageants* (Boston: Walter H. Baker Company, 1925), pp. 83–84.
14. Felix Clay, "The Renaissance of Dancing," *The Edinburgh Review*, vol. 219 (January 1914), p. 132 (reprinted in *Living Age*, vol. 281 [April 1914]).
15. P.G. Wodehouse, *Uneasy Money* (New York: Methuen, 1917. Reprint, Penguin Books edition, 1958), p. 56.

Chapter 6

1. Anne Campbell Rinehart, *What Pittsburgh Junior High School Pupils Read*, vol. 3, no.1, in the series The Heart of Youth (Pittsburgh: Henry C. Frick Educational Commission, 1931), pp. 60–61.
2. "The Radio in May Festivals," *The Playground*, vol. 20, no. 12 (March 1927): 667.
3. Richard Hofstadter, *The Age of Reform: From Bryan to F.D.R.* (New York: Alfred A. Knopf, 1972), p. 178.
4. Thomas E. Watson, cited in ibid., pp. 82–83.
5. Laurence W. Levine, *Highbrow/Lowbrow* (Cambridge, Mass.: Harvard University Press, 1988), p. 206. For more on the fin de siècle anxieties and the recoil from "overcivilized" modern life to the supposedly more intense forms of physical or spiritual experience supposedly embodied in medieval or eastern cultures, see T.J. Jackson Lears, *No Place of Grace: Antimodernism and the Transformation of American Culture, 1880–1920* (New York: Pantheon Books, 1981).
6. Levine, p. 214.
7. Constance Cary Harrison, *The Anglomaniacs* (New York: Cassell Publishing Co., 1890. Reprint, New York: Arno Press, 1977), pp. 127–132, passim.
8. Levine, p. 221.
9. Robert M. Crunden, *Ministers of Reform: The Progressives' Achievement in American Civilization, 1889–1920* (New York: Basic Books, 1982), pp. x, 96.
10. Mabel Potter Daggett, "The City as a Mother," *The World's Work*, vol. 25 (November 1912): 114.
11. Ernst Hermann, "Recreation and Industrial Efficiency," *The Playground*, vol. 4, no. 10 (January s1911): 322.
12. Lillian D. Wald, *The House on Henry Street* (New York: Henry Holt & Co., 1915), pp. 95, 96.
13. Dominick Cavallo, *Muscles and Morals: Organized Playgrounds and Urban Reform, 1880–1920* (Philadelphia: University of Pennsylvania Press, 1981), p. 2.
14. Allen F. Davis, *Spearheads for Reform: The Social Settlements and the Progressive Movement 1890–1914* (Oxford: Oxford University Press, 1967), p. 47.
15. George E. Johnson, "Report of the Superintendent of Recreation," *Twelfth Annual Report of the Pittsburgh Playgrounds, Vacation Schools and Recreation Parks* (Pittsburgh: Pittsburgh Playground Association, 1907), p. 38.
16. Gulick, "Teaching American Children to Play: Significance of the Revival of Folk dances, Games and Festivals by the Playground Association," *The Craftsman*, vol. 15 (November 1908): 192.
17. Ibid., p. 198.
18. Cavallo, p. 37.
19. John M. Glenn, Lilian Brandt, and F. Emerson Andrews, *Russell Sage Foundation, 1907–1946, Vol. 1* (New York: Russell Sage Foundation, 1947), p. 75.
20. Gulick, *The Healthful Art of Dancing*, p. 198.
21. Lawrence Cremin, *The Transformation of the School: Progressivism in American Education 1876–1957* (New York: Alfred A. Knopf, 1962), p. 279, Hall citation p. 306.
22. Cavallo, pp. 57, 60.
23. Ibid., p. 81.
24. Gulick, *The Healthful Art of Dancing*, p. 17.
25. Gulick, "Folk Dancing: Illustrating the Educational, Civic, and Moral Value of Folk Dancing," Bulletin No. 118 (Russell Sage Foundation, n.d.), pp. 14–15.
26. Gulick, *The Healthful Art of Dancing*, p. 155.
27. John M. Glenn, Lilian Brandt and F. Emerson Andrews, *Russell Sage Foundation, 1907–1946, Vol. 1* (New York: Russell Sage Foundation, 1947), p. 75
28. Gulick, *The Healthful Art of Dancing*, p. 157.
29. William Inglis, "Folk-Dances for Health," *Harper's Weekly*, vol. 55 (July 8, 1911): 13.
30. Lily Watson, "Athleticism for Girls," *The Girl's Own Paper*, vol. 24, no. 1191 (October 25, 1902).
31. Burchenal, Elizabeth, untitled essay in Russell Sage Foundation Child Hygiene Department, Pamphlet No. 37, p.10.
32. Gulick, *The Healthful Art of Dancing*, pp. 33–34.
33. Ibid., n.p. (Introduction).
34. Ibid., pp. 36–37.
35. Gulick, "Folk Dancing," p. 19.
36. Ibid., p. 36.
37. No author, no title, *The Playground*, vol. 4, no. 1 (April 1910): 31.

Chapter 7

1. "Merry May-Day as in Merrie England," *IDS*, April 16, 1908, p. 1, column 4; "First Dress Rehearsal," *IDS*, April 30, 1908, p. 1, column 3 (both courtesy of the Indiana University Archives).
2. Gulick, *The Healthful Art of Dancing*, p. 70.
3. Charles H. Farnsworth and Cecil J. Sharp, *Folk-Songs, Chanteys and Singing Games* (New York: H.W. Gray Company, n.d.), p. i.
4. Luther Halsey Gulick, "Folk Dancing: Illustrating the Educational, Civic, and Moral Value of Folk Dancing," Pamphlet No. 118 (Russell Sage Foundation, 1912), p. 1.
5. Ibid., p. 4.
6. Grace Kimmins, *The Guild of Play Book of National Dances* (London: J. Curwen & Sons, 1910), pp. 7, 16, 54, 65.
7. Gulick, "Folk Dancing," pp. 5–6.
8. Gulick, *The Healthful Art of Dancing*, p. 34.
9. Kimmins, *The Guild of Play Book of National Dances*, pp. 5, 4.
10. Tomko, *Dancing Class*, p. 195.
11. Gulick, *The Healthful Art of Dancing*, p. 66.
12. Hinman, cited in Gulick, *The Healthful Art of Dancing*, p. 79.
13. Gulick, *The Healthful Art of Dancing*, pp. 76–77.
14. Burchenal, Elizabeth, "Folk Dancing as Social Recreation for Adults," *The Playground*, vol. 14 (October 1920): 405.
15. Ibid., p. 406.
16. Elizabeth Burchenal, "Reviving the Folk Dance," *National Education Association Journal*, vol. 15 (November 1926): 241.
17. Helen Storrow, "Folk Dancing as a Means of Family Recreation in the Home," *The Playground*, vol. 6, no. 4 (July 1912): 139.
18. Gulick, *The Healthful Art of Dancing*, pp. 213–214.
19. Elizabeth Burchenal, *Dances of the People: A Second Book of Folk-Dances and Singing Games* (New York: G. Schirmer, 1913), p. 1.
20. Caroline Caffin and Charles H. Caffin, *Dancing and Dancers of Today: The Modern Revival of Dancing as an Art* (New York: Dodd, Mead and Co., 1912. Reprint, Cambridge, Mass.: Da Capo Press, 1978), p. 295.
21. Gulick, *The Healthful Art of Dancing*, pp. 60–61.
22. William Inglis, "Folk Dances for Health," *Harper's Weekly*, vol. 55 (July 8, 1911): 26.
23. Gulick, *The Healthful Art of Dancing*, pp. 39, 40.
24. "Report of the Committee on Folk Dancing," Pamphlet No. 77 (Russell Sage Foundation), p. 6.
25. Gulick, *The Healthful Art of Dancing*, p. 28–29.
26. Helen Storrow, Chairman, The Committee on Folk Dancing of the Playground and Recreation Association of America, "Folk Dancing," *The Playground*, vol. 5, no. 5, August 1911, p. 165.

Chapter 8

1. Cited in Naima Prevots, *American Pageantry* (Ann Arbor: University of Michigan Press, 1990), pp. 89–90.
2. Lotta Alma Clark, "The Development of American Pageantry," *American Pageant Association Bulletin*, no. 9 (November 1, 1914): n.p.
3. David Glassberg, *American Historical Pageantry: The Uses of Tradition in the Early Twentieth Century* (Chapel Hill: University of North Carolina Press, 1990), p. 122.
4. "Report of the Committee on Festivals," *The Playground*, vol. 4, no. 11 (February 1911): 379.
5. Account by Mary Vida Clark, cited in August H. Brunner, "Suggestions for Celebrating Independence Day" (Department of Child Hygiene, Russell Sage Foundation), Report presented to the Third Annual Conference of the Playground Association, 1909, pp. 6–8.
6. George P. Baker, "What the Pageant Can Do for the Town," *Ladies Home Journal*, vol. 31 (April 1914): 44.
7. Prevots, p. 4.
8. Ibid., pp. 29–33.
9. The Editor, in a preface to "Festivals in American Colleges for Women," *The Century: A Popular Quarterly*, vol. 49, issue 3 (January 1895): 429.
10. Esther Willard Bates, *The Art of Producing Pageants* (Boston: Walter H. Baker Company, 1925), pp. 240–242.
11. Percy MacKaye, "American Pageants and Their Promise," *Scribner's Magazine*, vol. 46 (July 1909): 240.
12. William Chauncy Langdon, "The Pageant of Thetford," *The Playground*, vol. 5, no. 9 (December 1911): 302–318.
13. Bates, p. 244.
14. Percival Chubb's *Festivals and Play* (New York: Harper & Brothers, 1912), p. xix.
15. "List of Pageants of the Year 1914," *American Pageant Association Bulletin*, no. 13 (January 1, 1915).
16. Prevots, p. 133.
17. *The Chimes: The Year Book of the Junior Class of Mills College*, 1915, n.p. (Archives, Mills College Library).
18. Vesper L. George, Problems of Color and Costume in Pageantry," *American Pageant Association Bulletin*, no. 21 (July 1, 1915): 1.
19. "Report of Committee on Festivals," given at the Fourth Annual Congress of Playground Association of America, June 10, 1911; printed in *The Playground*, vol. 4, no. 11 (February 1911): 373.
20. J. George Becht, "A Normal School Commencement," *The Playground*, vol. 4, no. 11 (February 1911): 367–369.
21. Elizabeth Burchenal, "May Day Celebrations," Pamphlet No. 53 (Russell Sage Foundation, Child Hygiene Department), p. 9.
22. Bates, p. 18.
23. "Frick to Give $500,000 Park," *The Playground*, vol. 3, no. 4 (July 1909): 17.
24. Prevots, p. 102.

Chapter 9

1. Zona Gale, "Robin Hood in Jones Street," *Outlook*, June 26, 1909, p. 443.
2. Constance Cary Harrison, "American Rural Festivals," *The Century Magazine*, vol. 50, no. 3 (July 1895): 333.
3. David Lansing, "Mimic Royalties of May Day," *Outing*, vol. 48 (May 1906): 143.
4. Ibid., p. 144.
5. William Inglis, "Folk-Dances for Health," *Harper's Weekly*, vol. 55 (July 8, 1911): 26.
6. Mabel Travis Wood, "Maytime in Manhattan," *The Playground*, vol. 21, no. 4 (July 1921): 206.
7. Mary Fanton Roberts, "The Value of Outdoor Plays to America: Through the Pageant Shall We Develop a Drama of Democracy?" *The Craftsman*, vol. 16, no. 5 (August 1909): 495.
8. Lansing, p. 150.
9. Gale, p. 446.
10. For examples, see the listing in *Recreation*, vol. 30, no. 1 (April 1936): 43.
11. Constance D'Arcy Mackay, "Imaginative Rural Recreation," *The Playground*, vol. 15, no. 6 (September 1920): 382.
12. Constance D'Arcy Mackay, "Festival Producing in Parks and Playgrounds," *The Playground*, vol. 15, no. 6 (September 1921): 369.
13. Ernest Bradley, "A Rural Experiment," *The Playground*, vol. 5, no. 6 (September 1911): 198.
14. "Five Thousand in May Festival," *The Playground*, vol. 20, no. 5 (August 1926).
15. "A May Day Revel on Nottingham Green," *The Playground*, vol. 20, no. 12 (March 1927): 666–667.
16. Katherine Peavy, "Palo Alto's May Festival," *Recreation*, vol. 30, no. 1 (April 1936): 28–29.
17. Letter, *New York Times*, May 7, 2003, Section D, p. 5.
18. David M. Herszenhorn, "Styles Change, but Dance Tradition Endures in Schools," *New York Times*, June 20, 2006, p. A 18.

Chapter 10

1. "1937 May Day Festival at Indiana College Revives Memories for Local Woman," *Santa Anna Daily Register*, April 9, 1937, n.p. (courtesy of the Earlham College Archives).
2. Sophia Kirk, cited in "College Girls," by Shirley Marchalonis, *Research/Penn State*, vol. 17, no. 2 (June 1996): 1.
3. Thomas Woody, *A History of Women's Education in the United States, Vol. 2* (New York: Octagon Books, 1966), p. 164.
4. Ibid., p. 182..
5. Mary Caroline Crawford, *The College Girl of America, and the Institutions Which Make Her What She Is* (Boston: L.C. Page & Co., 1905), p. viii.
6. Elaine Kendall, *"Peculiar Institutions": An Informal History of the Seven Sister Colleges*, (New York: Putnam, 1976), p. 126.
7. Lynn D. Gordon, *Gender and Higher Education in the Progressive Era* (New Haven: Yale University Press, 1990), pp. 194, 195.
8. Roberta Frankfort, *Collegiate Women: Domesticity and Career in Turn-of-the-Century America* (New York: New York University Press, 1977), p. 83.
9. William D. Jenkins, "Housewifery and Motherhood: The Question of Role Change in the Progressive Era," in *Woman's Being, Woman's Place: Female Identity and Vocation in American History*, edited by Mary Kelly (Boston: G.K Hall & Co., 1979), pp. 142–153.
10. Barbara M. Solomon, *In the Company of Educated Women: A History of Women and Higher Education in America* (New Haven: Yale University Press, 1990), p. 53.
11. Ibid., p. 46.
12. Morris Bishop, *A History of Cornell* (Ithaca, NY: Cornell University Press, 1962), p. 151.
13. Lida Rose McCabe, *The American Girl at College* (New York: Dodd, Mead & Co., 1893), p. 1.
14. Ibid., p. 432.
15. Lavinia Hart, "A Girl's Col-

lege Life," *Cosmopolitan*, vol. 31, no. 2 (June 1901): 191–192.

16. "Life at a Girl's College," *Munsey's Magazine*, 1897, pp. 6, 867.

17. McCabe, pp. 138–139.

18. Shirley Marchalonis, "College Girls," *Research/Penn State*, vol. 17, no. 2 (June 1996).

Chapter 11

1. From *The Jayhawker Yearbook*, 1912, University of Kansas, p. 364 (University Archives, University of Kansas, Spencer Research Library).

2. Opal Thornburg, *Earlham: The Story of the College, 1847–1962* (Richmond, Ind.: Earlham College Press, 1963), pp. 161–163, passim.

3. Ibid., p. 223.

4. "The First May Party at Rockford College," Alumnae *Bulletin*, n.p, n.d. (Rockford College Archives).

5. Cornelia Meigs, *What Makes A College? A History of Bryn Mawr* (New York: MacMillan Co., 1956), p. 226.

6. Evangeline Walker Andrews, "The Elizabethan May-Day Festivals of Bryn Mawr College," *American Pageant Association Bulletin*, no. 26 (October 1, 1915): n.p.

7. Meigs, pp. 226–227, passim.

8. Christopher Morley, "Round the May Pole," *Saturday Review*, May 2, 1936, p. 14.

9. Letter to the author from the college librarian, 2/27/2003, as well as a typescript of a speech given in 1943 by Edward M. Holder, "Salem's Traditional May-Day," n.d. (The Gramley Library, Salem College).

10. Jean Q. Watson and Frances L. Brown, "The Partheneia of the University of California," *Overland Monthly*, vol. 67 (May 1916): 364.

11. "Festivals in American Colleges for Women," *The Century: A Popular Quarterly*, vol. 49, issue 3 (January 1895): 429.

12. From a typescript account written by (Mrs. S.C.) Hathaway Alaman, March 18, 1964, n.p. (courtesy of the Newcomb College Archives).

13. "May Festival is Co-Eds' Way to Get Golden Shekels," *Silver and Gold* (CU History Subjects, Box 25, Student Activities, May Fete, Archives, University of Colorado at Boulder Libraries), n.p., n.d. (in context probably referring to first festival.)

14. *The Bomb* (Iowa State University Yearbook), 1909, n.p.

15. Joy Winstead, "Polishing the Gem: Tradition of Excellence Maintained at Westhampton for 75 Years," *The University of Richmond Magazine*, vol. 52, no. 2 (Winter 1990): 17.

16. From Lucy Sprague Mitchell's *Two Lives* (1953), cited in "Dean Lucy Sprague, the Partheneia, and the Arts," by Janet Ruyle, *Chronicle of the University of California*, no. 2 (Fall 1998): 65.

17. Ibid., p. 68.

18. Watson and Brown, pp. 359–360.

19. Clifton J. Phillips and John J. Baughman, *DePauw: A Pictorial History*, on-line version at http://www.depauw.edu/library/archives/ehistory/chapter3/women.html.

20. "Commencement," *The Utah Westminster*, vol. 8, no. 8 (June 1922): 1.

21. "University Pageant, May 18th," *Alumni Weekly*, vol. 10, no. 31 (May 1, 1911): 5 (courtesy of the University Archives, University of Minnesota).

22. Mary Watters, *The History of Mary Baldwin College* (Mary Baldwin College, 1942), cited in a letter to the author from William C. Pollard, College Archivist, October 8, 2002.

23. Leah A. Headley and Merrill E. Jarchow, *Carleton: The First Century* (Northfield, MN: Carleton College, 1966), p. 399.

24. "Sixth Biennial May Fete in Natural Amphitheater Today Largest in School's History," *Silver & Gold*, May 19, 1923 (CU History Subjects, Box 25, Student Activities—May Fête, Courtesy of the University of Colorado Archives), p. 1.

25. "Regularization of May Fête," Scripps College *Student Handbook*, 1947, 1948 (courtesy of the Denison Library, Scripps College), p. 29.

Chapter 12

1. Frances Westcott, "Every Girl," 1926 May Fête *Program* (Iowa State University Library Archives), n.p.

2. Peter Wilde, "English Country Dances on 78rpm Gramophone Records, Part I," *English Dance & Song*, vol. 61, no. 4 (Winter 1999): 15–18.

3. *The Victrola in Physical Education, Recreation, and Play* (Victor Talking Machine Company, handbook published in 1916, 1918 and 1924), p. 4.

4. *Silver and Gold*, May 11, 1914, p. 1, CU History Subjects, Box 25, Student Activities—May Fete (Archives, University of Colorado at Boulder Libraries).

5. May Pageant *Program*, June 14, 1920, Grinnell College, n.p.

6. Program, "Historic Wooster," May 1916 (Courtesy of the Department of Special Collections, the College of Wooster Libraries), n.p.

7. From "Pembroke Holds Festival of May," *Providence Sunday Journal*, May 16, 1937, n.p; and "Mary E. Dull is May Queen at Pembroke," no citation available (Brown University Archives).

8. Compiled from "350 Students to Take Part in May Day," *The Bucknellian*, May 10, 1945, p. 1; and May Day Program, 1945 (Special Collections/University Archives, Ellen Clarke Bertrand Library, Bucknell University).

9. The Fairies of Freya, "My Wife Is a Suffragette," 1911 May Day *Program*, Hollins College.

10. May Day Program reproduced in the Iowa State College Yearbook, *The Bomb*, 1917, (Iowa State University Archives), n.p.

11. Margaret Mead, "The Choice of American Girlhood," 1920 May Day *Program* (Archives of DePauw University and Indiana United Methodism), n.p.

12. *The Bomb*, 1919 (Iowa State University Archives), pp. 135–136.

13. *The Bomb*, 1920 (Iowa State University Archives), pp. 267–268.

14. 1945 May Day *Program*, Berea College.

15. "Will Celebrate May with Roman Pageantry," unidentified newspaper article ca. 1925, (Mount Holyoke College Archives and Special Collections).

16. May Day *Program*, "A Fantasy of Nations: A Pageant, May 11, 1946" (Mount Holyoke College Archives and Special Collections), n.p.

17. May Festival *Program*, May 15, 1920, n.p. (Milne Special Collections and Archives, University of New Hampshire Library, Durham, N.H.).

Chapter 13

1. Jean Q. Watson and Frances L. Brown, "The Partheneia of the University of California," *Overland Monthly*, vol. 67 (May 1916): 364.

2. Lida Rose McCabe, *The American Girl at College* (New York: Dodd, Mead & Co., 1893), p. 30.

3. This information, by date, comes from "First Queen of May to Return to Campus for Celebration," *Richmond Palladium and Sun-Telegram*, April 24, 1937, n.p.; O.M.B., "May-Day Celebration," *The Earlhamite*, June 1886, p. 211; and "Beginning of the May Day Festival," *Richmond Palladium and Sun-Telegram*, May 12, 1911, n.p.

4. Helen Lefkowitz Horowitz, *The Power and Passion of M. Carey Thomas* (New York: Alfred A. Knopf, 1994), p. 326.

5. Kate Sheeran, "'May' We Celebrate?" The Albright College *Reporter*, Winter 2001, n.p.

6. "May Day," in 1946 *Ruby* (college yearbook), pp. 108–109 (Ursinus College Archives).

7. Helen Lefkowitz Horowitz, *Campus Life: Undergraduate Cultures from the End of the Eighteenth Century to the Present* (New York: Alfred A. Knopf, 1987), pp. 41, 39.

8. Cited on the DePauw University website at *http://www.depauw.edu/library/archives/ehistory/chapter2/Customs.html*.

9. Lavinia Hart, "A Girl's College Life," *Cosmopolitan*, vol. 31, no. 2 (June 1901): 198.

10. Joy Lichtenstein, *For the Blue-and-Gold: A Tale of Life at the University of California* (San Francisco: A. M. Robertson, 1901), p. 77.

11. Ibid., p. 38.

12. Ibid., p. 154.

13. *The Jayhawker Yearbook*, 1903 (University Archives, University of Kansas, Spencer Research Library), p. 64.

14. Henry J. Fortunato, "Mayday Mayhem," at *http://www.kuhistory.com/proto/story*.

15. Summarized from "May Day Exercises," *The University Weekly Courier*, University of Kansas, May 8, 1891, p. 1; *The Jayhawker Yearbook*, Spring 1965, pp. 250–251; *The Jayhawker Yearbook*, 1903, p. 64; *The Kansas University Weekly*, May 7, 1904, p. 1, and *The Graduate Magazine of the University of Kansas*, vol. 3, no. 8 (May 1905): 312–313 (University Archives, University of Kansas, Spencer Research Library).

16. From *The Kansan* (University of Kansas newspaper), vol. 4, no. 68 (May 21, 1908): 1, and *The Kansan*, vol. 4, no. 69 (May 23, 1908): 1 (University Archives, University of Kansas, Spencer Research Library).

17. Untitled ms. dated January 21, 1966 (Courtesy of the University Archives, University of Kansas, Spencer Research Library [71/10/1966]), p. 2.

18. Walter Havighurst, *The Miami Years, 1809–1969* (New York: G.P. Putnam's Sons, 1958, 1969), p. 203.

19. Virginia Wolf Briscoe, "Bryn Mawr College Traditions: Women's Rituals as Expressive Behavior" (University of Pennsylvania, Ph.D. dissertation, 1981), vol. 2, p. 765.

20. Ibid., vol. 2, pp. 766–768.

21. Arlene Cohen '94, "Hoops, Trees, and Steps: The Role of Traditions at Wellesley College," a student paper (courtesy of the Wellesley College Archives), pp. 28–29. (Internal citations from the Wellesley *News*, 5/4/1939, no pages cited.)

22. Ibid., p. 29.

23. Anne Maynard Kidder, "In Maytime," in *A Book of Bryn Mawr Stories*, edited by Margaretta Morris and Louise Buffum Congdon (Philadelphia: George W. Jacobs and Co., 1901), pp. 77, 86–87.

24. Untitled ms. dated January 21, 1966 (University Archives, University of Kansas, Spencer Research Library [71/10/1966]), p. 2.

25. "May Day Festival: Dainty Maids in Picturesque Garb Will Tread the Light Fantastic, and Wind the May-Pole," *Indiana Daily Student*, April 22, 1908, p. 2 (University Archives, Indiana University).

Chapter 14

1. Roy Judge, "Tradition and the Plaited Maypole Dance," p. 2.

2. Ibid., p. 16.

3. Both quotations from Maureen Needham, *I See America Dancing: Selected Readings, 1685–2000* (Champaign: University of Illinois Press, 2002), p. 161; reprinted from Gary D. Engle, *This Grotesque Essence: Plays from the American Minstrel Stage* (Baton Rouge: Louisiana State University Press, 1978), pp. 122–127.

4. Elizabeth Burchenal, *Folk-Dances and Singing Games* (New York: G. Schirmer, 1909), p. 71.

5. "Girls' Athletics," an account in *Etosian*, vol. 6 (1923): 123 (Westminster College Archives).

6. Jennette E. Carpenter Lincoln, "How to Give a Maypole Dance," *Ladies Home Journal*, vol. 28 (March 15, 1911): 33.

7. E.M. Willard, *The Favorite Book of Drills* (Chicago: T.S. Denison & Company, 1907), p. 91.

8. Ibid., p. 10.

9. The song, "Staines Morris," was called "Bluff King Hal" at this time because that was the name of the morris dance set to it. This dance was apparently choreographed in about 1885 by pageant-master D'Arcy Ferris for his team of performers from the village of Bidford. The tune had been printed in William Chappell's *Popular Music of the Olden Time*, and represented therein as a sixteenth-century dance. While Ferris used elements of the morris dance that the old men from Bidford still remembered, he was particularly anxious to re-create the Elizabethan morris dance, as he understood it (or imagined it to be). "Bluff King Hal," as choreographed by Ferris, is a mock combat dance, with pretense fisticuffs. In 1907 Cecil Sharp and H. MacIlwaine "collected" the Bidford dances, not realizing Ferris' creative involvement with them, and held up both the dance and the tune as a prime example of the survival of the morris from the depths of antiquity. When Ferris apprised Sharp of his mistake, the latter hastily rejected the dance (but not his theory), since he was anxious to promulgate only "pure" folk material. However, across the ocean, the correction was apparently not as well recognized. The tune "Staines Morris" continued to be used under its name of "Bluff King Hal" as a morris tune as well as a tune for the maypole dance, and several of the early folk dance manuals contain the morris dance Bluff King Hal. For more information on D'Arcy Ferris and his involvement with historical pageants and the morris, see Roy Judge, "D'Arcy Ferris and the Bidford Morris," *Folk Music Journal*, vol. 4, no. 5 (1984): 443–480.

10. Anabel Kindersley, *Celebrations*, published in the Children Just Like Me series, a Unicef-sponsored publication (1997); Yasmine Galenorn, *Dancing with the Sun* (St. Paul, Minn.: Llewellyn Publications, 1999), p. 83.

11. For the hula maypole, see the archived activities at *http://www.waiau.k12.hi.us*.

Chapter 15

1. Poem found in the 1923 May Day program found in an on-line essay by Elizabeth McAllister, University Archives, at *http://www.wam.umd.edu/-emcallis/708u/FinalProject/frames.html* (University Archives, Special Collections, University of Maryland Libraries).

2. Virginia Hunt, "May-Day Frolics," *The Ladies Home Journal*, vol. 33 (May 1916): 44.

3. Amy E. Blanchard, *Dimple Dallas* (New York: Hurst & Co., 1900), pp. 180–181.

4. Headley and Jarchow, *Carleton: The First Century*, p. 400.

5. "May Day Tradition Begun at Seminary in 1894," *The Purple Parrot*, 1931–32 (Rockford College Archives), n.p.

6. *Program*, May Day 1962 (Rockford College Archives), n.p.

7. *The Collegian*, 1937, cited in Dan Morrell and David Pulizzi, "The

Lost Traditions," *The Penn Stater*, January/February 2005, p. 26.

8. "Meredith May Queens: Models '26 to '38," unidentified newspaper clipping, n.p. (Carlyle Campbell Library, Meredith College).

9. Compiled from the Program for May 9, 1938, and a student newspaper account, "First Annual May Day Festival Set Thursday May 5; Mary Nell Black to Be Crowned as First Queen in Phys Ed Affair," *The Orange and White*, April 22, 1938, n.p.

10. "May Day Queen at Denver U. Crowned Following Victory by the Juniors," *Daily News*, May 12, 1911, n.p. (University of Denver Archives).

11. Lois W. Banner, *American Beauty* (New York: Alfred A. Knopf, 1983), pp. 253–254.

12. Louise Pethis, "May Day at Winthrop," typescript summary, one page, n.d. (courtesy of the Winthrop University Archives).

13. Grace M. Burt, "May-Time at Mount Holyoke," *St. Nicholas [Magazine] for Boys and Girls*, vol. 47 (May 1920): 587–588.

14. May Fête *Program*, 1923 (University of Colorado Women's League, Associated Women Students' May Fete, courtesy of the Archives, University of Colorado at Boulder Libraries), n.p.

15. Mary Louise Couch, "Report of the General Chairman of May Day 1929," Elmira College, Gannett-Tripp Library Archives, typescript report, n.p.

16. Lillian Adele Kibler, *The History of Converse College: 1889–1971* (Spartanburg, S.C.: Converse College, 1973), pp. 237–241.

17. Cited in Nancy Woloch, *Women and the American Experience* (New York: Alfred A. Knopf, 1984), p. 500.

18. *Sweet Briar News*, May 12, 1932, cited in a student paper by Sonya Lynn Truman titled "May Day: The History and Ritual Performance at Sweet Briar" (Archives, Sweet Briar College), p. 39.

19. Woloch, pp. 468–470.

20. 1955 *Yearbook* (Archives, Sweet Briar College), n.p.

21. Christie Ann Farnham, *The Education of the Southern Belle: Higher Education and Student Socialization in the Antebellum South* (New York: New York University Press, 1994), passim.

22. All comments and quotations from Molly Roper Jenkins, "To Be the Queen: Evolution to Extinction ... Tradition Dies a Natural Death in a Changing World," Randolph-Macon Woman's College *Alumnae Bulletin*, vol. 94, no. 4 (Summer 2002): 16–20.

23. From the May Queen's Blue Book, n.p. (courtesy of the Sweet Briar Archives and Special Collections).

24. Melissa Booth Cook, interview with the author, September 26, 2002.

25. Dr. Carolyn Wilkerson Bell, "The May Queen," Randolph-Macon Woman's College *Alumnae Bulletin*, vol. 11, no. 1 (Fall, 1977): 14–15.

26. Jenkins, pp. 16–20.

27. Bell, p. 16.

28. Carolyn Wilkerson Bell, *A History of Randolph-Macon Woman's College* (ms. draft), n.p.

Chapter 16

1. Memo to Meredith Student Body from the Student Life Committee, "Continuation of Springs Court," Spring 1975 (Carlyle Campbell Library, Meredith College), pp. 2–5, passim.

2. Mary C. Lynn, *Make No Small Plans: A History of Skidmore College* (Saratoga Springs, N.Y.: Skidmore College, 2000), pp. 205–206.

3 Virginia Wolf Briscoe, *Bryn Mawr College Traditions: Women's Rituals as Expressive Behavior* (Ph.D. dissertation, 1991), passim; see especially vol. 2, pp. 863–880.

4. Letter to the author from Librarian Judy Harvey Sahak, January 23, 2003.

5. Compiled from the college photograph albums and conversations with Carol Yeager, Parents' Weekend Coordinator; Joann Staples Rose, May Queen of 1952; and Alice Bryant Ketler, May Queen of 1939 (January 28, 2005).

6. Briscoe, vol. 2, pp. 901–902.

7. Deborah Skinner Davis, *Valdosta State University* (Charleston, S.C.: Arcadia Publishing, 2001), p. 8.

8. Letter from Dean Jonn R. Hubbard to Mrs. S. C. Alaman, April 21, 1964 (courtesy of the Newcomb College Archives).

9. Lynn, *Make No Small Plans*, p. 203.

10. "May Day Queen," *Cleveland Press*, May 6, 1954, n.p. (22WM, Box 4, folder 6; courtesy of the Case Western Reserve University Archives).

11. Paper by Arlene Cohen, Class of 1994, "Hoops, Trees, and Steps: The Role of Traditions at Wellesley College," p. 29 (Wellesley College Archives). Ms. Cohen added that by the mid–1980s, the custom of the male imposter had become passé, but the winner still finds herself in the lake, usually voluntarily.

12. Bell, ms. notes, p. 21.

13. Cited by Meredith Minter, class of 1984, "The Past Master," *The Sundial*, vol. 66, no. 24 (April 23, 1982), formerly on-line at what is now Randolph College. It appears that when the college changed its name and began admitting men, the Web pages discussing the women's past traditions were taken down. I also observed this phenomenon at the Wells College Web site after that college admitted men.

14. Bell, ms., p. 26.

15. Minter, n.p.

16. Student Life Committee Minutes, September 8, 1975 (Carlyle Campbell Library, Meredith College).

17. Ray Warner, "At Small Quaker College, the Old Values Survive," *New York Times*, May 25, 1973, p. 10.

18. Ibid., p. 12.

19. Hamm, *Earlham College: A History, 1847–1997*, p. 320.

20. Ibid., p. 321.

21. Jenkins, p. 20.

Chapter 17

1. Lillian Thomas, "Holiday's History a Lesson in Contradiction, Struggle," Pittsburgh *Post-Gazette*, September 1, 2003, p. A-18.

2. See http://www.marxists.org/subject/mayday.

3. William Frederick Bigelow, in an editorial in *Good Housekeeping*, vol. 92 (April 1931): 4.

4. See http://www.publiccom.com/14850/9595/history.html.

5. "May Day 2007: Hundreds of Thousands March for Immigrant Rights." Democracy Now, May 2, 2007; see http://www.democracynow.org/article.pl?sid=07/05/02/1426257 (accessed November 2007).

6. Stephen G. Christianson, editor, *The American Book of Days*, 4th edition (New York: H.W. Wilson Co., 2000), p. 337.

7. Ibid., p. 337.

8. For the 2006 Mississippi Bar Association Law Day celebration, see http://www.msbar.org/lawday.php (accessed November 2007).

9. Dr. S. Josephine Baker, "May Day — Child Health Day," *Ladies Home Journal*, vol. 47 (May 1930): 112.

10. "May Day for Children," *The Independent*, vol. 112 (April 26, 1924): 213–214.

11. *May Day Festival Book: Some Suggestions for Celebrating Child Health Day* (New York: American Child Health Association, 1929), p. i.
12. Ibid., p. 41.
13. Ibid., p. 56.
14. Ibid., p. 54.
15. Ibid., p. 56.
16. Ibid., p. 6–7, 70.
17. Ibid., pp. 49–53.
18. Baker, p. 112.
19. Ibid., p. 130.
20. Summary of American Child Health Association Papers, Hoover Presidential Library, found at *www.ecommcode2.com/hoover/research/hooverpapers/hoover/commerce/acha5.htm*.
21. See the archived activities at *http://www.waiau.k12.hi.us*.

Chapter 18

1. See the May Day pages at *www.mendonutah.net*.
2. See *www.bluffton.edu/stories/mayday*.
3. See Carolyn's Page, *http://www.blight.com/^scarlett/traditions/mayday.html*.
4. Ibid.
5. Jane M. Dieckmann, *Wells College: A History* (Aurora, N.Y.: Wells College Press, 1995), a three-page typescript (Louis Jefferson Long Library, Wells College).
6. Michelle York, "Wells College: Newly, and Uneasily, Coed," *http://www.nytimes.com/2005/09/06/education/06wells.html*.
7. See *http://www.uoregon.edu/~uocomm/newsreleases/latest/apr98/P042198.html*.
8. For more on Shady Hill School, see *www.shs.org/news*.
9. See, for example, *www.waldorfschoolofcapecod.org/festivals-mayday.htm*.
10. Compiled from an article by Florence Dean, "'Round the Maypole," published on-line by *Dance Spirit*, April 2000, as well as videotapes and photos provided to the author in 2003.
11. Preschool May Day curricula can be found at *http://www.preschooleducation.com*.
12. For more on Dancing the Sun Up in the Bay Area, see *http://rgoldman.org/morris/mayday.htm*.
13. For more on the Basset Street Hounds' May Day, visit *http://bassett-street-hounds.org/mayday*.
14. For more on The Washington Revels, see *www.revelsdc.org*.
15. For more on In the Heart of the Beast, see *www.hobt.org*.
16. Yasmine Galenorn, *Dancing with the Sun* (St. Paul. Minn.: Llewellyn Publications, 1999), p. 83.
17. Hutton, *The Pagan Religions of the Ancient British Isles*, pp. 340–341.
18. For more on Hastings' maypole dances, see *http://www.smat.us/maypole*.
19. For more on Geyersville's annual May Day, see *www.geyservillecc.com/Events/MayDay.htm*.
20. For more on Westville's May Day, see *http://www.westville.org/mayday.htm*.
21. Fremont's 1999 May Day festival is described at *www.seattlepressonline.com/article-919.html*.
22. Fairfax's tenth annual May Day festival is described at *http://www.sonic.net/~mamazon/index.html*
23. "Great-grandmother Is May Queen," Pittsburgh *Post-Gazette*, July 19, 2005, p. C-5.
24. P.G. Wodehouse, *Uncle Fred in the Springtime* (New York: P.F. Collier & Son, 1939), p. 138.

Conclusion

1. Nissenbaum, pp. 315, 317.
2. Richard Handler and Jocelyn Linnekin, "Tradition, Genuine or Spurious," *Journal of American Folklore*, vol. 97, no. 385 (1984): 288.
3. For more on Bryn Mawr's traditions, see *http://www.brynmawr.edu/activities/traditions.shtml*.
4. Carolyn's Page, *http://www.blight.com/^scarlett/traditions/index.html* (accessed 2007).
5. For more on Wellesley's traditions, see *http://www.wellesley.edu/Welcome/Traditions/traditions.html*.
6. Katrina Cartwright, "USU Sets the Pace for College Traditions," published in the *Utah Statesman Online*, October 16, 2002.
7. J.D.A. Widdowson, "Trends in the Commercialization of English Calendar Customs: A Preliminary Study," in *Aspects of English Calendar Customs*, edited by Theresa Buckland and Juliette Wood (Sheffield: Sheffield Academic Press, 1993), pp. 23, 25.
8. Keith Thomas, *Perception of the Past*, p. 24, cited in Judge, "May Day and Merrie England," p. 144.
9. Washington Irving, *Bracebridge Hall*, ed. Andrew B. Myers (New York: Library of America, 1991), pp. 214–215.

Part II

1. All citations and the list of pageant programs come from "History of May Day," typewritten ms. of alumnae memories, n.d., pp. 1–4 (Archives, Agnes Scott College).
2. Kate Sheeran, "'May' We Celebrate?" The Albright College *Reporter*, Winter 2001, n.p.
3. Letter to the author from John Varner, Special Collections/Archives, Auburn University, January 30, 2003.
4. Letter to the author from Elaine Ardia, Archives Assistant, Edmund S. Muskie Archives and Special Collections, Bates College, January 27, 2003.
5. "Bates Holds May Day Festival," *The Bates Student*, vol. 44, no. 17 (May 25, 1916): n.p.
6. "Y.W. Presents May Festival Thursday Eve," *The Bates Student*, May 27, 1927, p. 1.
7. Summarized from May Day programs as well as the "Annual Report to the President by K. Helen McKinstrey, Director of Women's Physical Education," ca. 1935, and information provided by the archivist in a letter of October 27, 2002 (Berea College Archives, Record Group 6.32: Physical Education and Health Department).
8. *http://www.bluffton.edu/stories/mayday*.
9. See *www.brenau.edu/studentlife/activities/traditions/default.htm*.
10. Letter to the author from Debbie S. Thompson, Director of Alumni Affairs, Brenau University, November 2, 2004.
11. From the transcript by Paula Ogletree, "May Day: A Lasting Tradition at Brenau University," © 2003 Daydream Productions, n.p. (Archives, Brenau University).
12. Martha Mitchell, *Encylopedia Brunoniana* (Brown University Library, 1993), pp. 370–371.
13. Briscoe, vol. 2, p.752.
14. From "350 Students to Take Part in May Day," *The Bucknellian*, May 10, 1945, p. 1, and May Day *Program*, 1945 (Special Collections/University Archives, Ellen Clarke Bertrand Library, Bucknell University).
15. The account of Carleton's May Day festival and all citations come from Leah A. Headley and Merrill E. Jarchow, *Carleton: The First Century* (Carleton College Press, 1966), pp. 398–400. They based their work on an alumna account, "The History of the Development of the Annual May Fete [of] Carleton College," written by Gertrude C. Stork, February 1926, typescript account, 12 pages. Sample pageant titles post 1926 come from May Day programs provided by the Carleton College Archives.
16. Sue Geiger and Jean Vayo,

"Report on May Fête Poll, Spring, 1959," typescript account, one page (Archives, Carleton College).

17. *Program*, May 1911, 22WM, Box 4, folder 5, Case Western Reserve University Archives).

18. *Program*, May 1914, 22WM, Box 4, folder 5, Case Western Reserve University Archives.

19. No title, *The Cleveland Plain Dealer*, May 16, 1943, n.p., 22WM, Box 4, folder 6 Case Western Reserve University Archives.

20. "Adelbert-Mather in Spring Frolic," *Cleveland Plain Dealer*, n.d., n.p., 22WM, Box 4, folder 6, Case Western Reserve University Archives.

21. "May Day Queen," *Cleveland Press*, May 6, 1954, n.p., 22WM, Box 4, folder 6 Case Western Reserve University Archives.

22. Martha Ruley, Sophomore General Chairman, "May Day Report, Friday May 1, 1964," pp. 7, 12, 22WM, Box 4, folder 4, Case Western Reserve University Archives.

23. From "May Day's History at P.C.W," *The Arrow*, May 3, 1935, p.1; Laberta Dysart, *Chatham College: The First Ninety Years* (Pittsburgh: Chatham College, 1960), p. 224; various May Day programs (Archives, Chatham University, Pittsburgh, Pa.).

24. Summarized from *The Colby Echo*, May 18, 1910, p. 159; May 31, 1911, p. 204; May 29, 1912, p. 6; June 11, 1913, p. 6; June 10, 1914, pp. 2–3; June 5, 1918, p. 1; May 27, 1925, n.p.; and May 29, 1929, p. 1 (Miller Library, Special Collections, Colby College).

25. Lucy Lilian Notestein, *Wooster of the Middle West, Vol. 1* (New Haven: Yale University Press, 1937), pp. 211, 268.

26. Ibid., 2:248.

27. Ibid., 2:342.

28. 1946 Color Day *Program*, n.p., College of Wooster (Special Collections, the College of Wooster Libraries).

29. Unidentified newspaper clipping, n.d., n.p. (Special Collections, College of Wooster Libraries).

30. "College Color Day Pageant to Salute Wooster's Sesqui," *The Daily Record*, March 28, 1958, n.p. (Special Collections, College of Wooster Libraries).

31. Betty Sadler, "May Queens Return to Columbia College," *The State*, May 4, 1967, n.p.

32. All citations from Lillian Adele Kibler, *The History of Converse College: 1889–1971* (Spartanburg, S.C.: Converse College, 1973), pp. 237–241.

33. Summarized from the college's Web site *http://www.converse.edu/Overview/OnlineViewbook/converse_traditions.asp* (accessed November 2007).

34. Clifton J. Phillips and John J. Baughman, *DePauw: A Pictorial History*, on-line version at *http://www.depauw.edu/library/archives/ehistory/chapter3/women.html*.

35. Letter to the author from Thomas F. Harkins, Associate University Archivist, Duke University Archives, November 8, 2004.

36. O.M.B., "May-Day Celebration," *The Earlhamite*, June 1886, p. 213.

37. "Beginning of the May Day Festival," *Richmond Palladium and Sun-Telegram*, May 12, 1911, n.p.

38. "Students Hold a Rehearsal on the Campus Saturday," *Richmond Palladium*, May 1, 1911, n.p.

39. "Old English May Day 1977: From 1906 to Now," unidentified newspaper clipping, May 12, 1977, p. 3.

40. Julia E. Schult, "May Days at Elmira College," *American Morris Newsletter*, vol. 23, no. 2 (Summer 2000), p. 7.

41. Summarized from Schult, pp. 2–8, as well as "May Day at Elmira College," a brief typescript account prepared by College Archivist H.A. Wisbey, Jr., March 15, 1985, n.p. (Archives, Elmira College).

42. Anna Heubeck Knipp and Thaddeus P. Thomas, *The History of Goucher College* (Baltimore, Md.: Goucher College, 1938), p. 527.

43. Ibid., p. 632.

44. Ibid., p. 632.

45. Ibid., p. 527.

46. Ibid., pp. 527–528.

47. *The Scarlet and Black*, vol. 16, no. 52 (April 24, 1909): 2 (Grinnell College Archives).

48. Compiled from the college photograph albums and conversations with Carol Yeager, Parents' Weekend Coordinator; Joann Staples Rose, May Queen of 1952; and Alice Bryant Ketler, May Queen of 1939 (January 28, 2005).

49. Francis J. Niederer, *Hollins College: An Illustrated History* (Charlottesville: University Press of Virginia, 1973, 1985), p. 1.

50. "May Day, 1903 — May Day, 1928," *The Hollins Alumnae Quarterly*, vol. 3, no. 1 (April 1928): 3 (Archives, Hollins University).

51. "May Day," *The Semi-Annual*, Hollins University, June 1902, pp. 110–111 (Archives, Hollins University).

52. Niederer, p. 69.

53. *The Hollins Alumnae Quarterly*, vol. 3, no. 1 (April 1928): 3–5 (Archives, Hollins University).

54. Niederer, p. 67.

55. Ibid., p. 73.

56. Ibid., p. 133.

57. Pauline Newton, "Traditions of May Day," *HC*, May 8, 1995, n.p., Hood College Archives).

58. *The Lesbian Herald* (college yearbook), June 1915, p. 237 (Hood College Archives).

59. *The Lesbian Herald*, May 1917, pp. 379–381 (Hood College Archives).

60. *The Lesbian Herald* June, 1919, p. 387 (Hood College Archives).

61. May Queen information taken from a compilation of Queens and attendants made by the archivist; other information about the Hood celebration from student newspaper articles: Barbara Hufham, "History of May Day Reveals Varied Observances of Spring," *Blue & Grey*, May 3, 1959, n.p.; "Pageant, Horse Show, Dance to Highlight 'Roman Holiday,'" *Blue & Grey*, May 9, 1958, n.p. (Hood College Archives).

62. Letter to the author from Dina M. Kellams, Assistant Archivist, Indiana University Archives, November 6, 2002.

63. "Delightful Times Promised," *Indiana Daily Student*, May 23, 1905, p. 2 (University Archives, Indiana University).

64. "The May Festival," *Indiana Daily Student*, May 14, 1906, p. 2 (University Archives, Indiana University).

65. "May Day Festival: Dainty Maids in Picturesque Garb Will Tread the Light Fantastic, and Wind the May-Pole," *Indiana Daily Student*, April 22, 1908, p. 2 (University Archives, Indiana University).

66. "May Festival Program Committees Get Busy," *Indiana Daily Student*, April 20, 1922, p. 2:4 (University Archives, Indiana University).

67. From various May Day programs and letter to the author from Dina M. Kellams, Assistant Archivist, November 6, 2002 (University Archives, Indiana University).

68. *The Bomb* (University Yearbook), 1909, n.p. (Iowa State University Libraries).

69. *The Bomb*, 1919, pp. 135–136 (Iowa State University Libraries).

70. *The Bomb*, 1920, pp. 267–268 (Iowa State University Libraries).

71. *The Bomb*, 1923, p. 116 (Iowa State University Libraries).

72. For more on VEISHA visit *http://www.veishea.iastate.edu* (accessed November 13, 2007).

73. Raymond C. Dingledine, Jr., *Madison College: The First Fifty Years, 1908–1958* (Harrisonburg, Va.: Madison College, 1959), p. 198.

74. Nancy Bondurant Jones, "In the Merry Month of May," *Montpelier, the James Madison University Magazine*, vol. 21, no. 2 (Spring 1998): 36.

75. Frances Dew Hamilton and Elizabeth Crabtree Wells, *Daughters of the Dream: Judson College, 1838–1988* (Marion, Ala.: Judson College Press, 1989), p. 147.

76. Summarized from May Day program titles and contents provided by the Archives, Judson College.

77. "A Change of Face," *The Triangle*, April 16, 1966, p. 2 (Archives, Judson College).

78. *Industrialist*, May 28, 1910, p. 462 (Kansas State University Archives).

79. *Industrialist*, May 25, 1912, n.p. (Kansas State University Archives).

80. *Industrialist*, May 27, 1916, n.p. (Kansas State University Archives).

81. *Industrialist*, May 24, 1922, n.p. (Kansas State University Archives).

82. *Industrialist*, May 8, 1929, n.p. (Kansas State University Archives).

83. May Day *Program*, May 16, 1914, found in *The Chestnut Burr*, 1915, p. 137 (Kent State University Archives).

84. Philip R. Shriver, *The Years of Youth: Kent State University, 1910–1960* (Kent State University Press, 1960), p. 51.

85. "Campus Day History," *Out of This World*, Campus Day Program for 1966, p. 4 (Kent State University Archives).

86. See the Lebanon Valley College Web site page on "Traditions Now and Then," *www.lvc.edu/l-online/traditions.aspx* (accessed November 2007).

87. Letter to the author from William C. Pollard, College Archivist, October 8, 2002.

88. Quotation from *The History of Mary Baldwin College by Mary Watters* (Mary Baldwin College, 1942), n.p.; other information from letter to author from William C. Pollard, College Archivist, October 8, 2002.

89. Mary Lynch Johnson, *A History of Meredith College*, 2nd edition (Raleigh, N.C.: Edwards & Broughton Co., 1972; originally published 1956), p. 129.

90. From various May Day programs as well as "Meredith Presents the Sensational Sixties in Traditional May Day Festivities, May 2," *The Twig*, no. 13 (April 23, 1970): 1 (Carlyle Campbell Library, Meredith College).

91. From a memo to the student body and minutes of the Student Life Committee, n.p. (Carlyle Campbell Library, Meredith College).

92. Letter to the author from Bob Schmidt, Miami University Archives, March 10, 2004.

93. *The Chimes: The Year Book of the Junior Class of Mills College*, 1915, n.p. (Archives, Mills College Library).

94. Information summarized from May Day program titles and photographs provided courtesy the Archives, Mills College Library.

95. Crawford, p. 87.

96. Letter from the Office of the Dean of Residence, June 6, 1947, n.p. (Mount Holyoke College Archives and Special Collections).

97. Summarized from by Grace M. Burt, "May-Time at Mount Holyoke," published in *St. Nicholas [Magazine] for Boys and Girls*, May 1920, as well as information provided by the Mount Holyoke College Archives and Special Collections: in particular, a one-page typescript summary prepared by Jennifer Allison, class of 1981; an unidentified newspaper article ca. 1930 titled "Will Celebrate May with Roman Pageantry"; and an article titled "May Day at Mt. Holyoke," from the *Holyoke Daily Transcript*, June 3, 1904, n.p. (Mount Holyoke College Archives and Special Collections).

98. From May Day programs and typescript accounts provided by Robin Hanson, Librarian, Muskingum College Library, December 3, 2002.

99. From a typescript account written by (Mrs. S.C.) Hathaway Alaman, March 18, 1964, n.p. (Newcomb College Archives).

100. Summarized from Mrs. Alaman's account (see note 99) as well as May Day programs provided by the archivist (Newcomb College Archives).

101. Letter to author, April 24, 2003, from Bill Boehm, Curator of Unpublished Materials, Archives and Special Collections Department, New Mexico State University Library.

102. *The Oberlin Review*, May 12, 1897, n.p. (Oberlin College Archives).

103. In a letter to the author dated February 14, 2002, Melissa Gottwald, Project Archivist, noted that *The Oberlin Observer* (a staff newspaper) on May 9, 1991, printed a photograph of dancing in front of the chapel "with a note that May morning festival had been held in Oberlin for almost two decades and that they had been started after a trip to Oxford by the Dean of Students. There was also 'May Fair,' a day of music, crafts, and other activities which appears to have begun May 11, 1971 (the 1971 event was reported on in the July/August issue of *The Oberlin Alumni Magazine*."

104. Patrick Murphy, *A History of Oklahoma State University Student Life and Services* (Stillwater: Oklahoma State University Press, 1988), pp. 75–76.

105. Letter to the author from Jennifer Paustenbaugh, head of Special Collections and University Archives, Oklahoma State University Press, April 30, 2003.

106. Letter to the author from Lawrence Landis, University Archivist, Oregon State University, August 25, 2005.

107. Dan Morrell and David Pulizzi, "The Lost Traditions," *The Penn Stater*, January/February 2005, p. 26.

108. Roberta D. Cornelius, *The History of Randolph-Macon Woman's College* (Chapel Hill: University of North Carolina Press, 1951), p. 162.

109. Citations are from "The Past Master," a column written by Meredith Minter Dixon, class of 1984, in the student newspaper, *The Sundial*, vol. 66, no. 24 (April 23, 1982), as it appears on the college website *http://faculty.rmwc.edu/fwebb/traditions/mayday.html* (accessed October 2007).

110. Grace Sherman Dorcass, "Origin of the May Party at Rockford College," typewritten m.s., p. 1 (Rockford College Archives.)

111. Hortense E. Johnson, "May Party at Rockford College, 1900–04," typewritten m.s. (Rockford College Archives).

112. "History of May Party Reveals the Traditions of Rockford College," *The Purple Parrot*, May 17, 1924, p. 3 (Rockford College Archives).

113. May Day Tradition Begun at Seminary in 1894," *The Purple Parrot*, 1931–32, n.p. (Rockford College Archives).

114. "Big Program Preparing for May Day Celebration," *The Rollins Sandspur*, April 27, 1918, p. 1; "Gala Day Will Show War-Time May Spirit," *The Rollins Sandspur*, May 4, 1918, p. 1

115. Julia Patton, *Russell Sage College: The First Twenty-Five Years* (Troy, N.Y.: Press of Walter Snyder, 1941), p. 48.

116. Bunny Propper, "Queen of May Crowned in Gala Ceremony," *The Russell Sage Quill*, vol. 19, no. 26 (May 7, 1942): 1.

117. From information provided by the college librarian 2/27/2003, as well as a typescript of a speech given

in 1943 by Edward M. Holder, "Salem's Traditional May-Day," p. 4 (Archives, Gramley Library, Salem College).

118. Summarized from the 1952–1953 Student *Handbook* and a letter to the author from librarian Judy Harvey Sahak, January 23, 2003 (Ella Strong Denison Library, Scripps College).

119. Summarized with permission from the Simmons College Web site, *http://my.simmons.edu/library/collections/college_archives/traditions/mayday.shtml*.

120. Mary C. Lynn, *Make No Small Plans: A History of Skidmore College* (Saratoga Springs, N.Y.: Skidmore College, 2000), pp. 53–55.

121. Ibid., pp. 53–55.

122. Ibid., pp. 109–111.

123. Letter to the author from Sara Street, Smith College Archives, January 30, 2002.

124. From the *Briar Patch*, 1909, cited in a student paper by Sonya Lynn Truman titled "May Day: The History and Ritual Performance at Sweet Briar" (Sweet Briar College Archives), p. 36.

125. Ibid., p. 41.

126. Ibid., p. 42, citing the *Sweet Briar News*, February 26, 1958.

127. Ibid., p. 44.

128. Summarized from photograph captions in the 1915 and 1916 *Souvenir* as well as the 1924 May Day program, "The Quest of Youth: A Masque of May" (Waxahachie Photo Box, Folder 26, Special Collections and Archives, Elizabeth Huth Coates Library, Trinity University).

129. Summarized from "The Partheneia of the University of California," by Jean Q. Watson and Frances L. Brown, *Overland Monthly*, vol. 67 (May 1916): 359–364, and "Dean Lucy Sprague, the Partheneia, and the Arts," by Janet Ruyle, *Chronicle of the University of California*, no. 2 (Fall 1998): 65–70.

130. References come from "May Queens at Morris Harvey College," *Maroon & Gold Magazine*, n.d. (post–1970), pp. 14–15. On November 1, 1938, Morris Harvey College celebrated its first Sadie Hawkins Day celebration, named for a cartoon character developed by Al Capp for his Li'l Abner comic strip, which featured hillbilly characters. Sadie was so ugly that her father, the Mayor of Dog Patch, U.S.A., feared he would never marry her off. In desperation he called for a race in which all the unmarried men in Dogpatch would get a ten-minute head start before Sadie and the other girls started running after them.

The college celebration was held between halves of the football game. All female residents — given names from the comic strip — were allowed to chase their men, who got a ten-second start, but could not run out of bounds. Once captured, the couples would line up to be married by Marryin' Sam. Participants dressed in the skimpy, "hillbilly" outfits of the comic strip, a fact that concerned some parents. Sadie Hawkins Day at Morris Harvey College faded out after the 1963 celebration, in part because football had ended there in 1956. (From the University of Charleston web site, *http://www.ucwv.edu/eagle/about_uc/saide_hawkins.aspx*.)

131. "May Festival Is Co-Eds' Way to Get Golden Shekels," no newspaper identified (probably *Silver and Gold*), no date (presumably 1912) (CU History Subjects, Box 25, Student Activities — May Fête (Archives, University of Colorado at Boulder Libraries).

132. *Silver and Gold*, May 11, 1914, p. 1 (CU History Subjects, Box 25, Student Activities — May Fête (Archives, University of Colorado at Boulder Li-braries).

133. *Silver and Gold*, April 24, 1916, p.1 (CU History Subjects, Box 25, Student Activities — May Fête (Archives, University of Colorado at Boulder Libraries).

134. *Silver and Gold*, May 12, 1921, p. 1 (CU History Subjects, Box 25, Student Activities — May Fête (Archives, University of Colorado at Boulder Libraries).

135. *Silver and Gold*, May 19, 1923, p. 1 (CU History Subjects, Box 25, Student Activities — May Fête (Archives, University of Colorado at Boulder Libraries).

136. May Fête *Program*, 1923, n.p., University of Colorado Women's League, Associated Women Students' May Fête (Archives, University of Colorado at Boulder Libraries).

137. "May Day Queen at Denver U. Crowned Following Victory by the Juniors," *The Daily News*, May 12, 1911, n.p. (University of Denver Special Collections).

138. Information from various May Day programs, University of Denver (University of Denver Special Collections).

139. Keith C. Petersen, *This Crested Hill: An Illustrated History of the University of Idaho* (Moscow: University of Idaho Press, 1987), p. 92.

140. Letter to the author from the Archivist, University of Illinois at Urbana-Champaign, February 2002.

141. From *The Kansan*, vol. 4, no. 68 (May 21, 1908): 1, and *The Kansan*, vol. 4, no. 69 (May 23, 1908): 1 (University Archives, University of Kansas, Spencer Research Library).

142. From *The Jayhawker Yearbook*, 1912, University of Kansas, p. 364 (University Archives, University of Kansas, Spencer Research Library).

143. The citation comes from an on-line essay by Elizabeth McAllister, University Archives, found at *http://www.wam.umd.edu/~emcallis/708u/FinalProject/frames.html*. This site also includes the listing of May Day program titles (University Archives, Special Collections, University of Maryland Libraries).

144. See *www.umd.edu/traditions/past/* (accessed October 2007).

145. General information from the 1911 May Day Pageant program; concern about tights in "May Fetealism [sic] vs. Higher Education," *The Shevlin Record*, May 1, 1911; procession citation from "Campus Scene of Old English May Festival," *The Minnesota Daily*, May 18, 1911, p. 1, as well as information provided by Karen Klinkenberg, Archives, in letters of 1/4/2005 and 1/31/2005 (University of Minnesota Archives).

146. Summarized from "May Day at Mizzou," an on-line article at *www.system.missouri.edu/archives/mayday1.html* (accessed October 2007).

147. Mylinda Woodward, "Springtime Follies," *UNH Magazine Online*, Spring 2003, *www.unhmagazine.unh.edu/sp03/historypage.html* (accessed October 2007).

148. Information provided in correspondence January 9, 2003, to the author from Donna Bachmann, Archivist, University of Puget Sound.

149. Joy Winstead, "Polishing the Gem: Tradition of Excellence Maintained at Westhampton for 75 years," *The University of Richmond Magazine*, vol. 52, no. 2 (Winter 1990): 17.

150. Summarized from May Day program titles provided by the Virginia Baptist Historical Society, University of Richmond.

151. Larry Wood, "Campus Traditions," *The Carolinian*, at *www.sc.edu.carolinian.features.fea_01apr_01.html* (accessed October 2007).

152. Compiled from the Program for May 9, 1938, and a student newspaper account: "First Annual May Day Festival Set Thursday May 5; Mary Nell Black to be Crowned as First Queen in Phys Ed Affair," *The Orange and White*, April 22, 1938, n.p. (University Archives, University of Tennessee).

153. Ursinus College Archives Finding Aid, January 2001.

154. Deborah Skinner Davis, *Valdosta State University* (Charleston, S.C.: Arcadia Publishing, 2001), p. 8.

155. *The WAHSA, the Biennial Publication of the Senior Classes at Wartburg Normal College*, vol. 1 (1919): n.p. (Archives at the Vogel Library, Wartburg College).

156. *The WAHSA, the Biennial Publication of the Senior Classes at Wartburg Normal College*, vol. 9 (1929): 100 (Archives at the Vogel Library, Wartburg College).

157. Alice Payne Hackette, *Wellesley, Part of the American Story* (New York: E.P. Dutton & Co., Inc., 1949), p. 146.

158. Ibid., p. 200.

159. Florence Converse, *The Story of Wellesley* (Boston: Little, Brown, and Co., 1915), pp 208–209.

160. Arlene Cohen, "Hoops, Trees, and Steps: The Role of Traditions at Wellesley College" (student paper courtesy of the Wellesley College Archives), pp. 29–30.

161. Jane M. Dieckmann, *Wells College: A History* (Aurora, N.Y.: Wells College Press, 1995), a three-page typescript (Louis Jefferson Long Library, Wells College).

162. Ibid., p. 3 (Louis Jefferson Long Library, Wells College).

163. "The Merry Month of May: of Queens, Courts, Music, and Verse," an on-line article, Winter 2004, found at *www.wells.edu/pdfs/winter2004_41.pdf* (accessed October 2007).

164. Michelle York, "Wells College: Newly, and Uneasily, Coed," *New York Times*, September 6, 2005.

165. "Commencement Events," *The Utah Westminster*, vol. 4, no. 7 (May 1918): 1–2.

166. Compiled from May Day Programs provided by the Archives, Westminster College.

167. *The Pharetra*, Wilson College, May 1908, pp. 159–161 (C. Elizabeth Boyd '33 Archives, Hankey Center, Wilson College).

168. From May Day program titles reviewed by the author (C. Elizabeth Boyd '33 Archives, Hankey Center, Wilson College).

169. "May Day at Winthrop," *The Johnsonian*, April 27, 1929, n.p. (Winthrop University Archives).

170. May Day *Program*, May 18, 1923, n.p. (Elmira College Archives).

Selected Bibliography

Holidays

In *The Battle for Christmas* (New York: Alfred A. Knopf, 1997), Stephen Nissenbaum examines the origins of the sentimental, family-oriented holiday that we know today; a private holiday that was created at the same time as the more communal May Day. Another interesting analysis of the invention of a holiday is Mike Cronin and Daryl Adair's *The Wearing of the Green: A History of St Patrick's Day* (New York: Routledge, 2002), that addresses, among other points, the fact that the holiday was and still is more popular with the Irish of the diaspora in the New World than with those of old Erin.

Pagans

Two invaluable sources are Ronald Hutton, *The Pagan Religions of the Ancient British Isles: Their Nature and Legacy* (Oxford: Blackwell Publishing, 1991; 2nd ed., 1993), and Stuart Piggott, *The Druids* (New York: Frederick A. Praeger, 1968. Reprint, London and New York: Thames and Hudson, 1975).

The English Ritual Year

Much has been uncovered in the last few decades about the origins and evolution of morris and sword dances as well as various English customs and rituals that were formerly thought to be "ancient pagan" relics. Three works by Ronald Hutton are very helpful in understanding documented rituals and customs, including the many May Day customs: see *The Stations of the Sun: A History of the Ritual Year in Britain* (Oxford: Oxford University Press, 1996; 2nd ed., 2001); *The Pagan Religions of the Ancient British Isles* (cited above); and *The Rise and Fall of Merry England, The Ritual Year 1400–1700* (Oxford: Oxford University Press, 1994).

May Day in Merrie England

In addition to Hutton's works, the late Roy Judge's publications have greatly informed my understanding of the creation of Merrie May Day and Merrie England, the history of the maypole dance, and the evolution of morris dance in the late nineteenth and early twentieth centuries. Judge's *The Jack-in-the-Green: A May Day Custom* (Cambridge: D.S. Brewer for The Folklore Society, 1979; 2nd ed., 2000) is a fine study of a May-time tradition; other useful works include his "May Day and Merrie England" (*Folklore*, vol. 102 [1991]); "Merrie England and the Morris, 1881–1990" (*Folklore*, vol. 104 [1993]); "Theatrical Morris" (*Traditional Dance*, vols. 5 and 6, edited by T. Buckland [Sheffield: Crewe and Alsager College of Higher Education, 1988]); "D'Arcy Ferris and the Bidford Morris" (*Folk Music Journal*, vol. 4 [1984]); and "Tradition and the Plaited Maypole Dance" (*Traditional Dance*, vol. 2 [Sheffield: Crewe and Alsager College of Higher Education, 1983]); and "'The Old English Morris Dance': Theatrical Morris 1801–1880," (*Folk Music Journal*, vol. 7, no. 3 [1997]). Mark Girouard's *The Return to Camelot: Chivalry and the English Gentleman* (New Haven: Yale University Press, 1981) aided me in understanding the cult of chivalry in nineteenth-century England.

Ring Tournaments

See E.J. Crooks and R.W. Crooks, *The Ring Tournament in the United States* (Richmond, Va.: Garrett and Massie, 1936). For more information on the Maryland Jousting Tournament Association, on jousting as that state's official sport and for pictures of galloping riders aiming their lances at two-inch rings, visit *http://www.geocities.com/marylandjousting/*.

Dance

Linda Tomko's *Dancing Class: Gender, Ethnicity, and Social Divides in American Dance 1890–1920*

(Bloomington: Indiana University Press, 1999) was extraordinarily valuable in helping me understand the changing attitudes of women toward their bodies in this period, in the use of dance in the Progressive reform movement, the teaching of folk dance in the settlement houses and more. While not strictly covering the period of study of my book, Kate Van Winkle Keller's *Dance and Its Music in America, 1528–1789* (Hillsdale, N.Y.: Pendragon Press, 2007) is also recommended. Important information about the history of morris dancing is found in John Forrest's *The History of Morris Dancing, 1458–1750* (Toronto: University of Toronto Press, 1999) and on sword dancing in England and the continent in Stephen Corrsin's *Sword Dancing in Europe: A History* (London: Folklore Society, 1997). I also benefited by Daniel Walkowitz's article "The Cultural Turn and the New Social History: Folk Dance and the Renovation of Class in Social History," published in *The Journal of Social History* (vol. 39, no. 3 [Spring 2006]), as well as draft chapters of his forthcoming work, currently titled, *City Folk: The Politics of Folk and Urban Liberalism in English Country Dance Revivals*.

The American Pageant Association

For more on the American pageantry movement, turn to David Glassberg, *American Historical Pageantry: The Uses of Tradition in the Early Twentieth Century* (Chapel Hill: University of North Carolina Press, 1990), as well as Naima Prevots, *American Pageantry* (Ann Arbor: University of Michigan Press, 1990).

The Playground Association of America

In *Muscles and Morals: Organized Playgrounds and Urban Reform, 1880–1920* (Philadelphia: University of Pennsylvania Press, 1981), Dominick Cavallo provides an analysis of the early urban reformers and their focus on organizing, and thereby improving, children.

The Progressive Reform Movement

There has been much written about the Progressive movement, and works that I found helpful include (but are not limited to) Daphne Spain, *How Women Saved the City* (Minneapolis: University of Minnesota Press, 2001), and Allen F. Davis' *Spearheads for Reform: The Social Settlements and the Progressive Movement 1890–1914* (Oxford: Oxford University Press, 1967).

Understanding the College Girl

The history of education for women has received much attention of late, and several useful recent works include Lynn D. Gordon, *Gender and Higher Education in the Progressive Era* (New Haven: Yale University Press, 1990), as well as Roberta Frankfort's *Collegiate Women: Domesticity and Career in Turn-of-the-Century America* (New York: New York University Press, 1977). I found both Frankfort's, *Collegiate Women* and *No Small Courage: A History of Women in the United States*, edited by Nancy F. Cott (Oxford: Oxford University Press, 2000) to be particularly useful and insightful in understanding what a young woman of the time might expect from life. Also useful was Helen Lefkowitz Horowitz's *Campus Life: Undergraduate Cultures from the End of the Eighteenth Century to the Present* (New York: Knopf, 1987). *Woman's Being, Woman's Place: Female Identity and Vocation in American History*, edited by Marry Kelly (Boston: G.K Hall & Co., 1979), contains many helpful essays.

For more on the making of the College Girl, and for analysis of the nature of the Girl at the turn of the last century, see Shirley Marchalonis, "College Girls" (*Research/Penn State*, vol. 17, no. 2 [June 1996]), and her longer work, *College Girls: A Century in Fiction* (Rutgers, N.J.: Rutgers University Press, 1995). I also found *The Girl's Own: Cultural Histories of the Anglo-American Girl, 1830–1915*, edited by Claudia Nelson and Lynne Vallone (Athens: University of Georgia Press, 1994), to be particularly interesting. Christie Ann Farnham's work, *The Education of the Southern Belle: Higher Education and Student Socialization in the Antebellum South* (New York: New York University Press, 1994), examines the making of the Southern Belle, and includes analysis of the popularity of May Day festivals in girls' schools and colleges in the South.

Beauty and Image

Two works that informed my understanding of the Cult of Beauty in late nineteenth-century America are Lois W. Banner, *American Beauty* (New York: Knopf, 1983), and Martha Banta's *Imaging American Women: Ideas and Ideals in Cultural History* (New York: Columbia University Press, 1987).

College May Day Festivals

Some of the information about specific college May Day festivities came from the published histories of these colleges, while much more came from the programs, newspaper accounts, memoirs and images provided by the college archivist. Over the course of my research, an increasing number of colleges put photographs or some information about their May Day festivals on-line, and these can be found through an Internet search using the words "May Day" or "maypole" or even "college traditions" in conjunction with the college name.

One of the most extensive sites is that of Valdosta State University, *http://books.valdosta.edu/arch/imagecollection.html*. The University of Maryland also maintains several pages on their May Day tradition, including a complete list of pageant titles, at *http://www.wam.umd.edu/~emcallis/708u/FinalProject/frames.html*. Of all the women's colleges, Bryn Mawr College in Bryn Mawr, Pennsylvania, has some of the most elaborate and longest-lived traditions. For more about them, turn to Virginia Wolf Briscoe, *Bryn Mawr College Traditions: Women's Rituals as Expressive Behavior* (Pennsylvania State University, Ph.D. dissertation, 1981). See also the college's Web page describing its traditions at *http://www.brynmawr.edu/activities/traditions.shtml*.

Index

Numbers in ***bold italics*** indicate pages with photographs.

The Abbey Girls 37
Acteon and Diana 177
Adams, Charles Francis 41
Adams, John 40
Adams, John Quincy 40
Addams, Jane 36, 58, 60, 62–3
aesthetic dances *2*, ***55***, ***56***, 56–57, 195
African American May Queens 152, 189, 194, 201; Miss America contest 141*n*; participation in pageants 77, 118, 238
Agnes Scott College 89, 98, 102, 113, 185–186; influencing Newcomb College 219–220
Albright College 122, 187
Alcott, Louisa May 46
Alford, Violet 21, 32, 130
American Child Health Association 159–162
American Pageant Association 7, 58, 60, 75–84 *passim*, 98; bulletin on Bryn Mawr's May Day 101; health pageant 160–161; principles of symbolism 88
American Women 115-6
The Anglomaniacs 9–60
Anthony, Susan B. 44
Arts and Crafts movement 59, 88; *see also* craftsman, ideals of
athletics for girls 52; attire for 51; decried 65–66
Auburn University 187

Baby's Godmothers 160
Baggins, Bobo 4, 110
Baillie-Cochrane, Alexander 28–29
Baker, George Pierce 77, 79
Ballroom dances 56, 69
Barnard College 185
Bassett Street Hounds Morris 171
Bates, Esther Willard: on folk dance 56; on pageants 42, 77–78, 80, 83
Bates College 187–188
battle of Spring/Summer and Winter 21, 170, 220
Baylor College 98
Bean, John 110

beauty, cult of 141–142
Bell, Dr. Carolyn Wilkerson 146–147, 153
Bell, Elizabeth Turner 67
Bell, Nora Kizer 146
Beltane 17, 22
Beowulf 60
Berea College 52, 80, 116–117, 162, 188–189; African American May Queens 152, 189
Betty Wales college stories 96
Bidford Morris 30, 254*n*9
The Black Crook 131
The Black Crook Burlesque 131
Blandings, Don 162
Blood, Sweat and Tears 213
Bluffton College 165, 189
Bolshevists 59, 158–159; *see also* Communists
Bond Queen 238
Boy Scouts of America 62, 162
Boys Clubs of America 62
boys, team sports for 60–61; *see also* play
Brenau University 189–190
Brewster, Mary 60
Brown University 114, 190
Bryn Mawr College 89, 98, 102, ***108***, 121, 124, 127, 139, ***166***; description of first May Day 100–101, 79, 190–191; influencing University of Minnesota 237; and Mark Twain 51; men's experience of festival 127; physical education attire 51; step-singing 166–167; and tradition 17, 103, 149; Traditions Mistresses 103, 165–167
The Buccaneers 89
Bucknell University 114–115, 191
Burchenal, Elizabeth 8, 53–55, 67–74 *passim*, 82–83, 133; on athletics for girls 65; Central Park May Day 8, 86, 136; folk dance collections 73–74, 135–136; maypole dance 131; on performing folk dance 66, 72; recording folk dance music 110; student of Gilbert 133
Burchenal Athletic Club 70
Burne-Jones, Edward 33, 35

California 80–81, 216
Camp Fire Girls 62
Canaletto, Giovanni 129–130
Carleton College 105, 191–193; qualities of May court 140
Case Western Reserve University 193–194; African American May Queen 152; Tree Day 102
Castleton Garland 177
Catholic church and May Day 18, 174
Catt, Carrie Chapman 44
Cave Life to City Life 77
Celts 15–17, 22
Cervantes, Miguel 26, 45
Chalif, Louis H. 233
Chappell, William 177*n*
character dances 54–55, 67
Charles I 18, 20
Chatham University *2*, ***55***, ***73***, ***80***, ***81***, 81–82, ***95***, 168, 194, ***195***
Chaucer, Geoffrey 18
Child Health Day 11, 159–162
Child Hygiene Department, Russell Sage Foundation 58, 79
chivalry: cult of in England 28, 123, 145; in the South 44–46
The Choice of American Girl-hood 116
Christmas 152, 180, 240; celebrated before 1820 24, 39; creation of 24–25; as invented tradition 4–5; Queen 30; Revels 31, 171; tournaments 46; tree 25, 39–40, 129
A Christmas Carol 25
Christy's Minstrels 131
Chubb, Percival 78–79, 80, 82
Churchill, Lady Randolph (Mrs. George Cornwallis-West) 28
Cinco de Mayo 11, 163
city, problem of 58–63
Clarion State Normal School drills and pageants 82–83
Clark, Lotta 75, 79
Clarke, Dr. Edward H. 49
Claremont Colleges *see* Scripps College
classical dance *see* Gilbert, Melvin Ballou
Cleveland, Grover 158

265

Colby, Grace 54
Colby College 195–196
College Girl, defined 9, 91–97
college, girls' fun at 95–96, 98, 102
college girls' stories 96–97
College Man 120, 122–123
College of Wooster 113–114, 121, 196–197; Korean May Queen 152
college scraps 123; *see also* Maypole Scrap
college traditions: daisy chain **92**, 111, 206, 238–239; development of 9–10, 95–96, 103–104, 149–151, 190, 239; junior-freshman wedding 239; junior-senior friendship chain 116; men changing 225n13; statue-scrubbing 226–241; step-singing 127, 166–167; strawberry (shortcake) breakfast 165, 167, 227–228
college yell 123
colleges founded by religious groups 99
Collier, John 75
Collier, Norma 141–142
Columbia College 197–198
Columbia Gramophone Company 110
Columbia University Teachers' College 49, 76, 80, 102, 133
Communists 4, 158–159, 213, 221
Converse College **56**, **76**, **79**, 98, 143, **199**, 199–200
Coolidge, Calvin 159
Corinna's Going a-Maying 23, 25, 30, 201
Cornell University 94
Country Dance & Song Society of America 71, 225
The Court of Love 18
Cox, Robert 177
The Craftsman 62, 62n, 76, 86
craftsman, ideals of 29, 33n62
Crampton, Dr. C. Ward 74, 133, 137
Crane, Walter 156, 157
Crawford, Caroline 82
Croce, Jim 170
Curie, Marie 82
Curtis, Henry 62–63

Daddy-Long-Legs 96
Daggett, Mabel 60
Daisy Chain *see* college traditions
dance *see* aesthetic; folk; Greek; national
dance halls 66, 71, 72
dancing the sun up 171
Deedy, Joseph 30–31
Deep Sea Caverns **95**
Delsarte exercises 59
A Democracy Calls for Intelligence at Work 116-7
DePauw University 104, 199–200; college yell 123; Margaret Mead pageant 116
Dewali 179
Dewy, John 60
Dickens, Charles 25

Dimple Dallas 139
DisMay court 10, 10n, 153
Disraeli, Benjamin 28–29
Dodge, Grace Hoadley 62
Dole, Elizabeth, as May Queen 201
Don Quixote 26, 45
drill, defined **50**, **52**, 53
Druids *see* Celts
Duke University 200–201; African American May Queen 152, 194
Duncan, Isadora 56, 66
Duryea, Oscar 135

Earlham College **109**, **110**, 146, 201–202; dispute over ending 149, 154–155; engraving inspiring 48; first May Day festival 28, 48, 100, 139, 120–121; 1977 May Day 2, 118–119; Prune Queen 12, 155
Easter 180
Edward IV 48
Edward VI 18
Eglinton tournament *see* tournaments
Eisenhower, Dwight D. 159
The Elephant and Maypole 20n
Elizabeth I 18, 19
Elizabethan England 12, 118, 154–155, 237, 244
Elmira College **5**, 107, 143, 151, **180**, 202
Esperance Society 137
Every Girl 107

Fairies of Freya 115, 206
The Fairy Queen 45
fancy dances 54, 69
Fantasy of Nations 117
Father's Day 160
Ferris, D'Arcy 30, 254n9
figure dances 54, 67
Flora 16, 40, 48
Floralia see Flora
Flower, Jessie Graham 96
folk dance 67–74; agent of democracy 70–71; defined 54–55; difference folk and national dance 55–56; gramophone recordings for 107–110; representing national characteristics 67–68; social benefits of 69–70
folk dances: Ace of Diamonds (Danish) 74, 214, 241; Alley Cat 89; American Indian dances 72–73; Bean Setting (morris) 74, 171; Bleking (Swedish) 74, 233; Blue-Eyed Stranger (morris) 225; Bluff King Hal (morris) 30, 133, 135, 137, 254n9; Bobbing Joe (morris) 233; Bocastle Schottische (English) 214; Bounding Heart (Finnish) 74; Carrousel (Swedish) 72; Castleton Garland (English) 225; Clap Dance (Swedish) 74; Comarinskaia (Russian) 74; Country Gardens (morris) 170, 233; Csardas (Hungarian) 74, 118; Csebogar (Hungarian) 28; Dal Dance (Swedish) 58; Dance of Greeting (Danish) 74, 82; Dargason (English) 225; Firetue (Danish) 71; Fjalnas Polka (Swedish) 74; Gathering Peascods 12, 118, 202, 225; Harvest Dance (Finnish) 74; Highland Fling **69**, 72, 74, 86; Highland Reel *see* Scottish Reel; Highland Schottische 74; Hokey-Pokey 89; How Do You Do, My Partner? (Swedish) 74; How Do You Do, Sir (morris) 58, 74, 241; I See You (Swedish) 74; Irish clog 86; Irish Jig 58, 69, 74; Irish Lilt 74, 214, 241; Irish Reel 214; Javanese dance 72; Kentucky Mountain Running Set 225; Kirkby Malzeard (English sword) 225; Klappdans (Swedish) 89, 241; Komarno (Bohemian) 74; Kull Dance (Swedish) 74; Laudanum Bunches (morris) 74; Little Lassie (Swedish) 74; London Bridge188; Looby-Loo 83, 89; Macarena 89; Ma's Little Pigs (Swedish) 74; Morris dance **73**; Mountain March (Norwegian) 74, 203; Newcastle (English) 225; Nigare Polska (Swedish) 74; Nonesuch (English) 225; Oxdansen (Swedish) 72, 74, 225; Parson's Farewell (English) 241; Portland Fancy (American contra) 214, 233; Portsmouth (English) 133; Reap the Flax (Swedish) 72, 74, 82; Rigs O' Marlow (morris) 225; Roman Soldiers (Swedish) 72; Rufty Tufty (English) 118, 225; Russian dances 68–69; Sailors' Hornpipe 55, 68, 117, 233, 241; Scottish Reel 68–69, 71, 72; Sellenger's Round (English) 12, **109**, 117, 118, 133, 171, 202; Seven Jumps (Danish) 118; Shoemaker's Dance (Danish) 74; Sir Roger de Coverley (English) 72, 135; Spanish dances 68–69; Square dance **68**; Step Stately (English) 225; Strasak (Bohemian) 74; Tarantella (Italian) 55, 72, 74; Tretur (Swedish) 225; Trollen (Swedish) 74; Varsouvienne (Swedish) 74, 82; Virginia Reel 72, 116, 224, 135; Wyresdale Greensleeves (morris) 225
Fourth of July 24, 46, 180, 182
Frick, Helen 83–84
Frick, Henry Clay 58, 83–84

Galenorn, Yasmine 138, 172
garlanding 18, 21, 25; *see also* Jack-in-the-Green
George I 20n
George III, coronation of 28
German, Edward 30
German gymnastics 51
Gibson, Charles Dana 86
The Gift 116
gifts for May Queen *see* May Queen, gifts to

Gilbert, Melvin Ballou 53–54, 66, 133, 135, 136–137, 212
girl-break dance 210
Girl Scouts 62, 162
Girls' Branch of the Public School Athletic League of New York 65–66
Glenn, John M. 63
The Gods and the Golden Bowl 79
Gorme, Eydie 213
Goucher College 98, 202–203
Grace Harlowe college stories 96
Greece, athletic ideals of 65
Greek dances *see* aesthetic dances
The Green Man 21, 174
Greenaway, Kate 34, 35
Grinnell College 113, 203
Grove City College 36, 122, 146, 150–151, **169**, 204–206
Guild of Play 68, 70, 134, 137
Guild of the Poor Little Brave Things 134
Gulick, Dr. Luther Halsey 8, 54, 61–2, 107, 121; on folk dance 54–56, 63–67 *passim*; and pageant movement 79; on play 61–66 *passim*

Haines, J.R. 29, 130
Haley, Alex 238
Hall, G. Stanley 88; on folk dances 67–68, 70; on play 63–64
Hansen, Howard 42
Harrison, Constance Cary 59–60, 85, 91
Harvard University 94; disrupting hoop-rolling 126–127
Harvest Queen 30, 190
Haverford College 126
Hawthorne, Nathaniel 6, 25
Haymarket Riot 59, 157
Health Pageant, Berea KY 161
Heart of the Beast Puppet and Mask Theatre 171–172
Henry VIII 16, 18, 21, 48, 165, 201
Henry Street Settlement 60; *see also* settlement houses
Hepburn, Katharine 166
Here We Go Round the Maypole Tree 170
Herrick, Robert 15, 23, 25, 30, 201
Hinman, Mary Wood 54, 57, 66, 70, 74, 133, 137
Historic Wooster 113–114
Hobsbawm, Eric 4–5, 178–179
Hodge, Grace Hoadley 62
Hofer, Mari Ruef 83, 133, 137
Hollins University 46, 98, 115, 146, 206, 230
Holt, Ardern 134
Homecoming Day 151, 212
Homecoming Queen 36, 189
Hood College 98, 207–208; Prince Robin Hood 143
hoop-rolling 126–127, 158, 241–242; protests during Vietnam War 152–153
Hoover, Herbert 159, 121
Hoover, (Mrs.) Lou 196

hostility to women on campus 94
hula maypole dance 138, 162
Hull House 60, 137; *see also* settlement houses
The Hunt Is Up 165
Hutchinson, Susan Nye 46

Idylls of the King 45
Imbolc 17
Immigration, concerns over 59
Indiana University 67, 127, 208–209
interpretive dances *see* aesthetic dances
The Invention of Tradition 4–5, 178–179
Iowa State (College) University 102–103, 107, 115–116; in wartime 116, 209
Irving, Washington 6, 24–27, 181
Ivanhoe 28, 183
Ivy Day 96, 102, 195, 228; *see also* Tree Day

Jack-in-the-Green 21–22
James, Henry 59
James I 18, 20
James Madison University 210
Jazz dance 56, 69, 70, 71, 79
Jefferson, Thomas 40
jousting state sport of Maryland 44–45, 261
Judson College **68**, **111**, 210–211, **211**; girl Prince 143

Kalendar of Amusement 47
Kansas State University 211–212
Keats, John 23
Kennedy, Helen 37
Kennedy, John F. 214
Kennedy, Robert 214
Kent State University 121, 212–213; massacre 4, 147, 153
kilt, invention of 178
Kimmins, Grace 68–69, 70, 134–135
King, Martin Luther, Jr. 214
Kingston Trio 213
Knickerbockers 24–25
Knutsford Royal May Day festival 30
Kwanzaa 179

Labor Day 11, 82, 156–158, 180
Langdon, William Chauncy 78, 79
Langstaff, John 170, 171
Law Day 11, 159
Lawrence, Elizabeth 110
Lawrence, Steve 213
Lebanon Valley College 213
Lee, Joseph 62
Lei Day 11, 162
Leslie, Charles 27–28
Lewis, Dio 51
Lewis, Sinclair 206
Liberty Pole 43–44
Lichtenstein, Joy 123
Lincoln, Jennette E. Carpenter 26, 49, 54, 133–135 *passim*, 212

Lord of Misrule 121–122, 240; D'Arcy Ferris as 30; Thomas Morton as 40
The Lost Poem 216–217
Low, Juliette 62
Loyalty Day 11, 158–159
ludi Floralia see Flora
Lughnasadh 17

MacKaye, Constance D'Arcy 88
MacKaye, Percy 75, 78–79
Malory, Thomas 18
Manners, Lord John 28–29
Marmion 24, 28
Mary Baldwin College 104–105, 213–214
Mary I 18
May Ales 18
May baskets 83, 227, 229, 246
May Bishop 47, 206
May carols 25
May Court **5**, **109**, **142**, 143–144, **169**, **180**, **199**, 205, 208, **211**, **216**, 235, 243; procession of 112, 197, 216, 224, 244
May Day: as Bank Holiday 22; and Bolshevists 59, 158–159; burlesques 122, 193, 215, 226, 230, 231, 240 (*see also* DisMay court); as calendar holiday 178, 180–181; and Catholic church 18, 174; as Child Health Day 11, 159–162; and Communists 4, 158–159 213, 221; as community holiday 179–181 (*see also* May Day community festivals); as Law Day 159; as Lei Day 11, 162; as Loyalty Day 158–159; as Moving Day 38–39; in nineteenth century England 29–30, 46–48; origins of in England 15–22 *passim*; as Play Day 161–162, 241–242; rural festivities 87–89, 161; and war *see* Vietnam War; World War I; World War II
May Day community festivals: Buffalo NY 47; Fairfax CA 174; Fremont OR 174; Geyserville CA 173; Hastings MN 173; Mendon UT 47, 164, 173–174; New Orleans LA **39**; New York City 8, 66, 85–86, 89, 136; Omaha NB 8, 58; Palo Alto CA 89; Parkersburg VA 89; Pittsburgh PA 8, 83–84, 169–170 (*see also* Chatham University) ; Portales NM 170; St. Thomas USVI 173; San Francisco CA 47; Southern Marin County CA 89; Toronto Canada 89; Westville GA 173–174; Hawaii 11, 138, 162
May Day festivals: celebrated in schools 169–170; celebrated today in UK 22, 31, 37; celebrated today in US 138, 164–175, 194, 199, 204–206, 228; at colleges 100, 150; components of 110–112; dispute over ending 145–155 *passim*, 193–194, 202, 214–215, 223,

230; first college celebration 48; large-scale performances 8, 58, 66, 83, 85–86, 89; men's disruption of 125–176; music for 107–110, 192, 204, 208, 213, 218, 224, 239; plays performed at 112, 118; purpose of 179–180; for urban children 85–90; use of funds 102, 207, 209, 212, 222, 232, 234, 236, 245; value of tradition 190
May Day in Town; or New-York in an Uproar 38
May Day pageants, sample titles 185–186, 218–219, 236, 245
May Day poems, index of first lines: Come lasses and lads, take leave of your dads 129, 133; Come, let me crown thee Queen of May 207; Come ye young men come along 177 (*see also* "Staines Morris"); England was merry England when 24; Gone the merry morris din 23; The hunt is up, the hunt is up 165; Kind friends, we have met this lovely day 164; The maypole is up 15; Sherwood in the twilight, is Robin Hood awake? 38; Up oily in de mornin' we 85, 87; Who shall be Queen of the Maye? 139; With dew-drenched roses in her hair 91; World Workers, whatever may bind ye 156–157; You must wake and call me early 1, 27, 30, 100, 174
May garlands *see* garlanding; Jack-in-the-Green
May Hole **166**, 191
May King (female) 121, **144**, **199**, **211**; at Brenau 189; at Case Western 193; at Converse 199; at Hood 207–208; at Judson 143, 144, 210–211; at Newcomb 220; at U. Colorado 143, 232–233
May King (male): at Albright 122, 187; at Bluffton 165; at Brenau 189; burlesque 121–122; at Grove City 122, 167, 204; at Oberlin 221; at Oregon State U. 222; at Rockford 225; Tammany 43–44; at U. Puget Sound 238; at Westminster 243; at Whitelands 37
May Lady 18, 83
May Lord 18, 83
May Queen: African American 152, 189, 194, 201; cake 174; coronation of 144; as Daisy Mae 193; drink 174; escorts of 197; gifts to 33, 36, **142**, 244; gown of 33–34, 36, 198, 201; Korean American 197; publicity about 197; qualities of 139–143, 214–215, 224–225, 226, 233, 246; reactions of 10–11, 145–147; returning 36, 167, 198, 204; as Rosie the Riveter 193; selection of 139–143, 218, 230, 233, 239; as Spirit of Columbia 114, 204, 209;

as Spirit of Liberty 114, 117, 188; to be unmarried 142
The May Queen 1, 1*n*, 27, 30, 100
May Queen's Coach 135
May Revels 171
The Maypole 15
Maypole: and Canaletto 129–130; as fertility symbol 15, 18, 172–173; as Liberty Pole 43–44; origins of 18; restored with Charles II 43; and Socialism 156–157; symbol opposition Puritan rule 43; used in advertising 11, 129; workers' 156–157
maypole dance **11**, **19**, 74, **105**, **111**, 118, 129–138, **130**, **132**, **135**, **140**, **157**, **173**; hula 158, 162; modern Pagan fantasies about 137–138; origins of 29, 129–131; as rite of passage 169–170; and Ruskin 32
Maypole of Merrymount 39–43
Maypole Scrap 123–125, **125**, 235
Mead, Margaret 116, 200
Memorial Day 180
Mendes, Sergio 213
Mendon UT 47, 164, 173–174
Meredith College 98, **109**, 141, 214–215; controversy over ending 145, 148, 153–154
Merrie England (operetta) 30
Merrie England movement 6, 20, 23–31 *passim*, 34, 48
Merrie England Society 30–31
Merry Mount (opera) 42–43
Metropolitan Opera 43
Miami University 125–126, 215
Mills College **105**, **130**, **132**, 215–217, **216**, **217**; pageant at 80–81
Miss America contest 141*n*, 153
Moore, Clement 24–25
Morley, Christopher 101
Morrill Act 92, 92*n*, 93
Morris, William 33, 35
morris dance **73**; in America today 170–171; in nineteenth century 25, 29; origins of 20–21; *see also* Basset Street Hounds; Bidford Morris; folk dances
Morris Harvey College *see* University of Charleston
Morte d'Arthur 18
Morton, Thomas 40–41
Mother's Day 180
Mount Holyoke College 209, 217–218; fun at college 95, 98, 102; voting for Queen 142–143; wartime pageants 117
Muskingum College 113, 218–219
My Wife Is a Suffragette 115
Mysteries of Udolpho 6

National Child Health Day 162
national dances defined 54–55
natural dances *see* aesthetic dances
Neal, Mary 137
New Hampshire College *see* University of New Hampshire
New Mexico State University 220–221

Newcomb College 98, 102, 219–220; dispute over ending tradition 152
Norris, Kathleen 89
Norton, Charles Eliot 59
Now and—When? 114
Noyes, Alfred 3, 38, 198, 203, 232

Oberlin College 221
Oklahoma State University 222
Olde Englande 244–245
Oregon State University 222
Ormandy, Eugene 213
Oxenham, Elsie J. 37

Padstow May Song 170
Padstow 'Oss 171, 177
pagans 15–17, 22
Pagans (modern) 3–4, 15, 19, 164, 180; and maypole dance 137–138, 172–173
Pageants: **76**, **79**, **80**, **81**, **95**, **99**, **111**, **195**; books on 80; courses in 80, 239, 240; definition of 75, 77; effort to produce 201; ending in Depression era 119; importance of location to 77, 81, 105–106, 110–112, 232–233; movement in America 79–84; suffrage 80, 115; and symbolism 81–82; value of in society 75, 77–78, 214; in wartime *see* Vietnam War, World War I, World War II; and women 77
Pageant and Masque of St. Louis 75
pageant-writing contest 240
Parthenia 101, 103–104, 120, 125, 127–128, 231
Paskkennodan, or The City of Smoke Vapor **81**, 81–82
The Passing of Winter and the Coming of Spring 216
Pembroke College (Brown University) 114, 190
Pennsylvania State University 222–223; qualities of Queen 140–141
Pentecost 171
The Philadelphia Story 166
play 41–42, 60–66 *passim*, 78
The Playground 68, 78, 80, 82, 87–88
Playground Association of America 7–8, 42, 55–56, 58–66 *passim*, 68, 80, 82–84, 98
playgrounds, establishment of 61
Portales High School 170
Powell, Sir Baden 62
Presidents' Day *see* Washington's Birthday
Princeton University 94, 104
Progressive reform movement 7–8, 58–66 *passim*, 76, 159–162
Prune Queen 12, 155
Puritans and May Day: in America 38–43; in England 15, 20, 41, 246
Pyle, Howard 25, 27, 60

Queenhoo-Hall 26, 28
Queens *see* Bond; Christmas; Har-

vest; Homecoming; May; Prune; Summer
Queen's Coach 135, **136**
The Quest of Youth for Happiness 216

Radcliffe, Ann 6
Radcliffe College 98
Ramadan 180
Randolph College *see* Randolph-Macon Woman's College
Randolph-Macon Woman's College 98, 141, 223; controversy at ending celebration 145–147, 153, 155; DisMay Court 10, 10*n*, 153
Rath, Emil 53–54
Reeves, Boleyn 47
Reformation 19
Renaissance Faires and festivals 175
Revels, Inc. 170–171
rhythmic dances *see* aesthetic dances
Richard Plantagent 29, 130
Riis, Jacob 62
Ring Tournaments of the South 6, 44–46, 141
The Road to Wellville 160–161
Robin Hood 23; see also *A Song of Sherwood*
Robin Hood, origins of 21, 27; *see also* Pyle, Howard
Robin Hood in Jones Street 85, 87
Rockefeller, John D. 121
Rockford College 36, 100, 140, 223–225
Roehampton University *see* Whitelands College
Rollins College 225
Romans 15–16
Roosevelt, Theodore 62, 121
Rosie the Riveter 145; May Queen as 193
Ruskin, John 6, 60, 71, 224; and craftsman ideal 20, 29, 33, 62*n*; ideal of May Queen 33–34, 139–140; ideals influencing American colleges 36, 100; and maypole dance 32; and Whitelands College Festival 32–37
Russell Sage College (The Sage Colleges) 226
Russell Sage Foundation 7, 58, 63, 79

Sadie Hawkins Day 231, 259*n*130
The Saint-Gaudens Masque 79
St. Patrick's Day 24; as invented tradition 4–5
St. Tammany Societies 44
Salem College 98, 101, 226
Samhain 17
Santa Claus 25, 39
Sargent, Dr. Dudley 51
Scott, Sir Walter 6, 24, 26–28, 44, 45, 60
scraps 123; *see also* Maypole Scrap
Scripps College 106, 150, 227
Sedgwick, Catherine 25, 39–40
Seton, Ernest Thompson 62
settlement houses 61, 70, 87–88, 137

Severn, Arthur 33
Shady Hill School 170
Shakespeare tercentenary 28, 91–92
Sharp, Cecil 20–21, 30, 37; singing well showing moral character 67, 107–110, 170, 254*n*9
Shaw, Walter 136
Sigurd the Volsung **99**, 105, **105**, 192
Simmons College 227–228
Skidmore College 228–229; ending of tradition 149, 152
Smith, Dr. A.L. 49–51
Smith, Horatio 26
Smith College 93, 102, 229; girls' fun at 95–96, 98
Smythe, George 28–29
A Song of Sherwood 38, 31, 198, 203, 232
Sorensen, Bishop Henry C. 164
Sorensen, Rodney 250*n*28
Spenser, Edmund 45
The Spirit of Americanization 74, 117–118, 237
The Spirit of Grinnell College 113
Sprague, Lucy 103–104; *see also Partheneia*
Springfield MA (Independence Day) 76–77
The Squire of Bracebridge Hall 24, 26–27
"Staines Morris" 133, 134, 135, 177, 177*n*, 254*n*9
Standish, Miles 40
Stanford University 94
Staniland, C.J. 48
Starr, Ellen Gates 60
statue-scrubbing 226, 241; *see also* college traditions
Steiner, Rudolf 170
step-singing 127, 166–167; *see also* college traditions
Stevens, Thomas Wood 75
Stickley, Gustav 62*n*
Stokes, Richard L. 42–43
Storrow, Helen 71, 74
strawberry (shortcake) breakfast 165, 167, 227–228; *see also* college traditions
Strutt, Joseph 26–28, 83
Stubbes, Philip 19, 172
suffrage movement 93–94, 96, 110; pageants of 80, 115, 206
Sullivan, Sir Arthur 30
Summer Ladies 18, 21, 172
Summer Lords 18, 21, 172
Summer Queen 30
Swarthmore College 169
Swedish gymnastics 51
Sweet Briar College 98, 144–146, 193, 229–230
Sweet Country Life 23

Tammany King 43–44
Tarbell, Ida 55
Tennyson, Alfred 1, 1*n*, 6, 27, 45, 100, 150
Thanksgiving 24 129, 180; as invented tradition 4–5
Thetford VT 63

Thomas, M. Carey 103, 121
Tolkien, J.R.R 4, 110
Time in a Bottle 170
Tournaments: African American 45; burlesque 45; Eglinton 28, 45; Maur 45; Ring *see* Ring Tournaments
Tradition: invention of 2, 4–5, 177–179; value of 164, 179, 189, 190–191; *see also* college traditions
Traditions Mistresses 103, 165–167, 179
Tree Day 102, 228, 193, 242; *see also* Ivy Day
Trinity University **50**, 230
Tulane University *see* Newcomb College
Turnvereine 51, 53
Twain, Mark 44, 51
Tyler, Royall 38

Under Three Flags 114–115
University of California at Berkeley 101, 103–104, 123, 125, 127–128, 231; *see also Partheneia*
University of Charleston 231*n*150
University of Chicago 70
University of Colorado 89, 102, 106, **112**, 121, 143, 231–232
University of Denver 233–234; selecting Queen 141
University of Idaho 234
University of Illinois at Urbana-Champaign **69**, **136**, **140**, 234
University of Kansas 98, 123–125, **125**, 127, 235
University of Maryland 103, 139, 235–236; dispute over ending festivities 149
University of Michigan 94
University of Minnesota **52**, 104, 236–237
University of Missouri 94, 237; and creation of Homecoming 151
University of New Hampshire 74, 117–118, 237–238
University of Oregon 168
University of Puget Sound 238
University of Richmond (Westhampton College) 98, 103, 238–239
University of Rochester 94
University of South Carolina 239
University of Tennessee 94, 141, 239
Ursinus College 43; men's parody of pageant 122; pageantry courses at 80, 240
Utah State University 179

Valdosta State University 240–241; Christmas festival 152; ending May Day 151–152
Valentine's Day 129, 180
Vanderbilt, Constance (Lady Randolph Churchill) 91–92
Vassar College 96, 98, 102, 120, 121
VEISHEA 209
Veterans' Day 180

Victor Gramophone Company 110
Victoria, Queen 28, 30
Victoria and Merrie England 30
Victory Through Conflict **80**, ***195***
Vietnam War 147, 150–154 *passim*, 158, 202, 227, 229, 241–242
A Visit from Saint Nicholas 25

Wald, Lillian 60–62
Waldorf schools 170
Warde, Margaret 96
Wartburg College 241
Washington's Birthday 24; Ring Tournaments during 46
Webster, Jean 96
well-dressings 29
Wellesley College 93, 98, 102, 146, 168, 226; dispute over ending festival 152–153; men disrupting race 126–127; valuing traditions 179; Vietnam War protests 153, 241–242
Wells College 102, 242–243; dispute over ending May Day 167–168; reinstatement of festival 168n149
Wesleyan College 98
Westhampton College *see* University of Richmond
Westminster College 104, 243
Wharton, Edith 91
Whitelands College May Queen Festival 6, 29, 30, 32–37; influencing Rockford College 100
Whitsun 171
Wicca *see* Pagan
The Wild Man 21
Willard, Emma 226
Wilson College **99**, 113, ***135***, ***142***, 146, ***150***, 244–246; qualities of Queen 140, 142
Winchester Thurston School 169–170
Winthrop University 142, 246–247

Wizard of Oz 4, 113
Wodehouse, P.G. 57, 174
Woodcraft Boys 62
The Worker's Maypole 156, 157
working girls' clubs 62
World War I: disrupting May Day 187–189, 191, 193, 196–198, 204, 206, 209, 212, 225, 231, 237–238, 241–242; and end APA 84; pageants during 110, 113, 116–118, 159
World War II 145; Bond Queen 238; disrupting May Day 198, 202, 218, 221, 231, 240; pageants during 114–117, 179, 187, 189, 191, 193, 196, 210, 212, 238
Wright, Frank Lloyd 60

Yale University 94
Yom Kippur 180
Young England movement 28–29

Ziegfeld, Florenz 104, 200